FROMMER'S

AUSTRALIA
ON $25 A DAY™

by John Godwin

1986–87 Edition

Published by Prentice Hall Press
A Division of Simon & Schuster, Inc.
Gulf + Western Building
One Gulf + Western Plaza
New York, New York 10023

ISBN 0–671–55604–5

Manufactured in the United States of America

CONTENTS

MAPS

READ THIS FIRST

The first reaction of every Australian who heard the title of this book was, "Sounds great—but can you do it?"

The answer is *Yes,* absolutely, within the terms laid down for this entire long-standing series of budget guides. These terms stipulate that the $25-a-Day covers only your basic expenses of a clean bed and three solid meals. All other outlays count as extras. Here my job was to collect the information that will enable you to get the most for your money as far as all those extras are concerned. This also applies to the "splurge" opportunities I've included in each chapter. They may be above our budget bracket but are economical in terms of value offered for the price.

The $25 of the title is U.S. currency. *All other amounts mentioned are in Australian money*—and here you're in for a very happy surprise. For currently the American dollar fetches around $1.40 in Aussie money, which means that your basic $25 actually amounts to $A35. A nightly hotel charge of $A20 comes to only about $US14.50

Budget travelers Down Under also enjoy another big advantage over tourists in Europe and America: they can disregard "hidden costs." Every price displayed anywhere is exactly what you pay. There are no additional taxes or tips to reckon with, additions which elsewhere may increase your bills by 25% or more. This goes not only for services but also for store purchases and makes a mighty difference in the long run.

This book took five months to research, even though I was already familiar with most of the areas described. I personally checked out every establishment mentioned. A large number of "possibles" were dropped by the wayside for a variety of reasons, sometimes merely because the vibes were bad. So what you're getting is a selection—not a listing. Whenever I have included a place solely because it was ultra-economical, I say so plainly in the text. The purpose for including them at all was to give you a downward margin, just as the splurge spots provide you with an upward one.

All prices, therefore, are accurate for the time at which they were gathered. Unfortunately they won't stay that way. We're caught in an age of inexorable inflation, a constant edging up of living costs that operates Down Under as it does everywhere else. Since the tourist industry is the sector in which food, wage, and fuel increases are sharpest felt, it's more than likely that some of the rates will have grown by the time you get there. However, since all the managements involved are essentially budget-oriented, they will still offer you, relatively speaking, the best deals available.

Money value is a basic consideration of this book, but not the only one. Australia has things that cannot be assessed in dollars: dramatic beauty, a sense of newness and adventure, the fascinating dynamics of a young and free society shaping its future, and a wonderful spirit of "mateship" that enfolds natives and visitors alike.

I hope that by helping you extract the most from your money I can enable you to take a close-up glimpse of an exciting human experiment in a part of the globe that has long been veiled by the "tyranny of distance."

John Godwin

Acknowledgments

Thanks to the people of the Australian Tourist Commission, the most dedicated, hardworking, painstaking, and efficient bunch of government employees I have ever encountered. My special thanks go to John Rowe, Peter Harding, and Jennifer Price in Melbourne; to John King and Myriam Savides in Sydney; and to Alan Drew in Los Angeles. Without their unflagging assistance, all-around know-how, and talent for time schedules, this book might have been a decade in the making. On the transportation side I want to thank J. Patrick Clark, Jr., and Ernest Beyl of Qantas, and John Tilton and Allan Williams of TAA for smooth flights, gentle landings, and arrivals punctual enough to operate a very tight itinerary.

INFLATION ALERT: I don't have to tell you that inflation has hit Australia as it has everywhere else. In researching this book, I have made every effort to obtain up-to-the-minute prices, but even the most conscientious researcher cannot keep up with the current pace of inflation. As we go to press, I believe we have obtained the most reliable data possible. Nonetheless, in the lifetime of this edition—particularly its second year (1987)—the wise traveler will add 15% to 20% to the prices quoted throughout these pages.

A DISCLAIMER: Although every effort was made to ensure the accuracy of the prices and travel information appearing in this book, it should be kept in mind that prices can and do fluctuate in the course of time, and that information does change under the impact of the varied and volatile factors that affect the travel industry.

Introduction

AUSTRALIA ON $25 A DAY

1. Why Australia?
2. A Capsule History
3. The Aborigines
4. Flora And Fauna

THE DISTINGUISHED BRITISH AUTHOR James Cameron wrote: "One doesn't come to Australia by chance. When one arrives it means that one most definitely has meant to come."

This puts the tourist's angle in a nutshell. Australia isn't a transit point to anywhere. You don't get off there en route to your main objective. Nobody tours it as part of a package containing half a dozen other attractions. Australia is, decidedly, a destination.

1. Why Australia?

Why should it be yours? The prime reason, perhaps, is uniqueness. Australia is the only country that also happens to be a continent. It contains the only society that ever developed from a penal colony—and developed into one of the freest, happiest, and most progressive on earth. It is a place where plants and animals are primeval, unchanged since the time—millions of years ago—when the continent drifted loose from Asia, cutting off the flora and fauna from the processes of evolution.

For most of its brief recorded human history, Australia lay almost beyond the orbit of world traffic. It was the remotest of inhabited islands, virtually exiled from world affairs by what Geoffrey Blainey called "the tyranny of distance." By windjammer the 10,000-mile journey from England took eight months and considerable luck. In the days of steam the trip still required six weeks. The jet age has shrunk the traveling time to a matter of hours, but the *feeling* of remoteness remains. So does the astonishing degree of ignorance about the place.

Most Americans and Europeans tend to lump Australia together with New Zealand, simply because they share the same hemisphere. Yet the two countries are separated by 1,300 miles of turbulent ocean and are so different in character and appearance that virtually their only similarities consist of the English language and membership in the British Commonwealth. Few foreigners can name the capital of Australia or more than one of her large cities or have any idea of her size—roughly that of the United States minus Alaska. Australia, to most people, is a land of immense deserts, scores of tennis champions, a couple of great sopranos, and the Sydney Opera House.

And this is precisely the reason why you should go there. For Australia is a vast surprise package, a place that keeps astonishing you for being so similar and yet so entirely different from what you imagine. The gigantic interior deserts are there alright—but so are snow-capped mountains with ski lifts and alpine huts. The tennis champions do proliferate—but alongside symphony orchestras, a superb national ballet, avant-garde artists, and a remarkable film industry that is now gaining worldwide recognition.

The great, stark "Australian loneliness" exists. This is a land where cattle ranches, worked by a few dozen people, are as large as entire nations in Europe. Where, through the "School of the Air," teachers and students stay in touch by two-way radio in a classroom covering nearly a million square miles. Where the "Flying Doctor" makes housecalls by aircraft. Where only ten years ago explorers came upon Aboriginal tribesmen who had never seen a wheel, a pair of shoes, or a white skin.

But it is also a land of huge teeming cities: Sydney is bigger than Los Angeles, Melbourne has more people than Philadelphia, Brisbane more than Baltimore. The ratio of automobiles per head of population is as high as in the United States. Canberra is one of the few *totally* planned national capitals in the world and could serve as a blueprint for urban development. There are traffic jams and skyscrapers, giant department stores and trendy little boutiques, experimental theaters, gourmet restaurants, ear-splitting discos, suburban cocktail parties, and McDonald's hamburger chains. But there's also the world's largest monolith, Ayers Rock, glowing scarlet at sunrise and dusk in the midst of barren emptiness that looks like the surface of the moon.

In other words, Australia is exactly what you imagine and nothing like it, depending on what part you're in. And because the place is so vast and so varied it's important for prospective tourists to do their homework—meaning that you should know where you want to go and what you want to see. Otherwise you risk missing precisely those aspects that interest you most. Which is probably why you're reading this book.

Australia has a more subtle magnetism as well, based on the curious mixture of familiarity and strangeness you'll encounter. Thus the language is English, but of a kind you very likely haven't heard before. To the natives their country is "Orstylia," a newspaper a "piper," the Victorian capital "Melbrn," and anything unpleasant "bloody." This is delivered in a soft, slightly twangy timbre with retracted vowel sounds that take a bit of getting used to. As does the general habit of using the feminine gender to describe situations as well as places, conditions, or persons. Remarks like, "She's beaut" or "She's bloody crook" can refer to his wife, his hometown, the weather, or the outcome of an election.

Strictly speaking, the country is a monarchy, with titles like Sir and Dame bestowed by the queen, large numbers of "Royal" parks, gardens, and public buildings, and a degree of sentimental attachment to the British Crown. Yet simultaneously it is one of the most democratic societies extant, imbued with a fierce egalitarianism that falls heavily on anyone who may doubt that Jack is as good as his Master.

Australia is strongly Americanized, but in patches rather than universally. Sydney is deceptively American in spirit as well as appearance and might lead you to think that the entire country is likewise. But the moment you get to Melbourne or Adelaide you'll note the unmistakably British heritage. And so it goes, a bit of this and a bit of that, throughout the continent. The mixture is symbolized by the fact that while Australians now deal in dollars and cents, they still drive on the left. And even though Christmas falls into the hot antipodean summer, they faithfully eat plum pudding with brandy sauce for the occasion.

Some aspects of Australia fill Americans with a strange nostalgia for their own more secure past. Australia is a *safe* country, a place where street crime is minimal, people trust each other to an amazing extent, and where news vendors leave honesty boxes for buyers to deposit their coins while they go to the pub for a drink. You won't get short-changed, you're not likely to get robbed, and you can walk in peace in any part of town at any hour of the day or night.

But you do run one grave risk—you may not want to return home.

2. A Capsule History

Dreamtime . . . that's the past. The way, way back shrouded past, half lost, half remembered, when anything could happen and nothing was recorded except by a faint imprint in the recesses of man's subconscious.

The original Australians have no chronicled history; only the Dreaming. The misty spectral memories of a time before the coming of the white man, when the world was young, the land was infinite, and life was beautiful and free. It could have been a thousand years ago, or a million, or a hundred million years —who knows? But once, they dream, the earth was flat and featureless, and roaming across it at will were the ancestors, the heroes, the Creative Beings. As they wandered they created the country's topography: here a mountain range, there a forest, yonder a gigantic pebble—Ayers Rock.

Deep in the cavernous heart of the Rock lived the Rainbow Serpent, hundreds of yards long, fanged and bearded, whose scaly skin reflected all the colors of the rainbow. As the Serpent crawled along, it furrowed the riverbeds, which still wind and twist like a snake's body.

That's how they dream it in Central Australia. They dream it differently in the south and in still other ways in the north and west. The original Australians were too isolated from each other to conceive a universal Genesis. But all their dreams contain the image of endless space and unfenced horizons, of a world where time and distance didn't matter.

The dream ended, abruptly, with the arrival of people who trapped the unmeasured space with instruments and carried time in their pockets.

THE UNKNOWN LAND: In the second century A.D., the learned Ptolemy of Egypt designed a map of the then-known world. Into the southern region of what we now call the Indian Ocean he placed a huge misshapen blob and labeled it *Terra incognita*—Unknown Land. And during the next 1,500 years mankind's information about this particular *Terra* hardly advanced beyond Ptolemy's. It remained solidly *incognita*.

The reason was distance. For the transportation methods of our ancestors the Antipodes were nearly as remote as another planet. Marco Polo's journey to China and Columbus's cruise to America were mere hops compared to the traveling time required to cross the uncharted immensities of the Indian and Pacific Oceans.

You can argue *ad infinitum* about who "discovered" Australia. The Spaniards and Portuguese traced the northern coastlines, the Dutch landed on the west coast in 1616 and promptly christened the inhospitable wilderness New Holland—a name it carried for 150 years. The first Englishman set foot there in 1688. He was the buccaneer (a polite word for pirate) William Dampier. But Dampier saw only the barren northwestern shores and decided that the country wasn't worth either plundering or exploring.

Thus it was left to Capt. James Cook, one of the greatest navigators of all times, to become the new continent's founding father. His Australian landfall was simply another stop along the road of his historic cruise of discovery that opened up the last unknown area of the globe.

AUSTRALIA

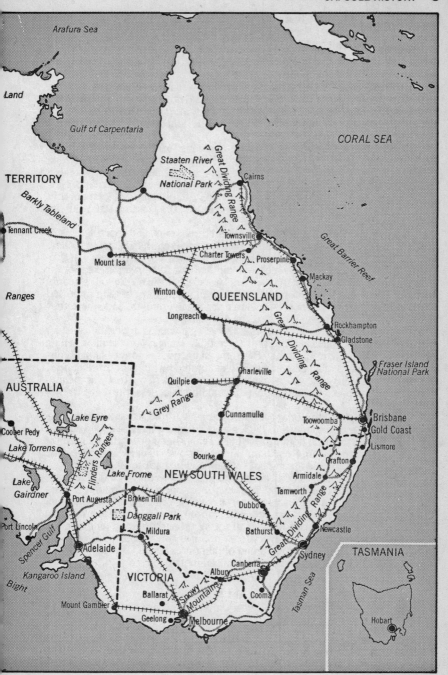

Arafura Sea

Land

Gulf of Carpentaria

CORAL SEA

TERRITORY

Barkly Tableland

Tennant Creek

Ranges

Great Dividing Range

Staaten River
National Park

Cairns

Townsville

Charter Towers

Mount Isa

Proserpine

Mackay

Great Barrier Reef

Winton

QUEENSLAND

Longreach

Great Dividing Range

Rockhampton

Gladstone

Fraser Island
National Park

AUSTRALIA

Charleville

Quilpie

Grey Range

Lake Eyre

Cunnamulla

Cooper Pedy

Toowoomba

Brisbane
Gold Coast

Lake Torrens

Lismore

Bourke

Lake Frome

NEW SOUTH WALES

Grafton

Lake
Gairdner

Flinders Ranges

Armidale

Tamworth

Great Dividing Range

Port Augusta

Broken Hill

Dubbo

Port Lincoln

Danggali Park

Mildura

Bathurst

Newcastle

Lake

Bourke

Sydney

Spencer Gulf

Adelaide

VICTORIA

Canberra

Albury

Kangaroo Island

Ballarat

Snowy Mountains

Cooma

TASMANIA

Bight

Mount Gambier

Geelong

Melbourne

Tasman Sea

Hobart

On April 29, 1770, Cook's *Endeavour* sailed into Botany Bay, and four months later the captain formally claimed the entire eastern seaboard of the continent for His Majesty King George III. Dreamtime was over. The men with watches, measuring rods, and muskets had arrived.

THE COMING OF THE CONVICTS: Australia owed its initial settlement to the success of the American Revolution. At first the British government had been totally uninterested in their new acquisition. Only after the American Colonies broke away did the Crown think of a use for the continent—as an alternative dumping ground for convicts!

Deportation for life was considered a "humane" sentence for such desperate lawbreakers as poachers, pickpockets, Irish rebels, trade union organizers, prostitutes, and cardsharps. Murderers, coiners, and highwaymen were still publicly hanged. Thus the fleet of 11 ships that brought the first governor of New South Wales, Capt. Arthur Phillip, also carried 1,500 people—half of them convicts. In January 1788 they founded a settlement at Port Jackson, today the site of the city of Sydney.

A second and a third fleet arrived within three years, and soon there were 4,000 whites in the colony commonly called Botany Bay. In England that name became synonymous with hell—and for good reasons. The settlement was supposed to be self-supporting, which was tantamount to starvation, scurvy, or death in the bush. How could the "settlers" wrest a living from the soil in a country where the seasons were turned upside down, where most of their imported seeds wouldn't grow, where they couldn't predict the rainfall, and where they didn't know what lay behind the next chain of hills?

And, worst of all, half of them had to work in chains under the constant threat of the whip, which was used with incredible savagery on the most trifling pretexts. The early years of Botany Bay were an unending agony of hunger, disease, floggings, and killings, made barely endurable by bouts of drunkenness. The only commodity that was in reasonable supply was rum. Rum was the universal balm, the precious relief from pain and homesickness, the real currency of Botany Bay.

Captain Bligh, of the *Bounty* Mutiny fame, was to discover that when he became governor of the colony in 1805. The brilliant but heavy-handed captain tried to suppress the illicit liquor traffic in his realm—and promptly sparked yet another mutiny, the "Rum Rebellion," among his own officers. They threw the governor out of office and ignominiously shipped him back to England.

When transportations finally ended in 1853, more than 100,000 convicts had been dumped into the country. By then the prisoners were already outnumbered by free settlers, and the struggle for survival in the new environment won. But the convict pioneers left an indelible imprint on the Australian national character. They bequeathed a heritage of strong antiauthoritarian sentiments, a fierce egalitarianism that made every Jack and Jill as good as their master, and a peculiarly sardonic, self-mocking brand of humor, expressed by the jingle that was something like the early colony's unofficial motto:

> *True patriots all, let this be understood,*
> *We left our country for our country's good.*

But while the convicts had a strong influence on Australian history, the original inhabitants had none. While New Zealand's past is interwoven with Maori wars and peace treaties, the role of the Australian Aborigines was simply that of victims. They were brushed aside, excluded from the mainstream, either ignored or massacred, but never taken seriously as part of the nation. Australia's history is the chronicle of its white usurpers.

EXPLORATION: The new continent began without either a name or a definite shape. Nobody could even be sure it *was* a continent, not just a cluster of large islands. It was a vague amorphous outline, variously known as New Holland, New South Wales, or Botany Bay. Not until 1803 did Capt. Matthew Flinders circumnavigate the entire landmass, establishing that it was indeed a continent —three million square miles of it, roughly the size of today's mainland United States.

Flinders was also the first to adopt the name Australia for his discovery. It means "Southland."

But although the settlements which later became state capitals were springing up along the coast, they lay in complete isolation. Between them stretched thousands of miles of unknown wilderness and their only means of contact was by sea. Small parties of explorers set out to scout links between the townships. As long as these men hugged the shoreline their progress was hard but bearable. Once they struck inland, however, it became nightmarish. For the farther away they marched from the coast the more barren the countryside grew, until at last it changed to absolute desert. By then many of the explorers were out of supplies and couldn't make it back. They perished in droves—of hunger, thirst, sheer exhaustion, snakebite, bushfires, fever, and, occasionally, the spears of hostile Aborigines.

Edward Eyre, who pushed through the broiling waterless Nullabor to the West Coast in 1841, made it . . . reduced to a walking skeleton. The German naturalist Ludwig Leichhardt, who tried to cross the continent from east to west seven years later, did not. Not a trace of his party was ever found. Neither did the heroic trio of Burke, Wills, and Gray, who attempted to reach the far north Gulf of Carpentaria overland from Melbourne in 1861. All three died en route. One of the finest books written about Australia's past, Alan Moorehead's *Cooper's Creek,* describes their tragedy.

The exploration of the continent is still going on. Even today certain portions of Arnhem Land in the Northern Territory remain *Terra incognita.*

GOLD: Australia was peopled not so much by steady immigration and procreation as by a series of frantic rushes. The first was the mass transportation of convicts from Britain. The second came with the discovery of fabulously rich goldfields at Ballarat and Bendigo in 1853. The timing was perfect—just at the stage when the great gold rush in California was petering out, thereby luring thousands of American miners to try their luck Down Under. Within ten years the population of the country jumped from 400,000 to 1,400,000. Some came to dig for gold, others to help them get rid of whatever they found. They came from every corner of the globe in every conceivable vessel—and they nearly wrecked the country in the process of populating it.

The Colony of Victoria, where the goldfields were located, was both materially and psychologically unprepared for the rush. The administration of Governor Hotham, still accustomed to dealing with helpless convicts, applied somewhat similar methods to the newcomers. They levied a crushing license tax on each claim, and then proceeded to collect taxes by means of the whip, bayonet, and musket butt. Mounted troopers indulged in "Digger hunts" through the goldfields, riding down prospectors in front of their comrades, who watched with clenched fists.

But there were rifles in many of those fists, and the Diggers were a fighting breed. (The term "Digger," in fact, became the generic label for all Australian soldiers.) A clash was inevitable. It turned out to be the only battle fought on Australian soil to date.

The Diggers issued a ringing proclamation of "Right and Justice," and elected a fiery young Irishman named Peter Lalor as their commander. The famous Eureka Stockade—a rough barricade of logs and rifle pits—went up at Ballarat, manned by an ill-armed but determined bunch of Irish, English, Italian, German, American, and native-born defenders. Some had rifles, others had pikes, pistols, or pitchforks, and above them floated a brand-new banner showing the Southern Cross on a blue field—the rebel flag that has since become the country's national emblem.

Governor Hotham's reply was to send a regiment of foot and squadrons of mounted police to crush the rising. On the morning of December 3, 1854, the troops charged the Eureka Stockade. The battle was brief and bloody. The Diggers stood no chance against the precision-drilled redcoat regulars who advanced, fired, advanced, fired, like rows of robots. The log palisade went down under the bayonet charge, the blue banner fell, riddled with bullets. Some 34 men were killed, hundreds wounded. Peter Lalor escaped, wounded and with a price on his head, and went into hiding. The cause of the Diggers seemed lost.

But the British authorities had learned quite a lot since the American Revolution. They had learned, above all, to recognize a dangerous situation when it confronted them. Instead of making a martyr of Lalor, they pardoned him. Less than a year after being outlawed, Lalor was elected to the Victorian Parliament and most of the demands he had fought for were granted.

Mark Twain wrote about the Eureka battle: "It was the Barons and John, over again; it was Hampden and Ship-Money; it was Lexington and Concord; small beginnings, all of them, but all of them great in political results, all of them epoch-making. It is another instance of a victory won by a lost battle."

Australians gained more than a flag, a hero, and recognition of some basic rights from the gold rush. They gained a wholesome infusion of cosmopolitan blood for their population base, including thousands of Chinese, many of whom came as camp cooks for the diggings. When the golden stream dwindled, some of them opened restaurants instead . . . the country's first relief from the accustomed dismal Anglo-Irish cuisine.

BUSHRANGERS: Banditry was an inevitable by-product in a colonial frontier society. Australia very quickly developed its own special brand, which closely resembled the outlaws of the American West. At first these were mainly escaped convicts, who robbed in order to survive in the bush. But soon they acquired professional flair at the banditry business, together with fast horses, good weapons, and an organized intelligence service that was often far superior to that of the authorities. These bushrangers, as they were called, plundered gold transports, homesteads, banks, railroads, and the Cobb & Co. stagecoaches that were Australia's equivalent of Wells Fargo.

For a time the bushrangers multiplied at a frightening rate. There were white, black, and yellow bushrangers, "gentlemen" bushrangers and half-demented maniacs. There was even a Jewish bushranger, one Edward Davis, whose gang terrorized the Hunter River region.

Law enforcers were badly handicapped by the absence of a regular police force in the colonies. The towns had army garrisons (almost useless in the bush) while the immense wilderness was patrolled by a handful of mounted troopers who hadn't a hope of controlling their colossal territory. When things got serious police work had to be done by posses of armed civilians—and they invariably included men whose sympathies lay with the bandits. The law suffered from a pretty poor profile in the early days of the colonies. This was aptly expressed by the popular folksong, "The Wild Colonial Boy," whose rollicking refrain runs:

> So come, all my hearties, we'll roam the mountains high,
> Together we will plunder, together we will die.
> We'll wander over valleys, and gallop over plains,
> We'll scorn to live in slavery, bound down with iron chains.

Bushrangerdom reached its peak with the Kelly Gang—the brothers Ned and Dan Kelly and two friends—whose exploits became as legendary as those of Frank and Jesse James in America. Ned Kelly possessed a certain rough chivalry, a wonderful flair for dramatics, and some genuine grudges against the authorities, including the alleged assault of his sister Kate by a trooper. He achieved a Robin Hood aura that still lingers. Even today you can buy into a fight in certain country pubs by making derogatory remarks about Ned, and "Game as Kelly" remains the highest tribute to a man's bravery in the Australian vocabulary.

The Kellys graduated from horse stealing to bank robbery and the holding up of entire country towns, where Ned made speeches to his literally captive audience redolent with Irish patriotism, Australian republicanism, and sentimental pathos. The locals loved it. For five years the Kelly gang ran the authorities ragged. Then, in June 1880, they overreached themselves. The four outlaws raided the town of Glenrowan, herding most of the population into Glenrowan Inn, where they wined and dined them liberally—at the management's expense.

Told that a trainload of troopers was heading up from Melbourne, the Kellys sabotaged the railroad track, hoping to wreck the police train. But the scheme failed, and the troopers swarmed into town. The gang barricaded Glenrowan Inn for their last stand. Three of them died in the gunfire—Ned came out fighting. He appeared, his head encased in a crude iron helmet, his chest armored with beaten ploughshares. For a while he seemed invulnerable, the hail of police bullets bounced screeching off his armor. Then the troopers aimed lower—at his unprotected legs—and Ned Kelly went down.

He was taken to Melbourne, sentenced to death, and duly hanged the following November—despite nationwide public petitions appealing for mercy on his behalf. His mother, a Ma Barker type, admonished her 25-year-old son: "Now mind that you die like a Kelly!" He did. Ned Kelly's ploughshare armor, pockmarked with bullet dents, is still on display in Melbourne.

ON THE SHEEP'S BACK: The bushranger plague faded out with the Kellys leaving Australia one of the most law-abiding countries on earth. The reason for this was not so much improved police work as the coming of prosperity, accompanied by an astonishing rise in the standard of living.

The substance behind the good life was wool. Australia rode to prosperity "on the sheep's back." Poor sheep—an animal few people love and even fewer find interesting, it was nevertheless the factor that transformed a cluster of struggling colonies into one of the wealthiest nations in the world. Cattle, and later minerals, played their parts, but the initial miracle was wrought by wool.

Some 428 rams and ewes came to Australia with the first convict fleets, a miserable runty lot, purchased partly in England, partly in the African Cape

Province. Both their numbers and their wool clip were laughable by today's standards. The Commonwealth now boasts around 165,000,000 sheep, and whereas their forebears yielded an average of less than three pounds of wool per head, the current clip is over nine pounds.

In 1801 a Capt. John Macarthur began to experiment with the breeding of fine-wool sheep, using Spanish merinos and English animals. In the meat-hungry colonies it took tremendous determination and foresight to breed for wool rather than mutton chops, but the effort paid off royally. By skillful hus-bandry Macarthur and his successors eventually succeeded in developing a kind of super sheep—the Australian merino—a walking mountain of wool of a quali-ty no breed in Europe or America could match. Such was the demand for Aus-tralian wool overseas that the exporters could take the huge shipping costs in their stride and still beat all competitors in the international wool market.

Sheep raising was—and is—a risky business. A single one of the devastat-ing Australian droughts can ruin a middling sheep farmer. Only immense flocks and enormous grazing lands offered some security—hence the tendency toward bigness in the industry. In the early days land ownership was established simply by occupation of "squatting." The big pastoralists were known as squatters, and as they grew bigger and richer the term "squattocracy" came into use for these sheep and cattle barons who, until industrialists and mine owners caught up with them, formed the country's financial and social elite.

COLONY TO COMMONWEALTH: For 80 years the British government fol-lowed an eminently sensible policy of granting limited home rule—including elected parliaments—to the Australian colonies. As the population increased, new colonies were carved out of the original ones and also granted constitu-tions. Thus by the end of the 19th century, Australia consisted of six separate colonies, each with its own constitution and legislature.

This pattern worked nicely from the viewpoint of the London Colonial Of-fice, but not so well for Australia. Among other drawbacks it saddled the young country with three different railroad gauges—which took several generations to standardize. It also fostered a psychology of separatism that might have been fatal to any form of concerted national effort.

The demand for unity and continental self-government became over-whelming with the approach of the 20th century. Federation was the watchword in every colony except Western Australia, which—isolated from the rest—had no desire to federate with anyone, but found itself forced to join by migrant gold miners.

The stage was set for Queen Victoria's proclamation issued on September 17, 1900. It established the Commonwealth of Australia as a united Dominion of the British Empire, a self-governing nation in every respect, but owing a largely traditional allegiance to the Crown as represented by the governor-general. The Commonwealth Constitution, worked out by a special convention, did a splendid job of picking the raisins from various pies. It adopted the best of British parliamentary procedure, large helpings of American Federalism, and a few snippets of French democracy. Added to this melange were some progres-sive touches that made it the most advanced political document of its time.

Women, for instance, received equal voting rights with men—20 years ahead of Britain and America! Voting was not only universal and secret, but compulsory (anyone who did not vote was fined), thereby eliminating any par-ty's ballot victory through lethargy. And to prevent the rival cities of Sydney and Melbourne from battling for the honor of being the nation's capital, it provided that a new city—roughly halfway between them—should be built for the express purpose of housing the federal government. The city, Canberra, was founded 13 years later, superbly designed by the American architect Walter Burley Griffin. Canberra had a stroke of luck in the final choice of its name. Among the ghastly labels suggested by politicians were Wheatwoolgold, Democratia, and—so help me—Marsupalia.

WAR: The infant Dominion entered World War I simultaneously—and with the same naïve enthusiasm—as the mother country. But unlike Britain, Australia never had to introduce conscription. Her problem was to find room for the avalanche of volunteers flooding the recruiting stations. Not even the gruesome casualty rate—the highest among all the Empire forces—did much to dampen the fervor. The Diggers were bigger, healthier, more aggressive—though less well disciplined—than the Tommies, which made them ideal assault troops. They suffered accordingly.

On April 25, 1915, the Anzacs (from the initials of Australian and New Zealand Army Corps) landed at Gallipoli in Turkey. The date, commemorated as Anzac Day, is now an Australian (and New Zealand) national holiday, but the actual event was a tragedy. For eight months the Anzacs held the barren, shell- and fever-ridden peninsula in the face of crack Turkish infantry supported by German artillery, before they were finally evacuated.

The Australian Light Horse Brigade spearheaded the British conquest of Palestine, and there were two Anzac corps fighting on the Western Front in France. Among their claims to fame is the (still-disputed) bagging of Manfred von Richthofen, the legendary "Red Baron," the war's No. 1 fighter ace. It is still debatable whether Richthofen was downed by a Canadian Sopwith pilot in the air or by Anzac machine guns from the ground. But when the celebrated red Fokker triplane—with its dead pilot—crashlanded in the Allied lines, an Aussie gunner peered at the German's face and yelled: "Cripes, we got the bloody baron!"

World War II, for Australia, opened very much like the first. Again the Dominion enlisted a large enthusiastic volunteer force, again it sailed to the Middle East, leaving an apparently safe homeland behind. But then Japan struck at Pearl Harbor, and with one blow the entire situation changed—fearfully.

Australia lay bare, wide open, and virtually undefended as the Japanese proceeded to swoop down through Southeast Asia. Most of the country's trained troops were fighting Rommel in Libya, 7,000 miles away. The remainder were lost when "impregnable" Singapore fell in February 1942. In July the Japanese landed in New Guinea, the huge island straddling Australia's northern doorstep. Japanese bombers wrecked Darwin, capital of the Northern Territory. Submarines shelled Sydney Harbour. The lights blacked out from coast to coast, and citizens grimly dug air raid shelters in the backyards of their little suburban homes. War, at last, had reached the "Lucky Country."

What followed was a trauma that shook Australia out of its complacent isolation, its smug feeling of invulnerability. For the first time the country had to draft manpower—and womanpower as well. Australia learned what it was like to try and defend her immense coastline with barely 7,000,000 inhabitants. Conscription was enforced drastically. The motto was: "Don't check their eyes, count them!" By literally scraping the bottom of the barrel, Australia placed 800,000 men and women in the armed forces, a call-up ratio only surpassed by Israel.

In the dense mountain jungle of New Guinea's Owen Stanley Range, half-trained, badly armed militiamen tried to stem the Japanese advance toward Port

Moresby, the springboard for an invasion of the Australian mainland. In the air Aussie pilots in light Wirraway trainers battled the Japanese Zeros. The Australians had to retreat, but they fought every step of the way along the muddy hell of the Kokoda Trail. And by the skin of their teeth managed to slow the enemy long enough for help to arrive.

Help . . . that meant the seasoned veterans from the Middle East and the Americans. Over Churchill's violent protests, Australia's wartime prime minister, John Curtin, ordered his troops back home. When they arrived—and U.S. reinforcements began to pour in—the tide in New Guinea turned. Australia was saved. But it had been, as the Duke of Wellington said about Waterloo, "A damned close run thing." Too close for any future complacency.

THE LUCKY COUNTRY: This label was coined by Australian writer Donald Horne, but with a somewhat different connotation than foreigners assumed. It meant fool's luck, luck by geographical and historical fluke, the kind of luck liable to run out any day unless backed by something more solid. And in the postwar decades Australia set out to create that backing.

Above anything, the continent needed people. The slogan "Populate or Perish" had been bandied about for half a century without resulting in action. The birthrate was—and is—low. And on top of producing few natural citizens, Australia also shut herself off by severely restrictive immigration rules designed to keep "lesser breeds" at a distance.

This changed drastically after 1945. Australia launched an assisted immigration scheme, with the government paying fares for overseas newcomers and their families, regardless of whether or not they spoke English. Now began the third great influx in the country's history, and this was by far the greatest. More than 3,000,000 migrants came and settled. Within 30 years the population topped 13½ million—almost double the prewar figure. Today about 40% of all Australians were either born overseas or have foreign-born parents.

At the same time Australia managed to avoid the minority ghetto enclaves that proved such a curse to America. The newcomers were not left to sink or swim on their own. They were given accommodation (of sorts), language tuition, health care, and considerable vocational guidance. Sternly enforced working standards prevented the "sweating" of migrant labor. Over the years a process of fusion occurred between old and "New Australians" and—equally important—among the newcomers themselves. The majority of them hailed from Britain, but over a million originated in countries habitually hostile to each other: Greece, Italy, Poland, Germany, the Netherlands, Austria, Yugoslavia. It says much for the balm of their new environment that they quickly buried their feuds—their children are hardly aware of them.

Simultaneously the continent's economy was radically altered. Until the late 1940s Australia's prosperity depended on the land. Today she is still the world's leading wool producer and a major supplier of wheat, meat, sugar, butter, and fruit. But agriculture has now dropped to 7% of the total production, its place taken up by manufacturing (particularly iron and steel) and a boom in mining that quadrupled the value of the mine output within a decade.

Something else altered as well—the average Australian's self-image. Australia is actually the most urban nation on earth, with 61% of the population living in large cities (compared to 48% in the United States). If you consider that Sydney and Melbourne alone account for some 5½ million people between them, the other state capitals for around three million more, this leaves mighty few country folks. Yet until recently most Aussies believed themselves to be spiritually a rural nation, almost as if the teeming cities were mere aberrations hiding the "real" Australia—in the "outback"—where only a handful lived. Now, at last, they have accepted the facts of their demography and shed the illusion of a Down Under Ruralia.

Australia today is a young and very prosperous country, facing the future with a less nonchalant but more rational optimism than before. Her material living standard is enviable: 75% of all houses are owned by their occupants, there are two motor vehicles registered for every five people, her citizens' life expectancy is among the highest and infant mortality among the lowest in the world. As a semiwelfare state her people enjoy national health benefits (including the famed Flying Doctor Service of the outback), guaranteed minimum wages and holidays, old-age pensions, child endowments, and maternity benefits. While not as comprehensive as the welfare schemes of Sweden or New Zealand, they are well in advance of, say, America or Canada.

For the tourist, Australia puts out the largest welcome mat in the international cupboard. It reads: Welcome to the New World Down Under; Welcome to the least known, most explorable continent; Welcome to the Lucky Country.

3. The Aborigines

It is a sadly significant fact that the original Australians are the only people in the world without a name. Racially they form a special category of mankind, the Australoids, but ethnically they are simply called Aborigines—natives. This namelessness remains symbolic of their tragedy—they were the people nobody recognized.

The Aborigines are believed to have migrated to Australia at least 30,000 years ago, perhaps via a land bridge that once linked the continent to Southeast Asia and was later submerged by the ocean. When the Aborigines arrived they were Stone Age hunters and food collectors—as were all *Homo sapiens* then. But while the rest of humanity developed into shepherds and peasants, the Aborigines—cut off from the mainstream—stayed nomadic hunters.

The reasons for this lay in their environment. Australia had no indigenous animals suitable for domestication, no grain food that could be cultivated. It was a harsh, largely arid wilderness that forced its inhabitants to keep wandering in search of game and water, thus preventing them from establishing permanent villages. And their isolation was so complete that they had no opportunities to copy the methods of other societies.

There were an estimated 300,000 Aborigines before the coming of the white man, scattered throughout the gigantic continent in tiny groups that spoke 300 or more different languages. Unlike the New Zealand Maoris and the American Indians, the Aborigines were not organized for war, had no concept of warfare in our sense of the word. This was their particular misfortune, because it prevented them from offering large-scale resistance to the invaders.

The white man saw nothing except their backwardness, only noticed the things they did *not* have: such as agriculture, pottery, woven cloth, seagoing vessels, or a military establishment. He was blind to their very real accomplishments, which are only now getting some of the appreciation they deserve.

For the Aborigines had invented aerodynamic marvels in the boomerang and the woomera—a kind of wooden extension of the throwing arm that imparts a bullet-like spin to a spear, vastly increasing its range, hitting power, and accuracy. They had perfected an amazingly sophisticated sign language—"finger talk"—that overcame tribal language barriers and acted as a universal lingua franca such as Europe, for instance, never possessed. They were the world's greatest trackers and hunters, capable of trailing a snake across bare, solid rock and telling the age, sex, weight, height, and tribe of a person by a couple of footprints. Although they couldn't read or write they communicated by message sticks that related intricate details by means of a few carved grooves.

They had a highly developed sense of artistry and worked wonders with primitive paint mixtures. Above all, they had established an ecological life pattern that most civilized nations would envy. They kept their birthrate at acceptable levels through a complex system of marriage taboos that avoided indiscriminate breeding among the tribes. Another set of taboos forbade certain members to eat or hunt certain animals—thereby assuring the survival of all animal species, and their own survival as well.

But the entire delicate balance of Aboriginal existence was destroyed by the conquering white settlers. The Europeans either killed Aborigines outright or condemned them to death by starvation, imported diseases, and rotgut liquor. Periodically there were outbursts of mass slaughter, such as the systematic drive that exterminated the entire native population of Tasmania.

On reading the historical martyrdom of the "nameless people" it seems almost a miracle that any of them survived. Only about 50,000 full-blooded Aborigines are left today, although the total number of people with Aboriginal strains is around 150,000. And since their conditions began to improve, their numbers are once again increasing.

A small minority—a few thousand at best—still live the nomadic life of their forebears in the remotest regions of Queensland and the Northern Territory. About ten times that many are settled in mission stations and government-sponsored outback communities. Thousands more work as stockmen (cowboys) in the huge northern cattle stations, many of which couldn't operate without the specialized skill of their black herders. Small groups also live in and around the capital cities, mostly in slum conditions.

But although the plight of most Aborigines is still bleak, a new and brighter era is dawning for them. The change began in the 1950s, when white Australia discovered some of the extraordinary artistry of the Aboriginal heritage. The superb ballet "Corroboree" thrilled capacity audiences who had never before realized the wild, magical beauty of this ceremonial dance form. The Aboriginal painter Albert Namatjira achieved world fame with his dazzling bush landscapes and opened a ready market for an entire generation of black artists. Aboriginal poets, authors, tennis stars, educators, and politicians appeared on the scene, presenting an entirely new image of their people to the white majority.

In 1972 the first Aboriginal knight was created by the queen. Sir Douglas Nicholls, a champion athlete as well as a leading churchman and tireless fighter for the advancement of his people, symbolized a huge step forward for the entire Australoid race.

A new spirit of pride and self-awareness is stirring among the original Australians. For the first time since the discovery of the continent Aboriginal voices and demands are being heard . . . and are finding a sympathetic echo among thousands of whites who had hitherto hardly been aware of their existence. In January 1972, a group of militant young blacks pitched a tent on the lawn in front of Canberra's Parliament House and declared themselves the "Aboriginal Embassy." It was a dramatic move designed to catch the attention of politicians and public alike—and it turned out to be one of the most successful public relations gestures in the country's history. The "invisible people" had suddenly become very visible indeed.

Most Aborigines undoubtedly desire complete assimilation—on equal terms—into white society. But this goal may entail the sacrifice of their unique heritage, the oblivion of their special culture. Materially such a sacrifice might seem worthwhile, yet anyone who has had a glimpse of Australoid traditions would be saddened by their extinction.

As Kath Walker, Australia's leading black poet, versed it:

Pour your pitcher of wine into the wide river
And where is your wine? There is only the river.
Must the genius of an old race die
That the race might live?

4. Flora and Fauna

What the Aussies term "bush" covers a fabulous variety of scenery, from tropical hothouse jungles glowing with orchids to gently rolling grassland and mountain meadows carpeted with wildflowers. It's all "bush" to the locals.

Their continent harbors hundreds of native plants found nowhere else on the globe. Western Australia alone grows some 6,000 species of wildflowers, many of them unique. But the two plants that symbolize the country are the acacia (Australians call it "wattle") featured in the national coat-of-arms, and the eucalyptus gum. The eucalyptus is as Australian as the kangaroo. It grows in more than 700 varieties throughout the country, some of them rearing to heights of 300 feet, their pungent blossoms shining white, deep scarlet, and coral pink.

For eons of time the eucalyptus gums were isolated from the rest of the world's flora by immense oceans, but today they are probably the most transplanted trees anywhere. They were exported to California and Arizona, to Japan, Canada, South Africa, and the Middle East, chiefly because they make ideal and astonishingly hardy windbreaks. And their unmistakable sharp, medicinal scent is guaranteed to make any Aussie homesick the moment he catches that characteristic whiff.

Foreigners may not recognize the singularity of much of Australia's flora. But there's no mistaking the uniqueness of the animal life. Australia is a gigantic outdoor museum for furred, feathered, and scaled phenomena that developed only there and in no other portion of our earth. There is a curious lopsidedness about this development—Mother Nature went rampant in the marsupial department, but left out virtually every other branch.

Marsupials are animals that carry their young in pouches. Their prime representatives are the kangaroos and their close cousins, the wallabies. They come in an amazing assortment of sizes, from the tiny rat kangaroo to the hulking Great Grey, six feet tall when upright and strong enough to knock over a pony. There are tree-climbing kangaroos and rock kangaroos, nest dwellers, swamp inhabitants, and those that stick to the wide-open plains.

All of them share the habit of tucking their babies back into their pouches when danger threatens, and the ability to perform fantastic leaps. Jumps of 25 feet are routine stuff—when pressed they have been known to sail 40 feet in one leap. Kangaroos are a delight to watch, but unfortunately their hides can be turned into excellent leather, their tails into gourmet soup. And human greed being what it is, thousands of these gentle creatures are slaughtered yearly by professional hunters. So if you want to do Australia—and the world—a favor, *don't* buy kangaroo leather souvenirs. Because otherwise your only chance of seeing a live kangaroo may soon be in a zoo.

If the kangaroo is appealing, the koala is adorable. Although he closely resembles a teddy bear with fluffy ears, he's no bear but another marsupial. Slow moving and even slower thinking, koalas live in trees, dreamily munching gumleaves and rarely descending to the ground. When the young emerge from their pouches they ride piggyback on their mothers until old enough to start munching on their own. Koalas need no water, but get enough moisture from their leaf diet to stay aloft permanently.

Equally cuddly, but somewhat tougher, is the wombat. About the size of a fox terrier, wombats dig holes in the ground at amazing speed and emerge from them at night to search for roots and shrubs. They make gentle, affectionate house pets and never bite. But don't underestimate them. Wombats have been known to weigh 80 pounds, and their backs are strong enough to crush any dog foolish enough to pursue them into their burrows.

Most marsupials are harmless vegetarians, but the family includes a few pretty fierce carnivores. The native "cats," for instance, aren't feline at all, but remarkably catlike pouch animals. And the Tasmanian devil must rate as one of the most aggressive critters extant. They aren't very big—about as large as a cocker spaniel—with disproportionately powerful forequarters and massive teeth. The devils eat anything that won't eat them—dead or alive. They're remarkably noisy for predators, snarling and screaming like demons when angered. Today they are found only in the remotest parts of Tasmania, although they're in no danger of becoming extinct.

The most common predator in Australia, the dingo, remains something of a mystery. The dingo is no marsupial, but a genuine wild dog with every canine characteristic except the bark. Dingoes can only howl. Nobody knows for certain just how the dingo came to Australia. They were already there, although in small numbers, when the white man arrived. Most zoologists now assume that they entered the continent with the migrating Aborigines, about 30,000 years ago. The dingoes multiplied rapidly when the colonists obligingly imported rabbits and sheep, and today these silent, tawny yellow outlaws are the scourge of sheep farmers and cattlemen alike. Fast, strong, tough, and highly intelligent, the dingoes are holding their own against every attempt to exterminate them, which includes aerial, chemical, and bacteriological warfare.

If the dingo is a mystery, the platypus is a living conundrum. When the first platypus skins reached Europe in the 18th century, zoologists flatly refused to believe they belonged to a genuine animal. You can't altogether blame them. What do you say about a creature that has a duck's bill, a mole's fur, the tail of a beaver, webbed feet, one poisonous claw, and that lays eggs and then suckles its young?

The platypus is a very shy little aquatic animal living in quiet rivers and lakes, where it eats immense quantities of prawns and worms—nearly its own weight per night. While it hunts in the water, it sleeps on land, building long underground tunnels with entrances just above the waterline. At one time the platypus was killed extensively for its fine fur, but now it is heavily protected and off the danger list.

Yet another phenomenon in Australia's menagerie is the Queensland lung fish. This is a prehistoric "fossil," survivor of a primitive marine species that thrived during the Triassic Period—some 35 million years ago! The lung fish has a singular breathing apparatus that enables it to live out of the water—in dry mud—for entire summers.

Reptiles abound in Australia, including giant saltwater crocodiles, huge pythons (frequently employed as rat catchers in fruit warehouses), and one of the world's deadliest snakes. This is the—luckily very rare—taipan, a rather drab brownish serpent that can inject more venom than a cobra. The various lizards are all harmless, even the goannas that grow up to eight feet in length and can run like greased lightning. Despite their dragon-like appearance they make very fancy eating—if you'd care to try.

The emu has the distinction of sharing his country's coat-of-arms with the kangaroo. This is the most Australian of birds, although not exactly popular with farmers. Closely resembling an ostrich, the emu is incapable of flying, but hits running speeds of over 30 miles per hour and has a kick that could stun a mule. Emus travel in flocks and when they descend on cropfields it's goodbye to the harvest. Farmers have gone to great expense in stringing emu-proof fences around their land, but the birds seem to have a genius for finding weak spots in the barriers.

The kookaburra, on the other hand, is the most beloved bird in the Commonwealth. Chiefly because it's a snake killer that can handle the most dangerous reptiles, scooping them up and dropping them from great heights or cracking them like a whip against a tree. The kookaburra—also known as laughing jackass—has a sense of humor as well. It literally shrieks with laughter in the bush—and often seems to time its hilarity when someone below has fallen flat on his face. They're completely fearless and will divebomb people or cats who come too near their nests. But they are also easily tamed, and once they learn that you'll feed them they'll form a cackling, giggling reception committee at your doorstep.

There is a strangely mystical quality about the bird known as brolga. A member of the crane family, this handsome, graceful four-footer figures largely in Aboriginal legendry. Brolgas perform amazingly stately and intricate dances, tossing their heads back and stepping high like chorus girls while keeping rhythm in their hoarse trumpet voices. The brolga dances form the basis of Aboriginal corroborees, and more recently have inspired modern ballet choreographers.

Perhaps the most startling aspect of Australia's fauna is the role played by imported animals. The country grew rich through imported sheep and cattle—but it nearly ruined itself by importing rabbits. The half dozen or so originals multiplied—well, like rabbits. They grew into hundreds of millions of bunnies that gobbled up the grass meant for livestock and required ruthless germ warfare to keep under some kind of control.

Throughout the more rugged northern portions of the continent you'll come upon wild buffaloes, camels, and donkeys. None of these creatures was indigenous; all of them were imported for domestic purposes, but ran wild, multiplied, and frequently became pests. Buffalo hunting is still a prime sport in the Northern Territory, but you'd better be sure of your marksmanship before joining the hunt. A wounded buff can be one of the most lethal customers you're liable to encounter.

The camels date back to the prerailroad era. They were brought in, together with Afghan drivers, to carry goods through desert country. The bearded, turbaned Afghans vanished when tracks replaced hoofs. But the camels stayed and multiplied, and are still there in the thousands. All of which makes you feel grateful that the Aussie forebears never thought of importing a few prides of lions. No telling *what* might have happened.

AUSTRALIA: A BUDGET SURVEY

YOU WOULD BE WISE to read this chapter before you embark on your trip. It may be the most useful in the entire book. It tells you when to come, what documents you'll need to get in, what to pack, where to go and stay, where to make inquiries, what to eat and drink, as well as a few things to avoid.

Above all, it tells you how to enjoy the best Australia has to offer at the lowest possible cost. This doesn't mean that you should slavishly follow all the tips listed below. Most of them are merely money- and aggravation-saving guidelines, leaving plenty of leeway in all directions. The best travelers are always the creative ones—those who use guidebooks like compasses indicating a general target, but approaching it at their own pace and according to their own tastes and wallets. And since this book is deliberately money-oriented we'll start with—

THE CURRENCY: Australia, you'll be glad to know, reckons in dollars and cents. A dollar is a buck, there as here, but forget about terms like nickels, dimes, and quarters. The Australian dollar ($A) tends to float several points *below* the U.S. buck, but these points vary from month to month. Most of the time it hovers around the US 66¢ mark, so for simplicity's sake assume that all prices mentioned in this book are 34% lower than their American equivalents.

Coins come in 1¢ and 2¢ copper pieces; 5¢, 10¢, 20¢, and 50¢ in silver; and $1 in brass. Notes (*not* bills) are $2, $5, $10, $20, and $50. There is no limit on the amount of money you may take into the country. You may take out any unused foreign or Australian currency in the form of traveler's checks, but no more than $A250 in cash.

CLIMATE—WHEN TO COME: Keep in mind that Australia is a continent as well as a country and that the climate varies accordingly. The variations are not as great as in America, but sharp enough to make you regret wearing the wrong clothes during certain seasons. The seasons are the reverse of those in the northern hemisphere: September to November is spring, December to February summer, March to May fall, and June to August winter.

The climate regions are upside down as well. The tropics lie north, the temperate zones south. Tasmania, the island state off the southern tip of the continent, is the coolest, while north of Brisbane things get pretty hot most of the year. As a general rule you can assume that from November to March it's warm to broiling everywhere. In the far north—around Darwin—this is the monsoon season and definitely a time to stay away unless you enjoy getting drenched in lukewarm rainwater. But the northern winter offers close to ideal traveling weather—days of crystal-clear sunshine, strong enough to tan, and nights crisp enough to appreciate a fireplace. In the south, winter tends to be chilly, with plenty of snow and excellent skiing in the mountain ranges. But even in Melbourne, the most southerly of the mainland capitals, the mercury rarely hits freezing point. Tasmania, however, has an almost—not quite—European winter. All around, Australia can be said to have superb tourist weather, particularly in the capital cities which lie outside the extreme hot and cold belts.

1. Preparing for Your Trip

TRAVEL DOCUMENTS: You need a passport and a visa to enter Australia unless you happen to be a New Zealander or a citizen of another Commonwealth country with permission to reside in either New Zealand or Australia. Australian visas are free and valid for a stay of up to six months, although the period allowed may be shorter. Applications for visa extensions have to be made at an office of the Department of Immigration in Australia. Visitors must also produce a return ticket and "sufficient funds"—whatever that means. Visas can be obtained from Australian or British government offices in major cities.

You can't, however, immigrate to Australia on the strength of a visa. If that's in your mind you will have to apply from outside the country, stating your purpose. And permits aren't being handed out anywhere near as lavishly as they used to be, say, ten years ago.

You need vaccination certificates against smallpox and yellow fever *only* if you've visited a country infected with these diseases within the preceding 14 days of entering Australia. The World Health Organization designates such countries, which means that if you come from the U.S., Canada, Britain, or New Zealand you can forget about the certificates.

There are no Customs charges on your personal belongings which you intend to use in the country and take home again. In addition, you may import duty free 250 cigarettes, or 9 ounces of cigars, or 9 ounces of tobacco, and 35 fluid ounces of alcoholic liquor, plus goods up to the value of $A200 for your own use or as presents.

If you are either British, Canadian, or Irish and between 18 and 30 years of age, you *may* be eligible for a working holiday visa. This entitles you to stay a maximum of three years and take employment during that period. Applications for this visa can only be made in your home country.

You can get further information at the Australian government offices listed below:

U.S.A.	Australian Consulate-General, 360 Post St., San Francisco, CA 94108 (tel. 415/362-6160)
	Australian Consulate-General, One Illinois Center, Suite 2212, 111 East Wacker Dr., Chicago, IL 60601 (tel. 312/329-1740)
	Australian Consulate-General, 636 Fifth Ave., 4th Floor, New York, NY 10111 (tel. 212/245-4000)
Canada	Australian High Commission, 130 Slater St., Ottawa, ON K1P 5H6 (tel. 613/236-0841)
England	Australian High Commission, Australia House, The Strand, London WC2B 4LA (tel. 438-8000)
New Zealand	Australian High Commission, 72 Hobson St., Wellington (tel. 736-411)

WHAT TO PACK: The wearables you should pack naturally depend on what time of the year you come and what you want to do (consult the section on climate, above). But there are a few items you should bring under all circumstances, regardless of seasons and intentions. One is a washcloth in a plastic case—very few Aussie hotels supply them to their guests. A travel alarm clock—this makes you independent of hotel wake-up calls, which are pretty unreliable. You can miss a lot of flights by relying on the early-morning memory of desk clerks. Sunglasses. A very small screwdriver. (In 15 years of globetrotting I've found that to be one of the handiest gadgets extant.) A cigarette lighter—matches don't come free of charge anywhere outside America. (The standard Australian wood matches cost 12¢ a box.) One pair of light plastic shoe trees. A magnifying glass to read the tiny print on maps. Stationery and envelopes, since these items are much more expensive in Australia than in the U.S. The same goes for film.

Leave at home any kind of electrical gadgetry, unless you bring along a 220-240V, flat three-pin plug converter/adapter. Also tropical whites for men. They spot hideously and, anyway, in torrid zones Australian males wear khaki.

As far as clothing is concerned, include at least one warm sweater or jacket, even if you come in summer. You get occasional cold snaps everywhere except in the tropical north. Men should also bring a tie (an ascot will do as well), since there are still a few restaurants and hotel dining rooms around that won't serve you without one. Otherwise Australians are very casual dressers, although women tend to wear more skirts and fewer pants than their American sisters. But ladies' pants suits are now universally accepted even as formal wear.

The Australian warm-weather outfit for men is both smart and eminently practical. It consists of walk shorts, high socks, shoes, and a short-sleeved shirt with or without a tie. They wear this to the office and almost everywhere else. The shorts are tighter in the butt than the American versions, usually khaki or some other solid color, and *never* droopy or flowered. The whole ensemble looks faintly military and very neat.

Women needn't bother to stock up on pantyhose. They're sold everywhere—and cheaply—in Australia. But you should beware of taking any cosmetic liquid in glass bottles; stick to unbreakable plastic. Anyway, you don't have to bring a load of cosmetics. International brand names are sold throughout Australia and the local products are excellent and usually much cheaper.

If you come in winter, the handiest item either sex can bring is an all-weather coat with a detachable lining. That, combined with a scarf, gloves, and a small travel umbrella, should see you through whatever the Down Under winter has in store.

A final word on packing in general—*travel light*. Never bring more luggage than you yourself can carry without assistance. Porters aren't always available at air terminals and rail stations, and those handy little luggage carts have a knack of disappearing just when you need them. The ideal tourist baggage consists of one suitcase and a shoulderbag. In that respect those who follow this book are more fortunate than I, who wrote it. They don't have to lug a typewriter.

TOURIST INFORMATION: The **Australian Tourist Commission** is possibly the most helpful, patient, sympathetic, and painstaking outfit ever created by a government. You can approach them with just about any question related to travel, and if they don't know the answer they're almost sure to put you in touch with someone who does. You'll find the addresses of the state (as distinct from federal) tourist bureaus in the appropriate chapters. But the ATC also has overseas offices you can consult before starting your trip. You'll find them at the following locations:

U.S.A.	3550 Wilshire Blvd., Suite 1740, Los Angeles, CA 90010 (tel. 213/380-6060)
	489 Fifth Ave., New York, NY 10017 (tel. 212/687-6300)
England	Heathcoat House, 20 Savile Row, London W1X 1AE (tel. 434-4371)
New Zealand	Quay Tower, 29 Customs St. West, Auckland 1 (tel. 799-594)

2. The $25-a-Day Travel Club—How to Save Money on All Your Travels

In this book we'll be looking at how to get your money's worth in Australia but there is a "device" for saving money and determining value on *all* your trips. It's the popular, international $25-a-Day Travel Club, now in its 24th successful year of operation. The Club was formed at the urging of numerous readers of the $$$-a-Day and Dollarwise Guides, who felt that such an organization could provide continuing travel information and a sense of community to value-minded travelers in all parts of the world. And so it does!

In keeping with the budget concept, the annual membership fee is low and is immediately exceeded by the value of your benefits. Upon receipt of $18 (U.S. residents), or $20 U.S. by check drawn on a U.S. bank or via international postal money order in U.S. funds (Canadian, Mexican, and other foreign residents) to cover one year's membership, we will send all new members the following items.

(1) *Any two* of the following books

Please designate in your letter which two you wish to receive:

Europe on $25 a Day

Australia on $25 a Day
England on $35 a Day
Eastern Europe on $25 a Day
Greece including Istanbul and Turkey's Aegean Coast on $25 a Day
Hawaii on $45 a Day
India on $15 & $25 a Day
Ireland on $35 a Day
Israel on $30 & $35 a Day
Mexico on $20 a Day
New York on $45 a Day
New Zealand on $25 a Day
Scandinavia on $40 a Day
Scotland and Wales on $35 a Day
South America on $25 a Day
Spain and Morocco (plus the Canary Is.) on $40 a Day
Turkey on $25 a Day
Washington, D.C., on $40 a Day

Dollarwise Guide to Alaska
Dollarwise Guide to Austria and Hungary
Dollarwise Guide to Benelux
Dollarwise Guide to Bermuda and The Bahamas
Dollarwise Guide to Canada
Dollarwise Guide to the Caribbean
Dollarwise Guide to Egypt
Dollarwise Guide to England and Scotland
Dollarwise Guide to France
Dollarwise Guide to Germany
Dollarwise Guide to Italy
Dollarwise Guide to Japan and Hong Kong
Dollarwise Guide to Portugal, Madeira, and the Azores
Dollarwise Guide to Switzerland and Liechtenstein
Dollarwise Guide to California and Las Vegas
Dollarwise Guide to Florida
Dollarwise Guide to New England
Dollarwise Guide to New York State
Dollarwise Guide to the Northwest
Dollarwise Guide to Skiing USA—East
Dollarwise Guide to Skiing USA—West
Dollarwise Guide to the Southeast and New Orleans
Dollarwise Guide to the Southwest
Dollarwise Guide to Texas
(Dollarwise Guides discuss accommodations and facilities in all price ranges, with emphasis on the medium-priced.)

A Guide for the Disabled Traveler
(A guide to the best destinations for wheelchair travelers and other disabled vacationers in Europe, the United States, and Canada by an experienced wheelchair traveler. Includes detailed information about accommodations, restaurants, sights, transportation, and their accessibility.)

A Shopper's Guide to Best Buys in England, Scotland, and Wales
(Describes in detail hundreds of places to shop—department stores, factory outlets, street markets, and craft centers—for great quality British bargains.)

A Shopper's Guide to the Caribbean
(A guide to the best shopping in the islands. Includes full descriptions of what to look for and where to find it.)

Bed & Breakfast—North America
(This guide contains a directory of over 150 organizations that offer bed & breakfast referrals and reservations throughout North America. The scenic attractions, businesses, and major schools and universities near the homes of each are also listed.)

Dollarwise Guide to Cruises
(This complete guide covers all the basics of cruising—ports of call, costs, fly-cruise package bargains, cabin selection booking, embarkation and debarkation and describes in detail over 60 or so ships cruising the waters of Alaska, the Caribbean, Mexico, Hawaii, Panama, Canada, and the United States.)

Dollarwise Guide to Skiing Europe
(Describes top ski resorts in Austria, France, Italy, and Switzerland. Illustrated with maps of each resort area plus full-color trail maps.)

Travel Diary and Record Book
(A 96-page diary for personal travel notes plus a section for such vital data as passport and traveler's check numbers, itinerary, postcard list, special people and places to visit, and a reference section with temperature and conversion charts, and world maps with distance zones.)

How to Beat the High Cost of Travel
(This practical guide details how to save money on absolutely all travel items—accommodations, transportation, dining, sightseeing, shopping, taxes, and more. Includes special budget information for seniors, students, singles, and families.)

Marilyn Wood's Wonderful Weekends
(This very selective guide covers the best mini-vacation destinations within a 175-mile radius of New York City. It describes special country inns and other accommodations, restaurants, picnic spots, sights, and activities—all the information needed for a two- or three-day stay.)

Museums in New York
(A complete guide to all the museums, historic houses, gardens, zoos, and more in the five boroughs. Illustrated with over 200 photographs.)

Swap and Go—Home Exchanging Made Easy
(Two veteran home exchangers explain in detail all the money-saving benefits of a home exchange, and then describe precisely how to do it. Also includes information on home rentals and many tips on low-cost travel.)

The Fast 'n' Easy Phrase Book
(French, German, Spanish, and Italian—all in one convenient, easy-to-use phrase guide.)

Motorist's Phrase Book
(A practical phrase book in French, German, and Spanish designed specifically for the English-speaking motorist touring abroad.)

The New York Urban Athlete
(The ultimate guide to all the sports facilities in New York City for jocks and novices.)

Where to Stay USA
(By the Council on International Educational Exchange, this extraordinary guide is the first to list accommodations in all 50 states that cost anywhere from $3 to $30 per night.)

(2) A one-year subscription to *The Wonderful World of Budget Travel*

This quarterly eight-page tabloid newspaper keeps you up to date on fast-breaking developments in low-cost travel in all parts of the world bringing you the latest money-saving information—the kind of information you'd have to pay $25 a year to obtain elsewhere. This consumer-conscious publication also features columns of special interest to readers: **Hospitality Exchange** (members all over the world who are willing to provide hospitality to other members as they pass through their home cities); **Share-a-Trip** (offers and requests from members for travel companions who can share costs and help avoid the burdensome single supplement); and **Readers Ask . . . Readers Reply** (travel questions from members to which other members reply with authentic firsthand information).

(3) A copy of *Arthur Frommer's Guide to New York*

This is a pocket-size guide to hotels, restaurants, nightspots, and sightseeing attractions in all price ranges throughout the New York area.

(4) Your personal membership card

Membership entitles you to purchase through the Club all Arthur Frommer publications for a third to a half off their regular retail prices during the term of your membership.

So why not join this hardy band of international budgeteers and participate in its exchange of travel information and hospitality?

Simply send your name and address, together with your annual membership fee of $18 (U.S. residents) or $20 U.S. (Canadian, Mexican, and other foreign residents), by check drawn on a U.S. bank or via international postal money order in U.S. funds to: $25-A-Day Travel Club, Inc., Frommer Books, Gulf + Western Building, One Gulf + Western Plaza, New York, NY 10023. And please remember to specify which *two* of the books in section (1) above you wish to receive in your initial package of members' benefits. Or, if you prefer, use the last page of this book, simply checking off the two books you select and enclosing $18 or $20 in U.S. currency.

Once you are a member, there is no obligation to buy additional books. No books will be mailed to you without your specific order.

---

3. Where to Stay

Australia offers an immense range of accommodations, from super-deluxe to rock-bottom economy. However, during holiday periods you'll be competing for beds with half of the country's population (see the ABCs at the end of this chapter for holidays). The choice, particularly in the budget line, can then get pretty meager. So, if possible, arrange your travels outside the public holidays. You can always get accommodations of some kind through the various state tourist bureaus (you'll find the addresses listed in the appropriate chapters), but it may not be in the area and price range you want. Every chapter also contains my personal selection of budget hostelries, with a few higher bracket places thrown in for good measure. Most places in resort areas and some in the big cities charge higher rates during holidays.

ACCOMMODATIONS IN GENERAL: There is a certain degree of desperate confusion in the Australian terminology for hostelries. This is entirely due to the country's somewhat antiquated liquor laws (and if you think they're ludicrous now, you should have seen them 25 years ago). These laws were framed—way back—with two purposes in mind: (1) to prevent the populace from drinking at the times most convenient and agreeable to them, and (2) to restrict the profitable sale of liquor to as tight a monopoly as possible. The laws were backed and maintained by a formidable combination of "wowsers" and liquor barons.

For over 40 years this combination kept Australia in a kind of drinking kindergarten, a condition accepted by the natives with the same sheeplike docility with which Americans, for instance, submit to the tyranny of tipping. The laws were so ludicrous that restaurateurs could be—and were—prosecuted for serving sherry trifle dessert with real sherry while not possessing a liquor license. Rum-filled chocolates were likewise taboo—candy stores don't have liquor licenses either. Even today, while the wowsers' grip has been loosened, enough irritating restrictions remain to demonstrate that the black-shrouded bluenose brigade is still very much around.

And what has all this to do with accommodations? I'm coming to that. The laws stipulated that in order to qualify for a liquor license, a "public house" had to be a hotel. Meaning that it had to sleep guests and serve food as well as liquid refreshments. But for most hotels only the bar trade brought in profit; they hated the idea of houseguests. Therefore a great many of them operated as hotels in name only—they maintained a few rooms, but kept them permanently empty by informing would-be guests that they were occupied. And they got away with it partly through political pull, but mainly because nobody bothered to raise a big enough stink.

The trouble is that a lot of these hotels are still functioning in the same fashion. The word "hotel," therefore, can either mean a genuine accommodation place or simply a drinking establishment. You have no way of telling until you ask to sleep there. And to add to the confusion, both types of hostelries are known as "pubs." Only in the past few years have the powers that be grudgingly issued a few tavern licenses—permission to operate honest-to-goodness bars clearly distinguishable from hotels.

The term **hotel,** in Australia, still means an establishment that runs a bar and may—*or may not*—accommodate houseguests. A **private hotel** takes guests but does not have a license to sell liquor. There is no real difference between a private hotel and a **guesthouse,** except that the latter always serves at least breakfast, the former *may* not serve any meals. In my listings I make a point of informing you whether or not meals are available in a particular hostelry.

YOUTH HOSTELS: The **Youth Hostel Association** (AYHA) is affiliated with the International Youth Hostel Federation and honors international membership cards. The AYHA hostels can be found in every Australian state and territory. They range from modern specially designed hostels to a convict-built church in New South Wales, a former toll house in Tasmania, and a defunct railroad station in Western Australia. Comfort-wise they range from the cozy to the primitive.

Overnight charges vary from $3 to $8, depending on location and facilities provided. All hostels require that you use regulation sleeping sheets. You can either make one yourself or buy one from the AYHA for around $10. The hostels have no age limit, but all of them bar alcohol and most (not all) impose a 10 p.m. curfew on their guests. All provide cooking facilities of some kind, most have hot showers and laundry facilities. The AYHA's Australian head office is at 60 Mary St., Surry Hills, Sydney, N.S.W. 2010 (tel. 212-1151). The AYHA puts out an excellent annual brochure, the *Australian Youth Hostels Handbook,* listing every hostel in the country, its prices, rules, and facilities, together with a map showing you how to get there. Membership cards can be obtained in the U.S. through **American Youth Hostels, Inc.,** National Administrative Offices, 1332 I St. NW, Suite 800, Washington, DC 20005. They cost $10 for juniors (under 18), $20 for seniors (any age above 18). Some Australian hostels also charge lower rates for juniors.

THE Y's: Both the YMCA and YWCA have hostels/hotels scattered throughout Australia. But in certain cities one or the other has become defunct, with the result that most M's now also take women and most W's also accommodate men. Several—although by no means all—are real bargains at about $10 a night. You'll find a description of the Y's among my accommodation listings in the various city chapters.

COLLEGES: Both students and nonstudents can stay at certain university colleges during vacations—although *bona fide* students usually get priority. These dorms are mostly comfortable, congenial, and wonderfully relaxed as well as cheap. You'll find a selection of them listed in the city chapters.

CAMPING AND TRAILER PARKS: Many caravan camps hire out on-site vans (house trailers) at very reasonable rates. The trouble is that the majority of these camps are located way out of town, sometimes with only a poor excuse for public transport. They are universally practicable only when you have your own wheels. Get a list of campsites from the relevant state tourist bureau or state motoring association and pinpoint them on a map before you inquire about rental vans. If you're motorized or if the camp is near a bus stop to the city, this is the most economical group or pair accommodation you'll find. Rates start at around $12 per night, but go up according to time of year.

Campsites have been accused of catering only to the caravan folks, caring little or nothing for the "genuine" tent campers. This is probably true, but most of them still let you pitch your canvas and provide you with access to hot showers, electricity, drinking water, sewerage and laundry facilities for $5 to $7 a night.

FARMHOUSE HOLIDAYS: A great idea providing you really enjoy country life and can do without the "bright lights" and whatever goes with them. A number of farms (stations) throughout Australia offer accommodations for paying guests, usually no more than five to eight at a time. The host farms change frequently, so the best thing is to get a current list of choices from the state government tourist bureau, which also tells you conditions, facilities, and prices, and will arrange bookings. It can be a fascinatingly "different" experience, particularly if you have a modicum of interest in agriculture.

Accommodations vary considerably—as do the tariffs. Some homesteads offer independent cottages on their properties. Others put up guests in their house, which means that you take all your meals with the host families and, in some cases, share their bathroom. Still others provide completely independent guest wings with all private facilities. On some places you may—but don't have to—join in the farm activities. But all of them offer you the run of the place. You're free to fish in the creeks, ride the horses, swim in the waterholes (or the family pool). The hospitality is invariably warm, you're treated as a member of the family. And the meals are country style—meaning enormous. Rates depend on the standard of accommodations and on whether you take bed-and-breakfast only or dinner as well. The range hovers between $10 and $50 a day.

MOTELS: These are a relatively recent innovation in Australia, which means that most of them are modern, well equipped, and comfortable in their own plastic fashion. They also go under titles like "motor inn" or "motor lodge" but I've not been able to discern any difference. As in America, they run the gamut from little five-unit establishments to luxury high-rises with Olympic-size swimming pools and sauna baths. Unlike their American counterparts, however, they have no real budget bracket. The basic cut-price category is missing. I have listed some of the cheaper ones, but there just aren't very many of them about. If an establishment is called hotel-motel it usually means an older hotel with a newer motel patched on. And you can bet that the hotel portion will be less expensive.

Most motels provide tea- and coffee-making facilities and refrigerators for their guests. Breakfast is usually served on trays to each unit and *may* be included in the tariff. The majority offer family units taking up to six people and will give concession rates for children.

BED-AND-BREAKFAST: This lodging concept, the mainstay of budget travelers in Britain, Ireland, or the continent, is less clearly defined in Australia. As a general rule, you may assume that all higher priced hostelries will charge you extra for breakfast, while in *some* economy-class places it's included in the price. Thus a bed-and-breakfast place can be anything from an elderly guesthouse to a brand-new hotel, although mostly it's the former. In my listings I have separated the B&B establishments from the rest to make your selection easier. (Note the specialized outfit called **Bed and Breakfast Australia** in the Sydney chapter.) I also tell you what *kind* of breakfast they serve, since the difference may be between a three-course meal and a morning snack.

SERVICED APARTMENTS: For couples, groups, or families these are the greatest money-savers of them all. Such apartments (flats in local parlance) consist of one to three rooms, plus bathrooms and kitchens. They come fully equipped with cooking and eating utensils, refrigerators, etc., and enable you to set up house for days or weeks or months. Your food bills go down fabulously when you cook for yourself, quite aside from the fact that you can cook the way *you* like it.

Australia is not as well supplied with these establishments as, for instance, New Zealand, but there are proportionally far more of them than in America. In the resort and tourist areas they can make the difference between an economy vacation and a purse-breaking one. Serviced flats can be located in buildings containing nothing else, in motels, and—occasionally—in hotels. Sometimes the management also supplies breakfast (as an extra), but usually the only meals available on the premises are those you make. Tariffs are given either as a daily rate for one or two people, or as a weekly rental for the whole apartment which applies for the maximum number of persons it will accommodate.

Motel flats are usually more expensive than the other kinds, because they almost invariably include television, telephone, and laundry facilities. The other kinds *may* have these trimmings; mostly they don't. All of them get maid service, but while the maids will clean the rooms they will *not* wash your dishes. Furnishings range from the bare basics to the near-sumptuous, but they always include bed linen, towels, blankets, and the amount of dishes and cutlery required by the maximum number of tenants. See my listings in the city chapters for tariffs, locations, and quality.

HOTEL LANGUAGE: Some of the terms used in Australian hotel brochures may need explanation. Herewith, a glossary:

B&B: Bed and breakfast. This means that the tariff includes breakfast of some kind. (See the distinctions below.)

Casual: Guests paying by the night or week, as distinct from permanent or monthly residents.

Continental breakfast: Bears little resemblance to the European coffee-and-rolls article. Here it means juice or fruit, cold cereal, toast with butter and jam, coffee or tea.

Cooked or full breakfast: This is the works: juice, hot cereal, eggs, bacon or sausages or (sometimes) steak, plus tea or coffee. Where a "menu" breakfast is offered it means additional choices of fish, lamb chops, or spaghetti or beans on toast.

Morning tea: The curse of late-nighters like myself. It means that no later than 7 a.m. some excessively cheerful sadist comes charging in, bearing a cup of tea plus two biscuits (cookies) on a plate. Where offered you must make absolutely clear that you *don't* want it—unless, of course, you do.

H&C: Short for "hot and cold," denoting that the room has a sink with hot and cold water.

Guest kitchen: Communal kitchen shared by the house guests.

Fans: This indicates that the place is not air-conditioned. Few establishments in the budget bracket are. Some don't provide fans either.

Jug: Same as an electric kettle, but breakable. Provides boiling water for making tea or instant coffee and works within moments.

Private facilities: This means a private bathroom with shower and/or tub. Very often it stands for just a shower and toilet.

Surcharge: The extra fee frequently charged for holiday periods and/or room service.

Tea- and coffee-making facilities: An almost universal feature in Australian hostelries and one of their best points. These facilities consist of an electric jug, cups, saucers, spoons, a teapot, sugar, and mostly—but not invariably—free teabags or sachets of instant coffee.

Tray service: Room service.

4. Where and What to Eat and Drink

Australia has excellent food, but even her greatest admirers admit that the country has no such thing as a national cuisine. What passes as native cooking is an adaptation of English and Irish styles—bland, blah, and deathly dull, overcooked and underspiced, the tasteless vegetables barely balanced by the generally superb quality of the meat. The current excellence of the gastronomy is entirely due to the influx of non-English, non-Irish foreigners, who not only cook wonderfully themselves but have taught large numbers of Aussies their art. In my listing of good and cheap eateries the foreign establishments outnumber the native kind by about five to one—a ratio you will appreciate.

But Australia does have a small array of native dishes, ranging from great to gruesome. You should try at least some of them. Kangaroo-tail soup, by the way, is now difficult to obtain here. Kangaroos are a protected species in some states and what little soup is still being produced gets canned for export, mostly to Japan.

The Down Under equivalents of hamburgers are meat pies, which Aussies devour at the rate of 680 million a year! This is an amazing concoction: the outer crust consists of soggy pastry, the filling of anonymous meat, and the whole thing is drenched in tomato sauce before consumption. They're sandwich-size, weigh six ounces, and seem to weigh as many pounds after you've got them down. Everybody eats them, from members of Parliament to factory workers. A Melbourne football crowd gobbled 40,000 of them on a single memorable Saturday afternoon. Together with chips (french fries) they could be said to form the basic diet of a large segment of the population. To some people (like yours truly) these pies are the closest thing to culinary perdition. But they have found some unexpected champions. When Michel Guérard, one of the world's leading French chefs, tasted a sample he chewed thoughtfully, then pronounced it *"formidable!"*

Other national specialties include damper, a kind of bush bread originally meant to be baked in the ashes of a campfire. Dampers are made of unleavened wheat flour mixed with water and kneaded into flat cakes three inches thick and up to two feet in diameter. They taste pretty good, providing you put lots of butter and jam on them. And they certainly beat the standard American sliced bread, which seems to consist of equal amounts of cottonwool and blotting paper. But, meat pies aside, the great Australian addiction is to a dark and strong-smelling yeast spread called Vegemite. Addiction is the only word for the fanaticism with which Aussies will drag the stuff with them wherever they go, including Antarctica. Australians abroad have been described as jars of Vegemite closely followed by tourists. Much to their sorrow, this elixir of life is unobtainable anywhere beyond Down Under. And—well . . . it tastes no worse than peanut butter.

But now we come to a batch of Australian specialties I would wager against any delicacy devised in other regions. One of them is roast spring lamb in mint sauce. Others are rabbit pie and carpetbagger steak (beef tenderloin stuffed with oysters). And that simple but wonderful local combination, steak and eggs: a plate-size steak with two fried eggs on top, which *some* farming folks eat for breakfast. Also, there's a selection of seafood that sets me dreaming: The small, sweet Sydney rock oysters; Queensland snapper and the delightfully subtle-tasting barramundi; Moreton Bay bugs, an outrageously misnamed miniature crustacean; Tasmanian scallops and grilled John Dory, an absolutely delicious fish unique to Australian waters; Victorian yabbies—a small type of lobster—and their larger relative, the crayfish.

While I have strong reservations about Australia's national dishes, there's only one word to describe her beers and wines: *magnifique!*

First a word on beer. This is the national drink Down Under, and although in recent years the Aussies have learned to appreciate their wines, beer is still the native nectar. Statistically they down 30 gallons of beer per throat annually —a figure that becomes even more impressive when you remember that this national consumption total counts children and teetotalers. This puts them slightly below the Belgians and Bavarians—but only slightly. On the other hand, Australian beer is so much stronger than either the continental, British, or American brews that their intake should count about 20 points more. This seems a good place to issue a warning: you can get awfully drunk on Australian beer awfully quickly, as many unwary visitors have discovered to their astonishment.

The quality is among the world's highest, particularly in the Tasmanian, Victorian, and Western Australian brands. (Every state has its own breweries.) The only way you can decide for yourself is to taste them, a very pleasant experience. Beer sells in medium-size "middies" or large "schooners," with a middy costing 90¢ to $1.50, depending on what part of town and what manner of pub you're in. If you're drinking in company, tradition demands that you "shout" in turn—meaning that every *male* member of the group pays for a round in sequence. But *never* out of sequence. Australians take a dim view of anyone ramming largesse down their gullets—unless he's just backed a winner at the races.

I could wax poetic about Australian wines, but I'll spare you the embarrassment. The Australian wine industry is almost exactly as old as the Californian, and the grapes grow in a very similar climate. There is a striking similarity in both the virtues and the drawbacks of Australian and Californian wines: both are great in light table wines, not so good in the heavy varieties, fair in the champagne range. The Australian surprise is the outstanding quality of the vermouth, dry or sweet, and the sparkling hocks and moselles. Australian sherry is fine, by and large, the port less so. The claret, moselle, chablis, and sauterne are a joy, and cheap to boot—as long as you buy them over the counter. Once a restaurant markup goes on top it's a different story. Thus a bottle of good riesling, which may cost you $4 in a store, becomes $7 or so the moment it's served by a waiter.

We have a conducted tour of Australia's prime wine region, the Barossa Valley, in the chapter on Adelaide. Meanwhile, if you'd like to know more about the noble Aussie grape, contact the **Australian Wine and Brandy Corporation,** Box 3649, GPO, Sydney N.S.W. 2001.

Before we leave the subject, let me enlighten you about Australia's liquor laws. The darkness fell during World War I, when the government introduced 6 p.m. closing of hotel bars as a "wartime emergency measure." This "temporary" measure, it turned out, was still in force 40 years and another World War later, and looked like lasting for all eternity. Why? Mainly because publicans had discovered the delightful advantages of the "five o'clock swill." During the hour between people getting off from work and the closing of the bars they consumed about as much liquor as they ordinarily would have in a leisurely evening's imbibing. The fact that they did so in conditions resembling a one-hour cattle stampede didn't interest the grog dispensers in the slightest. They were saving staff wages, light bills, and all the money they would otherwise have had to spend in making their joints attractive. So why should they care if between five and six you needed two hand grenades and a shoehorn to get at the bar?

Consequently the liquor interests linked up with the wowser lobby in preventing any change of the drinking times. Not until the mid-1950s, after several state referendums and an enormous amount of media agitation, was the government persuaded to rescind the nursery hours. Today Australians will proudly point to their "liberalized" drinking spans, which are about as "liberal" as those of 19th-century Boston. (But before you start feeling superior, remember that Americans put up with the "noble experiment" of Prohibition for 15 years and a whole bunch of counties still do to this day.)

In most places, pubs now stay open from 10 a.m. to 10 p.m.; that is, they close at exactly the time when you're beginning to enjoy yourself. You then have a choice of either trotting off to bed or going to a restaurant with a license that permits selling drinks till midnight or later. The catch is that they're only allowed to do so if they sell you a meal as well. You don't have to eat it, but you must pay for it. Alternatively, some of the large hotels have cocktail bars where they serve liquor to their houseguests. If you amble in you can get drinks there as well—nobody will ask for your room number. But you'll pay double prices for the privilege, and this will be one of the few occasions when you'll be expected to tip the bartender as well . . . for letting you pass as a guest.

The only region in Australia unaffected by this legislative idiocy is Canberra, the federal capital. There the politicians have really liberalized the laws: hostelries serve drinks as long as they please.

To return to culinary generalities, Australia's cuisine owes its current quality to the thousands of small, family-run foreign restaurants that have sprung up during the past few decades—to Greek moussaka, Hungarian goulash, Austrian schnitzel, German sauerbraten, Czech meat dumplings, Polish sausages, Italian lasagne, Yugoslav razmici, Indian curry, French coq au vin, Mid-Eastern falafel, et cetera, ad infinitum, usually cooked by mom and served by pop and the sons and daughters. It is this influence that has raised the standard of Down Under pub lunches to their present heights as well, although pubs are overwhelmingly Anglo-Irish . . . but the chefs aren't.

You'll find a splendid lunchtime alternative in the delicatessen stores, among the best, cheapest, and most cosmopolitan I've seen anywhere. In Sydney and Melbourne today, you'll get far better salami, mortadella, rollmops, ham, liptauer, potato salad, camembert, and suchlike than in either New York or Chicago, and for considerably less money. The same goes for sandwiches, which are less elaborate but far tastier than their U.S. brethren. A first-rate meat, fish, or vegetarian sandwich costs between 80¢ and $1.50. (But stay away from the baked beans or spaghetti fillings. They're straight out of cans and taste accordingly.) You can follow the example of millions of Australian office workers, who take their delicatessen lunches stretched out on the lawn of the nearest park. There's always a park within walking range and usually enough sun to give you a tan while munching.

Finally some comments on coffee. Traditionally the Aussies were a nation of tea drinkers, and tea is still one of their best concoctions. But the triumphant invasion of the espresso machine has altered their coffee making beyond recognition. Nearly every eatery now boasts one of these miracle machines and when you order coffee you'll almost automatically get cappuccino. If you don't care for either the froth or the sprinkling of chocolate, make sure to ask for a "flat white." In the cheaper hotels and in small towns it's still safer to stick to tea. The price is the same, between $1 and $1.50 a cup.

Hotels providing cooking facilities will hardly ever include a coffee percolator among the utensils (but always a teapot). So here is the recipe for French-style open pan or "camp coffee"—in case you feel the way I do and regard instant coffee as a dirty word:

All you need is good-quality coarsely ground coffee. You put the required number of cups of cold water into a saucepan. You measure out one tablespoon of coffee per cup, plus two extra "for the pot." Stir well and heat until the first bubbles form—but *don't* let it boil. Turn down your heat until the brew just barely simmers and let it stand for eight minutes. Stir it again and pour into a cup through a tea strainer to catch the grounds. The whole trick lies in exact measurement and in *not* letting it boil. *Voilà*—French coffee!

5. What to Buy

Australia is not a happy bargain hunter's ground. Most men's and women's clothing costs more than in the U.S., and the same goes for toys, books, and gadgetry. But you can utilize your tourist status by buying at the **duty-free shops** at international airports and in the larger cities. You can get some real bargains there (providing you take time to look around) but can use them only after you leave the country.

In the souvenir field, it's a question of sifting through veritable mountains of junk to select some worthwhile objects. Every shopping street has stores crammed with stuffed koalas, plastic boomerangs, mulga wood maps of Australia, kangaroo-hide wallets and sheepskin coats, plus millions of color postcards of the "Having a Great Time in . . ." type. Fine, if you like that manner of stuff—only you'd better watch out for hidden "Made in Japan" labels.

If it's genuine Australiana you're after, look over some of the **Aboriginal art and crafts** outlets I mention throughout the book. Aboriginal artifacts are unique, a blending of forms and colors that seem to reflect the immense, haunting bushland that inspired them. They were primitive in the same way Haitian paintings can be called that, with an artistry that conveys moods and impressions rather than details. Their abstract ornamentation has a strikingly "modern" look—almost as if our contemporary taste had just caught up with their traditions.

Other good—although not necessarily cheap—buys are Digger hats, perhaps the most attractive military headgear ever devised and equally so on men and women. Australian art and travel posters and prints. Try to get hold of reproductions of some works by Russell Drysdale and Sir Sidney Nolan; no one has captured the *essence* of the "wide brown land" and its people like these two artists. Also Australian folk records, which can be remarkably good. You might even discover one with the *original* version of "Waltzing Matilda" instead of the hackneyed derivation that's been thumped to death.

Opals—these are Australia's national gemstones and nearly all the world's supply comes from here. They're on sale in special gem stores in every city and their variety is endless—from the famous iridescent black opals to the flashing fire opal with a light greenish base. Most opals are found at Lightning Ridge in New South Wales, and Coober Pedy and Andamooka in South Australia, scorched and arid regions that seem to guard their treasures. I tell you how to get there in the South Australian chapter, and you can even try a bit of fossicking yourself. Good luck, mate. Meanwhile the stores offer opals in every imaginable setting or loose rough specimens you can polish yourself. There are also mounted stones called **doublets** or **triplets,** which possess some of the richness of the full gems but come considerably less expensive. And visitors pay no duty or purchase tax on opals destined for export.

6. What to Do

Australians are a nation obsessed with sport. You have to be there to realize just how far this obsession goes. Some sociologists believe that this is due to a combination of an ideal sporting climate, a strong competitive instinct, plus a passion for gambling. Whatever the causes, Australians live in a sporting atmosphere that permeates every nook and cranny of their consciousness. Television, a pretty reliable gauge of public taste, devotes around 26 hours of viewing time a week to sporting coverage.

Although the Aussies are known mainly as tennis players, tennis is an also-ran when it comes to drawing crowds. The great spectator sports are horse-racing, cricket, and (in Victoria) Australian Rules football.

Racing, of course, is the major gambling sport and has a natural appeal to the world's greatest gambling nation. (Australians each spend $160 a year on *legalized* gambling, compared to $90 a head in the U.S., $50 in New Zealand, and $30 in Britain.) If you include the illegal forms it works out at a staggering $423 per man, woman, and child annually. You can bet with licensed bookies at the racetracks or at official off-track betting bureaus called **TAB.** On Saturday it is virtually impossible to escape the sound effects of horseracing—they come from thousands of transistor radios, car radios, and pub radios. And it's wondrous to hear the usually relaxed radio commentators break out in shrieking hysteria because Fufflebum is streaking half a length ahead of Nincompoop.

I'll give you a brief discourse on Australian Rules football in the appropriate chapter—Melbourne. But it's quite impossible to describe the intricate subtleties of cricket and its rules in the space available. Cricket has certain similarities with baseball, and Australians take the "Ashes" even more seriously than Americans the World Series. The closest Australia ever came to leaving the British Commonwealth was during the historic "bodyline" cricket row of the 1930s. Oddly enough, cricket is a rather slow game, eminently suitable for filling long and leisurely summer afternoons. For anyone not familiar with the fine technical nuances, it can be an experience akin to a tone-deaf person's attending a symphony.

ACTIVE SPORTS: The Aussies are passionate sports participants as well as spectators. As the wife of former U.S. ambassador Ed Clark wrote: "Living in Australia is like living in a gymnasium—there's always somebody practicing something."

Usually it's tennis. Australian urbanites have more public and private courts at their disposal than any other race of city dwellers. Boys and girls start playing tennis in school and stay more or less wedded to their racquets thereafter. If you fly over Sydney at night you'll notice hundreds of little illuminated rectangles below you. These are night tennis courts on which the locals are lobbing balls long after darkness has fallen. Wherever you are, you'll have no difficulty renting a court and a racquet. Winning a game may prove a bit more troublesome. Courts rent at around $8 per weekday morning.

Surfing and swimming are the other great passions, not surprising since virtually every large city has miles of superb beaches at its doorstep. (Sydney has 34 ocean beaches within the city limits.) A bit of advice to those unaccustomed to ocean swimming: Those warning notices aren't placed for fun. When they say "Bathe Between the Flags," you ignore them at the risk of your life. Even shallow water can have a terrific undertow and—well, I hate to lose readers.

This is where one of the greatest Australian institutions comes in: the **lifesavers.** Basically they are a body of highly trained volunteers who patrol the beaches, keep a lookout for sharks, and rescue swimmers in distress. Actually they're far more than that—they represent a kind of civil elite force, a mystique based on unpaid service for the joy of it. Unpaid in money, that is—Australians consider the practice of *hiring* professional lifeguards as vaguely indecent. The lifesavers' payment comes in the shape of glory, admiration, and vast numbers of bikini beauties—which ain't bad either. They do a magnificent job, including tasks that in America would have to be tackled by cops. Whenever there is an outbreak of rowdyism on Australian beaches, the lifesavers put a very fast stop to it.

Every summer weekend, throughout the country, the lifesavers stage **Surf Carnivals,** which are an absolute must for visitors. The competing clubs parade in multicolored bathing suits, using a curious form of goose step that enables them to march in soft sand. The competitions that follow are uniquely exciting: rescue drills executed with parade ground precision, surfboat racing, in which the rowing crews maneuver their specially built craft over the breakers, frequently getting tossed high into the air. Phone the local **Surf Life Saving Association** to find out on which beach the carnival is being held, and make sure of seeing at least one.

Yachting is very nearly as big as surfing. In Australia, during any one weekend, the number of yachts out on the water has been estimated at about 200,000.

The Sunday afternoon sailing races provide a wonderful—and free—spectacle. If you're lucky enough to be in Sydney on December 26, don't miss the start of the **Sydney–Hobart Yacht Race,** the greatest marine event of the season. The sight of this yachting armada streaming out through The Heads—en route for Tasmania—is one you'll never forget.

Australia's greatest canvas triumph occurred in 1983 with her capture of the **America's Cup.** The Cup, prime trophy of the yachting world, was originally English and known as the One Hundred Guinea Trophy. Won by an American schooner in 1881, it remained in New York despite all attempts at recapture. The Aussies attempted the feat seven times until the *Australia II,* skippered by John Bertrand, finally succeeded. You'll find more about the Cup in the chapter on Perth.

Sporting opportunities are pretty near universal in Australia, but each region has specialties of its own. Herewith a very brief rundown of their outstanding sporting attractions:

Adelaide. Safe, calm-water swimming, sailing. Farther afield, the Southern Ocean ports of Port Lincoln and Kangaroo Island offer some of the best game fishing in Australia—including great white sharks of *Jaws* fame.

Brisbane and the Gold Coast. Surfing, swimming, skindiving in tropical waters. International motor racing.

Great Barrier Reef. Skindiving, swimming, big-game fishing with world-record catches of black marlin.

Melbourne. The finest golf courses and handsomest racecourses in the country. Australian Rules football with fanatical fans. Close to skiing grounds in the Australian Alps, with the season running from June through September.

Perth. Surfing, swimming, and sailing. Harness racing (trotting) is exceptionally popular, and Gloucester Park the best trotting course in the Commonwealth.

Sydney. Surfing, yachting, skindiving, power boating. Offshore game fishing for marlin, sailfish, tuna, sharks. Within easy reach of skiing grounds.

Tasmania. The best trout fishing in the land. Also some of the best sea fishing, sailing, and mountain climbing.

Another "warning"—if you want to call it that. Australian beaches are topless, though the custom is entirely optional. But if the sight of bare suntanned bosoms offends thee, don't go near the water.

EVENING ACTIVITIES: Australians are essentially outdoors daytime people, as indicated by their ridiculously early dinner hours—on the average around six o'clock. Nightlife, therefore, is a fairly neglected field. But let me hasten to add, not everywhere. Sydney, that wonderful scarlet sister among municipalities, hums at night. Melbourne, too, has a goodly number of nightspots, scattered and overdiscreet though they may be. But as for Adelaide, Brisbane, and others, it's meager pickings. The locals will tell you that this is due to their being "small towns"—which is rather surprising since they're larger than, say, San Francisco. I suspect the temperament of the inhabitants has more to do with it than size. They simply prefer daylight action to the other kind.

All these places do have regular nightclubs; nearly all of them are both expensive and rather dreary. In the cheaper brackets I've done my level best to pick the raisins out of the pie on your behalf. Don't blame me if the result isn't exactly overwhelming. And think of how much cash and energy you'll save for other purposes.

Much of the after-dark action centers on pubs. Now that the Down Under publicans actually have to *compete* for customers (and they're still crying about that injustice) they've blossomed out in a variety of ways. You get rows of rock pubs, jazz pubs, folk pubs, and their offerings are listed in the weekend editions of the local papers. Some have $1 to $3 admission charges; most do not.

Every city also boasts her share of discos, but these are so youth-oriented that you're virtually disqualified if you *look* 30. There are, however, lots of dance halls that cater to the tango and foxtrot as well as the rock crowd. You'll see them listed in the entertainment columns, duly divided into "modern," "old time," and "50-50." The majority are very staid indeed—in contrast to the discos which pride themselves on their decibel levels.

Of recent vintage, but tremendously popular, are the theater restaurants. These are places where you eat, drink, and watch a show on a regular stage, a specialty of Victorian England now experiencing a worldwide revival. At their best they're magnificent, such as the **Last Laugh Theatre Restaurant and Zoo** in Melbourne. But even the second-graders can be a lot of fun, frequently on the raunchy side. The stage offerings vary, with oldtime melodrama or vaudeville or parodies thereof being the hot favorites. Some theater restaurants insist on an all-inclusive price while others allow you to eat elsewhere and merely turn up for the show, in which case you won't pay more than $8 to $10.

Every city also has coffee lounges, a few of which display immunity to the great Australian vice of early closing. They serve only soft drinks, snacks, and sweets, frequently feature some kind of musical entertainment, and *may* remain open till one or two in the morning.

Apart from standard professional theater, Australia boasts a thriving little-theater movement. By "thriving" I don't mean in the financial sense but in terms of spirit, talent, enthusiasm, and the dogged determination not to succumb to bankruptcy. Several of them, like Sydney's **Nimrod Theatre** and Melbourne's **La Mama,** present far more original and innovative productions than most of the legitimate stages. And very often these are the only showcases open to young unknown Australian talent, either in the acting, directing, or writing regions. They're also vastly cheaper than the professional houses, with tickets selling in the $7 to $8 range.

The Australian film industry rates a chapter to itself—if I had one to spare. A usually acid-penned U.S. movie critic recently stated, "There seems to be no such thing as a bad Australian film." Which, while not quite accurate, summarizes the reputation Down Under filmmakers have won over the last few years.

The renaissance of the Australian cinema is a wonder to behold. Originally due to enlightened government assistance, it developed into a kind of soul-searching venture: the process of a young nation establishing an identity via the camera. Until around 1970 Australia produced very few and middling dismal movies. Some of her screen artists—Peter Finch, Errol Flynn, Diane Cilento, Leon Errol, Margaret Wilson—achieved international fame, but her films were mostly mediocre copies of English and American strips, lacking any vestige of originality.

The first overseas success was *Walkabout,* followed by *Stormboy,* which won the Best Foreign Entry award at the Moscow Film Festival of 1977. Then, as if the floodgates had opened, came a whole series of cinematic gems, every one bearing an unmistakably national stamp sharply defined as an artist's signature. The age of imitations was over.

The filmic self-portraits were by no means prettified—they showed all the warts. *The Chant of Jimmie Blacksmith* ranks among the most searing indictments of racism ever screened; *Breaker Morant* featured a war crime committed by Australian soldiers; *Gallipoli*'s theme was a total military fiasco; *Winter of Our Dreams* cast a bleak eye at the seamiest side of Sydney. All of them breathed an almost ruthless artistic honesty, a dedicated determination to come to grips with what might be called the collective soul of a country.

Apart from honesty, this cinematic new wave offered glimpses of delicate sensitivity few people would have expected from an otherwise pretty brash nation. And most amazingly, several had settings that were feminine as well as feminist. *Picnic at Hanging Rock, My Brilliant Career,* and *The Getting of Wisdom* were women's films in the best sense of the word, insofar as females activated the plot instead of being acted upon.

Nobody knows how long the current standard of quality will last. Meanwhile make the best of it by seeing Australian movies that may never reach your hometown. The only trouble lies in tracking them down among the piles of imported stuff that make up the routine fare of most Australian movie-houses. Cinema prices, incidentally, are about the same as in the U.S., though a few small rerun houses charge as little as $4.

Since the first edition of this book appeared there has been a major upheaval in the realm of Down Under gambling. State governments discovered the wonderful tax revenue to be garnered from casinos and have encouraged their growth to the point where Australia is now one of the most casino-studded countries on earth. At the moment there are seven, with a couple more under way. And this does not include the scores of "service clubs" that live and thrive on the profits of their poker machines.

I deal with them in the appropriate chapters. But I must warn you that the national game of two-up, though universally played, is illegal outside casino premises and can get you caught in a police raid—if the organizers have neglected to grease the correct palms. In the Sydney chapter you'll also find listings of gambling clubs happily operating in a kind of legal twilight zone, enjoying a temporary immunity that may go with the wind the moment the first *official* casino opens there.

One final comment on Australia's after-dark scene—it's safe. Muggings are still rare enough to make newspaper front pages. And despite media complaints about a "rising crime wave," the degree of criminal violence is minuscule by American standards. You don't have to worry about entering parking lots at night, strolling through parks, or taking shortcuts through dark alleys. Australians don't have the furtive over-the-shoulder look that has become typical of the U.S. urbanite after nightfall. And in the suburbs they still leave their front-door keys under the mat.

7. Meeting the Aussies

Few people in the world are quite as "meetable" as Australians. They will strike up acquaintances anywhere, anytime, needing no more than an introductory "How's it going?" If they perceive you as a visitor, the second question is invariably "How do you like Australia?" And this is *not* the right moment for an in-depth discourse on the virtues and drawbacks of the Commonwealth. All you have to answer is "Beaut" and you've made a mate—for that moment.

It has been noted that the proverbial Aussie amiability is a somewhat shallow characteristic that may not extend further than a couple of shared beers. Nevertheless, it's a fact of life and a very agreeable one. You see fewer arguments and less backbiting here than in most countries (except New Zealand), and the general pleasantness covers behavior in long post office waiting lines and at motor accidents as well. It's a rare Australian who won't take time off to exchange a few cheerful clichés with a stranger.

They also have a spirit of genuine helpfulness that can be heartwarming. Example: I had a flat tire, but no jack with which to change the wheel. On top of that it was pouring rain. I stopped a passing cab and asked the driver to lend me his jack. He climbed out, viewed the damage, got his jack, and—without another word—proceeded to change the wheel for me. When he was finished, soaked to the skin, I offered him the fare he would have collected had he taken me to a garage. He said, "Aw, forget it, sport," and drove off.

Most visitors will experience incidents of this sort and treasure them. But some will notice that while Australians are quick to "shout" you drinks and do you favors, they take their time about inviting you to their homes. They don't have the spontaneous hospitality of, for instance, the Irish, who quite casually ask you home "to meet the missus" after an hour's conversation in a pub. For one thing the Australian's home is apt to be way out in the suburbs. And for another he'll want to know you a little better first.

This caution, however, vanishes if you have *any* kind of connection, no matter how remote. Knowing a friend of a friend of his second cousin in Baltimore or Birmingham is quite sufficient. Calling any phone number you've obtained overseas from someone who knows someone in Sydney will get you an instant invitation to "tea"—meaning dinner. And from that little "in" you'll be able to build a whole chain of acquaintances that may carry you right across the country. Don't forget, though—Australians assume that you'll do exactly the same for any of *their* remote friends should they visit your hometown.

GET IN TOUCH: It is my fond hope that I've collected as good a batch of budget establishments as is possible for one person to gather. I know that I haven't garnered all—or anywhere near all—of them. Which is the reason why I'd like you to get in touch with me. If you should hit on some hotel, motel, guesthouse, restaurant, or entertainment spot *within our price range* that you would like to see included in the next edition, drop me a line and let me know about it. Mention all the particulars I mention: location, tariff, phone number (if it's an accommodation), and a bit of description.

I would also like to hear your comments on the places I have chosen: favorable or otherwise. Let me know if the rates have gone up or the quality gone down. Have there been any drastic changes that should be mentioned? I promise to investigate any complaint you may wish to make or pass on your praises. Either way, you'll be doing me, the management concerned, and thousands of other budget travelers a favor. We're all partners in this.

Write to John Godwin, c/o Frommer Books, Gulf + Western Building, One Gulf + Western Plaza, New York, NY 10023. Be sure the office will track me down wherever I may be wandering.

8. The ABC's of Australia

Traveling in a strange country we tend to get stumped by the kind of basic details we don't even think about at home. This (very) basic ABC listing is designed to reduce some of the aggravations that stem from unfamiliarity—such as what to tip a porter, what kind of razor plug can I use, how do I send a telegram, and how much does a haircut cost? Consider this merely an opener. You'll find most of the relevant local information under the respective chapter headings.

AMERICAN EMBASSY: Located in Canberra. Address: Chancery, Yarralumla, ACT, 2600 (tel. 733-711).

AMERICAN EXPRESS: Main office is in the A.E. Tower, 388 George St., Sydney, N.S.W. 2000 (tel. 239-0666). Hours for business and mail distribution (clients only): 9 a.m. to 5 p.m. weekdays, 9 a.m. to noon on Saturday.

BANKING HOURS: 10 a.m. to 3 p.m. Monday through Thursday, to 5 p.m. on Friday. In central Sydney, some banks keep extended hours daily.

CIGARETTES: Expensive by American standards, costing around $1.95 for a pack of 25. But most large cities have cut-price tobacconists selling single packs for 6¢ to 8¢ less, bigger cuts for cartons. Watch for the signs announcing these reductions.

ELECTRICAL APPLIANCES: Voltage is 220-240V and plugs are flat three-pin affairs. The more expensive hostelries have wall plugs that fit U.S. razors, the cheaper ones usually don't. You'll need an adaptor-converter to make your gadget work.

EMERGENCIES: To alert police, the fire department, or call an ambulance, dial 000 anywhere in the country at no charge.

GAS: Called petrol here—gas is only what you cook with. Prices vary considerably—the farther outback you go the higher they get. In Sydney it's around 59¢ per liter (3½ liters make a gallon).

HAIRDRESSING: Prices vary greatly. A typical Sydney tonsurist charges $8 to $10 for either ladies' or men's haircuts, $10.50 to $12.50 for a shampoo and set.

HOLIDAYS: Australians celebrate plenty of holidays, most of them on Monday so as to prolong the cherished weekend. All banks, post offices, government bodies, and private offices close, as do most shops. The occasions listed below are national holidays. On top of these, all states—and some cities—have local holidays, such as the celebrated Cup Day in Melbourne on November 1.

> **January:** New Year's Day; Australia Day, January 31
> **April:** Good Friday and Easter Saturday through Monday; Anzac Day, April 25
> **June:** Queen's Birthday, June 13
> **December:** Christmas Day; Boxing Day, December 26 (all states except South Australia)

These holidays affect hotel bookings and transport reservations and most resort hostelries raise their prices on these dates. A similar situation arises during **school holidays.** These occur from mid-December until early February, in May, and August/September. Traffic as well as bookings are then at their peak in vacation areas.

LANGUAGE: Volumes could be—and have been—written about the Down Under derivation of the English language. An absolute *must* for those interested is Afferbeck Lauder's *Let Stalk Strine*—the title being the phonetic translation of how a native would enunciate "Let Us Talk Australian." (The author's nom de plume is "Strine" for "in alphabetical order.")

There are no regional variations in the Australian accent, the only distinction being that urbanites talk faster than their rural brethren. All Australians tend to speak nasally, shorten words of more than two syllables and then add a vowel at the end of it. Thus "compensation" becomes "compo" and a member of the Salvation Army a "Salvo." They also employ diminutives whenever possible, turning surfers into "surfies" and mosquitoes into "mozzies," and vegetables into "veggies." They use the word "like" in exactly the same meaningless manner in which Americans employ "you know"—simply to elongate sentences.

All this, however, is still not actual Australian slang, which has a vocabulary all its own. In "Strine" a *sheila* is a girl, a *chook* is a chicken, *back o' Bourke* the bush or outback, *daks* trousers, a *dill, ning-nong,* or *drongo* an idiot, *dinkum* is honest or real, a *galah* a loudmouth, a *pom* an English person, *poofter* a homosexual, a *ratbag* any manner of villain, *tucker* food, *crook tucker* bad food; and so on, ad almost infinitum. Unfortunately the most widely known slang terms have become completely archaic. Nobody these days calls anyone *cobber* or a *fair dinkum Aussie* unless they mean it sarcastically. The term most commonly used is *ocker*—but with a distinctly derogative flavor. Being an ocker means being an urban redneck. Australia herself is known as *Oz*—as in "The Wizard of."

A study of Aussie slang may be entertaining but isn't essential for American visitors. A few (nonslang) terms, however, do need translating since they fall into daily tourist usage. The list below has the Aussie expression on the left, American equivalents on the right:

bonnet (on car)	hood
boot (on car)	trunk
bumpers (on car)	fenders
crook (as adj.)	ill, bad
cut lunch	sandwiches
duco	car paint
fireplug	hydrant
flake	shark meat
flog	sell
good on yer	term of approval (sometimes ironic)
grog	liquor
knock	criticize
lay-by	buying on deposit
loo	toilet (in Sydney also *Wooloomooloo*)
lollies	candy
lift	elevator
middy	small glass of beer
pot	large beer mug
power point	light socket
schooner	large beer glass
shout	to stand treat
smoke-o	tea or coffee break
stone (weight)	14 pounds
stubby	small beer bottle
tram	streetcar
ute	pickup truck (for utility)
wowser	killjoy, puritan

LAUNDROMATS: Located in all major cities, most open daily, some round-the-clock. A load of wash costs 80¢ to 90¢; dryers, 20¢ per 5 to 10 minutes.

MAIL: Definitely the feeblest of Australia's public services, it manages to be expensive, slow, *and* unreliable in one breath. Mail delivery comes once a day, five days a week, usually late—unless there's no delivery at all because of strikes or holidays. The only good thing to be said about the post office is that the personnel is wonderfully helpful and goes to great trouble trying to find the letters they so frequently lose. Standard letters within Australia cost 35¢; overseas aerogrammes, 45¢; airletters to the U.S.A., 90¢.

MEDICAL ATTENTION: First class by any standard and far more patient-oriented than in America. Doctors actually make house calls. However, visitors are not covered by the Medibank national health insurance scheme.

METRIC MEASUREMENTS: Australia "went metric" some ten years ago and most locals are fairly comfortable with the new system. You may not be, but you'll be pleased to know that shopkeepers still sell as happily by the pound as by the kilo. If you memorize the small table below you shouldn't have any metric woes:

1 in. = 2.54 cm (centimeters)
1 ft. = 0.305 m (meters)
1 mile = 1.61 km (kilometers)
1 oz. = 28.3 g (grams)
1 lb. = 0.454 kg (kilograms)
1 ton = 1.02 t (tonnes)
1 m.p.h. = 1.61 km/h (kilometers per hour)

PUB HOURS: Vary in some states but generally run from 10 a.m. to 10 p.m.

SHOP HOURS: General trading hours for most stores are from 9 a.m. to 5:30 p.m. Monday to Friday and till noon on Saturday. In Tasmania most shops are closed on Saturday. Late shopping (till 9 p.m.) on Friday in Melbourne and on Thursday in Sydney and Canberra. Luckily not all stores stick to this schedule. Family-run food stores in certain resort and nightlife areas open every day and stay open till around midnight. So do some downtown bookshops, milk bars, souvenir stores, and tobacconists. Every large city has several chemist shops (drugstores) offering round-the-clock service seven days a week.

SIZES: Measurements for women's and men's clothes are generally the same as in America. But watch out for the exceptions: shirts and shoes are totally different and hats slightly so.

TAXES: The only one that concerns you is a $20 airport tax payable when leaving the country.

TELEGRAMS: Send telegrams by going in person to any post office or phoning 015, or through your hotel switchboard.

TELEPHONES: Local calls from a public booth cost 20¢ for an unlimited amount of time, although hotels will charge you up to 40¢. Long-distance (STD) calls can be made from gray-green STD phones on which you dial direct and only pay for the time actually used. You cannot, as yet, dial overseas calls.

TIME: The Australian continent has three time zones: Eastern Standard Time, 10 hours ahead of Greenwich Mean Time; Central Australian Time, 9½ hours ahead; and Western Time, 8 hours ahead. During the summer months all states except Queensland and Western Australia introduce daylight saving, which makes the two exceptions one hour behind.

TIPPING: Australians have an international reputation for being woeful tippers but they also have a good excuse: they haven't been brainwashed into accepting this form of legal blackmail. Down Under a tip is still what it was originally—a reward for exceptionally good service. Neither hotels nor restaurants add service charges to their bills. Only in the plushest eateries, where the service *is* outstanding, are you expected to tip about 10% of your check. Hotel porters usually get $1 if they've helped you with your luggage. Taxi drivers and porters at air and rail terminals have set scales of charges.

TRAVELER'S CHECKS: You'll have no trouble in cashing any overseas traveler's checks, although some banks ask to see your passport while others don't. Australian states impose an 8¢ to 9¢ stamp duty per check, so it's cheaper to stick to higher denominations.

WATER: Tapwater is perfectly drinkable throughout the country. In fact, it tastes considerably better (because less chemicalized) than the American brand.

WEATHER REPORTS: All temperature readings are given in Celsius. The conversion table below will help you follow them:

Celsius		Fahrenheit
0	=	32
5	=	41
10	=	50
20	=	68
30	=	86
35	=	95
40	=	104

Forecasts, you may be reassured, are every bit as haphazard here as at home. Your guess is as good as the weather bureau's.

Chapter II

GETTING TO AND AROUND AUSTRALIA

1. Getting to Australia
2. Getting Around

CERTAINLY THE MAJOR item in any Australian travel budget is the cost of getting there. However, the price can be minimized by careful planning. These days visitors to Australia are able to fly from San Francisco or Los Angeles to Sydney in 13 hours and 40 minutes and enjoy the varied climate and sites of a country about the same size as the continental U.S.

1. Getting to Australia

More than 20 international airlines serve Australia as well as several shipping lines and cruise companies. Most travelers wishing to visit Australia do so by air so they will have more time to spend on the island continent.

FARES FROM THE U.S.: There are a variety of possibilities for special budget airfares. Several are offered by Qantas, although the Australian airline, as do others, also offers regular full-fare economy, business and first class. It is advisable to check closely with the Qantas reservations department concerning fares since various conditions apply and, of course, fares are subject to change without notice.

When the visitor wishes to travel is a key factor in determining the cost of the air fare. Qantas has a 14-day advance purchase economy class seasonal fare which offers the greatest value for travel from the West Coast to the South Pacific. Called the "Circle Eight" fare, travel is from San Francisco or Los Angeles to Sydney, Melbourne, Brisbane, or Cairns, Qantas' newest destination and gateway to the Great Barrier Reef. Low season fares start at US $999 for travel during April through November, and peak season at $1,299 for travel in December, January, February, or March. Stopovers in Hawaii along with a choice of South Pacific destinations like New Zealand or Fiji are included at no additional charge.

Fares from Honolulu are slightly less. For travel to Adelaide add $120 roundtrip and Perth $200 roundtrip. Travel must be for a minimum of six days, a maximum of one year.

QANTAS ROUTES

A new Qantas development is the South Pacific Excursion Fare, with no advance purchase required. For one basic price, depending on the time of year, you can purchase flights from the U.S. to Australia, New Zealand, Tahiti, and Fiji. Travel to each of these destinations allows for unlimited stopovers enroute. The fare is determined by the city which has the highest fare on your itinerary. For instance, going to Australia, as many as seven stopovers may be made in Tahiti, New Zealand, Fiji, and Hawaii. Low season fares (April through November) from Los Angeles/San Francisco to Sydney, Melbourne, Cairns, or Brisbane are $1,103. In peak season (January, February, March, and December) it's $1,449.

For family travel to Australia, Qantas has introduced special rates which save as much as 70% off regular fares for children aged two through 11, and young adults from 11 through 20 years, who receive a 50% discount. Infants not occupying a seat can fly for 10%. Each child traveling at these discounts must be accompanied by an adult fare.

Qantas also offers a one-way 14-day advance purchase economy class fare for travelers who do not wish to purchase roundtrip transportation to Australia. This fare is available at the year-round level of $800 from San Francisco or Los Angeles to Sydney, Brisbane or Cairns. Fare is slightly lower from Honolulu and slightly higher to Melbourne, Adelaide, and Perth. This fare is very popular for migrant travelers as the advance purchase restrictions are waived and the normal economy class baggage allowance is doubled.

Increasing in popularity are Circle Pacific itineraries which include Australia and points in the North and Central Pacific. Qantas offers several Circle Pacific programs, in combination with Japan Air Lines, Northwest Orient, or United.

Circle Pacific with Qantas and United includes your choice of five free stopovers from eleven Pacific destinations, with travel commencing in Los Angeles, San Francisco, Honolulu, or Vancouver. Fares are based on class of travel—economy class roundtrip $1,870, business class roundtrip $3,394, and first class roundtrip $5,472. All ticketing must be completed 21 days in advance; minimum stay is ten days and maximum stay 180 days.

For those travelers interested in Around-the-World excursions, Qantas and four U.S. and Canadian carriers offer a 21-day advance purchase economy class fare of $2,599. Business class $3,999 and luxury first class $5,399. These fares allow you to fly around-the-world in 365 days, if you choose, visiting cities along the combined networks. You may choose from a score of cities within North America, Europe, Asia, and Australia.

A new development is that Qantas and American Air Lines have joined in a Frequent Flyer Bonus Program, so that flights on one airline earn bonus points for free or reduced rates on the other.

YOUR CHOICE OF AIRLINE: All the international airlines flying to Australia are good. On a hike like that they couldn't neglect your comfort and stay in business long.

Still we like Qantas for flying to Australia. For one thing, it's the fastest (nonstop) to Australia. Second, it's a specialist in long-haul travel and therefore offers excellent service, seating, and facilities on board.

And, if the traveler is going to Australia, well, Qantas is Australian. It provides the Australian experience in the air before the wheels touch the ground in the land down under. For information, Qantas Airways, 350 Post St., San Francisco, CA 94108 (tel. 415/761-8000).

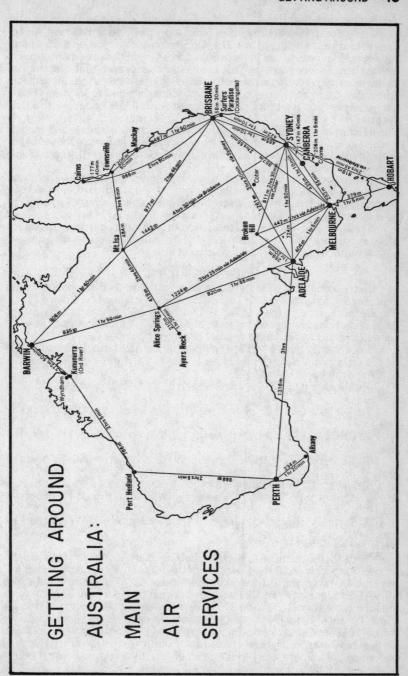

Advice for Your Flight

Let's face it, 15½ hours in the air is a l-o-n-g haul, more than most Americans have traveled before in one shot. During those hours you zip through four time zones, you pass through the tropics and arrive in the seasonally opposite climate from the one you left. What's more, the calendar gets slightly scrambled in the process. When you cross the Dateline into the southern hemisphere you lose a day. So in departing on a Monday, you arrive on Wednesday. On the return journey you get it back. That is, depart Australia on Friday—arrive U.S. on Friday.

Human bodies react to this kind of rapid transit with a curious 20th-century malaise called jet lag. In extreme cases it can ruin the first couple of days after your arrival if you don't plan your activities well. Here are a few tips for avoiding these consequences:

Go easy on food and liquor, especially liquor, even though there's no charge on board. Good airlines tend to overfeed you at a time when your body gets no exercise. Once in a while take a walk around the aircraft or stand in the aisle for a while. Have a drink of water or a soft drink every four hours.

The best idea, if possible, is to stretch out across the seats and get as much sleep as possible. But if you can't sleep and fly, make sure you catch up on your slumber after arrival. Don't push yourself at first.

2. Getting Around

Keep in mind that this is a very large country (nearly three million square miles) with a small population (under 15 million—less than New York State). Furthermore, most of the people live bunched together in five state capitals, leaving precious few for the immense hinterland. From the traveler's point of view this means vast distances to cover between population centers.

Since Sydney represents the entry point for most tourists, herewith a table of distances and traveling times between that city and some of the others described in this book:

To Alice Springs: 1,844 miles, 5½ hours by jet, 64 ½ hours by rail, 56 hours by bus.

To Adelaide: 885 miles, 2 hours by jet, 25¼ hours by rail, 23¾ hours by bus.

To Brisbane: 630 miles, 1¼ hours by jet, 15½ hours by rail, 17¾ hours by bus.

To Canberra: 192 miles, half an hour by jet, 5 hours by rail, 4¾ hours by bus.

To Hobart: 717 miles, 2½ hours by jet, 18 hours by rail, 19½ hours by bus.

To Melbourne: 557 miles, 1¼ hours by jet, 13 hours by rail, 14½ hours by bus.

To Perth: 2,717 miles, 5¼ hours by jet, 65¾ hours by rail, 72¼ hours by bus.

With these distances it is not surprising that Australians became air-minded very early on. Today their interior (as distinct from overseas) routes are serviced by two major domestic airlines, **Ansett** and **Trans-Australia Airlines** (TAA). In addition, there are five other regional operators and 25 small commuter airlines connecting some 170 centers throughout the country. These include the small but famous **Air Queensland** (formerly Bush Pilots Airways), which we'll meet again in the chapter on Cairns, their headquarters. All these airlines have outstanding safety records, due partly to strictly enforced government regulations but mainly to the generally ideal flying conditions. If ever a continent was made for air travel, it's Australia. So we'll start by getting you around—

BY AIR: TAA is government owned and Ansett a private airline, and a lot of people maintain that there aren't enough differences between them to call them competitors. They both fly American Boeing and Douglas jets, plus Dutch and Canadian twin-engine prop planes. They cover identical routes, serve similar meals, and charge identical prices. Frequently they also fly at identical times. But they do offer quite distinct and different economy packages, which we'll study a bit further on.

Standard airfares on some of the most heavily used routes (one way, economy class) are:

Sydney–Melbourne	$147.80
Sydney–Perth	$383.40
Melbourne–Adelaide	$139.80
Melbourne–Canberra	$116.40
Adelaide–Alice Springs	$218.50
Brisbane–Sydney	$152.90
Brisbane–Melbourne	$224.80
Perth–Adelaide	$294.40
Perth–Sydney	$383.40
Canberra–Sydney	$ 83.10

TAA

TAA (Trans-Australia Airlines) entered the annals of aviation with a humble hop from Melbourne to Sydney in September 1946, carrying 21 passengers in one of the 11 DC-3s that made up its original fleet. Today the airline commands an armada of jets serving 33 cities and centers throughout Australia and carrying more than four million passengers a year. It has a deserved international reputation for reliability and safety.

Latest additions to the TAA fleet are the A300s, which began to service some of the continent's busiest routes in 1981. They are larger than any other planes on Australia's domestic schedules and carry 230 passengers each. Because of their wider bodies and higher ceilings, these airbuses are also more comfortable—no passenger is more than one seat from the nearest aisle.

At present, the big buses fly the Melbourne–Sydney, Sydney–Brisbane, and Melbourne–Perth routes, and you'll notice the difference when you get on them.

TAA is also sole or part owner of several splendid holiday resorts, such as Great Keppel, Brampton Island, and Dunk Island off the tropical North Queensland coast. The airline operates specialty fly/stay packages to these spots, which can cut your costs considerably. Details are in the appropriate section of this book.

Right now we're only concerned with TAA's general economy offers. Thus children under 15 travel for 50% off—as do *bona fide* students aged 15 to 19. Full-time students under 26 (providing they can prove it by identification) pay 25% less.

Super-APEX Fares, booked and paid 30 days prior to travel, save you 35% on round-trip economy fares. You can get detailed brochures on these concessions from any TAA office in Australia or from the airline's overseas representatives.

Some of the best packages are fly/drive deals in conjunction with **Hertz**

Rent-A-Car. Since these deals tend to change from season to season, make sure to contact the airline before making plans. Currently TAA offers (among other goodies):

The **Fly-Drive**, which takes you from Melbourne to Tasmania, gives you a car with unlimited mileage, plus seven overnight stops at pleasant motels for $394.

TAA Air Pass gives you a choice of two dollar-saving packages, one of which is likely to be tailored for your particular touring plans. Fare A lets you travel up to 6,000 km (3,600 miles) with a minimum of two and a maximum of three stopovers for $500. Fare B lets you fly up to 10,000 km with a minimum of three and a maximum of seven stopovers for $800. Conditions for these fares include a minimum of ten nights and a maximum of 45 nights between start and completion of your holiday. Also that a stop *other* than a capital city must be made on at least four nights. (Learn your Australian capitals, mate.)

South Australia. Fly from Sydney and you can get seven nights in a Mediterranean-style, completely self-contained Adelaide hotel apartment for just $375. The price includes round-trip economy airfare, accommodation, and facilities like a swimming pool, private telephone, and laundromat.

See Australia Fares. These are specially tailored for overseas visitors. Available to all adult travelers arriving in Australia on any international airfare other than full economy, business class, or first class, they provide a 30% discount on all TAA jet routes for a total journey exceeding 1,000 km (600 miles). For information, contact Trans Australia Airlines, 50 Franklin St., Melbourne, Vic. 3001 (tel. 665-1333).

Standby Fares

Both major airlines offer these economy tickets, which save you up to 20% of the normal rate. No reservations—you buy your ticket at the airport and fly when there's a seat available. If you don't get on the first flight, you may wait for the next one. If you decide against this, your fare money is refunded.

Standby flying is a pretty good deal on heavily used routes with several flights a day between points. On routes with only one daily flight they're a serious time risk, since you stand a chance of losing an entire day waiting for the next connection. But the savings are considerable. On standby a Melbourne–Sydney trip costs only $118, Sydney–Brisbane, $122, and the long leap from Adelaide to Perth, $236.

Ansett

The interesting deals offered by Ansett include:

The **See Australia Fare,** available to overseas visitors only. If you've come from abroad on either an APEX or Excursion flight you can get a 30% discount on trips of over 1,000 kilometers. On certain very long hauls, such as the Sydney–Darwin leap, the saving can amount to as much as 40%. The offer is good all year, but you must show your passport and international ticket to qualify.

Kangaroo Airpass lets you fly either 6,000 km for $500 or 10,000 km for $800. On an average this saves you 40% of the normal airfare. Kangaroo Airpass holders are also entitled to special discounts when renting Avis cars or taking certain Ansett Pioneer bus tours.

For information, contact Ansett at 465 Swanston St., Melbourne, Vic. 3001 (tel. 342-2222).

Other Airlines

Some of the smaller airlines serving specific areas offer package deals as well. Contact the carriers concerned for the full lists. Here is one example:

East-West Airlines, 323 Castlereagh St., Sydney (tel. 219-5111) has the **Air Pass** available to overseas visitors only. The Pass costs $399 and lets you take any number of flights on the East-West network in Queensland, New South Wales (including Canberra), Victoria, Tasmania, and Sydney–Ayers Rock. It is valid for 14 days from commencement of travel.

BY RAIL:
Australian railroads represent the cheapest form of travel available—except your thumb. There are five distinct railway systems, four operated by state governments and one by the federal government, which eliminates even mildly incentive competition. As a result you get a few crack trains, comfortable but slow, and the rest, which are merely slow (the anthem of the Queensland state railroads is allegedly "I'll Walk Beside You"). The elite trains boast sleepers, parlor cars, bar service, good (although costly) dining-car meals, and attendants who bring you early-morning cups of tea or coffee in your berth. But even they run on tracks frequently resembling corrugated iron, suffer from fabulous delays, and are plagued by wildcat strikes that can leave you stranded at the flick of a union eyebrow.

Most of the iron horse's woes can be traced to amazing bungling in the colonial days. Australia, before federation and independence, consisted of six separate colonies. When the rails were laid, the featherbrains in charge managed things so that not one colony got the same rail gauge as a neighboring one! The system never quite recovered from that birth defect. It took 69 years after federation before the entire network was standardized and the celebrated Indian-Pacific run between Sydney and Perth could start operating.

With all their ailments, however, the railroads do offer bargain transportation, and some of their special economy deals are godsends for budget travelers. The table below, all single economy-class fares, will give you an idea of the normal price structure:

Sydney–Melbourne	$ 59
Sydney–Adelaide	$106
Melbourne–Brisbane	$118
Melbourne–Adelaide	$ 44
Adelaide–Brisbane	$165
Perth–Adelaide	$105
Alice Springs–Adelaide	$118

Some rail trips can also be spectacular in a way no air journey can match. The trans-Australian run, which links the Pacific Ocean port of Adelaide with the Indian Ocean port of Perth (Fremantle) spans 1,316 miles, taking two days and two nights. Most of it goes through the Nullarbor Plain, a colossal scrub desert, flat as a tabletop and not a tree in sight. The only structures en route are a few shacks and bungalows inhabited by railway workers, and they seem lost—engulfed—by the immense featureless solitude that stretches to the horizon day after day. This is the "Long Straight," the longest stretch of straight railway line in the world, where nothing exists except reddish-brown scrub, pale-blue sky, and telegraph poles. Once you've crossed the Nullarbor you'll know just how vast and how empty this continent is. The trip, incidentally, is both comfortable and convivial—the busy bar in the club car takes care of that.

The best railroad bargain available is the **Austrailpass.** You can buy one before you leave home at any travel agency in the U.S.A., Canada, Britain, South Africa, or New Zealand. The pass gives you unlimited first-class rail travel anywhere, anytime on the rail systems of Australia. The only extra charges are (optional) sleeping berths and meals. The Austrailpass costs: $400 for 14 days; $500 for 21 days; $620 for one month; $860 for two months.

The State Rail Authority of several states also operate combination tours by train, coach, launch, and ferry that can be great money-savers. The New South Wales SRA, Transport House, 11 York St., Sydney (tel. 29-7614), offers **DAYaWAY Tours,** combining every form of transportation the authority employs. As a sample, there's the **Canberra Luncheon Cruise.** Available Monday through Saturday, these 15-hour jaunts start with the air-conditioned Canberra–Monary express train. In Canberra you transfer to a launch for a cruise on Lake Burley Griffin, then to a coach for an afternoon's sightseeing through the capital and then back to the train for the return to Sydney.

In Victoria, the State Transport Authority (V/Line), 589 Collins St., Melbourne 3000 (tel. 619-1500), offers an outstanding bargain to rail travelers to Sydney. This is a three-night package including economy train fare plus three nights' accommodation at the Manhattan Hotel on an adult twin-share basis—the entire deal for $173, and you get breakfasts for that as well.

Victoria also has the **Off-peak Travel Saver** within the state. This is a 40% discount available for seven days of train travel anywhere in Victoria, providing it's done in off-peak periods.

Other states offer similar bargains—with the exception of Tasmania, which scrapped its last iron horse seven years ago, to the dismay of local rail buffs. I'll mention these deals when we come to the states concerned.

BY BUS: This is almost—but not quite—as cheap as rail travel. Here I must add that Australian bus terminals are considerably cleaner, more cheerful, and less dangerous than their American counterparts. The Aussies turf out the drug addicts, winos, panhandlers, and pimps that often frequent these places elsewhere.

All major cities are linked by express bus services. The coaches have air conditioning and adjustable seats, and all overnight buses come with washrooms and toilets. Two private companies operate interstate services and—unlike the airlines—their prices aren't always identical.

I have fond memories of my bus trip from Sydney to Canberra, a 4¾-hour jaunt costing $22. For a start the Pioneer terminal in Sydney's Oxford Square was spacious, modern, spotless, and every inch as comfortable as an airport lounge. The station adjoins the lobby of the Koala Inn, which places it handy to half a dozen shops in the hotel. The trip went through a gently rolling countryside, slowly rising in altitude. And the sights included some of Australia's oldest homesteads, churches and pubs, green fields, lush orchards, and small prosperous townships. Quite a change from the Nullarbor.

The driver, who had the kind of amiable gravel voice usually reserved for flight captains, was obviously enjoying his captive audience. And vice versa. He offered a running commentary on the landscape, sprinkled with historical, geographical, architectural, and political tidbits and little "in" jokes that invariably sparked a busload of guffaws. Once he referred to an extremely unpopular politician who had just lost his cabinet post. "Oh yeah, him," drawled the driver. "I hear he's been appointed ambassador to the Bermuda Triangle."

But I digress.

As mentioned above, bus prices vary slightly but this table will give you the pattern:

Sydney–Melbourne	$38
Sydney–Adelaide	$70
Melbourne–Brisbane	$70
Melbourne–Adelaide	$37
Adelaide–Alice Springs	$95
Brisbane–Cairns	$83

To get complete price lists, contact the three major operators either at their branch or their main offices:

Greyhound Coaches, 96 Victoria St., Westend, Queensland (tel. 240-9300).

Pioneer Express, 501 Swanston St., Melbourne (tel. 342-3144).

Pioneer Express, Oxford Square, corner of Oxford and Riley Streets, Sydney (tel. 268-1414).

Greyhound has the **Eaglepass** ticket, which allows you 14, 30, or 60 days of unlimited bus travel anywhere in Australia. The same ticket also gives you between 10% and 20% concession on sightseeing tours in approximately twenty cities, a 10% discount in the Homestead Motels, Flag Inns, Zebra Motels, Country Comfort Motels, Tas Pubs, and Royale Inns, and a 25% discount on car rental with Budget.

Pioneer offers the **Aussiepass,** which comes in two versions. For $430 you get 35 days of unlimited bus travel, for $640 you get 60 days. On either one you can pack in an awful lot of mileage.

AAT

A combined venture by TAA airline and one of the country's biggest transport companies, AAT coaches operate tours of capital cities as well as a vast variety of overland tours taking from 3 to 39 days. Some of them are fly/ride combinations that save you a lot of money in airfares. The **Accommodated Tours** entail overnight stops in motels. **Camping Tours,** considerably cheaper, are for those who enjoy sleeping under canvas.

Thus a nine-day camping jaunt across Tasmania—the AAT man takes care of your meals, but you pitch your own tent—costs $350, plus airfare from Melbourne, tents and meals included. For information, contact AAT, Shop 12, Wharf 6, Circular Quay, Sydney, N.S.W. (tel. 27-2066).

BY CAR: Before renting an automobile in Australia, there are a few things you should know about driving there. Traffic drives on the left-hand side of the road and most cars therefore have right-hand steering. Apart from that, the most important points to remember are to give way to all cars at "T" intersections if you're approaching on the stem of the "T," and to give way to cars coming from the right at intersections, unless they have traffic lights or "stop" signs. Also that the wearing of seatbelts is *compulsory* and failure to do so can earn you a $40 fine.

Overseas drivers licenses are valid throughout Australia for up to one year, but overseas insurance is *not.* Compulsory third-party insurance is automatically added to all car-rental charges, but more comprehensive coverage is an extra. You must be 21 years or over to rent a car, and you may be asked for a special reference if you're under 25. Members of overseas organizations affiliated with the Alliance Internationale de Tourisme or Fédération Internationale de l'Automobile are entitled to all services provided by the Australian Automobile Associations on production of a current membership card. These outfits have different names in various states. In New South Wales it's the National Roads and Motorists Association (NRMA), 151 Clarence St., Sydney (tel. 260-9222). It's a good idea to get the brochures on state road rules from any of them.

A word about driving conditions in general. Australian roads are not as good as those in the U.S., Canada, Britain, or New Zealand. In the outback they can be incredibly bad. Don't, for instance, attempt to drive from Adelaide to Alice Springs. In the Northern Territory you get road hazards you may not have bargained with—such as flash floods, wild buffalo, and equally wild camels. As mentioned earlier, distances between towns can be enormous, and you'll find far fewer service stations in between. The large metropolitan centers boast excellent freeway systems, but the network does not cover the country. Also, because some of these freeways are brand spanking new they may not be marked on city maps issued a few years before. This was a handicap I experienced in Brisbane and Perth, and it did gruesome things to my blood pressure. My Brisbane hotel was right alongside one of the new freeways, a tall landmark of a place, visible from blocks away. But . . . you could only approach it by *one* route and my city map was innocent of the pattern of one-way streets that had been instituted since it was printed. Consequently I kept driving all around my abode, trying first this approach, then that, without getting near the entrance. A cab driver finally showed me the only way to go home.

Traffic conditions vary from city to city. In Canberra they're ideal—the national capital was designed for motorists. Cairns and Alice Springs are easy; wide streets and not enough cars to congest them. Melbourne and Adelaide have heavy but highly disciplined traffic: stick to the rules or else. . . . Sydney is fast and furious, the drivers displaying an almost Parisian aggressiveness. Brisbane and Perth are chaotic, with traffic snarled in a maze of ill-planned one-way streets, badly marked freeways, and lousy signposting. Hobart, although a small town, is surprisingly difficult. Streets in the downtown area are narrow, thronged, and desperately short of parking spots. They are also marked with that small-town haphazardness that can't imagine anyone *not* knowing which street they're in.

Australian drivers, while not as maniacal as Spaniards, Italians, or Germans, are nowhere near as well trained as Californians. Bush motorists, in particular, have a deplorable habit of charging full speed from little dirt roads into main highways. And they only bother with signals if there's a police car in the vicinity. By and large, Australians are not as amiable behind a steering wheel as they are on foot, a metamorphosis that affects many other nationalities as well. I've seen impeccably courteous Swiss and Englishmen turn into replicas of Attila the Hun the moment they switched on their ignition.

Outside the city areas you must beware of highway monsters in the shape of timber trucks, oil tankers, and road trains. The last are the size of battleships and behave like such. They ignore speed laws with regal nonchalance and think nothing of blasting you into a ditch if you don't move over fast enough. But meet their drivers after they've stopped for a cup of tea and they're once again souls of benevolence.

Australia has four big nationwide **car-rental companies** and scores of small local ones. The Big Four are Hertz, Avis, Budget, and Thrifty, and you'll find their airport desks and downtown offices in virtually every major town. The small outfits are a bit cheaper, but they have definite drawbacks. They don't give you the service and trimmings of the big boys and—being local—they usually can't let you pick up a car in one state and return it in another.

The most economical of the Bigs is **Thrifty,** and they have promised to give special consideration to customers who arrive clutching a copy of this book in their hot little hands.

Thrifty rents seven categories of automobiles, including special nonsmoking vehicles for those who can't stand the smell of stale tobacco. Their cheapest cars currently are manual-shift Colts and Gemini, which you can rent for $38 a day or $228 a week. The weekly rates are real bargains since they actually give you seven days' rental for the cost of six. These rates include unlimited free kilometers.

Make a point of inquiring about the special weekend rates, which depend on spare cars being available and can save you considerable cash. Thrifty also rents camper-vans in their Tasmanian and Northern Territory locations, where these rolling homes are particularly handy.

It's important to remember that *all* rental companies, including the local outfits, charge higher rates in the Northern Territory and other remote areas where driving conditions are apt to be rougher. Thrifty's additional country rates come to $5 per day or $30 per week. You may also have to pay extra during certain holiday periods in certain resort regions. In compensation, Thrifty's Sydney, Gold Coast, and Perth offices give you booklets of 25 discount vouchers good for that number of local restaurants and attractions.

Also please note—for the sake of my reputation for accuracy—that rental-car rates in Australia, as elsewhere, are in a near-chaotic state of flux. All figures and conditions mentioned apply only to the time of writing and are so ephemeral that they serve as guidelines rather than measuring rods. In the hire-car business practically every month brings a new ballgame. Among the variables that drive travel writers up the wall are the peak-season rates that add charges to rental fees in resort areas like the Gold Coast and Tasmania—but at different times of the year.

Avis hands out a brochure asking "What lives in Queensland, looks like a tin of sardines, holds four people, and is a heap of fun?" This is an apt description of their Mini-Moke, a wide-open Jeep-like critter with no frills but lots of fresh air. It thrives not only in Queensland but in other balmy regions like Darwin and Alice Springs.

You may want to hire a **campmobile** in areas not mentioned above. They come in several makes and are fitted in caravan/trailer style. The Volkswagen vans take up to five persons. Contact:

Pound Motors, 116 Leicester St., Carlton, Melbourne (tel. 347-6822).

Westland Travel, 708 Canning Hwy, Applecross, Western Australia (tel. 364-5529).

Mobile Camper Van Hire Service, 459 North East Rd., Hillcrest, South Australia (tel. 261-9732).

BY SHIP: Time was when you could take a comfortable and leisurely sea journey from one Australian port to the next, and a lot of people did. But the coastal shipping services went the way of the mastodon, at least as far as passenger traffic is concerned. The one remaining maritime link is the ferry operating between the mainland and Tasmania.

The term "ferry" conveys a wrong impression. The *Abel Tasman* is a fully grown ocean liner of 19,200 tons, handsomely appointed and equipped with smoke lounge, bar, shop, and cafeteria. She takes 820 passengers, plus cars, motorcycles, and bicycles. The crossing from Melbourne to Devonport lasts 14 hours and can be fairly rough. The ship leaves Melbourne on Monday, Wednesday, and Friday at 6 p.m. You have a choice of four-berth, three-berth, two-berth, or single cabins. Transport from the terminals to the railway stations at each end is available.

The cheapest fare: a four-berth cabin in low season comes to $56 per person. Accompanied vehicles: cars up to 13 feet in length are $76, bicycles (Tasmania is ideal cycling country), $15.

For bookings and inquiries, contact **Tasmanian Tourist Bureau,** 256 Collins St., Melbourne (tel. 636-351).

HITCHHIKING. While perfectly legal, travel by thumb is frowned upon by the minions of the law. But if you're determined to locomote in that fashion, don't let the frowns disturb you—it's a legitimate practice. The only thing they can book you for is "hampering traffic"—which means don't stand out in the road.

Since I've been handing you advice about every other form of transport, I might as well pass the good word on this type as well. The following tips come from "reliable sources," people who've traversed the country by thumb propulsion. So treat them with the respect we owe to practical experience.

Have your national flag sewn prominently on your pack, particularly if you're American, Canadian, or Kiwi. It brings out the native instinct for hospitality. Two people are the ideal hitching number, preferably one male, one female. Two males may find it more difficult, two females take a degree of risk. And although hitching in Australia is a pretty safe custom, it is decidedly *not* recommended for solo gals. The best place to get rides is on the outskirts of a town, at a junction where vehicles travel slowly and can stop easily.

Don't carry much luggage, and nothing that looks breakable. And wear a clean outfit. Shabbiness is fine—even helpful—but dirt is taboo. After all, your friendly chauffeur is going to spend some hours cooped up with you in a confined space. Displaying your destination also helps—it makes you look like a reliable veteran at the game.

If your numbers and appearance are right, you'll find hitching remarkably easy. Australians are a gregarious lot and not prone to fear of strangers. You'll be able to pick and choose rides to a certain extent. Don't hesitate to turn down short lifts. It pays to wait for a long haul to come along. And if you were on a tight time schedule you wouldn't be hitching.

Chapter III

SYDNEY

1. The City and Surroundings
2. New South Wales

FOR ANY OVERSEAS VISITOR landing here for the first time, Sydney comes as a double surprise. The city is unexpectedly huge and astonishingly beautiful—a very rare combination. The bigness is a matter of statistics: Sydney has more than 3,000,000 people and sprawls over 670 square miles, making her considerably larger than, say, Rome or Los Angeles.

But the beauty is a kind of indestructible miracle, a gift of nature that has survived any amount of shoddy boom building, bad planning, and mindless wrecking. Nothing, it seems—not even real estate sharks and boneheaded bureaucrats—can mar that gem-like harbor setting. The blue Pacific embraces and caresses the city like a lover, protecting her against any disfigurement that human greed and myopia can devise. You could turn half the city area into cemented parking lots and she would *still* remain a pearl.

For Sydney Harbour is more than a harbor. It is immense enough to reduce any clutter of cranes, derricks, and dumps to insignificance—in Governor Phillip's words, "a thousand sail of the line may ride in the most perfect security here." Its configurations splinter the coast into hundreds of coves, bays, and inlets, creating a foreshore of 150 miles and putting much of the city within sight or walking distance of the sea. And since Sydney is hilly, the harbor gesticulates at you from the most unexpected places, providing an endless kaleidoscope of surprise views. With ruffles of white surf fringing golden beaches, with thousands of multicolored sails slicing through sparkling water, with deep-green foliage marking the shores, the harbor casts a spell of almost magic loveliness over the entire metropolis.

The natural magic has proved stronger than man's creations, which were frequently awful. The Harbour Bridge is a clumsy slab of steel and mortar. Most of Sydney's downtown streets are ill-designed warrens clogged with chaotic traffic. Portions of her suburbia could win booby prizes for drabness, resembling concentration camps for used cars. Even now, building speculators and freeway fanatics are trying to demolish the last of the little 19th-century terrace houses whose ornate wrought-iron balconies provide the only touch of charm in some areas.

Yet somehow the magic triumphed. The city remains irresistibly attractive, imbued with an almost feminine sex appeal that makes you forget all her sins and shortcomings. The spectacle of a white ocean liner berthed next to the gleaming wings of the Opera House, framed against green water and a dazzling blue sky, blots out all the industrial wastelands that stretch beyond.

Sydney is the largest, oldest, and liveliest city in Australia—a lady with a scarlet past and a tempestuous present. In 1800 she had a population of just 5,000—41% of them convicts and most of the females "transported" prostitutes. But even this unpromising start turned to her advantage: convict mementos are now among her best tourist attractions and convict labor created some of her finest buildings. And perhaps Sydney owes some facets of her hell-raising, hard-driving, slightly rakish, and tremendously convivial personality to those rough forebears who founded her against their will.

This, then, is the gateway to Australia, the first and often the final glimpse visitors get of this amazing continent. And no place on earth could wish for a more fascinating welcome mat.

KINGSFORD SMITH AIRPORT: Chances are that this will be your first touchdown in Australia. Located in Mascot, about five miles from the city center, this is the biggest air terminal in the country and one of the busiest in the world (more daily flights than Paris's de Gaulle Airport). Built on the shores of—and partly *into*—Botany Bay, the airport consists of an international and a domestic portion. In-transit passengers transfer from one part to the other by domestic airline coach for 50¢. Kingsford Smith has every conceivable facility for travelers: currency exchange, showers, round-the-clock cafeterias, restaurants and bars, shops, book stalls, boutiques, hotel information, etc., all run with what *Newsweek* magazine termed "Aussie-friendly" efficiency. The airport may be huge, but it has none of the sausage-machine spirit that makes others so nervegrinding. Here you'll also find the Big Four car-rental desks. Skybus coaches take passengers to their downtown hotels for $3.50.

1. The City and Surroundings

ORIENTATION: Sydney, capital of the state of New South Wales (a singularly misnamed state that bears not the faintest resemblance to its original), is divided into two major (and many minor) portions by the undulations of her harbor. The main divisions are Sydney proper and North Sydney, linked by the gigantic traffic-jammed Harbour Bridge. Some of the most glamorous suburbs and beauty spots lie north of the bridge, but nearly all tourist attractions—except Taronga Park Zoo and Manly—are in the southern part.

Focal point of the city is the pedestrian plaza on Martin Place. If you stand with your back to the pillared General Post Office you will be facing due north. That is the direction for Circular Quay—terminal for all ferry services—the Harbour Bridge and, at the tip of Bennelong Point, the Opera House. Northeast and east stretch the Royal Botanic Gardens and their southward extension, the Domain. Southeast of you lies Hyde Park, from which point William Street runs straight uphill to Kings Cross.

South of you, at the grubby end of Pitt Street, stands Central Station, the country and interstate rail terminal. Due west extends Darling Harbour, Sydney's main cargo receptacle. Two streets away from you to the northwest is Wynyard Station, the terminal for both the city's train and bus transport. And going either through or by Martin Place are all of the city's main shopping streets: George Street, Pitt Street, Castlereagh Street, and Elizabeth Street.

TRANSPORTATION: Sydney is serviced by electric trains (surface and underground), double- and single-decker buses, and ferries. The last concern you only for harbor cruises and fairly leisurely trips to the North Shore. The quickest

SYDNEY : CITY CENTER

Walsh Bay

NORTH SYDNEY

HICKSON RD.

LOWER FORT ST.

SYDNEY HARBOUR BRIDGE

The Rocks

ARGYLE

EXPRESSWAY

CIRCULAR QUAY WEST

Sydney Cove

Ferry Terminal

CIRCULAR QUAY EAST

Bennelong Point

Sydney Opera House

Government House

Farm Cove

Mrs. Macquarie's Point

MRS. MACQUARIE'S RD.

Woolloomooloo Bay

Potts Point

COWPER WHARF RD.

Elizabeth Bay

CHALLIS

Rushcutter's Bay Park

BAY RD.

GROSVENOR

Australia Square

BRIDGE ST.

SPRING

O'CONNELL

MARGARET ST.

YOUNG ST.

PHILLIP ST.

MACQUARIE ST.

CAHILL EXPRESSWAY

Botanic Gardens

HUNTER ST.

BLIGH

Mitchell Library

The Domain

Wynyard Underground Railway Stn.

Tourist Bureau

MARTIN PLACE

PHILLIP ST.

ELIZABETH ST.

ART GALLERY RD.

SIR JOHN YOUNG CRES.

King's Cross Area

MACLEAY ST.

ORWELL

BAY RD.

CLARENCE ST.

KING ST.

GEORGE ST.

PITT ST.

CASTLEREAGH ST.

YORK ST.

KENT ST.

SUSSEX ST.

MARKET ST.

Hyde Park

HAIG AVE.

CATHEDRAL ST.

DOWLING ST.

BROUGHAM ST.

VICTORIA ST.

ROSLYN ST.

DRUITT ST.

PARK ST.

Hyde Park

WILLIAM ST.

KINGS CROSS RD.

BATHURST ST.

DAY ST.

COLLEGE ST.

STANLEY ST.

BOURKE ST.

FORBES ST.

DARLINGHURST RD.

Liverpool ST.

LIVERPOOL ST.

BURTON ST.

OXFORD ST.

QUAY ST.

HAY ST.

GOULBURN ST.

ELIZABETH ST.

GOULBURN ST.

CAMPBELL ST.

VICTORIA ST.

BOUNDARY ST.

GLENMORE RD.

NEILD AVE.

PADDINGTON ST.

ORMOND ST.

RESERVOIR ST.

Belmore Park

EDDY AVE.

To Kingsford Smith Airport

Central Railway Stn.

RILEY ST.

CROWN ST.

ALBION ST.

DOWLING ST.

OXFORD ST.

To Bondi Beach

5 MILES

UNDERWOOD ST.

VT ST.

DEVONSHIRE ST.

FITZROY ST.

MOORE PARK RD.

and dullest way to get around is by the **underground rail system** which connects the city with the suburbs and operates from 4:30 a.m. till midnight. Travel is by sections, tickets start at 50¢, and you can use the same tickets on the buses. You can save quite a bit of money by purchasing a **Day Rover,** allowing you to travel on all trains, buses, and ferries around Sydney for one day. They cost $4.50. The **Weekly Rover,** costing $19, gives you the same privilege for a week. You can buy them at rail stations and bus depots.

Sydney also has some **gratis bus services.** Bus 666 takes you to the State Art Gallery in the Domain. Bus 777 does a circuit of the city and runs a shuttle service every ten minutes till 4 p.m.

Taxis are more numerous in Sydney than anywhere else in the country and the locals use them as casually as New Yorkers. Phone bookings add an extra 60¢ to the meter and crossing the Harbour Bridge costs an additional 20¢. Some of the main cab companies are **Legion Cabs** (20918), **Taxis Combined** (332-8888), and **RSL Cabs** (699-0144).

For car rentals there's **Thrifty,** 85 William St., Kings Cross (tel. 357-5399) or at Mascot Airport (tel. 669-6677).

USEFUL INFORMATION: All-night chemists (drugstores) are located at 197 Oxford St., Darlinghurst, and 28 Darlinghurst Rd., Kings Cross. . . . For dental emergency services on Sunday and public holidays, phone 267-5919. Emergency number for police, fire brigade, or ambulance is a delightfully simple 000. . . . The **Travellers' Aid Society** offers help to distraught travelers, including a lounge, day bed, and irons at the Central Railway Station from 6:30 a.m. to 9 p.m. weekdays, to 1 p.m. weekends. . . . Banking hours run from 10 a.m. to 3 p.m. Monday to Thursday, to 5 p.m. on Friday. Closed Saturday and Sunday. . . . For emergency medical attention at Sydney Hospital, phone 230-0111.

For information on current activities in town, consult *This Week in Sydney,* free from hotels and the Tourist Bureau. The *Sydney Morning Herald* gives a good roundup of nighttime doings. . . . **Suburban buses** leave from Circular Quay for eastern suburbs and beaches, from Carrington and York Streets at Wynyard Park for northern suburbs and beaches. . . . **Suburban trains** depart from Wynyard Station (entrances on York Street and George Street). . . . **Interstate buses** go from the Pioneer terminal, corner of Riley and Oxford Streets. Phone 268-1881 for information. . . . For **interstate trains,** go to the Central Railway at Eddy Avenue where George and Elizabeth Streets converge. For information, phone 219-8888. . . . **Ansett Airlines** coach terminal is at the corner of Riley and Oxford Streets (tel. 268-1111). **Trans-Australia Airlines** coaches leave from 16 Elizabeth St., between Martin Place and Hunter Street (tel. 693-3333). . . . The **General Post Office** (GPO) is on Martin Place, between George and Pitt Streets. Open Monday through Friday from 9 a.m. to 5 p.m., Saturday from 9 a.m. to noon.

ACCOMMODATIONS: The majority of Sydney's good budget establishments are clustered in two distinct areas: Kings Cross, one mile from downtown and the city's entertainment district; and Bondi, the most popular (although not particularly pretty) beach suburb, 15 minutes by bus from the center. If you're stuck for accommodation turn trustingly to the **Travel Centre of N.S.W.,** corner of Pitt and Spring Streets (tel. 231-4444). They'll find you something, but not necessarily in the bargain basement. The listing below is my own selection, organized *not* in order of preference but according to convenient subheadings.

A NOTE ON PRICES: All prices in this guide are in Australian dollars (A$). As we go to press, US$1 = approximately A$1.40. Thus a room listed at $20 a night actually costs only about $14.50 in U.S. funds—good news indeed for budget travelers.

Bed-and-Breakfast

The **Adlon Private Hotel,** 354 Edgecliff Rd., Edgecliff (tel. 328-6156), is a beautiful white villa-like building in one of the best residential portions, set among gardens and quiet winding hillside streets. The 16 rooms vary in size, from large family units to not-small singles. All rooms have hot and cold water taps, four have private facilities. Otherwise the house contains four impeccable bathrooms, a communal kitchen with gas stove and large refrigerator, and laundry facilities with dryer. The bedrooms are nicely furnished and well carpeted; all have bedside reading lamps, shaver plugs, and TV, plus tea-making facilities, good mirrors, and ample wardrobe space. The hotel has no lounge or dining room, so the continental breakfast is delivered to your bedside. Singles pay $22 a night, doubles from $30. Convenient bus connection (nos. 389 and 387) to downtown.

The **Hotel Bondi,** 178 Campbell Parade, Bondi, (tel. 30-3271), is a vast, rambling white structure built in what can only be described as "seaside architecture"—you'll find this style dotted along the oceanfronts of the entire civilized world. If it's action you want, this is your hostelry. The hotel has four bars, a beer garden, a disco, a bistro, and a billiard room, all fairly humming every weekend. Bedroom fittings are not exactly plush but ample, with bedside lamps, good wardrobe space, and carpeting. TV and refrigerator are in all units, and a telephone too. The hotel has a spacious guest lounge, and a bus stop to town at the front door. You also get the benefit of great bistro meals downstairs, prepared by a French chef, and mostly costing around $5. Rates run from $20 for singles, from $30 for doubles.

The **Canberra-Oriental,** 223 Victoria St., Kings Cross (tel. 358-3155), is in our price bracket in double accommodation ($34.50) and offers budget singles for $24.50 per night, full breakfast included. A rather sedate establishment in a decidedly unsedate neighborhood, this is a handsome white structure (nothing Oriental about it) with an attractive lobby, a roof garden, a charmingly appointed lounge, and a family restaurant on the premises. All rooms come with hot and cold water, and TV sets.

The Imperial, 221 Darlinghurst Road, Kings Cross (tel. 331-4051), is a brown brick five-story structure (with lift), showing a pleasant frontage of striped awnings and brass lanterns flanking the doorway. It has a busy welcoming lobby and nicely furnished public rooms: two TV and writing lounges and a dining room for breakfasts only. Most of the 110 bedrooms are on the small side and fairly simple. Eleven come with private facilities, all the rest with H&C handbasins. The walls are whitewashed, but the carpeting wall-to-wall and, although some of them only boast one chair, there is ample wardrobe and drawer space. One ceiling light and a couple of wall lights provide good illumination. An intercom system allows incoming calls. Two public bathrooms per floor and excellently maintained corridors. Breakfast here is English—meaning large and cooked. Singles pay $27, doubles $40.

Bed & Breakfast Australia, 18 Oxford St., Woollahra (tel. 33-4235). This is a remarkable enterprise aimed at letting you stay with Australian families while touring the country. It fulfills the dual purpose of meeting the Aussies and enjoying budget accommodation. Actually you get far more than the terms promise. As a "paying guest" you get the use of the living room, plus a lot of impromptu home hospitality not mentioned in the brochures. And the homes listed are carefully vetted beforehand.

The places listed are divided into homestays and farmstays (about 400 host families altogether), the former in various cities, the latter in country areas throughout four states. Farmstays usually entail full board (in lavish country style) instead of just B&B. All homes fall into one of three categories: economy, quality, and superior.

Economy homestays run from $28 for singles, from $22 per person for double accommodation. A hearty breakfast is included. Farmstays start at $50 per person for full board. Not calculable in cash terms are the warmth and personalized hospitality most of the hosts offer to their overseas guests.

For detailed information and reservations, contact the above address in Sydney (postal code 2025) or inquire at overseas airline or tourist offices.

Hotels

The next establishments are within the Kings Cross area, although both of them are on quiet streets with a minimum of traffic noise. The **Montpelier,** 39a Elizabeth Bay Rd. (tel. 358-6960), is simple, but clean and well managed, specializing in single accommodation. The 37 rooms are rather small, the furniture elderly, and the taps cold water only. Some—not all—have bedside lamps, and the wardrobe space is fair. The hotel offers a communal kitchen, fully equipped, as well as laundry facilities on the premises. Singles run from $12 per night, from $40 weekly; doubles are from $16 per night, from $60 weekly.

The **Bernly Hotel,** 15 Springfield Ave. (tel. 358-3122), stands tucked away in a calm corner and can pass as an example of what competent conscientious management can do for a hostelry. While by no means luxurious, it's well maintained and extremely comfortable. The 80 rooms are on the small side, the furnishings modern with wall-to-wall carpet, dressing table with color TV, *good* mirrors, bedside lamps, fridge, and H&C water in all of them. A few have private shower, but no toilet. The hotel has no food service, but there are scores of restaurants all around. The hotel has several family rooms plus two penthouses with fabulous views. The rate structure is: singles pay $18 per night; doubles pay $24 per night. The weekly rate, according to size, is respectively $95 and $145.

The **Waldorf,** 3 Milson Rd., Cremorne Point (tel. 90-2621), stands on the North Shore, seven minutes by ferry from Circular Quay and with a bus stopping at the front door. A quaintly handsome building surrounded by tranquil gardens, the Waldorf offers panoramic views of the city across the water, plus a lot of facilities including a TV lounge and games room, a fully equipped guest kitchen, laundry, drying and ironing equipment. The guest rooms have no hot and cold sinks, but are very well equipped otherwise and excellently serviced. Rates run from $18 for singles, from $25 for doubles. If you stay a full week, it's 10% less.

Springfield Lodge, 9 Springfield Ave. (tel. 358-3222). There's a distinct private-mansion air about this establishment, a pillared white frontage behind an outdoor terrace with tables and chairs overlooking a fairly sedate side street of the Cross. Its charming lobby is lit by small chandeliers and beautifully maintained corridors. The bedrooms are quite well furnished, most of them of good size and airy, with ample lighting and wardrobe space. Singles pay $20; doubles, $24 to $26. With private facilities it's $6 more.

The following two choices are in Bondi at—or close to—the famous surfing beach. The **Thelellen Beach Inn,** 2 Campbell Parade (tel. 30-5333), has 71 rooms, all good-sized, nicely carpeted, and quite attractively furnished. The four-story hotel (no elevator) boasts a panoramic sundeck and TV plus fridges in the rooms. No public rooms and no meals (except a light breakfast), but you'll find a handy seafood restaurant in the same building. The rates run from $12.50 per person.

The **Thelellen Lodge,** 11a Consett Ave. (tel. 30-1521), stands on a quiet residential street, just one block from the beach. A smallish, 14-room white stucco structure, fronted by a little lawn and palm trees, this place combines a high level of comfort with remarkably low rates. All rooms have H&C basins, fans in summer and heating in winter, radio, toaster, tea-making facilities, and refrigerators. Add wall-to-wall carpeting, overbed lights, light-pastel walls, bright bedspreads, and leafy potted plants, and you get the right picture of homey restfulness. Light breakfast (at $2.50 extra) is served to your room. A pay phone and washing machine are available to guests and the morning paper is delivered on request. The standard tariff is from $12.50 per person.

The **Park Hotel,** 20 Yurong St., East Sydney (tel. 357-5537), is the cheapest place in this bracket and should be viewed in that light. A basic budget hostelry, it doesn't offer much by way of service and facilities, but is very clean and efficiently managed. Most of the 106 rooms are singles. No elevator, cooking facilities, or meals served, but the eight bathrooms are nicely kept. Bedrooms are small and the fittings basic. H&C water and mirrors above the sink, small curtained wardrobes, fluorescent lights on the ceiling, and individual bedside lamps as well as wall-to-wall carpets. The rate is a standard $10 per person per night.

Over in Kings Cross is the **Maksim Hotel,** 40 Darlinghurst Rd. (tel. 358-6008). A smart, small, and new establishment, the Maksim has a tiny lobby, four floors, but no elevator—its only drawback. Modern and well groomed, the place has 22 bedrooms, three with private bath, all with H&C handbasins. All rooms are air-conditioned, medium-size, nicely carpeted, and equipped with color TV. The furniture is lightwood, and you get ample hanging space in two wardrobes, and bedside lamps as well as overhead lights. Soothing and tasteful color schemes are found throughout, plus excellent beds and handy little writing tables. No meals are served on the premises, but guests get a 10% discount at the Sweethearts Café, run in conjunction with the hotel (see the dining section). Standard rates are $20 to $25 for singles, $26 to $30 for doubles. The hotel also offers a special bargain in the form of three- to five-bedded rooms at $10 per person.

Pacific Coast Budget Accommodation, 400 Pitt St. (tel. 211-5777), is part of a nationwide chain we'll encounter again and again. A large cream-colored structure from the Edwardian age, it has a downtown location and all the spaciousness of its vintage. The lobby is large and inviting, equipped with comfortable—although oddly matched—settees and armchairs. It's flanked by a restaurant on one side, a snackbar on the other, both open seven days a week. The entire building positively sparkles with cleanliness, has 680 beds in bright, airy, spick-and-span rooms, sufficiently, although not lavishly, furnished. Some rooms have H&C taps. No curfew or suchlike petty regulations, but a strict prohibition against liquor on the premises. Singles run from $16 to $18, doubles from $28 to $32, family rates from $34 to $52.

The **C.B. Hotel,** 417 Pitt St. (tel. 211-5115), directly opposite the Budget, has no ban on liquor, although it doesn't sell any. Nor, for that matter, does it sell food. A large, ancient structure, recently renovated, the hotel has a brightly lit lobby with vending machines, piped music, and public phone. The TV lounge upstairs also boasts a piano that actually gets used. The 211 bedrooms are impeccably clean and airy, equipped with essential furnishings only. None has handbasin, radio, or bedside lamp, and the only razor plugs are in the communal bathrooms (four per floor). There is, however, a guest laundry and exceptionally friendly staff. Singles cost $15, doubles run $23 per night, and the weekly rates include two free nights.

Hostels

After years without any hostels, Sydney now has no fewer than six—but only two are operated by the **Youth Hostels Association.** The *official* pair are located at, respectively, 28 Ross St., Forest Lodge (tel. 692-0747), just across the road from Sydney University, and 407 Marrickville Rd., Dulwich Hill (tel. 569-0272). The first is a converted mansion dating from 1873, now equipped with hot showers and refrigerators, plus 30 beds. The second has 62 bedrooms. Both have full cooking facilities, but neither serves meals. Both charge $6.50 per night. Take bus 412, 438, or 461 from Railway Square to Forest Lodge, and bus 426, 446, or 490 to Dulwich Hill.

The **Young Travellers Hostel,** 15 Roslyn Gardens (tel. 357-3509), has four dormitories with bunk beds, a communal kitchen, laundry, bathrooms, TV room, and an atmosphere filled with good vibes. The place is just below Kings Cross, handy to the bright lights, and has neither age restrictions nor petty regulations. It boasts one of the handiest bulletin boards in town, crammed with budget grapevine intelligence. You pay $7 a night.

The **Young Cross Country Travellers Centre,** 25 Hughes St., Kings Cross (tel. 358-1143), gets a bit crowded occasionally, but is a warm, friendly, well-run place. The reception office is stacked with backpacks, the notice board brimming with budget tips, job offers, and items for sale. It has a capacity of 105 people, two or three per room. Also a communal kitchen and a rooftop TV lounge. There are H&C basins in all rooms, bunk beds, and fluorescent lighting. You pay $6 per night.

Wattle House, 44 Hereford St., Glebe (tel. 692-0879), is small (30 beds), friendly, and newly renovated. Located about 1½ miles from the city center (take bus 431 or 433) it provides a guest kitchen, laundry facilities, TV lounge, and a garden with outdoor barbecue. The bathrooms are bright and sparkling, and the amenities of the University of Sydney lie within walking distance. Rates come to $6.50 per night per person.

Backpackers Hostel, 162 Victoria St., (tel. 356-3232) caters to a lot of folks besides backpackers. A small elderly building in a charming tree-shaded street, the place has 23 rooms plus dormitory accommodation. The rooms come with H&C handbasins; there are shared bathrooms and cooking facilities but no TV sets. Space is a little cramped, but the location couldn't be more convenient—almost adjacent to the King Cross subway and within a few hundred feet of the bright lights. The management hands out maps gratis and a very thoughtful notice outside tells you when the next vacancy is due—other hostels please copy! Double rooms cost $7 per person, dormitory space goes for $6 per.

Motel Apartments

Sydney has few self-contained motel suites, but one quite outstanding establishment in that line, the **Florida Motor Inn,** 1 McDonald St., Kings Cross (tel. 358-6811). One of the Best Western chain, it stands tucked away at the end of a quietly elegant street, just off the city's nightlife center. A modern brown-and-white nine-story building (with elevator), the Florida encloses a palm-fringed lawn with a large swimming pool, hand-tennis court, table tennis, and barbecues. The 100 units range from singles to those sleeping five people, all of them spacious, bright, and exceptionally well equipped. Each unit has an all-electric kitchen with utensils (even egg cups), bathroom, refrigerator, telephone, color TV and radio, caressing carpeting, wide beds, electric heaters, and built-in wardrobes, as well as day couches and armchairs. Some are air-conditioned. The inn also serves breakfast (if desired), arranges babysitters, car rentals, and same-day dry cleaning, and has automatic washing machines on the premises. The weekly tariff is based on one *free* night out of seven. Thus a twin unit costing $62 per night comes to only $372 per week. And on top of that, travelers arriving with a copy of this book get a 15% discount.

Campus Accommodation

This is available on the two city campuses during school vacations (November through February, May, and August). The first is at the **International House** of the University of Sydney on campus at City Road and Cleveland Street (tel. 692-4114). Full board costs $25 per day for students, $40 for nonstudents. The **International House** of the University of New South Wales (tel. 692-2040) charges $20 per day full board for students, $30 for nonstudents. In both cases, expect facilities to be campus casual. And in both cases it's best to book ahead.

The Y's

The Sydney **YMCA** unfortunately no longer offers accommodations.

The **YWCA**, however, has brand-new premises and now takes women, couples, families, and groups—but no single men. Located at 5-11 Wentworth Ave. (tel. 264-2451), the place is easy to miss because it looks like an office building. Three floors are in fact offices; the other five comprise the Y. Centrally situated, the new establishment has a large cafeteria, TV lounges, laundry facilities, and excellent public bathrooms. The bedrooms are of fair size and functional, well carpeted and fitted with large wardrobes and mirrors, fluorescent ceiling lights and bedside lamps. Some also have H&C handbasins. Tariffs depend on whether or not you want a private bathroom. Without bath they come to $23 for singles, $35 for doubles. There's also a bunkroom, holding six persons, each paying $12.50.

MEALS: Sydney is one of the world's great restaurant towns, and this applies not only to the quality but also to the quantity and variety of her eateries. Thanks to the influx of "New Australians," Sydney now boasts a quite astonishingly cosmopolitan culinary scene. The only cuisine, in fact, I was *not* able to find was Mongolian—and that may have been remedied by the time this book comes out.

The most pleasing feature about the immense proliferation of international restaurants is their authenticity. Sydney establishments are run by first-generation immigrants who haven't learned to "modify" their cooking yet. So enjoy the tang of New Australian gastronomy—chances are it won't last.

Lunch

Because of the super-abundance of small, inexpensive restaurants all over town, hotel counter lunches play a far less important role here than in most of Australia. Their standard, however, is high and their prices usually very reasonable. In the accommodations section I have already mentioned the toothsome buffet spreads put on by the **Bondi** hotel in Bondi for $5.50. Downtown the main business streets are lined with pubs offering similar fare for similar prices. The norm is a choice of steak, mixed grill, or ham steak, with as much salad as you can eat, for around $5 to $6.

The **Valencia,** 781 George St., offers an outstanding lunch menu of Spanish omelet and a glass of wine for $5. Also in George Street, at no. 614, is the original **Fritzel's Schnitzels,** an attractively brown-paneled establishment that lives up to its name. You get a dozen varieties of schnitzel here from the traditional wiener to the way-out Russina (served with boiled eggs and caviar, so help me). A plain Fritzel's schnitzel, which comes with potato salad and hot damper, followed by ice cream and hot chocolate sauce, is $5.45.

The **Roma**, 189 Hay St., is a legend among Sydneysiders with either a sweet or a savoury tooth. Italian to the backbone, permanently packed, short on elbow space, and high on quality, this wonderful little coffeeshop serves cannelloni with spinach, lasagne, etc., for around $6, plus superlative cakes and pastries for around $1.20. Closes at 5:30 p.m.

El Sano, 14 Martin Pl., is vegetarian with a South American flavor. It's counter service here and the fare is intriguingly "different"—soya bean casseroles, cabbage rolls (minus meat), vegetable pies, and good rich soups. The cost runs around the $3.90 mark for a grass lunch, and the choice of cakes runs to aniseed and persimmon.

The **Hippodrome Café**, 274 Castlereagh St., has a menu festooned with French hippos, written in basic française, offering "Les Sandwiches" and drinks (soft only) from "Le Bar." A spacious, airy, tastefully furnished establishment, the Hippo shares premises with a theater booking agency, into which many patrons stray by mistake. The walls are decorated with celebrity posters and you get quiche Lorraine for $4.50 and very good "sandwich jambon"—served with little gherkins—for $1.90. Closed Sunday.

Dinner

The most remarkable selection of fine-quality, well-priced, well-mixed restaurants in all Australia is found in Darlinghurst, just south of Kings Cross. Take bus 399 from Circular Quay to Taylor Square. Get off and stroll up Oxford Street toward Darlinghurst Road, savoring the posted menus as you go. Most of these places invite you to BYO (Bring Your Own, bottle, that is) and there are plenty of good wine shops nearby. Among the multitude of choices, the following are my favorites:

The **Balkan Restaurant**, 209 Oxford St., has one dining room downstairs, another upstairs, both usually packed and with good reason. There's not much atmosphere to speak of: the long narrow premises have minimum decorations, plastic tables, and metal chairs, sliding doors to the street, an open grill kitchen in front sending out aromatic signals to your taste buds, fast, bustling, and usually breathless service. The food, however, is outstanding. The bean soup—a meal in itself for $3—is almost poetic. The saturas (beef goulash) costs $7.20 and is in the same class. It takes a very hearty appetite to manage more than one course in this place. The Balkan is open six days a week from 11 a.m. to 11 p.m. and between mealtimes doubles as an espresso café. Closed Tuesday.

At 129 Oxford St., the **Kaffee Mirabel** (correctly spelled Swiss style) is a small, charming Swiss eatery, featuring the brand of attentive service you usually encounter only in deluxe establishments. The decor is quite plain, but with neat touches of elegance, such as the half dozen outstanding prints of Swiss towns and landscapes that form the only wall decorations. Genuine little oil lamps flicker on the tables and the air conditioning really works. Wonderful fresh crusty bread comes with each meal. Apart from Zürich specialties with unpronounceable names, the Mirabel has subtly tangy chicken filets in walnut sauce and veal medallions hunter style with a rich cream sauce, both costing $9.10. The desserts—chocolate truffle slices or Linzer torte—are memorable but a rather pricey $2.50 to $3.50. Open till 10 p.m. six days a week. Closed Sunday.

Kim, 235 Oxford St., is a little Vietnamese BYO that qualifies as possibly the best of its breed in Australia, employing some of the most charming French-accented Vietnamese waitresses extant. It has no other Oriental trimmings, and only 13 tables downstairs and upstairs, but wood-paneled walls, softly gleaming lanterns beneath a beamed ceiling, and the subtle ambience produced by the mixture of Gallic finesse and Asiatic piquancy, which extends to the menu—printed in Vietnamese with English translations. The specialties are slightly spicier and considerably more startling than their Chinese counterparts, but this is a place for a little culinary courage—it pays dividends in the form of an outstanding meal at very gentle prices. Try, for instance, the pineapple soup with fish ($2.80), the braised chicken with ginger ($6), or the wondrously subtle pork satay ($6), and don't forget the savory rice cakes. Kim gets very crowded on weekends, not surprisingly. Open till 10:30 p.m. Closed Tuesday.

The historic area called the Rocks boasts a couple of eateries that provide fun along with the comestibles. **The Old Spaghetti Factory,** 80 George St., is a hilarious storage dump of oddball Victoriana, including an authentic 1898 trolley (tram) that did service on the tracks outside the building and now forms part of the dining room. Also hog scrapers, a confessional booth, slingshots, stereoscopes, love seats, etc., etc., as well as the dire warning to avoid spaghetti with chocolate sauce. Each spaghetti order includes green salad, a loaf of wholemeal bread, and garlic or plain butter. The spags with Romaine sauce cost $5.50, and there are eight other choices. Open seven days a week.

Pancakes on the Rocks, 10 Hickson Rd., features—among other amusements—games of chess, backgammon, and Trivial Pursuit. The breakfast menu here includes a "bottomless" cup of coffee. The savory pancakes include one called Tabriz for $5, pancake stacks (three for $3.90), and sweet Jewish blintzes with cheese, brandied sultanas, and sour cream. Open all day, every day.

Minerva, 285 Elizabeth St. in the city, is a Greek dinery open daily till 9:30 p.m. The place has a distinctly elegant air, brown-paneled in wood, lit by subdued chandeliers, cooled by whirring fans on the ceiling, and decorated with Hellenic landscape murals. The menu is obligingly printed in Greek on one side, English on the other. And the prices are happily budget: a three-course meal of soup, main course, and dessert comes to $5.10. The main dish may be braised beef, braised lamb, or fried squid; the dessert, rice custard or cassata.

No Name, 2 Chapel St., East Sydney. A real oddity and a very real find for economy travelers, this eatery is known to regulars as "Caesar's" but is officially nameless. You'll locate it off Crown Street and spot it by the American flag that flies next door. Originally established as an eating place for single Italian male migrants, it now caters lavishly to all comers, including family groups. Entrees go for around $3 (try the bean soup, which constitutes a meal by itself). Then, if you can, go on to the roast veal, boiled beef, or meatballs, all with salad and costing around $4. Orange cordial goes gratis with your meal—help yourself from the counter. No decorations and minimum furniture, but the food is tasty, authentic, and several notches above ample.

Steindler, 197 Campbell St., Darlinghurst. At the Taylor Square part of Oxford Street, this small eatery dispenses Czech cuisine at its solidest. The decorations consist of some maps and Prague posters, Czech wall calendars and oddly assorted statuettes. The furniture is metal covered with wax cloth, and the background music, pop. But the fare is tasty, the helpings positively monumental. Soup here constitutes a meal. A three-course repast of, say, beef-noodle soup, smoked pork with dumplings and sauerkraut, and apple strudel costs you $6.50, and you won't have to eat again for maybe a day. Open all week till 10 p.m.

Totally atmospheric, on the other hand, is the **Balalaika,** hiding underground at the Tank Stream Arcade, 175 Pitt St., in the city. It has a tiny dining room and a small menu, but is as authentically Russian as you'll find so far south of the Volga. Some of the items may puzzle you, but the lady behind the counter will be glad to explain that Siberian pelmeni are dough pockets stuffed with spicy meat, brizoll are beef rissoles with mushrooms and onions, and piroshki are the famous Russian meat pastries. Desserts are mouthwatering chocolate walnut, prune, raisin, and poppyseed concoctions, all baked on the premises and tasting accordingly. An entire meal will set you back about $8.50.

The Kings Cross region has by far the largest concentration of restaurants in Sydney, and they span the spectrum from super-deluxe to rock-bottom economy.

The **Belgrade Inn,** 116 Surrey St., is pure Yugoslav in fare. It's a small, plain establishment with an upstairs and downstairs portion, bare laminex tables, and an open kitchen range spreading the wonderful aroma of charcoal grilling. The lighting is as dim as the food is appetizing. Even the boxes of pink Kleenex that take the place of table napkins don't detract from the enjoyment. For your information, a Serbo-Croat hamburger is called pljeskavica and costs $6.80, the same as the chepavcici (beef, veal, and pork minced together and cooked on a barbecue). The raznici (tender chunks of pork cooked on skewers) $7, and the absolutely indispensable Turkish coffee costs 90¢. Open 6 to 11 p.m. Closed Sunday.

The **Fiesta,** 223 Victoria St., is a neat, modern Australian eatery with hardly a Latin touch in sight and none whatever on the plates. Decorated with hanging and standing baskets of potted plants and some straw mats, this establishment offers dishes like pork sausages with bacon and salad for $4.20, banana fritters with ice cream for $1.90. Open all week, but only from 6 to 9 p.m.

Korea House, 171 Victoria St., lies upstairs above a pretty plain pub with tiled exterior. But what a surprise! The "house" sparkles a welcome with a beautiful array of tropical fish tanks whose soft bubbling sounds provide the background music. There's also a display case in which colorfully arranged Korean delicacies are presented like shop-window jewelry. The fare is similar but more highly spiced than Chinese cuisine, and the place is licensed. The Korean barbecue is hot on the palate and wonderfully aromatic ($7.50); the soon man du (Korean version of dim sum), $4. Unfortunately you also have to pay for the excellent tea.

Una's Espresso, 286 Darlinghurst Rd., bears a misleading name because this is actually an unconventional restaurant open for breakfast, lunch, and dinner until midnight right through the week. The espresso bit is more of a sideline. There's a very small coffee bar and a much larger dining room, saved from plainness by pictures, candles on the tables, and a general air of comfortable conviviality, as befits a real neighborhood eatery. Very good continental meat loaf costs $4.70, wienerschnitzel is $5.70, and strong beef soup runs $1.80.

The **Astoria,** 7 Darlinghurst Rd., is *the* bargain dinery of the district, and one of the very few Australian establishments around. Small and narrow, with two rows of eating booths and a large standing fan as sole decoration, this establishment serves plain, well-cooked Anglo meals, devoid of alien spices, at unequivocal budget prices: barley broth for 30¢, Irish stew or lamb cutlets at $2.80, roast pork and apple sauce for $3.70. Closes at 8:30 p.m. sharp.

It's the cafés that give the Cross its special character and here they proliferate like aromatic caterpillars, indoors and out, spilling over the pavements in the best Parisian style. Their stock in trade is, of course, coffee, but some of them double very nicely as eateries.

The most famous is undoubtedly **Sweethearts,** on Darlinghurst Road, the inspiration for a song, "Breakfast at Sweethearts," turned out by the Australian rock group Cold Chisel. Sweethearts is strictly indoors, but offers you large street windows for people-watching. It's *the* rendezvous spot of the region and stays open for business around the clock seven days a week, serving pretty good Spanish omelet for $4.50 or lemon veal for $8. You can get an education along with your vittels.

Geoffrey Café, 1b Roslyn St., is more of the same, but with tables out on the pavement, partly shaded by trees, the better to watch from: a delightful spot late on a warm night or early for breakfast; a vantage point for the strolling, standing, occasionally rather rambunctious passing parade. Coffee—good and strong—goes for $1.50, main dishes for around $6. Open till 3 a.m., all night on weekends.

The **Cactus Café**, 150 Victoria St., lives up to its label by sporting desert murals, yellow-white furnishings, and a cactus plant on every table. Run by a Parisian gourmet chef, Bruno Le Glay, who thought that an economy eatery would be more fun than a deluxe den, the place specializes in unusual dishes at quite unusual prices. The hot bacon salad with cheese comes at $5.50, and a truly elegant three-course repast sets you back about $15. Do leave room for desserts—hot almond custard in puff pastry. This is a BYO, open Wednesday to Sunday till midnight.

Leaving the Cross for a moment, we'll wander to the venerable **Old Windsor Tavern,** at the corner of Castlereagh and Park Streets. A rather posh pub, decorated with rakishly Hogarthian murals depicting the naughtier aspects of Georgian England, the place also features live music every night. The main thing here, however, are the roast meals: lamb, chicken, pork, beef, steak, plus a free and sumptuous salad bar, costing just $4.90. Served continuously from 11 a.m. to 9 p.m.

North of Kings Cross huddles the much-quoted waterfront district of **Woolloomooloo** (try spelling it out over the telephone). Like several other regions, the 'Loo was once a rowdy slum patch to be avoided at night, but in recent years has become partly depopulated, partly fashionable, and wholly "in," thanks to urban renewal and squads of men and women artists who took over some of the decrepit terrace dwellings and magicked them into chic (and expensive) studios.

The oldest pub in the 'Loo is the venerable and hilarious **Lockup,** at 129 Dowling St. Outside and inside it looks like a jailhouse, decorated with police truncheons, handcuffs, chains, and rifles. The shingle is a very happy-looking convict peering out through painted bars. One wall is devoted to a fascinating display of pictures and newspaper clippings concerning Ned Kelly, the armor-plated bushranger. And there's comedy entertainment every Saturday night. The menu promises that "Chief Warder Charlie" will make your stretch a memorable one. The prison rations are pretty lavish: T-bone steak, deep-fried chicken, meat salads, or smörgåsbord, all at $10 per prisoner. As the manager points out, at those prices you don't have to rob a bank to eat there.

DAYTIME ACTIVITIES: Sunlit daytime in Sydney is for exploration. It's for delving into Australia's past, as carved by convicts into the stones of her first settlement, as read in the portraits of the founders at the Mitchell and Dixson Galleries. It's for enjoying the present—at the beaches and zoo, on the ferries, in the museums, and boutiques and shops. It's for seeing those futuristic showcases—the Opera House, Australia Square, Centrepoint—and then resting in the Domain, in earshot of the town's self-appointed orators, to contemplate from whence this society came and whither she goes. And at what pace!

All of which can be accomplished with remarkable ease, because the majority of Sydney's sights are clustered in the central city, and the balance can be easily reached by ferry from Circular Quay (which is not circular, just as Australia Square isn't square). As walking is the preferred propulsion to gain in-depth knowledge of any city, I've included a walking tour below.

But if you'd rather ride you can use one of the fleet of distinctive red Mercedes buses called **Sydney Explorers,** which run a continuous shuttle service between 20 of the most popular visitors attractions. For $7 per adult, $3.50 per child, you can spend from 9:30 a.m. to 5 p.m. any day of the week on these buses, getting on and off as often as you like. The buses stop at each location every half hour, so you can hang around as long as you please, then catch the next Explorer to the next highlight. These include Circular Quay, the Opera House, Parliament House, Kings Cross, Chinatown, The Rocks, and Pier One and you can buy your ticket as you board. Along with your ticket you'll also receive concession discounts to seven other attractions along the way.

Overviews of the harbor are also possible at refreshingly low prices. **Sydney Harbour Ferries,** Circular Quay (tel. 27-9251), provides a 2½-hour harbor cruise, with commentary, on Wednesday, Saturday, and Sunday at 1:30 or 2:30 p.m. Cruises leave from no. 4 jetty and cost $5.60 for adults, half fare for each child. The same economy rates pertain to the river cruise up Lane Cove and Parramatta River, which leaves no. 5 jetty on Sunday and public holidays at 2 p.m. Shoe leather costs more!

A Walking Tour

Start in **Martin Place** where you can pick up an excellent map at the Tourist Bureau. The most striking feature of the flower-filled mall is the **Cenotaph,** a memorial to Australia's fallen servicemen. Thursday at 12:30 p.m. the army stages a ceremony at the Cenotaph, then marches impressively to the Anzac Memorial in Hyde Park. Turn right into George Street and walk two blocks to . . .

Australia Square: Part of the Sydney skyline since 1967, the 50-floor (three below ground) **Australia Square Tower** is a circular cement, aluminum, and glass structure presently noted as the tallest building in the southern hemisphere. Take the fastest lifts in the southern hemisphere to the **Summit,** the largest revolving restaurant in the world, where prices are yet another Australia Square superlative. Descend to the sixth level and step into a simulated opal mine at the **Opal Skymine.** Continuous color films show life in the Andamooka Opal Fields, gem cutters and polishers at work. Masses of opals and other gems are on sale from $20 to upwards of $50,000. You are promised "in the field" prices, so experts should do some serious fossicking here. Open daily from 9 a.m. to 5:30 p.m.; admission is free to the showroom and exhibition.

Level 4, the **Shopping Circle,** is a colorful arcade of shops and services. Note the tapestries in the main entrance, which were woven at Aubusson in France from designs by Le Corbusier and Vasarely. A massive Calder sculpture squats on the George Street plaza. Exit to Pitt Street and turn left. In two blocks, you reach . . .

Circular Quay: Today the busy site of the ferry wharves and Overseas Passenger Shipping Terminal, this horseshoe-shaped quay embraces Sydney Cove, "the cradle of Australian history." Here it was that Capt. Arthur Phillip put in in 1788 with his flock of 1,500 (700 convicts) to begin building a colony. It was he who "honoured" the cove—and by extension the city—with its name, after Viscount Sydney. Sydney past, present, and future converge on this quay. Stand facing the harbor. To your right, jutting into the froth-tipped waves, is Australia's fabulous futuristic folly, the **Sydney Opera House** (details below). To your left arches the **Sydney Harbour Bridge,** linking the business district to the northern suburbs. Too massive and fussy for beauty, the bridge has been dubbed the

"Coathanger" by realistic Sydneysiders, who are nevertheless prompt to point out to foreign detractors that, while not the longest single span in the world, falling two feet short of the Golden Gate, struth, it's the heaviest! A full 52,800 tons of steel went into its 2¾-mile length, and that wasn't nice saying every ton shows. Just wait. The Harbour Bridge grows on you quickly. You become as affectionate toward that graceless structure as toward a floppy mutt with over-grown feet and a willing nature. It's a very efficient bridge, transferring commut-ers from shore to shore via eight traffic lanes, two railway lines, a footpath, and a lane for cyclists. And when viewed from the harbor entrance in the softening haze of dusk, framing the fragility of the Opera House shells in its stolid, protec-tive curve, it's a sight to strike joy from the most sight-hardened breast. Wel-come to Sydney!

Still standing on Circular Quay, picture the land along the peninsula to your left as it was in 1788, when Captain Phillip ordered his motley cargo to pitch tents and raise the Union Jack. The immense sprawl that is contemporary Sydney, over the hills behind you, along the coves in every direction, grew from this minute patch known as . . .

The Rocks: You could spend two hours, two days, or two weeks exploring this, Sydney's cradle. To simplify matters, stop into the Sydney Cove Redevel-opment Authority's **Information Centre** at 104 George St., one block west of the Overseas Passenger Terminal, and pick up their handy map/brochure enti-tled "Visit the Rocks." The Rocks is part of an imaginative long-term develop-ment program consisting partly of painstaking reconstructions, partly of new constructions, blending in a fascinatingly contrasting whole. May the creators not lose their vision.

Following this map, which details every item of interest along the route, here are the main points for those with limited time. From the Information Cen-tre, walk two blocks to:

The **Argyle Arts Centre,** 18 Argyle St. This is a complex of stores, work-shops, art galleries, and courtyards housed in a handsome three-story ware-house, convict-built in 1820 of durable sandstone and hand-hewn timber. Wander through the linked buildings and see beeswax candles made just as they were in the early colonial days, glass blowing, brass rubbing, pottery making, displays of flowers, stained glass, and antiques. You can buy or just look or stop and take in the free film show at the **Ampol History Centre,** showing the progress of the oil industry, together with dioramas, working models, and other exhibits. Take lunch or tea at **Mary Reibey's Parlour.** Mary was transported at the age of 13 for stealing a horse (and lucky she wasn't hanged for it) and died 60 years later, seven children and £120,000 sterling to the good. Her most profitable trading was done out of the rum stores in the cellars below. The shutters at the Parlour entrance once hung at the windows of her 'umble cottage.

Back on Argyle Street, turn right and head uphill through dusky **Argyle Cut,** the 300-foot tunnel hollowed out of the solid stone to give direct access to Miller's Point from Circular Quay. It was begun with convict labor in 1843, and you can still see the prisoners' marks on the granite. This used to be the riskiest spot in perhaps the toughest area of the southern hemisphere. For in its mid-history the Rocks was the gathering ground for a truly choice mob of convicts, soldiers, sailors, whalers, sealers, thugs, and prostitutes, and produced its per-sonal species of gangsters—the larrikins. A bit later San Francisco's Barbary Coast played host to some of these same gents and ladies, with the transplanted "Sydney Ducks" acquiring the reputation of being the most vicious mob in Cali-fornia.

At the top of Argyle Street, facing the leafy quietude of **Argyle Place,** Syd-ney's only village green, stands the Church of the Holy Trinity, better known as the **Garrison Church.** With a cornerstone reading June 23, 1840, this is the second-oldest church in Sydney, the first Official Garrison Church of the Colony, and the earliest example of Australian Gothic extant. In 1840, its parishioners included the redcoats of the 50th Queen's Own, stationed at nearby Dawes' Point Battery, who attended morning prayers regularly en colorful masse. Worshiping with the military were the well-to-do merchants who lived in the pastel houses fringed with cast-iron lace still sheltering under the trees of the green, shuttered tightly against the sunlight. And those living in the gracious town and terrace houses, so obviously derived from London and New Orleans that range along stately Lower Fort Street to the right of the church, also attended. The church is open daily for inspection—step in to admire the Gothic arches, mullioned windows, the early wine-glass pulpit of old red cedar, the century-old prayer desk—and you are welcome to attend Sunday services.

Circle the green and then head down Lower Fort Street. Immediately to your left is the oldest pub in Sydney, the **Hero of Waterloo Hotel.** Built in 1804 as a jailhouse, it was licensed in 1815 and gained notoriety in the Rocks' "Barbary Coast" days for the number of well-seasoned drinkers who disappeared through a trapdoor under the bar only to reappear days later doing unenthusiastic duty on some sea-bound merchant ship. The main pub is plain and fitted with the ubiquitous pool tables, but you can sip nostalgically in one rock-walled snug, complete with fireplace and hanging gas lamps, dubbed "The Duke's Room," or enjoy a home-cooked hot lunch for just $2.

The facades along Lower Fort Street are lovely to behold, spanning as they do the major architectural influences of the 19th century. Step behind one at no. 53, where the **Colonial House Museum** occupies two floors of a four-story terrace house dating to 1884. The six museum rooms, furnished in period style, look so lived in you can almost see some affluent Aussie forebear strolling through, ruffling a book open here, straightening a mannequin's costume there. The two display rooms feature a complete photographic record of the Rocks from 1880 to 1901, giving you a glimpse of those many buildings that have passed on. Open daily from 10 a.m. to 5 p.m.; admission is 50¢ for adults, half price for children.

At the end of Lower Fort Street, look to your right for an unexpected and breath-catching view of the Opera House on the opposite peninsula. Pass under the highway and into George Street. The first building on your left is the **Geological and Mining Museum,** 36 George St., built in 1902 as the Electric Light Station. Housing one of the finest displays of geological specimens—gemstones, minerals, rocks, and fossils—in the southern hemisphere, it is open free to the public weekdays from 9:30 a.m. to 4 p.m., 1 to 4 p.m. on Saturday, 11 a.m. to 4 p.m. on Sunday. The **Mercantile Hotel** on your right, erected in 1908, is notable mainly for its face of brilliant green tiles. The **Old Spaghetti Factory** on your left is notable for its fine spaghetti, prices, and funky decor (see "Meals"). Passing the Information Centre from whence you began, stroll to the corner of Argyle Street, turn left and view the recently restored **Cadman's Cottage,** Sydney's oldest homestead (1816). John Cadman was superintendent of government boats at a time when Sydney Cove virtually flowed to his door. Walk another block and you're back on Circular Quay.

Note: Should you be in Sydney in early April, join the **Argyle Annual Celebrations,** a "people's celebration" featuring street stalls, an organized pub crawl, free entertainment by name Aussie artists, a flashy parade, and a ceremonial appointment of the year's "Governor of the Rocks," complete to cannon and musket salute from Observatory Hill. Lively!

Back on Circular Quay, pass the ferry wharves on your left and continue around the quay to Bennelong Point, where perches the controversial **Sydney**

Opera House, looking very much, to quote Robert Morley, "like something that has crawled out of the sea and is up to no good." The trouble it has caused started over 30 years ago, but let me zip through the tale in case you've been adrift in a lifeboat for two decades.

In 1954, a group of noted Sydney citizens decided that the time had come in the city's maturity for a performing arts center. They chose the present site and began an international competition for a suitable design. In 1957, Danish architect Joern Utzon won the $10,000 prize for his unique sails-along-harbor design, a magnificent concept fraught with untried techniques. He also won the dubious right to direct construction on an estimated budget of $7.2 million. By 1966, after battling governments, unions, and his own unworkable plans, Utzon rejected the privilege and scooted for home. The government stepped in and the budget shot up to $50 million. From there on, the project supported the building trades through work stoppages and labor disputes, through blunders and oversights, until the final cost, when Queen Elizabeth cut the blue ribbon on October 20, 1973, was a staggering $102 million (US$140 million). Not that milk was swiped from children to pay the tab. It was all financed by lottery, and with Australian gambling fever what it is, the entire building was paid off by 1975. (Suggestion: Let's let the Diggers handle the U.S. federal budget deficit.)

A common expression among locals, since the first derricks thrust their giraffe necks into the skyline, has been "It'll never fly." It nearly didn't. The builders forgot to put in dressing rooms, planned no parking facilities, and paved the promenade with slabs of pink marble, not realizing that heavy trucks delivering the final equipment would crack it all. Everything had to be rectified.

And all this in full view of the verbal populace, spawning an avalanche of waggeries. The New South Whale, they called it, the Hunchback of Bennelong Point, the Operasaurus, a haystack with a tarpaulin, a pack of French nuns playing football, an opera house eight sheets to the wind. Then it was finished. The *London Times* said it was "the building of the century" (gee, Mom), and the Aussies shut up, looked again, and saw a pearl-pale sculpture glowing suspiciously like a national symbol on their waterfront. For the truth is, what man hath wrought in wrangling and union negotiations occasionally comes out right. The building is *exquisite.* From every angle. It has no contemporary peer.

Go along on a guided tour by day to view the remarkable workmanship of the interior, with its beautifully treated timber panels, its tinted glass merging into the sea beyond, its curtains woven in the bold hues of the Australian day and night. Then go back at night to sample the perfect acoustics and the first-class talent. In all, there are four performance halls (within a total of 980 rooms), one for concerts, one for opera and ballet, one for drama, and a smaller room for recitals. Pop groups and comedians make their appearances as well as classical musicians, the people throng to both, and the mischievous sea monster 30 years in the hatching has been embraced and turned into a prince.

Tours are held daily except Saturday from 9:15 a.m. Admission is $2.50 for adults, $1.20 for children.

Strike out now across the 125-acre **Domain** (if you're tired—and I wouldn't blame you—you might leave this walk for the next day), passing the sandstone keep and turrets of **Government House,** the white crenelated towers of the **Conservatorium of Music.** Stroll leisurely through the rolled lawns and labeled shrubs of the **Royal Botanic Gardens,** with hothouses filled with orchids and ferns, and aim toward the **Art Gallery of New South Wales,** diagonally across. On Sunday, the Domain is peopled with Sydney's self-proclaimed philosophers sounding off from the mid-rungs of their stepladders on the level of Australian intelligence (always lower than the speaker's), religion, communism, and sex. Listen and remain uninformed.

The two wings of the Art Gallery of New South Wales, one built at the turn of the century and the other in 1970, are admirably suited to their contrasting exhibits. The traditionally skylit, wine-walled galleries of the old wing contain European and Australian art dating from the Renaissance to the early 20th century. The new wing, all angled white walls and harbor-framing glass, houses impressionist and modern works, including some striking paintings by those most famed Australian artists, William Dobell, Russell Drysdale, and Sidney Nolan. Pick up a free guide to the collection in the bookshop to the left of the entrance. Open daily, except Good Friday and Christmas, from 10 a.m. to 5 p.m. Monday through Saturday, from noon to 5 p.m. on Sunday. Admission is 30¢ for adults, half price for children. Free to all on Tuesday and Sunday.

Within the museum is a licensed café serving hot dishes, sandwiches, and snacks. Exit from the front door and follow the winding path halfway across the Domain to the circular building trimmed with windowboxes and you can purchase inexpensive teas, lunches, and sandwiches at the **Domain Restaurant** (unlicensed). Both feature some items under $1.

Otherwise, turn left upon leaving the Gallery and follow Art Gallery Road into College Street. Turn left again at **St. Mary's Cathedral,** an excellent example of Gothic Revival architecture, and continue two blocks to the . . .

Australian Museum (College Street), where you can inspect natural history displays (masses of crawlies), an interesting study of Aboriginal life, and a gallery of Melanesian art. Open 10 a.m. to 5 p.m. Tuesday to Sunday, noon to 5 p.m. on Monday; closed Good Friday and Christmas. Snacks and light meals are available at the rooftop cafeteria. Retrace your steps down College Street into **Queens Square** and stop and get your bearings.

You are now in the most architecturally impressive part of Sydney, where the handsome structures provide a remarkable contrast to some of those seen at the day's beginning within the Rocks. As Sydney grew up, out, and prosperous, she evolved from ramshackle huts through the simple elegance of the late Georgian period headfirst into the voluptuousness of the long Victorian age. The loveliest legacy to the city was left by convict-architect Francis Greenway, who designed the fine proportions, handsome classical porches, and graceful copper-sheathed spire of **St. James' Church** (1819), to your left on the square. The **Law Courts,** to your right, originally planned by Greenway as convict quarters, so delighted then Governor Macquarie that he granted the gifted architect a full pardon.

Full speed ahead into Macquarie Street, passing on your right the **Old Mint** (1811–1816), one surviving wing of the old Rum Hospital, which served as a branch of the Royal Mint from 1855 to 1926. (The Rum Hospital, Sydney's first general hospital, was so named because the three philanthropic colonists who contributed the building did so in return for a three-year monopoly on the rum traffic.) Next comes contemporary Sydney Hospital and then the **New South Wales Parliament House,** another portion of the old Rum Hospital, much embellished. Meeting in a building older than itself (the oldest parliament house in the southern hemisphere), the Parliament legislates "for the peace, welfare and good government of the State in all matters not specifically reserved to the Commonwealth Parliament." Visitors are welcome to view the proceedings between 10 a.m. and 3 p.m. Monday through Friday. If Parliament is not in session, ask at the front desk and a guard will guide you through the chambers.

Next door to Parliament is the State Library of New South Wales, where you should definitely clamber up the long stone steps to view the **Dixson and Mitchell Galleries.** A repository of papers, prints, paintings, and proclamations dealing with the settlement of Sydney, the galleries mount various showings of the trove. I immensely enjoyed one called "Our Origins—From Penal Camp to

Parliament." It included over 300 fascinating items, but possibly the most telling was Governor Davey's Proclamation, circa 1828, a pictorial broadsheet explaining British justice to Aborigines. The potentialities are graphically expressed. Black chief and white chief shake hands (warriors to rear). Black man spears white man, white warriors hang black man. White man shoots black man, white warriors hang white man. Ultimate potential: black and white man with arms around shoulders, black and white child holding hands, black woman cradling white baby, white woman cradling black baby. Everybody happy—in white fella clothes. The galleries are open from 10 a.m. to 5 p.m. Monday to Saturday, 2 to 6 p.m. on Sunday.

From here you can continue down Macquarie Street admiring more impressive buildings (nos. 173, 171, and 145 are representative of the lovely residences once gracing this area) until you reach Circular Quay. Or backtrack to Sydney Hospital, cross Macquarie and, following Martin Place, return to the mall where you started. A fast walk through this circular trail would have taken you approximately two hours. Let me know if you did it in a day! (Alternatively, if the spirit is willing but the bunions ache, all the above can be seen independently and by public transport.)

The Beaches

Thirty-four glorious ocean beaches exist within the city limits, golden dashes along an undulating path leading from Port Hacking, 20 miles south of Sydney Harbour, to Palm Beach 20 miles north. Picking your patch of pine-shaded sand (only those born to it can bear the Sydney summer sun full strength) would take weeks of delightful testing. Rest assured that all border a sea where the average annual temperature is 68 degrees, all boast their quota of handsome, lightly draped bodies, and your major choices are between near and far, noisy or less noisy, crowded and not-so-crowded. Whatever you choose, be prepared for the fact that Sydneysiders *utilize* their beaches. They are capable of sitting, sunning, and getting sand in no crevices (a particularly Australian talent) for longer hours than any people I know. But they also toy with their roaring surf in any number of reckless ways—in surfboats, canoes, inflated rubber rafts, on a mere slip of a surfboard, or "body-shooting" with nothing but high spirits and skin for buoyancy.

The most popular beaches on summer weekends are **Bondi, Manly, Coogee, Maroubra,** and **Cronulla,** all easily reached by public transportation from downtown. **Whale Beach, Avalon,** and **Bilgola** have been characterized as "tranquil." To survey the northern beaches, you can catch the no. 190 bus from Carrington Street behind Wynyard Station to **Palm Beach,** which skirts an approximately 26-mile shoreline. If you only have one day to experience an Australian beach, then I'd say make it Manly.

To make the most of your half day there, choose two different modes of transport. When it's early and you're raring to leap into the spray, speed the seven miles in 13 minutes via **hydrofoil** (it's like a boat racing on waterskis) from no. 2 jetty, Circular Quay. Coming back, surfeited with sun and saltwater, cruise in on the slow boat. **Ferries** commute between Manly and no. 3 wharf, Circular Quay. It's a leisurely and quite wonderful chug, taking 35 minutes and costing 50¢ for adults, 25¢ for children.

Manly has four ocean beaches, two ocean swimming pools, and six (calm) harbor beaches. It also has a **Fun Pier,** with spinning wheels, dodge-'ems, whirlers, and a ghost train, where rides cost 60¢. Considerably more impressive is **Marine Land,** which has a 250,000-gallon tank, viewable from above and from three depth-levels. The pool is swarming with thousands of ocean critters, from tiny rainbow fish to enormous sea turtles, giant rays, groupers, and killer sharks.

At feeding time (twice on weekdays, thrice on Saturday and Sunday), divers descend into the tank with food sleighs and actually hand-feed the inhabitants. How they manage not to get their hands bitten off is one of the permanent puzzles and special thrills of the place. Admission is $5 for adults, half price for children.

The **Manly Waterworks,** across the park from the ferry wharf, consists of four giant waterslides that sluice you, twisting, turning, and yelling, from considerable heights into a gentle pool landing below. It feels nerve-tingling but is absolutely safe, and you vary the speeds of the rides. In action seven days a week. In cool weather they thoughtfully heat the water. The cost is $6 for an hour's slithering. If you're ready for a slower brand of locomotion, take the **Manly Horse Tram,** which dates from 1903 and is the only such vehicle surviving in Australia. Propelled by one four-legged horsepower, it costs $2 for adults, half price for children.

More Sights

Taronga Zoo, in Mosman, has the most beautiful setting of any zoological garden in the world. Perched on a hillside 12 minutes by ferry from Circular Quay, it offers harbor panoramas together with the animals and 75 acres of bushland park. Take the ferry from no. 5 wharf (adults pay 90¢, children 30¢), then the waiting bus to the top of the hill and sightsee downhill all the way. See koalas at their own treetop level in their specially designed enclosure. Check out the platypus house, the rainforest aviary where you walk *into* the cage and have the birds fly above and around you, and the friendship farm where you can pet a lamb or a wombat. In the underground building where special lights turn day into night you can watch the nocturnal denizens of Australia and New Guinea at their busiest. Plus the inevitable lions, tigers, gorillas, elephants, and reptiles. Admission is $6 for adults, half that for children, and the zoo is open from 10 a.m. to 5 p.m. seven days a week.

Victoria Barracks, Oxford Street, Paddington, is a living history of Australia's military forces. Built largely by convict labor and finished in 1848, the barracks were designed to house one regiment of British infantry. The British garrison troops were withdrawn in 1870, since there was no enemy imaginable who couldn't be handled by the Royal Navy. Since then Australia's own forces have occupied the barracks, which today are the hub and command post of the Commonwealth's field and supporting units. The place is a splendid example of late Georgian architecture, crammed with military memorabilia. Every Tuesday, at 11 a.m., there's a ceremonial changing of the guard, impressive to watch. Following this the barracks are open to tours. You can make arrangements by phoning 339-0455.

The **Entertainment Centre,** Haymarket, is Australia's largest auditorium, impressive though not particularly photogenic. Looking like an outsize airport terminal, the building is a marvel of flexibility: four different layouts allow the complex to be used for single star performers, theatrical productions, or giant sporting events. It can hold from 3,500 to 12,000 people with nary a pillar to block anyone's view of the stage.

Pier One, underneath the Harbour Bridge, adjacent to the Rocks, is a fun pier writ large: not stylish, but delightfully relaxed, inexpensive, and impressively cosmopolitan Pier One has so many attractions that you'd have to list them alphabetically. Based on a row of converted warehouses are dodge-'em cars, a movie theater, merry-go-rounds, an excellent bookstore (John Cookson), market stalls, shops selling anything from jewelry to junk, a colonial village from the turn of the century, and a bewildering array of restaurants, cafés, and snackeries. You can gorge yourself on sashimi, pasta, tabouli, tacos, sate, baklava, samosa, hamburgers, or Sydney rock oysters, while listening to strolling ballad-eers, brass bands, jazz combos, watching jugglers and dancers, or just the con-stantly changing harbor scene around you. The place also boasts an "astro analyst," a futuristic shooting gallery, and electronic games.

Fort Denison. You can't miss the little hump of rock with the round tower sticking out of Sydney Harbour. Officially named Fort Denison, the islet was known as "pinchgut" to thousands of convicts sent there on starvation rations as a "mild" form of punishment. Built and armed to protect Sydney from invasion (which never came), Fort Denison today is a maritime tide observation station as well as a landmark. The massive Martello Tower still houses the huge cannon and balls earmarked for an enemy (Russian at that time) who failed to test them. Tours leave no. 6 wharf, Circular Quay, from Tuesday to Saturday at 10:15 a.m., 12:45, and 2:15 p.m. The tours last 1½ hours and the ferry ride costs $3 for adults, $2 for children.

Elizabeth Bay House is an enchanting period mansion built for the colonial secretary of New South Wales in 1838. Laid out around a superb central stair-case, saloon lit by an oval lantern from above, the white villa shows in what tasteful splendor dwelled the colonial upper classes at a time when Australia's lower orders were somewhat less stylishly housed. The furnishings have the typ-ical elegant simplicity of the Georgian era—soon to be obliterated by the over-stuffed red-brick monstrosities of the Victorians, who spread their architectural ham-handedness all over the globe. Open for inspection Tuesday to Sunday. Admission is $1.50 for adults, 50¢ for students.

Sydney Tower is the newest landmark in a town that fairly bristles with 'em, a giant sky needle stabbing 1,000 feet up from Centrepoint, at the corner of Market and Pitt Streets. The spectacular views are aided by high-powered bin-oculars plus a television camera that zooms in on all the other landmarks of the city spreading below you. Also electronic guide paths illustrating Sydney's ship-ping and air traffic, a weather station, two nonstop audio-visual theaters, and two more revolving restaurants—which make Sydney the world's revolving res-taurant capital. Tickets cost $3.50 for adults, $1.50 for children.

Holdsworth Galleries, 86 Holdsworth St., Woollahra, is the largest *private* art gallery in the southern hemisphere. It is also one of the premier showcases for contemporary Australian artists, so beautifully designed and constructed that it could pass as an artwork itself. The exhibitions change—sometimes three shows simultaneously—but they invariably reflect the best efforts produced by local painters and sculptors. Names like Sidney Nolan, Margaret Olley, Sali Herman, and Arthur Boyd are regulars, with the new unknowns occasionally getting their meteoric start here. Admission is free and the gallery is open seven days a week till 5 p.m.

EVENING ACTIVITIES: The possibilities are endless. Light-hearted Sydney has no taste for early hours. The warm weather awakens a thirst and thickens the blood for the chase. "What's happening" in Sydney is what's happening in every other class city in the world—a little less subtly than in Paris, less frantically than in New York, fraught with fewer funky possibilities than in San Francisco, but quite a few at that.

The first step in successful Sydneyfication is to know the hideously complex local liquor laws. Wine bars and pubs close tight at 10 p.m. except in summer when it's 11 p.m. But everybody and her brother belongs to a private club where the slot machines clang out till midnight or beyond seven days a week, and the brew is cold and cheap (tourist directions are in the text, below). Dine in a li-censed restaurant and you can drink until the proprietor starts stacking the chairs. Bring your own to a nonlicensed eatery (purchase it before 10 p.m.) and do likewise. Finally, there are the discos, jazz joints, and nightclubs where you are required to order something trivial in the food line (often included in the admission charge) for the privilege of dancing and drinking to as late—or early —as 3 a.m. And ultimately there's Kings Cross, where rows of liquor joints operate by some special dispensation until dawn's early light.

Your best guide to after-dark activities is the daily newspaper, which lists the international artists and touring casts in town, the plays, movies, concerts, and Opera House programs. The *Sydney Morning Herald* prints a comprehensive "Amusements" page; dial the given numbers for ticket and price information. Scouting out pubs and wine bars takes little more than strong legs and motivation. City pubs are 20 to the mile in the center, although far too many are of the bare-board, badly lit, no-nonsense genre. If you want to sample 20 pubs under one roof, each with its separate strata of society, tipple through the first five floors of the **Menzies Hotel,** 14 Carrington St., a first-class hostelry straddling Wynyard Station that has the distinction of being Australia's largest single liquor dispenser—upward of $12,000 worth per day, 70% of that beer. Pre-wedding stag parties have attempted pub crawls through the layers but there is no record of anyone's lasting the route.

Wine bars have sprung up like daffodils in the Sydney suburbs since the mid-'60s. Wine bar owners, attempting to lure patrons from the private clubs, built in a bit of comfort and atmosphere, priced the food and red, white, or pink by the glass at reasonable levels, and frequently threw in live entertainment. The young and handsome flocked in, found each other, and stayed. Wine bars are the best places for unattached females to sip at their ease. They are also excellent at linking up those wishing to be attached. Among noted Sydney wine bars are: **Sweet Fanny's** on Elizabeth Street, **Soren's** in Woolloomooloo, the **Stoned Crow** in Crow's Nest, **Strata** at Cremorne Junction, the **Grape Escape** and **Dionysus' Bistro** at McMahon's Point, **French's** on Oxford Street, and on and on.

For my part, I intend to guide you to only one large area and several special spots where you can most easily join the perpetual party that is Sydney after sunset.

Kings Cross

Sydney's Soho, Montmartre, North Beach, or Greenwich Village—take your pick—deserves a heading by itself because it is the only such district in Australia. A concentrated cluster of bright and/or red lights, filled with more after-dark whoopee than you'll find anywhere west of Broadway and Columbus, the Cross contains every conceivable brand of nocturnal action within one square mile: from svelte international eateries to sleazy strip joints, from roaring discos to intimate little back-lane cafés. It's a place for drifting around and dropping into whatever tickles your fancy, and doing so in complete *physical* safety. For while you're likely to get propositioned every few yards, you almost certainly won't get assaulted.

The odd thing about Kings Cross is that, technically, it doesn't exist. The area is merely a vague geographical definition, the region where Darlinghurst, Potts Point, and Elizabeth Bay meet and join hands in a bit of heel-kicking before going their own businesslike ways. But to tens of thousands of GIs, who flocked here on "R & R" from the hell of duty in Vietnam, the Cross was a patch of sulfurous paradise to be dreamt about when you were back among the rice paddies. The locals, who had added a third "R"—for Remuneration—to the other two, deeply mourned the passing of this bonanza.

The two main thoroughfares, Darlinghurst Road and Macleay Street, are so chock-a-block with niteries, eateries, and stripperies that it's useless to try to list them. I can merely pick a few random raisins from the pie and assure you that there are dozens more where these came from:

The **Pink Panther,** Darlinghurst Road, has relays of long-stemmed ladies demurely dressed in smiles, although somehow Aussie peelers always seem strangely wholesome because of their suntans. At **Les Girls,** at the corner of Darlinghurst Road and Roslyn Street, the performers are boys. Young and not-so-young female impersonators, very talented and stunningly attired, they romp through a Rabelaisian variety show abrim with campy humor and awash with double entendres. All the singing is (superbly) mimed to pretaped voices. The two nightly shows include a three-course dinner and the whole thing costs $23 or $25 a head.

The **Village Centre** is another complex containing shops, cafés, restaurants, and the **Kings Cross Wax Works.** For $4.50 for adults, $2.50 for children, you can gaze at 89 life-size wax figures in 50 pretty realistic settings running the historical gamut from Captain Cook to Marilyn Monroe, from Henry VIII to Count Dracula.

Arthur's, 155 Victoria St., is a small white building housing a chic and decidedly "in" espresso bar in front, a beautiful restaurant with balcony tables in the rear, and a minuscule dance floor upstairs. Served by a trio of DJs spinning out New Wave sounds till 3 a.m., Arthur's spurns light plays and other disco gimmicks, but is the stomping ground for the way-outest dressers and coolest kids in town. On weekends there's a $3 admission charge.

The **Texas Hotel,** 44 Macleay St., houses an entire entertainment complex under one roof. In the basement there's the Civic Club with rows of slot machines. The San Antonio Bar, one floor up, has live jazz and a dance floor. Still further up the elevator are the Aircrew Club with a piano bar and the Lan Club, featuring Japanese entertainment.

The **Nevada,** Bayswater Road, looks as if it had been flown over from New Orleans' French Quarter. Its signs proclaim "Australia's Largest Bed" and "Exciting Hostesses"—some of whom can be observed waving and shouting from the upper balcony to pedestrians below.

The Cross has a number of pure gambling clubs, where the game's the thing, undisturbed by frivolities like bands and dancefloors. They are very well run and widely advertised. The games are cards only—no roulette, two-up or slot machines—and include poker, black jack, Russian poker, and gin rummy. Minimum stakes around $2, maximum around $100. They operate seven nights a week until the wee hours. The **Barclay Club,** 17 Bayswater Road, and **Club 77,** Darlinghurst Road, are both well established, plushly furnished and very amiably staffed.

The **Barrel Theatre,** Darlinghurst Road, warns patrons against attending its burlesque performances should they, per chance, be affronted by total nudity. And at the arterial hub of the Cross, **El Alamein Fountain** shimmers in the floodlights like a giant thistledown, dispensing delicate beauty in all directions, free of charge.

Just down the road there's a different kind of landmark. The **Wayside Chapel,** 29 Hughes St., was built with volunteer labor by a free-wheeling Methodist minister named Ted Noffs in 1964. Open "to all faiths and none," the chapel has since married more people than any other church in Australia, and probably helped more desperate souls as well. This is where you go when you're in trouble (it functions as a 24-hour crisis center), if you want to locate any group or association in Sydney (straight, gay, or otherwise), if you need a crash pad or a solo bed for the night, if you're sick in body or spirit, or pregnant or suicidal or lonely or broke. You'll get whatever help human goodwill and know-how can bestow and you'll get *no* hassles.

The chapel itself, welcoming behind plate-glass windows, is tiny. Instead of normal services it holds "Celebrations" every Sunday, featuring jazz, folk and rock music, Buddhist chants, whatever aids. Sunday evening is Question Time, when Mr. Noffs leads discussions on topics like drugs, racism, rape, or the relevance of religion. Upstairs is a coffeeshop selling "cuppas" for 50¢, meals from $1. In the theater behind the chapel, plays and films are shown—and not the "message" kind either—debates held, and problems of the day thrashed out. Phone the Wayside Chapel at 358-6577 to find out what's going on that evening. Or better still, drop in and deposit something in the donation box. It'll be your best-spent money in Australia.

And Elsewhere

Kings Cross may be best by night, but t'ain't bad by day (as the saying goes). Loads of continental delicatessens, shadowy arcades with signs reading "The Sex Aid Shop" and "Tattoo Parlor," picaresque characters and a perfectly proper community gathering place named the Village Centre where outdoor cafés surround an inner fountain and you can purchase a passionfruit gelati before browsing through the bookshops and health food stores. . . . **Paddington** ("Paddo" to you, mate) was a deteriorating suburb filled with rickety Victorian houses along narrow, winding streets just 20 years ago. Today it has been reclaimed by ardent householders who have restored the iron lace on their terraced houses and brought the area delightfully alive. Over and under the verandas are galleries, curio shops, avant-garde boutiques, small restaurants—all best discovered on foot. Oxford Street is the main thoroughfare (take bus 379 or 380 from Circular Quay). The Windsor Castle Hotel is the "in" drinkery for "in" types. . . . **Double Bay** never did much deteriorating—it has long been the haunt of Sydney's Westport types. The large family dwellings of the late 1800s now house select shops, the "better" galleries, antique shops, and haute couture boutiques, as well as the descendants of settlers. Take bus 306 or 324 from Pitt Street and ask to be dropped among the shops in New South Head Road. *Note:* The word "suburb," as anything outside Sydney's center is called, can be misleading. Kings Cross is one mile from downtown, Paddo about three, and Double Bay no more than four.

Theater

Although Sydney lacks an actual theater district (worse luck), standard "Broadway" theater is easy to locate through the newspapers and about as pricey Down Under as in America. A popular local alternative—and a window into Aussie life for foreigners—are the various theater-restaurants presenting topical revues, ribaldry, and political satire. They include dinner—mostly uninspired—in their ticket prices, as well as drinking privileges.

It may seem paradoxical to talk about off-Broadway productions in a town without Broadway. But that's the only way to describe the group of nonestablishment playhouses that give Sydney its theatrical dash of paprika.

The **New Theatre**, 542 King St., Newtown (tel. 519-3403), is not "new" at all, having started during the Depression as a platform for social commentary and continuing in that role today, although somewhat less earnestly. For over 50 years the New Theatre has played in homes, on street corners, at meetings, even down in a mine to striking miners, making dramatized comments on vital issues of the time. Success has mellowed the group, but only to a point. Its most famous production was Australia's first authentic musical, *Reedy River*, a lively if somewhat naïve depiction of life in the outback of the 1890s, with a score woven around genuine and wonderfully catchy old bush ballads. If on—it gets repeated at intervals—don't miss. The actors are non-professional and perform Friday, Saturday, and Sunday—sometimes beautifully.

Phillip Street Theatre, 169 Phillip St. (tel. 323-4900), originally made its reputation by staging Australia's sharpest and funniest topical revues. It still has them occasionally, but is now mainly a showcase for Aussie playwrights, budding and otherwise. Last thing I saw there was a hilarious study of the mating habits of a bunch of economy bus tourists visiting the "Red Heart" of the continent.

Seymour Centre, at the corner of City Road and Cleveland Street (tel. 692-3511), combines three stages and usually gives you a choice between comedy and drama. It often has visiting overseas companies, mostly excellent.

Genesian Theatre, 420 Kent St. (tel. 267-7774). One of the longest established Sydney groups, it puts on anything from local talent to imported hits from abroad.

Ensemble Theatre, 78 McDougall St., Milsons Point (tel. 929-0644), located just across the Sydney Harbour Bridge, specializes in Australian theater and "musical romps."

Q Theatre, Railway Street, Penrith (tel. 21-5735), used to be a lunchtime theater down by Circular Quay, but has now graduated to being the only fully professional stage in the western area of Sydney. The ideal time to catch a play there is when you're on your way to or from the popular Blue Mountains region (see "Day Tours"). Tickets cost around $9, considerably cheaper than city prices.

Belvoir Street Theatre, 25 Belvoir St., Surry Hills (tel. 699-3273). One of the best, most original and variegated showstages in Australia—or rather two stages because there's an upstairs and a downstairs portion. Located in a distinctly drab part of town, with decor that badly needs a facelift, this theater puts on sparkling performances that feature local playwrights, directors, and actors at their unvarnished finest.

Stables Theatre, Nimrod St., Kings Cross (tel. 33-5216), is the only fully clothed live show in the area and therefore discreetly tucked away in a backstreet. Specializes in original Australian works; mostly serious and frequently excellent.

There are many more where this selection came from, but the above will keep you busy enough during your stay.

Disco, Jazz, and Folk

Sydney fairly bristles with discos, most of them jumping at decibel levels that make wallpaper curl. However, they blossom and wilt so fast that anything I say about them is almost guaranteed to be passé within a year. Currently the two snazziest are **Juliana's,** in the Sydney Hilton, 259 Pitt St., and **Amy's,** in the Hilton International, 20 Levy St., Arncliff. The latter, named after aviatrix Amy Johnston, is appropriately located at Sydney Airport and decorated with aeronautical equipment. The **Paradise,** 39 Darlinghurst Rd., Kings Cross, roars seven nights a week till dawn, gives you some of the zaniest light play extant, and has no cover charge.

The **Musician's Club,** 94 Chalmers St., presents both rock and solid jazz on different nights, and frequently acts as a showcase for Sydney's "fringe bands" who haven't yet gained much public recognition. Interesting to watch for the hidden talents it brings to light.

Sydney's pubs have not succumbed to the rock 'n' roll avalanche and still present a rich and raunchy mix of rock, jazz, and folk music. The selection is quite enormous and changes so rapidly that even the weekly entertainment publications can't keep completely abreast.

The **Sydney Cove Tavern**, AMP Centre, 50 Bridge St., for instance, may put on five different bands in one weekend. A charming newish pub with a yesteryear flavor, a large stage, and a bistro, the tavern has a cover charge of between $4.50 and $6 on music nights.

A complete listing would fill the rest of this chapter, but the music pubs include **The Basement**, 29 Reiby Pl., Circular Quay; the **Marble Bar** of the Sydney Hilton; **Soup Plus**, 383 George St., which does dispense very good budget-priced soup and full meals as well as sounds; and **Bensons Wine Bar**, 101 Oxford St., Bondi Junction. Few of them charge admission prices and most sell beer and wine at around $1 a glass. My pet jazz pub is the **Old Push**, 109 George St., in the Rocks region. The word "push," I must hasten to explain, means gang in Down Underese. One of Australia's most celebrated (and quite unprintable) poems describes an epic duologue between the "Captain of the Push" and the "Bastard from the Bush." But I digress. Anyway, the Old Push is an intimate waterfront establishment featuring local jazz combos belting out Dixieland and occasionally swing. Lantern-lit, with two white-walled rooms—one for dining, the other for the bandstand—the place offers music nightly until midnight. No cover charge, but you have to eat something, which won't break you.

For music in the widest sense of the word there's the **Australian Music Centre**, 80 George St., The Rocks. There you'll find everything that relates to Australian music, from a library and listening room to listings of performers, composers, and compositions.

The Argyle Tavern

For a bit of communal jollity, decidedly tourist-oriented but fun nonetheless, opt for a Big Splurge evening of dinner, song, and dance at the **Argyle Tavern**, 18 Argyle St. (tel. 27-7782 or 27-1613). Occupying a basement room of the restored warehouse that contains the Argyle Arts Centre (see "Daytime Activities"), the tavern exudes early-Aussie atmosphere, complete to convict-hewn rock walls and long wooden tables lit by candles. Girls in calico gowns and white dust caps share the serving chores with boys in red sashes—and it's happy, willing service, if not overbrisk. They hand out souvenir menus printed under the masthead of *The Sydney Monitor* circa 1829 and tie paper bibs around your neck, which you can flip up come singalong time to read the words of "Click Go the Shears" and "Tie Me Kangaroo Down, Sport." Then they bring on your choices from the à la carte menu—generous servings of roast lamb, pork, crayfish, beef, or chicken, plump meat pies, possibly followed by blueberry pie or fresh strawberries with whipped cream to top off. All items on the menu are fresh, reasonably traditional, and prepared without risks. Food comes first, so go no later than 8 p.m. At 9:45 p.m., the band strikes up and leads the congregation in 30 minutes of stirring song, including the unofficial national anthem, "Waltzing Matilda," and such international oldtimers as "My Bonnie Lies Over the Ocean." With the ice (if there was any) truly broken, the rest of the evening is dedicated to lively dancing to popular music and fueling up on the tavern's specialty, rum punch. The dinner charge is $37.50.

Cabarets and Comics

This is our grab bag for a melange of basement dives and pub theaters devoted—more or less—to comedy, in which bracket I include male strippers. Charges range from a lowly $5 to a steep $26 (including supper) and the shows may feature unblooded amateurs or national celebrities. A whispered warning here: The humor dispensed can be either extremely raunchy or very "in." In the first instance you run the risk of being offended, in the second of not understanding the jokes.

Kirribilli Pub, Milsons Point (opposite the railway station), is inexpensive and frequently hilarious. Some knowledge of Aussie idiom is an advantage for spectators. Go on Thursday, Friday, or Saturday only.

Blue Cockatoo, 238 Crown St., Darlinghurst, puts on outstanding programs of folk/music/comedy/blues/jazz with rapidly changing performers. Open Wednesday through Sunday.

Kinselas, Bourke Street, Darlinghurst, offers mixed comedy/satire shows, often star-studded, Tuesday through Saturday.

The Comedy Store, Margaret Lane, off Jamison Street in the city center, specializes in stand-up comics. On Wednesday, Thursday, and Friday it's women's night with male strippers. It operates Tuesday through Saturday—on Tuesday you get amateurs.

The Gap, Sydney Trade Union Club, 111 Foveaux St., Surry Hills. Cheap admission prices for sharp, politically flavored comedy turns—very funny if you know what it's all about.

The above is merely a snap selection. There's about a dozen more where these came from.

The Leagues Clubs

Not too long ago, with the advent of the poker (slot) machine in New South Wales, the cry that arose from city publicans was: Where have all the young men gone? Where was obvious: to the private clubs. Why was equally so: flush from their gambling gains, the clubs offered low-priced food and drink, the finest nightclub entertainment in the country at virtually no charge, longer drinking hours, luxurious surroundings, and that eternally seductive chance to hit the jackpot—an irresistible combination to the Aussie mind.

Likewise to the mind of the visitor, but the word "private" has proved daunting. True, the clubs are open to members only on a day-to-day basis, but they also welcome tourists from overseas and out-of-state. Simply call the club and tell them where you are from and that you would like to see their show. Your name will be left with the doorman. Upon arrival, present your passport or out-of-state identification (driver's license, etc.) and you will be smoothly admitted. For the rest of your Sydney stay, you will be an honorary member.

Clubs can be founded on almost any pretext (although legalized gambling is the common thread), but the largest and most lavish are the athletic associations, or Leagues Clubs, open to any and all over the age of 21 regardless of sporting affiliation. These are vast casinos featuring rows of slot machines in all configurations, elegant restaurants where dinner can be purchased for under $6, bars where the beer sells at 70¢ per glass, showrooms where the entertainers are international names, and the admission ranges from low to free!

Australia's largest club, with 52,000 members, is the **South Sydney Junior Rugby League Club,** 556 Anzac Parade, Kingsford (tel. 349-7555). Here the show is staged in a 1,000-seat auditorium and the cast includes top level entertainers—all for gratis! Call for current program or consult the "What's On In Your Club" column in the Sunday papers.

The most lavish revues in the city are staged at the **St. George Leagues Club,** 124 Princes Hwy. (tel. 587-1022), with 36,000 members, whose glittering suburban edifice is known as the "Taj Mahal." Name artists appear—call for program and reservations (required). Shows at 8:30 p.m. Tuesday through Saturday night and Sunday afternoon.

Most clubs are open daily from 10 a.m. to midnight, weekends to 1 a.m.

SPECIAL EVENTS: Two of the happiest times to be happy in Sydney are at Easter (autumn in these here regions) and during January (mid-summer). Starting with a fireworks salute and running right through January is the **Festival of Sydney,** a somewhat zany and totally joyous hodgepodge of classical and pop concerts, out- and indoor theater, dancing in the streets, ethnic displays, art, poetry, and craft demonstrations, plus a score of events that defy rational classification. The center of Hyde Park becomes a kiddieland, the Opera House stages a chain of special performances, the beaches break out in a rash of crazy aquatic sports (like a regatta in which all craft are made from Pepsi-Cola cans), cycle races, ferry boat races, antique car races (with drivers sporting Edwardian gents' attire), wandering musicians and strolling actors in medieval garb, a Highland Gathering with a thousand pipes and drums, and a military finale on the last weekend—**Australia Day**—with the living descendants of the First Fleet wearing the costumes of their forebears who landed on these shores on January 26, 1788, to become the continent's first settlers—involuntary settlers, perhaps, but still the first.

Easter Week sees the **Royal Easter Show** in all its kaleidoscopic hyperbole: Rural Australia on Display! The Cream of Australia's Livestock Competing for Coveted Awards! Ride the Gondola Skyway! See Balloon Divers, Acrobats, Spectacular Fireworks! A stunning display of agricultural wealth, this 11-day event is the most important in the city's social calendar and the week toward which many a country person gears the year. The best the country has to offer is brought to the city—the best sheep, cattle, dogs, wool, wine. The best the city has to sell is exhibited to the country—tractors, trucks, household appliances. The three-day horse trial attracts former Olympic riders and those aspiring to represent their country overseas. Competing for championships and handsome purses are: polo teams, teams of tent peggers, international woodchoppers (a "must watch"), and rodeo riders of all specialties—buckjumping, steer and bareback riding, bulldogging. Artists, sculptors, and craft workers earn purses of their own (to be "hung" at the Royal Easter Show is prestigious indeed). A fashion show features local fabrics and designers; the horticultural section mounts ten glorious flower shows in as many days; the dog show is the largest in the southern hemisphere. An annual event since 1824, the Royal Easter Show, held at the 72-acre Moore Park Showground, boasts a record total of 33,853 entries, a record attendance of 1,232,413, and prize money exceeding $200,000 each year. Along with the serious showing and trading are all the carnival attractions of circus acts, rides, entertainers, and military bands. Puppet shows, children's theater, and a charming animal nursery keep the young ones fascinated. The grounds abound in picnic tables and snack booths, and all exhibits and most attractions are free. Go for a full day and cram in as much as you can. Be sure to stay for the Grand Parade of ribbon-bedecked animals at day's end. Overseas visitors can go to the Information Centre, identify themselves as visitors, and receive a special lapel ribbon, a colorful souvenir booklet, and all the guidance and help required. Cut rates are also available on grandstand seats—inquire. For advance information, write: The Royal Agricultural Society of N.S.W., Box 4317, GPO Sydney, 2001 (tel. 331-4781).

THE BLUE MOUNTAINS: Just 50 miles west of Sydney the **Blue Mountains** rise from the coastal plain and form a backdrop almost as spectacular as the harbor entry. For these rolling cliff-toothed ranges really *are* of a deep dreamlike blue, a natural phenomenon produced by countless oil-bearing eucalyptus. These trees constantly release fine droplets of oil into the surrounding atmosphere, reflecting the blue light rays of the sun and wrapping the whole landscape into a vivid azure haze.

The Blue Mountains National Park is fringed with resort towns, ribboned with magnificent waterfalls, and criss-crossed by trails. Each of the mountain townships has its own bag of scenic delights. **Katoomba,** heart and capital of the region, operates the **Scenic Railway** and **Scenic Skyway;** the former reputedly the steepest in the world (at least that's what it feels like while you're riding), the latter an aerial cable car suspended above a fabulous chasm. **Leura** has eight unforgettable gardens (admission 50¢) landscaped into the mountain ruggedness. West of Katoomba lies **Explorers' Tree Birdland,** swarming with brightly colored tropical birds. **Springwood** features the **Norman Lindsay Gallery,** a collection of paintings and statues by Australia's artistic sensualist who shocked a generation of his compatriots and still startles a few. **Wentworth Falls Deer Park** (admission 60¢), laid out in a gentle valley, has tame deer, black swans, hundreds of other waterbirds, and vast picnic areas. **Jenolan Caves** are the most famous and awesome underground limestone caves in the state, while the largest single-drop waterfall in the region is Govett's Leap near **Blackheath.**

Trains for the Blue Mountains leave several times a day from Sydney's Central Railway Station. The round-trip fare is $7.20.

Two companies offer full-day tours around the Blue Mountains. **AAT King's Tours,** 46 Kent Rd., Mascot (tel. 669-5444), has a coach leaving daily at 9 a.m. and returning at 5:30 p.m. This excursion includes an (optional) ride on the Scenic Railway and costs $24 for adults, $17 for children. The **Ansett Pioneer Gray Line,** Oxford Square (tel. 268-1881), takes in the Jenolan Caves as well as Katoomba, Blackheath, and Mount Victoria. The coach leaves from Circular Quay at 9 a.m. every Tuesday and Thursday, and returns at 7:30 p.m. Adults pay $32; children, $16.

WARATAH PARK: This area isn't a park but a wonderful patch of bushland carved out of the edge of Ku-ring-gai Chase National Park, about half an hour's drive north of Sydney. Most of the animals—wallabies, emus, koalas—are uncaged and roam around freely, ready to be petted and fed. Others, such as dingos and Tasmanian devils, you can watch through wire fencing. Waratah is also the home of one of Australia's top television stars, "Skippy the Bush Kangaroo," who loves meeting his fans and has never been known to throw star tantrums. For tourist coach reservations phone 241-1636. Admission is $5 for adults, half price for children.

HARBOR CRUISES: No city in the world utilizes its harbor setting for pleasure jaunts to the extent Sydney does. You can rent rides on virtually every kind of craft (including passenger sailing yachts) and with every kind of provisioning, including midnight champagne suppers. The samples below are merely some of the cheapest and most popular of a dozen similar water ventures.

Every Sunday, for instance, a ferry boat leaves no. 2 pier, Circular Quay, at 1:45 p.m. for a closeup view of the spectacular sailing craft races staged by the **NSW 18-ft Sailing Club.** The fares cost $4 for adults, $1 for children, and you can book by phoning 32-2995.

Captain Cook Cruises, no. 6 jetty, Circular Quay (tel. 27-4416), offers a 1½-hour mini-cruise of the harbor four times daily Monday through Friday, three on Saturday and Sunday, which takes in the major points of interest and costs $7 for adults, $4 for children. But if you can possibly spare the time go on the **Coffee Cruise,** which really shows you what the celebrated harbor is all about. (The sights include a closeup of a nudist beach, but watching is not compulsory.) Departs daily at 10 a.m. and 2 p.m., takes 2½ hours, and has a running sociohistorical commentary on Sydney's past, present, and future by a knowledgeable tourist hostess. Price is $13 for adults, $8 for children, coffee refreshments included.

The **Riverboat Mail Run,** where you ride along with Australia's last river postman, delivering mail, groceries, milk, etc., to the population along the scenic Hawkesbury River, is bookable through the Government Travel Centre, 16 Spring St. (tel. 231-4444). A tremendously popular three-hour chug, Monday to Friday, this costs $12 for adults, $6 for children.

MISCELLANY: Sydney has more than a dozen **duty-free shops,** one of them at the International Airport. Others are the **Downtown,** 84 Pitt St., **Sterling Nicholas,** 113 Oxford St., Darlinghurst, and **Mainland,** 125 King St. . . . The City Council operates the **Hyde Park Family Centre,** corner of Park and Elizabeth Streets. Children can be left in the nursery there for a fee of $1 per two hours. The Centre has a storage room for prams as well as a writing room, showers, irons, lounge, writing desks, etc. Open Monday to Saturday from 9 a.m. to 5 p.m. . . . The **Tourist Information Service** is a free telephone inquiry service for information of concern to visitors. Tells you where to find anything from Aboriginal artifacts to lady escorts by calling 669-5111. . . . **Paddington Street Market,** held every Saturday around Paddington Church, Oxford Street, offers bargains in a fantastic array of useful (or less) goods, from embroidered Tibetan boots to teaspoons. . . . Aboriginal boomerangs, both the returning and the nonreturning (hunting) kind, are sold, demonstrated, and taught through Duncan MacLennan's **Boomerang School,** 138 and 200 William St., Kings Cross. They cost from $5 to $10 each, and the lessons in throwing them are given gratis and expertly each Sunday morning at a nearby park. . . . **Bus 777** is a sightseeing special. Runs every day except Sunday and completes a circuit of places of interest around the city—and the ride is free.

Likewise free is the enthralling collection of mechanical marvels at the **Power House Museum,** Mary Ann Street, Ultimo, ranging from miniature steam locomotives and clockwork nightingales to musical snuffboxes and player pianos; open every day till 5 p.m.

2. New South Wales

New South Wales, as residents will be swift to inform you, is the "chief" state of the Commonwealth. Meaning it is the most populous and industrialized of all. But remember they're speaking in strictly Aussie terms. For New South Wales has just over four million people and measures a full third of a million square miles. And when you realize that 2¾ million are bunched happily into metropolitan Sydney, you get some concept of how much space is left to the rest.

The state boasts a greater variety (if not number) of beauty spots and tourist attractions than any other portion of the continent. New South Wales has four distinct geographical regions, each with its own brand of splendor: first there's the 1,000-mile coastal strip, offering some of the finest surfing and swimming beaches on the globe; then the inland mountain ranges and plateaus, with snowy peaks sweeping up to over 7,000 feet; third, the gold-green lushness of the western slopes, an area of warm lazy rivers and rich wheatfields, ideal for fishing and waterskiing; and finally the western plains, the "woolbelt" of the state, with immense flocks of sheep and horizons that stretch into eternity.

NEW ENGLAND: North of Sydney, stretching up to the Queensland border, run a series of verdant ranges and plateaus known as New England. The countryside doesn't really resemble England very much, but it's cool, green, lush, and pleasant, with a special patrician-academic flavor of its own. This is a region of prosperous sheep and cattle holdings, of European elms, oaks, willows, and silver birch trees, of red-breasted robins, waterfalls, and an almost British-style university town.

The town is **Armidale,** 352 miles north of Sydney on the New England Highway, and it radiates academic vibes over the entire region. Of Armidale's 17,000 people, over 2,000 are students and staff of the **University of New England,** and they go to remarkable lengths to live up to their reputation as a Down Under twin of Oxford. True, inside the campus park deer mingle with kangaroos in a most un-Oxonian fashion, but the collegians make up for it by having officials called Yeoman Bedells and talking in terms of "Town and Gown." The frequent fisticuffs between the two factions, which characterize the real Oxford, haven't happened in Armidale yet. But give 'em time.

The university has six established faculties and maintains very high standards. The town has a sprinkling of cathedrals with dreaming spires, excellent and numerous pubs, and the crispest, most multicolored autumn in the state. For visitors interested in educational facilities, there is also Australia's first country **Teacher's College.** It houses a remarkable art collection (including a Rembrandt etching) given to the college by a shipping tycoon who wound up being worth about $50, because he spent all his fortune on pictures and gave them to galleries. There are daily trains from Sydney to Armidale.

THE SNOWY MOUNTAINS: More peaks, but much higher this time, and (we hope) covered from June through September in superbly skiable snow. The Snowy Mountains start their climb 300 miles southwest of Sydney, and their tallest peak, Mount Kosciusko (7,314 feet), is the highest point in Australia. Mount Kozzie, as the natives know it, forms part of a vast winter playground that embraces all 2,100 square miles of the Kosciusko National Park and looks much like a patch of Switzerland transplanted to the southern hemisphere. The skiing capital is a brand-new, "all-mod.-cons." resort village called . . .

Thredbo

The brainchild of former Czechoslovakian ski champion Tony Sponar, Thredbo Alpine Village was founded in 1957 and built in the image of the famous European wintersport resorts. In similar style, it offers outdoor and indoor fun in roughly equal portions, but at less than European expense. You can share a room in an "economy" lodge or rent a holiday flat; all-inclusive, six-day "snow holiday" packages start as low as $120. In season, the whole village merges into one big party, scattered between the thumping disco of the Keller and half a dozen more intimate, but just as swinging, restaurants, bars, and bistros. Maybe it's the marvelously bracing mountain air, but most of the swingers manage to stumble onto a 2,000-foot chair lift next morning to zoom down the 25 miles of ski trails, jet-turning and paralleling as if they hadn't rocked through the night. Off-season, the attractions include glorious views—a 1½-mile chair lift operates year round to the top of Mount Crackenback (6,350 feet)—and such relaxing diversions as fishing, swimming, hiking, barbecuing, campfire nights, and dinner dances. Prices relax too, slipping even lower than winter levels. You reach Thredbo by bus, train, or plane to Cooma, 56 miles away. Coaches take you into the skifields. For information, contact New South Wales Travel Centre, 16 Spring St., Sydney (tel. 231-4444).

LIGHTNING RIDGE: A destination of opposite appeal, here you have the real outback—hot, dry, flat—but with a distinction unique among tourist lures: you might leave far richer than you came. Lightning Ridge, 480 miles northwest of Sydney, is the only place in the world where the most beautiful and valuable type of opal is found, the "black" opal, which actually blazes in a rainbow of colors from raven black to molten green, and which some connoisseurs consider the finest gem in the world. The first black opal was discovered in 1907; production peaked in 1914 and declined steadily thereafter. The population of approximately 1,000 today (plus 500 in the outlying opal fields) engages in sifting the old mullock, the rejected residue excavated by the pioneer miners, by means of a "puddler," a revolving colander type of metal sieve. "Puddlers" are for rent and visitors are invited to fossick on the heaps or dig in any "unoccupied" holes. Do they find anything? Many don't, some garner enough rough opal pebbles (called "nobbies") to pay for their vacation. A few—a very few—strike it rich, such as the schoolboy who picked up a nobby worth $3,000.

But even if you leave with no souvenir beyond the dirt under your fingernails, you will be richer for the experience. This is the frontier Australia so many of us come seeking. That taut, hot—broiling five months of the year—countryside where you can sip an ice-cold Fosters in a grand old pub called Diggers Rest beside men called Crank Joe, Shameless, and Spider Brown. For your (reasonable) comfort there is a caravan park with on-site vans for overnighting, plus several motels. Fresh bread and meat arrive four times weekly, mail comes five times weekly, the road into town has recently been paved and electricity installed throughout. A 24-hour artesian bore pool provides year-round warm swimming. Gemstones are on display and the friendly townspeople are only too willing to talk prospecting with other enthusiasts—and show their specimens. It is one of the few places left to "get away from it all" among people who have done just that. You reach Lightning Ridge by flying the Airlines of New South Wales to Walgett (three flights weekly) or going by rail. Between Walgett and the Ridge, 46 miles away, there is no public transport. Three taxis operate out of Walgett and you may be able to hitch a ride on the mail truck. Organized coach tours and charter flights also go to the Ridge. Best to discuss transportation with the carriers or tourist bureau.

Chapter IV

MELBOURNE

1. The City and Surroundings
2. Victoria

MELBOURNE—LIKE CHICAGO—is a Second City. Unlike Chicago she has never resigned herself to that position. One reason why Sydney moves so fast is undoubtedly because Melbourne is snapping at her heels and breathing down her neck, if you'll pardon my Irish.

Melbourne looks and behaves like the Senior City of the Commonwealth. No other town makes so much of its history or is so concerned about lineage and tradition. Yet Melbourne actually rates third on the seniority ladder, being outranked by Hobart as well. As a permanent settlement she's decidedly a latecomer, founded in 1835, and then only because her founding fathers had failed to obtain the required acreage in Tasmania and tried the mainland instead.

Be that as it may, Melbourne remains proudly aware that she was once the largest city in Australia and—for a brief heady spell—the acting capital. Canberra, in fact, was dreamt up chiefly in order to stop the incessant supremacy struggle between Sydney and Melbourne.

1. The City and Surroundings

Melbourne may have lost the population race and the seat of parliamentary power, but she won hands down in other fields. She is Australia's financial and commercial hub, home of the most prestigious schools and colleges, the social arbiter, the art, fashion, and culinary capital, and, incidentally, the breeding ground of the nation's most influential politicians, right and left.

The Victorian capital lacked the natural advantages of her rival. She had nothing like Sydney's breathtaking harbor, and her river, the Yarra, is a trickling brown apology. Melburnians therefore determined to create their own setting and succeeded so well that the inner core of Sydney appears tawdry by comparison. Melbourne was designed to *look* like the nation's No. 1, even though the whims of history deprived her of that place.

Nothing man-made in Sydney can match the majestic sweep of St. Kilda Road—one of the grandest boulevards on earth—or the tree-lined elegance of Collins Street. Melbourne's wide, handsome thoroughfares, meticulously laid out in chessboard pattern, pulsate with the best regulated traffic in Australia. Her 100-acre Royal Botanical Garden is the most beautiful in the southern hemisphere, her main department store, Myer Emporium, is the largest in the country (second largest in the world), her little boutiques the trendiest, her theaters, orchestras, and restaurants the best in the Commonwealth. And when Sydney flashed her vaunted Opera House, Melbourne replied with the Arts

MELBOURNE : CITY CENTER

Centre, superlatively designed and housing by far the finest exhibits on the continent.

All this was the result of much dedicated effort, and the strain shows a little. Melburnians have been accused of being snooty, stuffy, class-conscious, and money worshiping, with a certain degree of justification. Nowhere else in Australia is it considered so important to attend the *right* schools, live in the *right* suburbs, and—in some circles—have the *right* ancestry. Melburnians are indeed a nuance more reserved than their compatriots and suffer from an inability to let their hair down—except at sporting events.

The climate has a certain influence there. Melbourne is cooler than most Australian capitals and has a longer winter. But these characteristics were also instrumental in creating a city of 2,700,000 people afflicted with fewer urban woes and blights than any place of similar size on the globe.

ORIENTATION: The central portions of Melbourne are wonderfully easy to find your way around in. It's almost as if the city had been built for the benefit of postmen and foreigners. If you look down from the top of the **National Mutual Building** at 447 Collins St. (the view is gratis) you'll see why.

The city (as distinct from the suburbs) is laid out in a grid of vertical and horizontal main streets bisecting each other. Each of the horizontal main streets (but not the vertical ones) has a narrow "little" street running parallel and bearing the same name. Thus there is a Collins Street and Little Collins Street alongside, a Bourke Street and a Little Bourke Street, a Flinders Street and a Flinders Lane, and so on. There are no intruding squares or round-abouts, no freeways, and no railroad tracks to spoil the pattern. Some of these streets change their character several times along their way, but not their direction. You could lay a straight ruler down their entire lengths.

To the south the city is bordered by the gently curving Yarra River. On the south side of Princess Bridge (beside the immense Flinders Street rail station) starts St. Kilda Road, which runs all the way to the beach suburb of St. Kilda. Flanking St. Kilda Road to the east are vast expanses of parklands, bearing different names (Botanic Gardens among them) but actually forming one colossal green oasis on both banks of the Yarra. This contains, besides many other attractions, the 120,000-seat **Melbourne Cricket Ground** (home of Australian Rules football, Test Cricket, and the 1956 Olympic Games), the residence of Victoria's governor, and the **Shrine of Remembrance** to the fallen of two World Wars.

The western fringe of the city consists of the maze of railtracks emanating from Spencer Street Station. To the northwest lie the two major airports, **Tullamarine** and **Essendon.** Due north, across Victoria Street, starts the once-slummy but now passing-chic suburb of Carlton. To the east stretch Fitzroy Gardens and Treasury Gardens, parts of the aforementioned parklands. South of the parks lie the posh districts of South Yarra and Toorak, the "innest" of residential areas. Toorak Road counts as Melbourne's classiest shopping, dining, and dating strip although—true to local tradition—it is less showy than similar stretches elsewhere.

Not surprisingly, Melbourne's public transport system is by far the best and most comprehensive in Australia. In part she owes this edge to her innate conservatism. While other cities were scrapping their trams (streetcars, trolleys) as fast as they could manage and replacing them with buses, Melbourne not only stuck to hers but even updated them with new models. As a result she now boasts a tram network with much greater carrying capacity than equivalent numbers of buses. What's more, the trams don't pollute the air, run on cheap electricity instead of expensive gasoline, and generally give more comfortable rides. You can actually ride them for fun. Particularly no. 15, which rumbles down St. Kilda Road and stops at the beach, or no. 8, which takes you from the city to Toorak Road. Fares go by sections, the minimum 65¢, the longest, $1.10.

Melbourne also has a suburban electric train system, radiating from **Flinders Street Station,** a structure as ugly as it is efficient. A row of clocks above the main entrance indicate departure times for the trains and constitute the single most popular rendezvous spot in the country. "Meet you under the clocks," is probably the best-known assignation line in Australia.

For extensive sightseeing get the **TravelCard,** giving you unlimited travel by train, tram, and bus all day for $4. Available at all suburban stations, trams, and buses. For inquiries about timetables and fares call the **Met Centre** at 617-0900.

Melbourne transport suffers from one grave ailment: it curls up and dies around midnight. There is no late-night public transport service. After the witching hour it's either your legs, your thumb, or a taxi. And Melbourne's taxis are nowhere near as plentiful as Sydney's. Some major cab companies are: **Silver Top** (tel. 435-3455) and **Embassy** (tel. 329-9444).

THE AIRPORT: All planes for overseas and interstate travel leave from **Melbourne Airport** in Tullamarine, $5 by Sky Bus. (Remember the ancient days when airlines carried you to and from airports gratis?) The main interior airlines are **Ansett,** 465 Swanston St. (tel. 668-2222), and **TAA,** 50 Franklin St. (tel. 345-1333). The four major car-rental agencies have branches at the airport.

USEFUL INFORMATION: Of Melbourne's three daily newspapers two—the *Age* and the *Sun*—appear in the morning, the *Herald* in the afternoon. All three are hometown oriented, but the *Age* has a fair amount of overseas coverage. The handiest tourist publication is *This Week in Melbourne,* which can be picked up free of charge in hotel lobbies and at the Victorian Government Tourist Bureau, 230 Collins Street (tel. 602-9444).

Two useful telephone numbers in crisis times (major or minor) are the **Citizens Advice Bureau** (tel. 63-1062) for general information and **Link-Up** (tel. 94-8281) for psychiatric, medical, drug, or welfare problems.

Bicycles—known as pushbikes—seem to be rentable only in the suburbs: **Hoath's Cycle Store,** 527 Station St., Box Hill, and **Saddle and Bell Cycles,** 3 Link St., Kingsbury.

Late-night eateries are scattered far and wide. Best to know where some of them can be found before night starvation sets in: **Firenze,** 20 Myers Pl. (off Bourke Street), Italian budget food. **Ma's Hot Dog Stand,** outside Flinders Street Station, hot dogs, coffee, etc., until 4 in the morning. **Hole in the Wall,** 12 Bourke St., pizza and lasagne around the clock. **Johnny's Green Room,** 194 Faraday St., Carlton, combines pool playing and food dispensing 24 hours a day (foreign visitors get a gratis cup of coffee here).

A NOTE ON PRICES: All prices in this guide are in Australian dollars (A$). As we go to press, US$1 = approximately A$1.40. Thus a room listed at $20 a night actually costs only about $14.50 in U.S. funds—good news indeed for budget travelers.

ACCOMMODATIONS: Melbourne is well supplied with tourist lodgings (too well, according to some proprietors) but they are not arranged in convenient motel strips or guesthouse squares. Accommodations tend to cluster in districts rather than certain streets. The two areas most thickly sprinkled are the city and the beach suburb of St. Kilda, a ten-minute tram ride from downtown. If you're unable or unwilling to pick your own lodgings, **Victour,** at 230 Collins St. (tel. 602-9444), will do it for you, providing, that is, you get there on a weekday before 5 p.m., before noon on Saturday. They won't, however, guarantee you a budget berth. The **Travellers Aid Society** keeps longer hours and caters especially to the economy bracket. Their City Centre is at 281 Bourke St. (tel. 654-2600), and they also have facilities at Spencer Street Railway Station (tel. 67-2873).

The places I have selected all fall into the budget range, although in a few cases—when the value offered was particularly good—I've stretched the limits a little. They are *not* listed in my order of preference but according to categories, such as motels, bed-and-breakfast establishments, etc.

Motels

The **Carlisle Lodge,** 32 Carlisle St., St. Kilda (tel. 534-0316), is a kind of cross between a motel and an apartment block, but a find either way. A solid two-story red-brick structure, ten walking minutes from the beach, the Carlisle has units accommodating up to three persons and flats for up to five. All come equipped with air conditioning and TV set. The units have shower and kitchenette, the flats bathroom with tub and spacious kitchen. Carpeting is excellent throughout, there's a laundry on the premises, and the motel-style furniture seems brand spanking new. Single units rent for $28, doubles for $30—and don't forget how much eating money you save by doing your own cooking.

Hotels

The first two selections here are contrasting neighbors, both facing the looming edifice of Spencer Street Station, a decidedly unlovely street but in a convenient downtown location. The **Spencer,** 44 Spencer St. (tel. 62-6991), is a combination of old hotel and new motel, offering 200 units between them. The exterior is somewhat gloomy, but once you step inside, the impression changes completely. (In a lot of hostelries it works the other way around.) The hotel portion has lower rates because it lacks private bathrooms, but there are ample facilities on each floor. There are also two restaurants and a laundry. The motel part overlooks a charming garden courtyard, blue-lit at night, secluded from street sounds. All the units here have shower and toilet, telephone, refrigerator, tea- and coffee-making facilities, and color TV. They are small, compact, tastefully furnished in brown and orange with a rustic touch of wood paneling. The hotel has a licensed restaurant, but no bar trade. Different tariffs apply for the two portions. In the hotel part singles pay from $15; doubles, $20. In the motel it's from $38 for singles, $45 for doubles.

Almost next door, the **Great Southern,** 16 Spencer St. (tel. 62-3989), is one of the mementos of the golden age of railway hotels. The place has a colorful history dating back to Melbourne's wild 1920s, when it was the stomping ground of some of the most famous and notorious characters of the local underworld. The past glories still show in the huge ornate public rooms, but the 155 bedrooms are fairly basic in their fittings. None has a private bathroom (although there are plenty along the corridors) and only some come with H&C washbasins. Ceiling lights only (no bedside lamps), but the carpeting is wall to wall, and the rooms are spotless. The hotel also features such facilities as a lounge, TV and billiard rooms, a dining room, espresso bar, and a dry cleaner on the premises. Real bargain rates here: singles from $14, doubles from $20, family rooms from $26.

The next selection is in East Melbourne, just on the edge of the city and rubbing elbows with Fitzroy Gardens. **Magnolia Court,** 101 Powlett St. (tel. 417-2782), has a frontage as lovely as its name, with a glassed-in balcony breakfast room behind a stone terrace. A charming white building in a quiet street, the Magnolia houses 22 suites, all with private facilities (tub and shower). Also a community kitchen and laundry. The bedroom decor is kept in soft hues, the rooms have a telephone and large wardrobe, and the entire establishment shows the earmarks of good grooming. Rates for singles are $30, for doubles $36 (this fits our budget bracket), with special reductions for families.

City Lodge, 235 King St. (tel. 67-6679), stands in a pretty noisy street and has a rather stark and bare lobby. The breakfast room, however, is most attractive and the guests' TV lounge nicely decorated. Only three of the bedrooms have hot and cold water (the public bathrooms are meticulously kept), and in all of them the fittings are strictly no frills, except for wall-to-wall carpets. Singles run from $14, doubles from $20, with special concession rates for longer stays.

Bed-and-Breakfast

My favorite in this category is the **Miami,** 13 Hawke St., West Melbourne (tel. 329-8499), not so much for its facilities but for the tremendous pride management and staff take in the place. An attractively sturdy red-brick corner building, minutes from the heart of downtown, the Miami has 102 rooms, a welcoming reception area, and even more welcoming rates. The bedrooms are small and compact, the furnishings not lavish, but the care bestowed upon them is. All rooms have hot and cold water, double wardrobes offering ample hanging space, fluorescent bedside lights, and good carpeting. The hotel offers a TV guest lounge, drink machines, air-conditioned dining room, and a well-equipped laundry. You can choose between bed-and-breakfast and full board (meaning two meals) and get the manager's guarantee that "nothing out of tins is served here." With breakfast only, singles pay $17 a day; doubles, $24. A three-course dinner is just $5.

The **Regal Hotel,** 149 Fitzroy St. (tel. 534-5603), in the beach suburb of St. Kilda, is a small white building facing a park on a tree-lined and very busy street. It has a pleasant dining room where the large cooked breakfast is served, as well as a guest kitchen with refrigerator. You have a choice between renting your own TV set for 50¢ a day or watching communally in the TV lounge. The 80 bedrooms come with H&C washbasin and fairly basic furnishings; bedside lamps are supplied on request. There are seven good public bathrooms. Excellent transport to the city is right at the doorstep, and the beach is within easy walking distance. Singles pay $15; doubles, $24.

In Toorak, Melbourne's plushest residential quarter, the **Toorak Private Hotel,** 189 Toorak Rd. (tel. 241-8652), also happens to be one of the cheapest hostelries on our list. A green, three-story Edwardian structure, its doorway flanked with stone pillars, the Toorak is decidedly old-fashioned, which means it offers a lot of space and loftiness: a large bare lobby, large games room and TV lounge, and very high ceilings throughout the building. It has, however, no elevator, and none of the 90 bedrooms has a handbasin. Furniture is somewhat sparse, but all rooms come with wall-to-wall carpeting, wide beds, plus overhead and bedside lamps. The metal wardrobes are narrow and offer minimal hanging space. The public bathrooms are kept spotless, breakfast is served in a comfortable dinery, and the games room offers a billiard table. Singles here start at $14; doubles, from $18.

Our next find is in Melbourne's geographically most desirable neighborhood—the last place to expect budget accommodation. The **West End**, 76 Toorak Rd. West, South Yarra (tel. 26-3135), overlooks the palm-lined quiet end of Melbourne's poshest shopping street. It's a very attractive hostelry with large airy rooms, some with San Francisco–style bay windows, an elegant TV lounge, and a cozy dining room, where only breakfast is served. The rooms, mostly doubles, all have hot and cold water, plus dressing tables with mirrors big enough to do the job for which they are intended. The rooms are kept in deep-green color schemes, which makes for a soothing atmosphere. The rates here are $17 for singles, $26 for doubles, $8 for children under 12, and no charge for cots.

The **Gatwick Hotel**, 34 Fitzroy St., St. Kilda (tel. 534-0318), is an attractive white three-story structure in a tree-lined but very busy thoroughfare, St. Kilda's main drag, a hop from the beach. Large, old-fashioned, minus an elevator but nicely maintained, the Gatwick offers Edwardian spaciousness all around, particularly in the public bathrooms, which are positively huge. There's a TV lounge, laundry facilities, and a natty dining room serving breakfast and dinner. The 75 guest rooms give you lots of breathing space, H&C taps, and lots of pretty antique furniture. Overhead lights only, big wardrobes, new carpeting, and small mirrors. The B&B rates here are $20 for singles, $30 for doubles.

Back to the city for the **Kingsgate**, 131 King St., (tel. 62-4171), another old building with good grooming plus an exceptionally friendly staff. There are 250 rooms here, some of them with private baths, the others with H&C handbasins, plus six bathrooms per floor, a restaurant on the premises, two TV lounges, pinball machines, and laundry facilities, but a strict rule against liquor. The Kingsgate has a hospitable lobby, well carpeted, and a regular maze of corridors and passageways in which you can get lost with the greatest of ease. Bedroom furnishings are rather on the spartan side with narrow wardrobes and beds, but you get bedside as well as ceiling lights, a very central position, and a modern, spacious dining room. Rates vary according to whether you want a private bathroom: singles from $18 to $29, doubles from $29 to $39.

Now to the seaside suburb of Elwood and the **Bayside Hotel**, 65 Ormond Esplanade (tel. 531-4778), a handsome white-brown three-story structure with large windows overlooking the esplanade and the ocean beyond. A newish and very well-kept establishment, the Bayside houses 42 rooms, 12 of them with private bath. Also a large, rather bare, TV lounge and downstairs dining room. The bedrooms are of medium size, bright and airy; the furnishings are simple but attractive, and the fittings include wall-to-wall carpet, TV set, H&C handbasin in some rooms, generous closet space, and a handy little refrigerator. Rates here are *full board:* meaning a cooked breakfast and three-course dinner (on weekends breakfast only). Two laundromats are located just around the corner. Singles pay from $20, doubles from $30.

Holiday Apartments

The **City Gate Travel Flats**, 6 Tennyson St., St. Kilda (tel. 534-2650), have an ideal location in a quiet street opposite a rose garden. A friendly building, nicely kept, with a small courtyard boasting two palm trees, it contains 50 flats, each with bedsitter, fully equipped kitchen, shower, toilet, fridge, crockery, cutlery, and TV. Linen and blankets are also provided, but no telephones apart from a red public phone booth in the hall. The lobby is small and dark but the flats pleasantly furnished, with large beds and wardrobes, good carpeting and lighting. Rates for singles are $26 per night, $105 per week; for doubles, $30 nightly, $125 weekly.

The **Melbourne Gate Travel Flats,** 87 Alma Rd., East St. Kilda (tel. 51-5870), has the same owners and the same rates.

The Y's

The Melbourne YMCA offers no accommodation, worse luck. But the **YWCA,** 489 Elizabeth St. (tel. 329-5188), caters to both genders and occupies a large downtown motel complex. The building resembles a concrete garage, but the interior is a pleasant surprise. Each unit has shower and toilet, comfortable furnishings, and wall-to-wall carpets. The building also contains a swimming pool, a fairly cozy TV lounge, laundry facilities, and a restaurant open seven days a week. Singles cost $23; doubles, $34. The complex is two walking minutes away from the domestic airlines terminal.

Youth Hostels

Melbourne's **Youth Hostel** is situated at 500 Abbotsford St., North Melbourne (tel. 328-2880), about two miles from downtown, but with good tram connections. The bus from Tullamarine International Airport passes the hostel and will stop if requested in advance. The 42-bed hostel has a fully equipped communal kitchen. Charges are $7.50 a night for seniors, $3.50 for juniors.

The second hostel stands 80 feet away at 76 Chapman St. (tel. 328-3595).

Caravan (Trailer) Park

One of Melbourne's most centrally situated caravan parks is the **Footscray Caravan Park,** 163 Somerville Rd., West Footscray (tel. 314-6646), about 4½ miles from the city center by direct train service, so you don't need a car to get downtown, and there's a shopping center right near the gate. This park rents on-site caravans only and provides hot showers, washing machines, and refrigerators.

Campus Accommodation

Melbourne has a regular bonanza of good economic college accommodations—no less than 19 colleges to choose from. Most, however, are available during vacations only; that is, January, February, May, August, and December. The sample below is the *only* one available all year round:

International House, University of Melbourne, 241 Royal Parade, Parkville (contact the bursar at 347-2351), is located about 2½ miles from downtown. It has single rooms, shared bathrooms, plus TV room, common room, billiard room, laundry, and tennis courts. Rates include breakfast and dinner and come to $12.60 per day. Take trams 18, 19, 20 from Elizabeth St., City, to tram stop 21.

MEALS: I have referred to Melbourne as Australia's culinary capital, and this is as much a fact of life as her financial supremacy. It has nothing to do with her half dozen or so world-class luxury restaurants, which don't concern us here and which in any case have their counterparts in other cities. What establishes Melbourne's title is the quality of local cuisine in the lower price regions, right down to greasy-spoon-plastic-tabletop levels. Sample any given counter lunch in Melbourne and, say, Brisbane, and you'll instantly note the contrast unless you've had your tastebuds lobotomized beforehand.

Melbourne's preeminence was achieved despite the city authorities, who for 50 years have passed many nitpicking ordinances that might well have hampered the restaurant business. The local entrepreneurs even managed to turn to advantage the liquor laws that make the granting of wine licenses to restaurants costly and difficult. Their alternative was the BYO (which sacred initials stand for Bring Your Own) which allows patrons to bring along their own liquor to drink with their meals. Those bottles are bought at over-the-counter prices, say $4 instead of the $7 or $8 a restaurant would charge. The result is a considerable saving in meal expenses, since few establishments have the temerity to charge for glasses or corkage. So watch for the initials BYO. You may assume that any hostelry that boasts a license is automatically more expensive than a BYO.

Melbourne's culinary reputation rests on the small mom-and-pop restaurants, mostly—although not always—foreign. Unlike Sydney, Melbourne has no real restaurant district—these establishments are scattered all over town. And there are certain exceptions. By and large Chinese restaurants run below par, and those in Melbourne's miniature Chinatown, Little Bourke Street, are often overpriced as well.

Counter and Other Lunches

Melbourne's pub grub is of almost universally high standard, so all I can do here is give you a few pointers with the proviso that these are merely a handful out of a hundred. The **Casa Mañana**, 348 St. Kilda Rd., known to habitués as "Case of Bananas," is actually a whole complex of dispensaries, including a rather posh carvery and piano bar upstairs. But the midday crowds throng the ground-level bar, decorated with "celeb" photographs. Try the lasagne for $4. And, naturally, a middy of beer.

The **Tok H,** Toorak Road, functions as a mild kind of body exchange, where people of various different lifestyles mingle in a very congenial atmosphere. You can switch from the chic pub portion to the elegant carvery, glass in hand, and find your social life falling into shape en route. At 52 Toorak Rd. West is the equally stylish **Fawkner Club.** This has the added advantage of a garden terrace surrounded by a green hedge combined with an old-fashioned club-like interior. The counter lunch features specials for $5.50.

The **Café Nostalgia,** 319 Swanston St., has white iron tables on the pavement outside and umbrellas overhead. It serves four types of equally good quiches at $5.50, and excellent percolated coffee (in case you're weary of the omnipresent cappuccino). So far, so continental—but it closes at 7:30 p.m. and stays closed Saturday and Sunday . . . most uncontinental.

Mac's Hotel, on Franklin Street between the TAA and Ansett offices, is a beautiful old colonial bluestone building, with an upstairs veranda and glass-encased bistro in the rear. Counter lunch here is swarming with airline personnel, who know a good thing when they taste it. Fried whiting goes for $4; the rest of the menu comes equally economical.

Young and Jacksons, at the corner of Flinders and Swanston Streets, is Melbourne's most venerable pub, hallowed to the memories of departing soldiers since the Boer War. No thing of beauty from the outside, the hotel nevertheless houses Australia's best known nude who now glories in her very own parlor. *Chloe,* painted by French artist Jules Lefebore in 1875, is a shapely and eternally young lady dressed in nothing but a fashionable pallor, an object of barfly desire for over a century. Take a look at her, then drift over to the formidable counter lunch served from noon to 2 p.m., which includes braised steak and mushrooms or roast chicken at $4.20 a serving.

Gibby's, 263 Little Collins St., is a small quiet coffee shop with unique wall decorations. All surfaces are covered with Victorian and Edwardian artwork, from lovely to ludicrous. The objects range from gold-framed oil paintings to postcards, most of them depicting coy maidens and excruciatingly arch kiddies, all of which will keep you busily gazing throughout lunch. For good measure, a few religious themes have also strayed in. You get five breeds of salad for $5, Danish open-faced sandwiches with delicious spreads for $3.50. Also excellent coffee and service. Open seven days a week.

Dinner

The **Tamani Bistro**, 156 Toorak Rd., features Italian cooking and a charming Australian proprietor—Margaret Benassi, who acquired her taste along with an Italian husband. Functionally modern yet remarkably cozy, the Tamani offers minestrone soup for $2, lasagne for $4.80, and an almost artistic salad bar where selections range from $2 to $5. Open seven days a week from 9:30 a.m. to 9 p.m., this bistro draws an intriguing cross section of customers, senior executives clashing forks with junior road repairmen. Still in Toorak Road and also Italian is the **Barolo**, at no. 74, another example proving that you can find inexpensive eateries in a deluxe shopping area. Very plain with crude wooden tables and benches and brick-lined doorways to give it a Paris Left Bank cellar touch, the Barolo is decorated with Italian scenes on posters quite in keeping with its bistro air. The fare is, happily, gargantuan: tagliatelle avocado, senoppine con funghi, or trippa parmigiana, all equally excellent, at between $6 and $8 per huge helping. Open daily from 9 a.m. to 9 p.m. seven days a week. Both the above places are BYOs, as are most of the others I'm mentioning.

At 152 Toorak Rd. is **Pinocchio's Pizza,** which has a fanatical following that swears it produces the best pizza in town—a much-debated claim. Pinocchio's is considerably fancier than most of its clan, loaded with atmosphere, and decorated with superb illustrations from the children's classic it is named after—all with the original Italian texts. The famous pizzas come in large and small editions, respectively $3 and $5, while osso buco sells at $4.50.

Moving into the city we come upon the local representative of a national chain, **The Pancake Parlor,** 25 Market Lane (opposite the Southern Cross Hotel). These parlors are distinguished by their inspired menus, which make excellent mealtime reading, plus the fact that they're open all day, every day. This one covers five levels, including an "attic," and devotes as much attention to pulchritude as to pancakes. All the walls are covered with bosomy 1890s-vintage ladies performing remarkably sexy gyrations while tossing pancakes. Don't miss the huge *Police Gazette*-style mural depicting the "Great Colonial Pancake Tossing Race for Ladies," in which all contestants seem to be Victorian-brand *Playboy* bunnies. Ah, yes, the pancakes . . . they come in 33 varieties, from Canadian with bacon and eggs ($5.80) to the apricot jam kind ($4.30). The place also serves breakfast from 7 a.m., offers a secluded bower for chess players, and waxes apologetic about every surcharge they have to make on weekends and public holidays.

Campari, 25 Hardware St., is considered by some to be the best Italian restaurant in the city. It's certainly genuine; you hear more Italian than English spoken on the premises, always a sign of ethnic authenticity. A large, handsomely decorated place, it has an upstairs and downstairs portion, red-brick floors, walls hung with gleaming copperware beneath shelves of olive oil bottles, giving the establishment the air of a grandly stocked country kitchen. This is not an economy restaurant, but you can pick some excellent budget dishes from the extensive menu: cannelloni for $5 or lasagne at $4.50. Closes 8:30 p.m.

Robs Carousel, overlooking Albert Park Lake in Aughtie Drive, is a fun place, particularly if you have kids along. Apart from the lake view the pièce de résistance here is the circular food bar that slowly revolves while you're eating, like some of those panoramic rooftop places. You can ride the dining carousel for just a cup of coffee or order the Hawaiian-style chicken salad for $6.95 and listen to the golfers from the course across the road talking up their scores. Closes 10 p.m. weekdays, midnight on Saturday.

In the center city, 142 Russell St. is the abode of one of Australia's pioneer Mexican eateries, **Taco Bill.** Up a flight of stairs and usually thronged with youthful clients, this taco temple has a pretty authentic air and the aroma to go with it. For Mexican palates the spices are on the gentle side, though by Anglo standards they're red-hot. A platter of nachos costs $7, and the place stays open till 10 p.m., closed Sunday.

BYO Pellegrini's, 66 Bourke St., is a contestant for the honor of serving the best cappuccino in Melbourne, which is saying something. Neither elegant nor atmospheric, the place is nevertheless aflutter with good-looking people. The excellent risotto primavera is $4.50 and pasta dishes run $4, but don't miss having a cup of coffee along with a slice of cheesecake here. The cappuccino comes in the correct style—in a glass—and the treat costs $1.

Now we're off to Carlton, an inner suburb that has undergone a remarkable transformation. Once considered a predominantly Italian semislum, it has developed into the "in" stomping ground for Melbourne's gilt-edged set while retaining most of its ethnic backbone. The Italian flavor still predominates (notice in shop window: "Never mind if you don't speak Italian—we speak good broken English"). And there's still a sprinkling of very "out" all-male cafés, where elderly Sicilians brood over their dominos. But the young business, art, and university crowd has definitely taken over and most of the local eateries now reflect their tastes.

Genevieve, 233 Faraday St., is a popular rendezvous spot as well as dinery. It looks like an ice cream parlor decked out in bright orange and browns, but serves some of the finest economy meals in town: risotto bolognese for $3.96 and a dreamy torta gelato (ice cream cake to you, mate) for $1.30. At 376 Lygon Street there's an entirely different **Pancake Place.** With a clientele heavily on the student side, the walls here are covered with sketches and posters proclaiming various left-wing causes and rallies as well as yoga lessons, ballet performances, and products of the underground film industry. Pancakes run the gamut from savory to sweet: from honey and cinnamon at $2.90 to spinach and cheese at $5.10. All sweet pancakes are served with cream, and the Vienna coffee (more cream) is outstanding. Open till midnight. At 331 Clarendon Street in South Melbourne, you'll find the **Chinese Noodleshop.** As the name indicates, it specializes in noodle dishes, either to take out or eat there. Take your pick at the food counter with stools. The place is spotless, serves mighty portions, and charges some of the lowest prices in the business: roast pork noodles for $5, soy sauce noodles with beef for $6.50, and the biggest, hugest, most variegated wonton soup extant.

The **Paradiso,** 370 Lygon St., has a near-fanatical college clientele who account for the happy vibes as well as the permanent shortage of table space. With two rooms, *Casablanca*-style ceiling fans, the walls festooned with posters proclaiming classes, concerts, and causes, the main decoration consists of a painted glass window. You can eat at a food bar or a table; the cuisine is equally excellent at both. Not even the bare floors and high noise volume detract from the quality of the fare. Spinach cannelloni costs $4.80, and brains and bacon runs $6. Conclude with an outstanding crème caramel for $1.80. Eat and you'll join the throng of Paradiso fans. Open seven days until 10 p.m.

The **Paragon,** 651 Rathdowne St., is housed in a beautifully restored Victorian building, now air-conditioned and supplemented with outdoor tables set beneath the shelter of an antique lace-iron verandah. The menu matches the setting—an intriguing melange of Mediterranean, Asian, and vegetarian goodies: pinenut cannelloni for $5.80, beef saté in peanut sauce for $6.80, plus an imposing array of desserts made on the premises. You have a choice of food bar or table service (a rarity) and the place stays open till 10 p.m. every day.

The next selections are both in St. Kilda, the seaside suburb that was once *the* eating scene but has nearly succumbed to the onslaught of what must be among the most repulsive rashes of junkfood dispensaries in the world. However, some of the old gastronomic quality still survives; it's merely a matter of tracking it down.

One such survivor is the **Danube,** 107 Acland St. The plainest of dineries, with plastic flooring, bare metal tables, and whitewashed brickwalls, the Danube's only ornamental touches consist of a few impressionist prints. But it has a staunchly devoted clientele of Europeans, and when you sample the fare you'll know the reason for their loyalty. Chicken soup here is the real thing, the different species of goulashes (all $8) carry the tang of Budapest, as does the stuffed paprika at the same price. Open till 9:30 p.m. every night.

Leo's Spaghetti Bar, 55 Fitzroy St., serves a great many things besides spaghetti, among them possibly Australia's greatest gelati ice. At 60¢ per cone it's memorable, and the mocha is tops. A big, modern (but not plastic) establishment, Leo's has a coffee lounge in front, a restaurant in the rear, and an excellent salad bar in between. Spaghetti alla marinara is $5.80, the ravioli runs $4.40, and the place stays open till 12:30 at night with a Latin American band playing on weekends.

For your dining splurge I'd suggest you venture to drably industrial North Melbourne and head for the delightful **Café Popolare,** 7 Leveson St., which is even more "popolare" than its name implies. A simple bluestone cottage structure with a Latin awning, this outstanding BYO seems to have strayed into its street setting through a faulty compass. Roomy and simple, almost bare of decorations, the Popolare is half café, half restaurant, and all Italian. The menu gets chalked up on a blackboard and always features around eight varieties of antipasta, a memorable scaloppine al vino bianco ($9.10), and intriguing, figure-wrecking "dolci" for $4—worth every cent and calorie. The shady courtyard garden is a pleasant choice in the summer. Open nightly until about 10 p.m., but pleasantly flexible. Closed Sunday.

DAYTIME ACTIVITIES: The **Victorian Arts Centre,** St. Kilda Road. This is Melbourne's answer to the Sydney Opera House, Victoria's top tourist attraction, and one of the great showpieces of the southern hemisphere. The entire vast complex embraces the National Gallery of Victoria, the Melbourne Concert Hall, an opera, two theaters, plus bars, restaurants, an outdoor stage, a functions center, and shops, the whole crowned with an abbreviated version of the Eiffel Tower transformed into a silvery beacon at night. The only way to do justice to this edifice is to describe its separate components.

The **National Gallery,** which draws 750,000 visitors a year, looks like an immense granite slab from the outside, but the interior is a wonderfully sensitive blend of the severely monastic and the light-hearted artistic. Gray granite courtyards, green with shrubbery and sparkling with fountains, entrance windows with water flowing permanently between the thick panes, unexpected shafts of sunlight—all add to the happy cross between classical restraint and playfulness. The entire ground floor is devoted to Asian art, the second floor to Australian. There's a European section covering the period before 1800, and a European and American floor taking in the time since 1800, including works by Manet, Degas, Pissarro, and Frank Gallo. The third floor houses photography in all its artistic phases. There are also changing exhibitions on loan from America, Japan, China, Austria, and Germany.

The **Melbourne Concert Hall** is an acoustic marvel on three levels. The sound is honed by 24 perspex shells and 24 acoustic banners that can be altered for different sound requirements. The Hall's Grand Concert Organ, built by Canadian Casavant Frères, has 4,189 pipes. The organist, invisible to the audience, communicates with the stage through closed-circuit TV. The decorations are nothing short of magnificent: a melange of paintings, sculptures, and harmonized color schemes that act like a symphony for the eyes. The foyer blazes with the 100 frames of a mammoth creation by Sir Sidney Nolan titled *Paradise Garden*, depicting Australian flora from its organic beginnings, pushing through the earth, and following seasonal cycles. The hall seats 2,600 people amid visual as well as audial splendor.

The theater complex comprises the huge **State Theatre,** designed for opera, ballet, and large-scale productions; the *Playhouse* for drama; and the intimate *Studio*, a multi-purpose space for experimental shows, dance, and music. All mirror the architectural brilliance of the Concert Hall and contain some of the most advanced technical equipment in the world.

You can spend a wonderfully variegated day in this complex, visiting the Gallery first, dining at one of the restaurants (which include a budget eatery), going on to a concert, and finishing off with a late-night show. Conducted tours of the Concert Hall, daily between 10 a.m. and 5 p.m., cost $2.50 for adults, half price for children. The Art Gallery is open six days a week (closed Monday) with admission costing 80¢ for adults, half price for children.

The **Museum of Victoria,** Russell Street, concentrates on natural history, with sections on anthropology, zoology, geology, etc. What makes the place a pilgrimage spot for turf addicts are the mounted remains of Phar Lap, Australia's greatest-ever racehorse, allegedly poisoned while running in America. Open six days a week (closed Sunday) from 10 a.m. to 5 p.m. Admission is free.

City Square, extending from the Town Hall to St. Paul's Cathedral, is the new hub of the city, a kind of architectural goulash garnished with lawns, shops, cafés, plus waterfalls that remind you irresistibly of flushing toilets. It's a great gratis spectacle and seems to draw a large percentage of the city's working population around lunchtime.

The **Saona** is a romantic paddlesteamer that plies the Yarra River from Princess Walk to the Botanic Gardens, Como Park, and Fairview Park. These are leisurely two-hour cruises, giving you ample shore leave at the stops and opportunity to view Melbourne from the river, probably the best vantage point for a city that lovingly cherishes its green arteries. Cruises between 10 a.m. and 4 p.m. For details phone 51-8748.

The Old Melbourne Gaol and Penal Museum, appropriately situated opposite Russell Street police headquarters, is an old bluestone prison built in 1841. It contains relics from the grimmest and wildest pages of Australia's history. Prize exhibit here is Ned Kelly's—the king of the bushrangers—bullet-dented armor made from ploughshares (see the introductory chapter) and the scaffold on which he was hanged . . . uttering the not very original words "Such is life." The gaol is carefully restored and you can wander through the cells and see what conditions were like. Open six days a week (closed Sunday) from 10 a.m. to 5 p.m. Admission is $3 for adults, half price for children.

Captain Cook's Cottage, Fitzroy Gardens, is the residence of one of mankind's greatest explorers and the discoverer of Australia (see the introductory chapter), brought over from England in pieces and reassembled here. Open every day. Adults pay 60¢; children, 20¢. **La Trobe Cottage,** Domain, by the Botanical Gardens, was Victoria's first Government House. Quite small and simple on the outside (as befitted the power center of a colony with fewer than 6,000 settlers), it has a remarkably elegant interior. Governor La Trobe, who ran the colony until 1854, was as much a visionary as an administrator. He conceived, among other projects, the Melbourne Botanical Gardens, which now bloom in his memory. Open daily; admission is $2. The **Shrine of Remembrance,** St. Kilda Road, dedicated to Australia's war dead, has a great dome with an opening so contrived that precisely at "Armistice Hour 1918" a single ray of light shines on the Stone of Remembrance below.

The **Melbourne Zoo** is situated in Royal Park (take the electric train from Flinders Street Station) and has undergone a very extensive facelift. Most of the enclosures are set in natural environments, charmingly landscaped. The zoo has 3,000 beasties from every part of the globe, but the main attraction is the native fauna—koalas, wombats, kangaroos, emus, echidnas, and others. Visitors can stroll among them in a bushland setting. Other Aussies—snakes, crocodiles, and giant lizards—are kept safely screened. Open daily from 10 a.m. to 5:30 p.m. Admission is $4.40 for adults, $2.20 for children.

Luna Park, St. Kilda Esplanade, is a handily compact amusement park, crammed with devices to shake, whirl, rattle, bump, swing, slide, and bounce for squealing patrons willing to pay money for these pleasures. Rides cost a dollar each.

Como, Como Avenue, South Yarra, is a century-old mansion preserved by the National Trust. On view inside is the entire lifestyle of the Victorian rich—coaches and kitchen gear, furniture, drapes, and bathroom utensils. The house is enchanting, with wonderful white verandas and delicate wrought railings, set among five acres of manicured lawns, flower gardens, and fountains. Catch the no. 8 tram from Swanston Street. Open daily till 5 p.m. Admission is $3.50 for adults, $1.50 for children. More ornate, but equally stylish is **Rippon Lea,** 192 Hotham St., Elsternwick, another Victorian mansion in 13 acres of gardens and lakes populated by strutting peacocks. Admission is $3.50 for adults, $1.50 for children. Open daily till 5 p.m.

The **Royal Botanical Gardens,** between Alexandra Avenue and Domain Road, are unreservedly the most beautiful in Australia and among the world's finest examples of classical landscaping. They comprise three lakes, some 43 acres of flowerbeds, and 35 acres of lawns. The **King's Domain,** between the Botanical Gardens and the city, embraces several gardens and displays a flower clock containing 10,000 plants. It also contains the **Sidney Myer Music Bowl,** a huge but strangely graceful auditorium amid glorious parkland surroundings where free symphonic and modern concerts are performed from November to February. Check the newspapers for the programs. Melbourne has half a dozen other great parks and Melburnians utilize, cherish, and enjoy the "green lungs" of their city like few other urbanites. To help the enjoyment, several parks feature 10¢-operated gas jets for barbecue picnics—a unique innovation. Throughout the summer months the City Council sponsors free outdoor concerts —classical, jazz, folk, and rock—in various parks and squares. Find out what's on where by dialing 63-0421.

Sports

Sporting events are just about the only occasions when Melburnians "let fly" en masse. But then they do it with a vengeance, breaking out in positive orgies of inhibition shedding. There is a story about two Russian (or Chinese, or German, or Japanese) agents who allegedly visited the town in order to spy out invasion possibilities. They reported back that it would be better to drop the idea. Melburnians, they explained, were so bloodthirsty that they spent Saturday afternoons maiming each other for fun.

What these mythical agents had witnessed was undoubtedly **Australian Rules football,** a remarkable melange of rugby, soccer, Gaelic football, and guerrilla warfare. Players wear no protective gear, which accounts for the fabulous casualty rate. What's more difficult to explain is why this native version of football became popular *only* in Victoria, but there to a degree that borders on religious frenzy. Begun in 1858, Australian football now has 12 clubs (the Victorian Football League) battling for the annual premiership. Between April and September each year the Melbourne media is saturated with football coverage (six matches are held each Saturday) climaxing with the six Finals. Four of the Finals take place in the Melbourne Cricket Ground and pack in more than 100,000 fans.

For comprehension of the rules, get the special brochure published by the VFL, Jolimont Street, Jolimont, Vic. 3002—it's complimentary. Free conducted tours of the colossal MCG (yes, they play cricket there too) are held every Wednesday morning at 10 a.m.

Melbourne's other great passion—horse racing—is shared by most of her compatriots. Horse racing may be called the "Sport of Kings" but in Australia it's very much a sport of the butchers and bakers and candlestick makers, with audience participation to the outer limits of lung power. It goes all the year round on Melbourne's metropolitan courses at Flemington, Caulfield, Moonee Valley, and Sandown.

On the first Tuesday in November, the entire nation grinds to a halt for the running of the **Melbourne Cup,** Australia's richest horse race. Traffic stops in the streets as a million radios pour out the race description in tones ranging from anguish to ecstasy. The Melbourne Cup is also *the* fashion event of the season, and it's astonishing to behold thousands of exquisitely coiffed and gowned ladies abandoning their poise as the horses head into the homestretch.

AFTER DARK: Sydneysiders are wont to sneer that "Melbourne shuts up with the shops" but—like most such sneers—this is basically untrue. Melbourne merely *seems* to curl up because she has no nightlife district. Her nearest facsimile thereof, St. Kilda, does such a dismal job that you're afraid to turn your head in case it flickers out behind your back, like an anemic candle. The fact is that Melbourne has a large array of nightspots—some of them quite gloriously boisterous—but they're scattered all over the map. Isolated and introverted, they bestow no glow on their surroundings and have to be pinpointed and targeted. You can't just stroll along and drop into something you fancy, because the Via Veneto this ain't.

For a start, Melbourne has the most active live stage in Australia. Not merely the standard legit theaters, but some remarkably avant-garde establishments of both the raunchy and the earnest variety. The **Russell Street Theatre,** 19 Russell St., frequently performs unknown but hopeful Australian playwrights. The **Universal Theatre,** 13 Victoria St., Fitzroy, runs to pretty sharp political satire. The **Anthill Theatre,** 199 Napier St., South Melbourne, has experimental material and occasionally foreign-language productions. The **Atheaneum Theatre,** 188 Collins St., stages major overseas plays, mainly drama, while the **National Theatre,** at the corner of Barkly and Carlisle Streets, St. Kilda, acts as a showcase for different theatrical groups that range from classical dancers to grand opera.

La Mama, 205 Faraday St., Carlton, is heavily into novelty and occasionally brilliantly innovative. The **Palais Theatre,** St. Kilda Esplanade, has a mix of concerts and live theater. It's on the expensive side, but usually worth every cent. You get more good theater at the **Comedy,** 240 Exhibition St., and the **Princess,** Spring Street, though these shows are mostly successful overseas productions surfacing in Australia.

Then there are an amazing number of theater restaurants, some of them delightful, all fairly expensive because you have to pay for an obligatory dinner as well as the show. The two funkiest were both launched by a local genius named John Pinder. He started with the **Flying Trapeze Café,** which became so popular that you couldn't get in. So Pinder picked up his marbles and moved to the larger, zanier, absolutely Mad-Hatterish **Last Laugh Theatre,** 64 Smith St., in distinctly unchic Collingwood. The shows vary, but rarely in laugh volume, which can be almost painful. Upstairs on the same premises is the economy-geared **Le Joke,** which offers stage room for try-out talent and, of course, varies considerably more in quality. You have to take pot luck—not too risky at tickets starting at $4 Tuesday to Saturday.

At last count there were 17 other theater restaurants in operation around town, including **Dirty Dick's,** 23 Queen's Rd., for some of the raunchiest sing-alongs and wenchiest wenches extant; **Dracula's,** 7 Drewery Lane, for black-comedy gems like *Fangs for the Memory;* and the **Stage Door,** 1 Wynyard St., South Melbourne, which is BYO and puts on first-class gourmet meals as well as straight comedy productions.

Bunratty Castle, 127 Dorcas St., South Melbourne, is a happy transplant from Ireland. You get a suitably modified Medieval Banquet (no titlark pies or roast swan) enlivened by ballad singers, winsome damsels, and court jesters, regally chaired by the illustrious "Earl of Thomond" and his lady. The cost is $23 Tuesday to Friday, $25 on Saturday. The **Naughty Nineties,** 675 Glenferrie Rd., Hawthorn, is a characteristic local phenomenon: a theater-restaurant BYO —where but in Melbourne? And certainly the actual Naughty Nineties wouldn't have dreamt up such an establishment. Anyway, it cuts down your liquor bill. You get 2½ hours of variety entertainment plus a four-course dinner Wednesday to Saturday, starting at 7 p.m.

Note that the above are merely samplings of the scene, which has a dozen more and new ones emerging constantly.

Discos
The Melbourne discos are as inconsistent as those elsewhere. Meaning that some actually rely on platters (as the name implies), others feature live bands continually or occasionally. The "ins" change with breathless rapidity. At the moment it's probably the **Broadway,** 14 Claremont St., South Yarra, which has supper, a light show, and a formidable DJ. Weeknight prices are reasonable, with a minimum of $6, rising to $20 for Saturday dinner. **Club Chevron,** in the Chevron Hotel, 519 St. Kilda Rd., has the most spectacular light and video shows in town and it flashes seven nights a week till 3 a.m. The minimum here is $5 to $9, depending on the night. The **Melbourne Underground** (it's not), 22 King St., in the center city, is an entire restaurant complex, including eight bars. The disco forms only a part of the establishment. Admission here is $9—but only $6 if you mention this book. **Filliers,** Lower Esplanade, St. Kilda, combines supper, floor show, and disco in one noisy bundle, costing $12.50.

Piano Bars
Melbourne has several of these, the most memorable in the **Old Melbourne Hotel,** 5 Flemington Rd., North Melbourne. The hotel itself offers an absolutely superb setting: a Victorian courtyard with gaslights and wrought-iron balconies fronting public rooms crammed with genuine antiques glittering in the candle-light. The walnut-pillared, ornately Edwardian "Norman Lindsay" cocktail bar is decorated with sketches by the Australian artist considered "outrageous" by a consensus of grandparents. The actual piano bar is only one attraction here, lit by a silver candelabra that seems to flicker in time to the chords. The back-

ground may be Edwardian, but the patronage is predominantly young and beautiful.

Rock, Jazz, and Folk

Melbourne is Australia's undisputed rock 'n roll center, boasting a widespread net of pubs, clubs, and bars rocking from two to seven nights a week. They range from hangar-size monsters in the suburbs to trendy little dives around the inner city, and in quality from highly talented local groups to mere eardrum assassins. Check the *Herald* on Friday evening to find out who's rocking where. Door charges run from zero to $6, depending on the band and the night. Drinks are mostly at bar prices.

The **Albion Hotel,** 356 Lygon St., Carlton, varies rock fare with Dixieland jazz and charges no admission. The **Bombay Rock,** at the corner of Sydney Road and Phoenix Street, Brunswick, operates until the early hours and offers a tremendous variety of groups. The **Warehouse,** located in the New Prospect Hill Hotel, 299 High St., Kew, rocks seven days a week (including Saturday afternoon) and has free admission nights at least thrice weekly. The **Prince of Wales Hotel,** 29 Fitzroy St., St. Kilda, offers a quiet piano bar as well as "mega venues" which are very mega indeed. The **Grainstore Tavern,** 46 King St., in the center city, has imported outfits as well as locals six nights a week. **The Venue,** Earls Court, Upper Esplanade, St. Kilda, charges $2 on weeknights, $7 on weekends, for a disco and live-band mixture that goes on till 3 a.m. And so forth for at least two newspaper columns. . . .

Jazz sounds (every night of the week) at the **Victoria Hotel,** Beaconsfield Parade, Albert Park, and at **Banjo's,** 55 Chetwynd St., North Melbourne, founded by a late all-time great of Australian jazz and specializing in authentic 1920s syncopation. This, by the way, is a licensed restaurant instead of the usual pub, open Thursday to Sunday nights.

Folk and country music still abounds, but tends to shift from place to place at a rate that makes it difficult to record for anything as durable as even a softcover book. Among the more consistent folk platforms is the **Dan O'Connell Hotel,** Princess Street, Carlton, where the accent is heavily on Irish airs, as befits the name, usually from 8 to 10 p.m., with an occasional $4 admission fee. Also the **Green Man Coffee Lounge,** 1221 High St., Malvern, which puts on an interesting Open Talent Night every Tuesday, apart from its usual nightly lineup of semiprofessionals.

SHOPPING: As stated earlier, Melbourne is Australia's commercial capital and the country's shopping center par excellence. This applies to the entire retailing range from monumental department stores to plush little boutiques, from flea markets to budget emporiums. The two main shopping drags are Bourke Street and Collins Street. Bourke is the site of most of the *big* stores: **Myer** (after Chicago's Marshall Field's, the world's largest department store), **David Jones,** its more traditional neighbor, and **G. J. Coles,** specializing in an enormous range of budget goods. Collins Street is more exclusive (ergo more expensive) and has **Georges,** plus a legion of small trendy specialty stores, from fashions and jewelry to chocolates and rare books.

All of Melbourne's downtown thoroughfares show the growth pattern of the city: 19th-century colonial brick next to the soaring glass and concrete cloud scrapers of the Nuclear Age. But, unlike Sydney, they somehow blend into an amazingly harmonious whole, their basic starkness relieved and hidden by boulevard trees, unexpected patches of mini-parks, and lighting effects.

Then there are the shopping arcades, which should be explored individually. They vary from tawdry gimcrack to blazing elegance, but all of them contain surprising little stores that reveal that dazzling range of goods this town has to offer. (See especially the **Royal Arcade,** Bourke Street, where Gog & Magog strike the time, the **Australia Arcade,** and **Block Court,** off Collins Street).

Melbourne also has a host of street markets, where shopping is a matter of sharp eyes and good luck. The **Flea Market,** Drummond Street, Carlton, opens Friday nights and Saturday mornings. **Victoria Market,** Victoria Street, North Melbourne, is open Tuesday, Thursday, Friday, and Saturday morning. At **Prahran Market,** Commercial Road, you find a vast array of European goods, edible and otherwise. There are about half a dozen more, including the **St. Kilda Art Banks,** Upper Esplanade, on Sunday, featuring sidewalk displays of paintings, pottery, jewelry, and leatherwork, running the gamut from talented to terrible.

Australian Specialties

At every step you'll come across shops selling stuffed koalas, plastic boomerangs, sheepskin rugs, Aboriginal art, and kangaroo skins. Some of this is plain junk, homemade or imported from Japan and Hong Kong. You'll have to use your own taste and expertise when buying.

For Australian opals it's **Altmann & Cherny,** 120 Exhibition St. This is as much a showplace as a store. Their prize exhibit is the "Olympic Australis," the largest, costliest gem opal in the world, duly recorded in the *Guinness Book of Records*. Found in the Olympic year of 1956 (hence the name) at the Coober Pedy field in South Australia by a prospecting oldtimer, the stone weighs 17,700 carats or seven pounds, sparkles white, brown, silver, and amber, and is definitely *not* for sale. Other stones are. You can watch the entire process of sorting, cutting, and polishing the gems, and the products sell at anything from 10¢ a gram to $100 a gram: opal pendants from $20 upward, gold opal rings from $60. Tourists get a 20% discount here, apart from there being no local sales tax for overseas visitors.

Regent Jewellers, a subsidiary of the above, has a dazzling exhibit in the shape of the world's most valuable black opal. The "Aurora Australia" hails from Lightning Ridge, weighs 180 carats, and is valued at $1.5 million—a trifle beyond our budget bracket.

But you can ogle it gratis at **Collins Place,** Australia's costliest real estate development to date. The place is actually a super-deluxe shopping center incorporating the Regent Hotel in upper Collins Street. It houses boulevard-style cafés and restaurants, galleries of swank little stores, and a transparent elevator to waft you from level to level. You can spend half a day there window shopping in almost sinful comfort.

An opal trove of a different hue is Nick Le Souef's **Lightning Ridge,** at 330 Little Collins St. Mr. Le Souef is an opal miner, stunt man, naturalist who combines expertise with gems with a fascination for poisonous critters. He once spent a couple of nights in a tank swarming with stingrays and appeared in the American TV show "That's Incredible" swimming in a pool alive with piranhas. His basement gem store and showroom is "guarded" by deadly funnel-web spiders, blue-ringed octopi, scorpions, and assorted tiger snakes—all safely behind glass, of course.

Duty-Free Shops

For overseas visitors only, these special stores offer a substantial saving on retail prices. They offer jewelry, perfume, liquor, watches, etc., at what—for *bona fide* travelers from abroad—are bargain rates. One tip for the unwary: there is no such thing as Australian jade. The stones so misnamed (and sold) are actually inferior gems that *look* like jade without being in the same class. The special tourist stores include the **International Duty Free Stores,** 53 Queen St., and the **Downtown Duty Free,** 128 Exhibition St.

SPECIAL EVENTS: Two of Melbourne's top annual events—the Melbourne Cup and the Football Finals—have already been mentioned. The third is **Moomba.** Although not in the quality bracket of the Adelaide Arts Festival, Moomba offers Melburnians ten days of highly versatile festivities each year from February 28 to March 8. And versatile is the word. There are 175 events attracting around 4½ million people and covering every conceivable brand of taste.

There are waterski revues and regattas on the Yarra River, outdoor art shows, numerous concerts, and free entertainments in the parks, more concerts in galleries and music halls, the National Music Awards, a Moomba King and Queen competition, and sporting events from Moomba greyhound racing to Moomba woodchopping. Parts of Alexandra Gardens are turned into a fantasyland—the Magic Gardens—swarming with clowns, magicians, jugglers, acrobats, mimes, and dancers. There's a Moomba Writers Week and a Chess Week, art shows and minstrel shows, plus the inevitable Moomba procession of floats and a grand fireworks in conclusion.

MELBOURNE MISCELLANY: Stroll along and observe the way Collins Street changes character en route without ever losing its highly individualistic stylishness. At the western end, near Spencer Street Station, it's high-finance territory, boardroom land, flanked by the towering business edifices, banks, insurance companies, and brokerage houses that govern Australia's commercial ledgers. At the center—between the Queen Street/Swanston Street intersections—it becomes a hustle of hotels, restaurants, and smart retail stores. Above that starts the upper or "Paris" end of the street: tree-lined and slightly subdued, sprinkled with small cafés, bistros, and petite boutiques competing with Toorak Road for the patronage of Melbourne's formidable suburban matrons in their British or German chariots. . . . The **Melbourne University Theatre** runs irregular "classic films" weeks, as do the suburban **Dendy** cinemas. For two weeks in June the **Palais,** St. Kilda Esplanade, features the entries of the **Melbourne Film Festival.** Watch the newspapers for the respective programs. For rock-bottom price re-runs there's the **Carlton Theatre,** 235 Faraday St., where tickets sell at less than half the rates elsewhere. . . . For genuine Australian Digger hats (new), go to **Mitchell's,** 134 Russell St., which specializes in military disposals. With the martial spears-and-bayonets emblem removed, this is possibly the only military headgear that flatters men and women alike. . . . For vintage photo buffs, the **Photographic Centre,** 384 Church St., Richmond, has a wonderful collection of antique Australian photographs, the kind you admire on restaurant and pub walls but can never get for yourself.

DAY TOURS AROUND MELBOURNE: While Melbourne's immediate setting is not spectacular, she has some enchanting patches within easy reach.

The Dandenongs
Known as the "Blue Dandenongs," this is a range of rolling hills and timbered valleys, so close that they form a natural backdrop to the city. The hills are gray-green with gum trees, ablaze with fields of tulips, daffodils, and gladioli, and studded with panoramic lookout spots and wildlife preserves.

The most popular point is **Mount Dandenong Lookout** (over 2,000 feet high), which presents a view over all of Melbourne and suburbs spread out below. Running bravely from Belgrave to Menzies Creek is **Puffing Billy,** a delightful little narrow-gauge steam train that seems imbued with a personality of its own. Billy may be a relic, but he's the real thing, not a replica, and there's something very endearing about the way he huffs and blusters his way up and down the ranges, pulling the original wooden passenger cars packed with tourists. A round trip costs $6.50 for adults, $4.30 for children. Suburban electric trains from Flinders Street take you directly to Billy's station at Belgrave.

My personal favorite in the Dandenongs is the **William Ricketts Sanctuary** at Churinga. William Ricketts was a musician who turned to sculpture to express his overwhelming love for nature and the people closest to it—the Australian Aborigines. Ricketts purchased a tract of steep forest land and set about populating it with the Aboriginal theme—clay figures of men, women, and children that seem to grow among and out of the trees. The union between plants and people is so wonderfully demonstrated in these sculptings that you suddenly grasp the true meaning of Aboriginal mythology: its timelessness that doesn't divide eternity into human life spans but thinks in the endless growth cycles of evolution. There is both innocence and knowingness in Ricketts's carvings, tremendous joy, and inherent sadness. The only word that describes them is "unforgettable."

Sherbrooke Forest, near Upper Ferntree Gully, is a nature preserve crisscrossed by some of the prettiest trail walks I've ever trodden. (It also has picnic facilities and a snack kiosk.) This is the home of the lyre bird, an amazing feathered mimic that imitates the sounds it hears with uncanny accuracy—including machinery noises. Your best chance of either seeing or hearing one is by taking a forest trail. You may also come across a waddling wombat or an echidna, the little spiky marsupial version of the porcupine.

Healesville

Tucked away beneath the mountains some 40 miles northeast of Melbourne, Healesville is an idyllic pleasure resort in the valley of the Watts River. In or around the town you'll find just about everything in the spectrum of holiday fun: smart hotels and budget guesthouses, picnic and camping grounds, horse racing, horse riding, golf, and nature unspoiled and carefully preserved.

Healesville's top attraction is the **Sir Colin Mackenzie Sanctuary,** internationally famous as a wildlife haven. Originally developed as a research station, the sanctuary is now open to the public every day. The green scrub and tall grass rustle with emu families, the trees harbor neon-colored parrots and leaf-munching koalas, clusters of kangaroos prick their ears at your approach and close in for a cuddle, and occasionally you get a glimpse of a giant goanna lizard scuttling through the grass, black tongue flicking. The platypus, which remains practically invisible under normal circumstances, can be seen close up in glass-sided observation tanks. What it does, nearly all the time, is search for worms and yabbies along the rocky bottom. If there's one way to describe a platypus, it's an elongated piece of fur stretched over an appetite.

Phillip Island

Located at the entrance of Westernport Bay, Phillip Island is now connected to the mainland by a concrete bridge. You can get there by road, by sea (hydrofoil or ferry boat from Stony Point), or by air (twin-engine planes fly from Melbourne International in Tullamarine, Essendon, or Moorabbin Airports). The island, lying about 90 miles southeast of Melbourne, is the finest wildlife preserve Victoria can offer, apart from boasting its own fishing fleet, sheltered, safe, and sunny beaches, and every marine sport in the book, plus a famous motor racing circuit.

But the animals are the real draws. There's a colony of fur seals to be seen at close range at the Nobbies, where they bask in the sun with the total flipper-fanning abandonment only seals and humans can muster. There are mutton birds, looking quite small while resting but demonstrating enormous wing span once they take off—during November they seem to blacken the sky when they return from their astonishing migratory flights to Japan, Alaska, the American coast, and back to their island rookeries. The island is patterned in individual sanctuaries, one of them marked by a sign "Travel Slowly—Watch for Children and Koalas." The koalas, incidentally, were in danger of becoming extinct. The islanders saved them by importing and planting manna gums—the only species of gum leaf (out of hundreds) the cuddly little blighters will eat.

Many tourists visit Phillip Island for just one sight: the **Penguin Parade.** This is held every evening of the year around dusk, so regularly that the starting time is posted outside the fence of the motor racing circuit. The performers are waves of fairy penguins splashing ashore at Summerland Beach after hunting fish all day. They head back to their burrows in the sand dunes, waddling ceremoniously and determinedly, oblivious of the spotlights turned on them. If you sit quietly they'll march past within arm's reach like so many fat little men in dinner jackets filing out of a banquet. The parade lasts from half an hour to an hour—there are more than 2,000 penguins participating, all with very full tummies.

For economical overnight stays on the island there's the **Boomerang Caravan Park,** 121 Thompson Ave., Cowes (tel. 059-52-2348). The park rents on-site caravans equipped with cooking facilities, refrigerators, water, electricity, color TV, and foam-rubber mattresses, and has showers and toilets, gas barbecues, and washing machines. You have to supply your own linen, blankets, and pillows—or rent them. Rates for two persons run from off-season (May to November) at $20 to tourist season (mid-November till May) at $22.

Conducted Tours

There are large numbers of organized tours available in and around Melbourne. The examples quoted merely give you an idea of the prices and areas visited.

Australian Pacific, 181 Flinders St. (tel. 631-511), offers half-day City Sights tours on Monday through Friday afternoon. Adults pay $14; children, $10. Half-day trips to Healesville Sanctuary, highlighted by watching the platypus feed (and feed); return at 5:35 p.m. Adults pay $19; children, $14. Full-day trips to Phillip Island every day except Sunday, from $26.

Gray Line, 465 Swanston St. (tel. 668-2422). The Melbourne sights tours (morning or afternoon) are arranged to complement each other and visit different places. Available daily. Adults are charged $18; children, $5. The Blue Dandenongs tour starts at 1:45 p.m. and returns at 5:30 p.m. Adults pay $18; children, $5. Tours to Sovereign Hill, Ballarat (see the section on the state of Victoria), run from late September to May every Tuesday and Sunday, leaving at 9:15 a.m. and returning at 6 p.m. Trips to Geelong and Lorne along the Great Ocean Road are available late September to May every Friday. They depart at 9:15 a.m. and return 5:45 p.m. Adults pay $32; children, $5.

2. Victoria

This is the smallest state on the mainland, but "small" only by Australian standards. Victoria could comfortably hold Kansas plus Connecticut, with some acreage to spare. The climate is what tourist brochures call "equable," meaning it lacks the desert sizzlers you encounter farther north, although you can experience four seasons in one day along the coast.

Because of its relative compactness, and the excellent transportation system radiating from Melbourne, Victoria is an ideal field for tourist exploration, offering colorful variety within an easily manageable area. Just 75 miles from Melbourne, for instance, bubble the mineral springs of the spa country around **Hepburn Springs,** where you imbibe mountain air and medicinal water along with lashings of resort fun. Or for a complete change of pace, try a trip by paddlesteamer along the lazy **Murray River,** the most relaxing mode of travel since Huck Finn's raft. Or visit the **Grampians** in springtime, when carpets of wildflowers turn the mountain slopes into painters' palettes.

But Victoria owes her start to one of the wildest gold rushes in history. During the 1850s one-third of all the gold in the world was mined here! If you want to relive some of the excitement of those rip-roaring days head for—

BALLARAT: Seventy miles west of Melbourne by rail or road, the otherwise sedate city of Ballarat has re-created its gold and gunpowder past on **Sovereign Hill.** For $5 admission you walk into 36 acres of gold rush ground, correct in every detail, but with the violence removed.

Stroll along re-created Main Street and you're back in 1855. There's the Gold Office where Diggers took their gleanings to be weighed and stored until the heavily armed Gold Escort transported the stuff to Melbourne—with one wary eye on the bush from which "Captain Moonlight" could pounce any moment. There's the *Ballarat Times* building, whose editor was publicly horsewhipped by the fiery Lola Montez for writing that she "danced like a hussy." There's the Chinese Joss House, Johnny Alloo's famous restaurant, a blacksmith forge in full operation, livery stables, Diggers' huts, and a quartz mine.

You can actually pan for gold in the creek—don't expect any nuggets, but you may get some yellow flakes if your pan "comes up smiling."

A short distance away you come to **Eureka Stockade,** the site of Australia's one and only armed rebellion (see "A Capsule History"). A vivid diorama now tells the story of that brief and bloody clash between Diggers and redcoats, and a museum full of muskets and bayonets explains who won—and why.

SWAN HILL: At Horseshoe Bend on the Murray River, 214 miles northwest of Melbourne, lies Australia's finest theme park. **Pioneer Settlement** is a community enterprise of Swan Hill that grew from the idea of converting an old paddlesteamer into a folk museum. The steamer is now the **Riverboat Restaurant,** a unique and delightful hostelry serving culinary adventures like billabong platter, grilled yabbies and bacon, kangaroo tail soup, and witchetty grubs, and has hosted not only Queen Elizabeth and a couple of prime ministers, but also every gourmet in the Commonwealth.

Around the lagoon-locked riverboat has grown the faithful replica of a pioneer community. A Cobb & Co. stagecoach office—the Down Under equivalent of Wells Fargo—a century-old weatherboard bank, saddler's shop, bush schoolhouse, barbershop, mud-brick kitchen, pioneer log cabin, fire station, and printer's workshop, all equipped with the utensils and crudely ingenious machinery of the period. On the streets and river you can see the vehicles of another age: firefighting contraptions, gigs, buggies, drays, log carts, horse omnibuses, steam-powered tractors, penny-farthing bicycles, and massive wool barges. One section is devoted to Aboriginal displays—the black man's hunting weapons, musical instruments, and carved canoe trees.

Four times a night Swan Hill puts on its own version of a **Sound and Light** spectacle. But this is a mobile performance, with visitors being guided through the area by special lighting effects linked dramatically by atmospheric music, narration, and authentic wildlife sounds.

You can reach Swan Hill by train or bus from Melbourne or zoom by Biz-jet, a daily air service flying from Essendon Airport and taking less than an hour for the trip.

GIPPSLAND LAKES: "Two holidays for the price of one" could be the slogan of this resort region. The Gippsland Lakes, starting 100 miles or so east of Melbourne, form a connected chain running parallel to the ocean, some of them separated from the sea only by narrow strips of sand dune. So in a manner of speaking, you can wade with one foot in saltwater and the other in fresh, enjoying ocean beaches and lakefronts simultaneously.

A lot of locals have discovered this, and around **Lakes Entrance** the area is awash with neon-glaring motels, caravan parks, and diners. But the lakes and beaches stretch on and on, offering scores of uncrowded coves, bays, and inlets, hedged in green, flanked by blue, with nary a neon to mar the horizon. The scenery is lush, the picnicking great, the fishing wonderful. (Just off the coast lie the happy hunting grounds of Australia's largest trawler fleet.)

You can chug or sail or paddle or zip from one lake to another in every conceivable type of watercraft, heading out into the Pacific when the weather is calm. Occasionally you run into schools of sleek bubble-spouting dolphin, and if you throttle your motor way down they'll play games around your boat.

Thousands of black swans dot the lakes, and some of the lake islands have kangaroos and koalas. But most of the visitors come for the fishing. And if you make friends with the natives—which isn't hard—they'll give you the recipe for bream fried in beer batter.

BENDIGO: Some 92 miles north of Melbourne along the Calder Highway stands **"Golden Bendigo,"** with the gold in the past tense. By Australian—or Californian—standards this is a city "steeped in history." At the height of the gold rush of the early 1850s there were 20,000 Diggers (including 4,000 Chinese) working in the fields around the town and spending the yellow dust on women, dice, cards, and liquor considerably faster than they found it.

Today Bendigo is a prosperous and smugly respectable provincial center, but still sprinkled with reminders of its hectic youth. It has the **Chinese Joss House** at Emu Point, where the "Diggers in pigtails" used to pray for a rich strike. There is the **Central Deborah,** the last mine to cease production when the gold petered out. Today the mine has been restored as a museum piece. You can see the primitive shower rooms where miners were stripped and searched. Or sit in the engine driver's huge seat which hauled the miners' cage up the 1,385-foot-deep shaft.

From the same era dates the 115-year-old **Bendigo Pottery** at Epsom, the oldest in Australia. Unlike the gold rush relics, this place is still in full production —you can watch the entire process, from the wet clay stage and firing in the kilns to the finished article.

Chapter V

ADELAIDE

1. The City and Surroundings
2. South Australia

ONCE UPON A TIME—a dozen or so years ago—Adelaide was known as **Wowserville** or, a little more politely, as the "City of Churches." What both titles meant was that this was the metropolis the bluenoses and killjoys had built in their own image and ran accordingly. Everybody admitted that the place was beautiful, but a dead loss as far as even a modicum of *joie de vivre* went. Adelaide's reputation resembled that of Boston a few decades back: a locality where they rolled up the pavements after sunset.

But Time has a knack of marching on. Today Adelaide counts as perhaps the most liberal and enlightened Australian city—having duly adopted most of Sydney's virtues and few of its vices. The churches are still there in dazzling profusion, but the wowsers no longer rule the roost.

There were various reasons behind this transformation. The immense cultural impact of the biennial Adelaide Arts Festival, with its explosion of artistic creativity, a new generation of natives and the influx of overseas migrants, a change of government, rapid growth (Adelaide now tops 900,000 people), and the influence of abundant local wine on people's lifestyles. For the amazing thing was that although Adelaide had been sitting atop one of the world's greatest wine barrels for a century, few locals drank the stuff. It took the example of the European newcomers to educate their palates.

Whatever the reason—Adelaide has altered almost beyond recognition. Perhaps the most telling proof of this metamorphosis was the fact that Adelaide opened the *first* nudist beach in Australia a few miles south. And it didn't even cause an earthquake!

1. The City and Surroundings

Somehow Adelaide has managed to retain its leisurely charm, its natural dignity, and the air of tranquil calm that has always been its chief attraction. It didn't join the neon-lit rat race that makes Sydney so stimulating and frazzling at once. Adelaide is still a city of strollers and smilers, catering to pedestrians rather than to motorists, to amblers rather than to speedsters.

No other city boasts proportionately more parkland or pedestrian malls that make shopping (window or otherwise) such unhassled pleasure. And no other place goes to such pains to enhance these facilities. In Rymill Park (which harbors one of the world's greatest rose gardens) replicas of native birds perch in the trees. Press a button on the trunk and the birds sing! And in order to reduce the number of private cars clogging downtown, Adelaide launched Australia's first free bus service—the Bee-line. Hop on and the buses take you on a shopping circuit on the house, or rather the municipality.

Adelaide owes much of its pleasant layout to an army officer—Col. William Light—who designed the city in 1836 and happened to be a genius in town planning. He projected the central area inside one square mile, encircled it with parks, stipulated wide avenues bisecting at right angles, and made all five city squares into gardens. As a result you virtually can't get lost in the city and you walk beneath shady trees or awnings almost wherever you go.

The main shopping strip, Rundle Street, is the most compact commercial center in the country. For half a kilometer it's a mall, closed to traffic, and most of the large retail stores, boutiques, cafés, and movie houses are either on this street or in the arcades or small side alleys adjoining it.

ORIENTATION: The exact center of Adelaide is Victoria Square, not in the least Victorian but marked by a very handsome modernistic fountain. From there, incidentally, you catch Adelaide's last remaining streetcar to the beach resort of Glenelg. The city proper forms an almost perfect square, bounded on four sides by North, East, South, and West Terrace. North Adelaide, an intriguing area of restored bluestone cottages, old hotels, and plush new restaurants, actually forms part of the city but lies three-quarters of a mile north. The two parts are separated by parklands and the Torrens River, connected by King William Road. Due west lies the seashore with 20 miles of beaches and a string of resort towns as well as Adelaide Airport. To the east and south the suburbs stretch endlessly, right to the foot of the rolling Mount Lofty Ranges. To the north beckon the wineries of the Barossa Valley (see our special tour). The entire city is separated from the suburbs by an unbroken green belt of parks and recreation areas—the lungs of Adelaide and the joy of visitors from less thoughtfully designed municipalities.

Adelaide Airport lies about five miles to the west. It's a smallish, comfortable terminal, with showers, a cafeteria, and a bar, plus the inevitable **Avis** car-rental desk. Most facilities close at 9:30 p.m. Watch for the illuminated display of the famous Vickers Vimy bomber that carried four men on the first-ever England-Australia flight (28 days) in 1919. The coach fare to the city is $3.50.

Except for its solitary tramline, Adelaide is serviced by buses. Fares go by sections, starting at 60¢, the average ride costing 90¢. A trip to Maslins Beach—the famous first nudist reserve—is $1.30.

You can rent bicycles from **Elliotts** (tel. 223-3946) for $5 a day, $10 weekly.

There is a **State Transport Authority** information booth in the railway station, on North Terrace (tel. 218-2345).

The main office of **Thrifty** rental cars is 100 Franklin St. (tel. 211-8788).

A NOTE ON PRICES: All prices in this guide are in Australian dollars (A$). As we go to press, US$1 = approximately A$1.40. Thus a room listed at $20 a night actually costs only about $14.50 in U.S. funds—good news indeed for budget travelers.

ACCOMMODATIONS: Adelaide has very few budget hotels or guesthouses in her downtown area, and most in this category are scattered throughout the inner suburbs. (In some Australian cities the situation is reversed). But the **Youth Hostel** here is the most central of all—about a mile from the city. The **YH,**

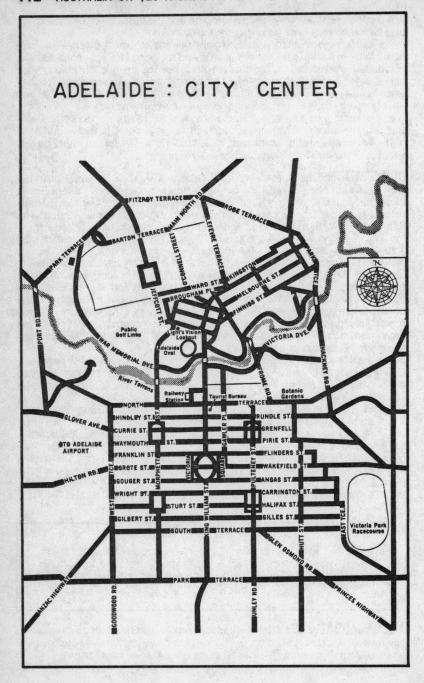

ADELAIDE : CITY CENTER

290 Gilles St. (tel. 223-6007), is near a bus stop, post office, and several stores in adjacent Hutt Street. Overnight fees are $6.50 for seniors, $4.50 for juniors. Sheet bags are for rent at $1.50. Only members may stay at the hostels, but it's possible to join at the door. Sleeping bags are not permitted.

Adelaide University used to be a gold mine in either providing or finding student accommodations during the holidays, thanks to its sympathetic and enterprising welfare officer, Barry Heath. Alas, the situation has changed. Chances for accommodations have become slighter, but it's still worth a try. Contact Mr. Heath at 223-4333, ext. 2915, Monday to Friday from 9 a.m. to 5 p.m.

Accommodations can also be arranged through the **South Australian Government Travel Centre,** 18 King William St. (tel. 212-1644), which is open Monday to Friday from 8:15 a.m. to 5:30 p.m., Saturday and Sunday to 2 p.m.

Adelaide has about 20 **caravan (trailer) parks** within a 15-mile radius of the city. Some of the closest with on-site caravans for rent (at around $20 a night) are: **Adelaide Caravan Park,** Bruton Street, Hackney (tel. 42-1563); **Sturt River Caravan Park,** Brookside Road, Darlington (tel. 296-7302); **West Beach,** Military Road on the seafront (tel. 356-7654).

The Y

Adelaide's **YMCA,** like so many institutions, has dropped its sex barriers and now caters to men, women, and family groups. Centrally located at 76 Flinders St. (tel. 223-1611), it's a very modern building with glass walls overlooking a small rock garden. The rooms are bright and airy, nicely carpeted, and equipped with fair-size wardrobes, although lighting fixtures are not lavish. Rates are $6 per day for dormitory accommodation, $10 daily ($60 weekly) for a single room, and $8 daily ($48 weekly) for a twin. The Y has vending machines dispensing hot and cold edibles and drinkables, a TV lounge, reading room, and laundry, as well as squash courts and a sauna. The rates do not include breakfast —which comes à la carte—but prices on the premises are among the lowest in town. You can get cereal and milk, poached eggs, buttered toast, and tea or coffee for $2.50.

Bed-and-Breakfast

Most B&B establishments in central Adelaide are pubs; large or small but all with a busy bar trade. One of the most economical is the **King's Head Hotel,** 357 King William St. (tel. 212-6657). A lovely old colonial structure, stone-fronted, with brass coach-lanterns above the doorway and an overhanging balcony providing shelter from rain or sun. The place exudes 19th-century charm, but has very limited facilities for houseguests: only 9 rooms accommodating 16 people. The rate is a straight $16 per person.

Another downtowner, our favorite in this category, is the **Brecknock Hotel,** 401 King William St. (tel. 51-5467). A mellow white corner building with a round tower on top, the Brecknock is run by an enthusiastic Aussie-Canadian couple who have turned it into a budget showpiece. The lobby and stairs are nicely carpeted, half the rooms are air-conditioned, the hotel beer garden is charming, and the TV lounge spacious. The restaurant on the premises provides three meals six days a week—on Sunday, breakfast comes via room service (it's continental but ample). There are also three bars downstairs, plus a snooker room and a guest laundry. Despite lots of action below, the guest rooms are remarkably quiet and tranquil. Not luxurious but well equipped with H&C handbasin, ceiling fan, electric blanket, large wardrobe, bedside mirrors, wall-to-wall carpet, tea and coffee-making equipment, and ceiling lights. The entire house is immaculately kept, the management bends over backward to please, and the rates are $18 for singles, $25 for doubles (room only).

Hotels and Motel

The **Sunny South,** 190 Glen Osmond Rd., Fullarton, (tel. 79-1621), is about 1½ miles from the city center. Recently redecorated, the establishment has 18 units, all air-conditioned, with private bathroom, telephone, and electric jug, plus refrigerator. The carpeting is foot-soothing, the decor light green and walnut, the beds delightfully springy, and there's TV in the rooms. Breakfast is served in your unit. Rates vary according to season. Too high for singles ($30), it's a fine deal for two persons ($33). Not to forget: The establishment has its own beauty salon. I should also add that Glen Osmond Road is busy and therefore tends to be noisy.

Out in Glenelg again is the **Bay Motel-Hotel,** 58 Broadway (tel. 294-4244). About 500 yards from the beach, the Bay has a restaurant with a large handsome bar that also serves counter lunches. The 42 units are air-conditioned and equipped with color TV, refrigerator, and tea-making facilities, and they're handy to fishing, boating, golf courses, and tennis courts, as well as a seaside shopping center. The tariff is $25 for singles, $30 for doubles, and $7.50 for each extra person. Continental breakfast comes at $4.50.

Right in central Adelaide, at the corner of Gawler Place and Flinders Street, stands the **Earl of Zetland Hotel** (tel. 223-5500). A small white building at a very busy location, the hotel is fully air-conditioned and has a main front bar and two more intimate—and comfortable—saloon bars. The 30 rooms are nicely decorated and well furnished, all with private shower, tea- and coffee-making facilities, telephone, and TV. All rooms have a radio as well. It's above our budget for singles, but the doubles, at $37, just make it.

The **Plaza Hotel,** 85 Hindley St. (tel. 51-6371), an oldish building with a lot of charm and a youngish clientele, is maintained with a great deal of tender loving care. The interior balconies look down on a palm-studded courtyard that gives the place a distinctly New Orleans air. The 62 rooms come with H&C water handbasin, innerspring mattresses, telephone, and bedside lamps. The bathrooms, although shared, are excellent and colorful as well. Rates run to $20 per single room, $29 per double, and $14 per person in three- or four-bedded rooms.

The majestic white Edwardian **Grosvenor Hotel,** 125 North Terrace (tel. 51-2961), directly opposite the railway station, would appear squarely in the luxury class. And so it is, except for its "budget sleepers," an arrangement other establishments should copy. These rooms are simpler—and very much cheaper —than the Grosvenor's standard accommodation. But their guests get all the trimmings of a deluxe hostelry—bars, restaurants, hall porters, and a very svelte atmosphere. The building is air-conditioned, has a guest laundry, gymnasium and sauna, plus two of the finest dining rooms in town. Breakfast here is an event: apart from juices, coffee, cereals, toast, honey, and jams, it includes an absolutely sumptuous hot buffet guaranteed to tide you over lunch. The whole feast costs $8. Rates for the budget sleepers (*not* the standard rooms) are $35 for singles, $48 for doubles.

Serviced Suites

The **Powell's Court Motel,** 2 Glen Osmond Rd., Parkside (tel. 271-7995), is a real find for budget travelers, particularly groups of three or more. Apartments there come in eight different types of layout, so you can pick one that fits your exact requirements. All are surprisingly large and have spacious, fully equipped kitchens—*not* kitchenettes. The flats have separate sitting rooms, bedrooms and bathrooms, big refrigerators, air conditioning, color TV, telephones, and excellent beds fitted with allergy-free mattresses. Furnishing is not lavish but ample, providing good wardrobe space, wall-to-wall carpets, and bedside lamps. The morning paper is on the house and you can arrange daily fresh bread and milk deliveries. The white four-story building has an elevator and a fine view of the surrounding green hills. Singles go from $30 per day, doubles from $32 a day; three people pay from $36 daily, and four persons, from $40.

MEALS: Being much smaller, Adelaide does not have the volume or variety of eateries found in Sydney and Melbourne. But the local culinary standards are remarkably high, particularly in the realm of pub grub. You'll probably agree with this providing you don't start off by sampling the South Australian specialty —floaters. This is a meat pie floating on or in pea soup, and it tastes nearly as gruesome as it reads.

Apart from counter lunches, most of the good cheap establishments are non-Australian, which is pretty much the rule throughout the country. Because of pleasantly liberal licensing laws, Adelaide has no BYOs. Which is nice on the one hand, because you can have the great local wines with almost every meal. On the other hand, it tends to work out more expensively because no restaurant sells liquor at store prices. Ah, well, you can't win 'em all. . . .

Lunches and Such

Mary Brown's Café, 19a Rundle Mall, has a charming balcony overlooking the bustling shopping mall below. Up one flight of stairs, this is a pleasantly subdued eating place with soothing amber lights, ferns hanging from the ceiling, and wonderful old photos, depicting Adelaide around 1900, on the walls. The menu is simple and economical: bacon and eggs costs $3.70; a hefty steak sandwich, $2.30; omelets, $4. Closes at 6 p.m.

The best counter lunches are encountered along Hindley Street, which is studded with hotels competing for the city crowds at midday. The **Royal Oak** at no. 208, **Royal Admiral** at no. 125, and the **Princes Berkeley** at no. 58 put on equally substantial bar lunches. If you're out in Glenelg around lunchtime, sample the fare at the **Pier Hotel,** opposite the Town Hall on Pier Street. It serves lunch at tables instead of the counter in two large, pleasant dining rooms at very reasonable prices. A thick grilled steak and mushrooms for $4.50, "bangers and mash" (sausages and mashed potatoes to you, mate) for $3.

Also on Glenelg's Pier Street is the **Rice Bowl,** which offers a choice of Chinese combination lunches for $2.85. The fare is simple and tasty (try the fried rice and beef chop suey), the portions generous.

Dinner

Chief Charley's, 12 Grenfell St., is the downstairs abode of a mythical (and somewhat villainous) redskin boss "who spoke more bull than Sitting Bull." Chief Charley, however, has a perfectly genuine offer to feed you all the filets of fresh fish you can eat for just $5.80. The fish in question varies, but freshness and quality are permanent and the helpings unlimited. Despite its Wild West label, this is a small, cheerful family restaurant, happily devoid of Western paraphernalia but with fast friendly service and a vast menu of marine delectables. Apart from the daily all-you-can-eat offer, you can get brimming fisherman's baskets for $7.40 and highly imaginative "seafood shashlik" (fish, shellfish, onion, bacon, banana and pineapple) for $6.90. A small carafe of wine to help it float comes for $2.90. Charley's stays open seven days a week from 10:30 a.m. "until late."

It's pasta territory at **Lino's Restaurant,** 23 Gilbert Pl., one of the best values in its price range in Australia. Big and brown-paneled, with fine chandeliers and a magnificent photo montage of a Florentine bridge on the wall, the place looks surprisingly stylish for a budget restaurant. It was founded, allegedly, by one Mick Marrinelli when he discovered that all he could get in an Adelaide restaurant was "steak and bloody chips"—that must have been quite a few years ago. Anyway, Mick set about rectifying the situation by opening his own eatery. No chips on the menu, but a very thoughtful lesson on the correct way of pronouncing c-a-n-a-l-o-n-i and l-a-za-n-a. The positively gargantuan minestrone soup (it could pass for a meal) is $2, spaghetti pizzaiola is $4.90, and the outstanding espresso $1.10 per cup. Open Monday to Saturday till 9:15 p.m. Directly opposite, the enterprising Mr. Marrinelli has another—costlier—establishment, the **Arkaba Steak Cellar.** A beautiful place, looking exactly like a European cellar bistro, with heavy wooden tables, tiled floors, and wine cask ends set into the walls. A club or rump steak served with jacket potato, coleslaw, and potato salad sets you back $9.

Also on Gilbert Place is the **Pancake Kitchen,** humming in what was originally a small cottage, now extended into four oddly shaped dining rooms. The management provides gratis magazines in case you like reading with your meals. The majority of the young and very lively clientele prefer talking or flirting, which they do enthusiastically in the booths set aside for that purpose—maybe. The menu offers a lot besides pancakes—Russian or Jewish blintzes at $4, for instance. Open round the clock, seven days a week—a haven for hungry wayfarers. The **Ceylon Hut,** 27 Bank St., is a richly carpeted (walls and all) Indian hostelry, redolent with the aroma of curry and kindred spices. Curry dishes go from $6.50 for beef, chicken, and pork to $8.50 for the most expensive prawn concoction. Open Monday to Saturday till 10 p.m.

Our next two choices are both on North Adelaide's Melbourne Street, proving that trendiness does not necessarily mean deluxe prices. **Zapata's,** 42 Melbourne St., ranks among the most charming Mexican transplants: white-washed adobe walls beneath low ceilings, suitably revolutionary photos as decorations, but soft Spanish background music for mellowness. Candles cast their flickers on red tablecloths and the straw-matted ceiling. The fare is not particularly spicy, but manager Norm Frohnert will pepper it up on request. Try a pair of beef and cheese enchiladas followed by flan de queso—a rich cheese custard coated with caramel. Total cost is $10.20. So you can afford a classic margarita Zapata cocktail—served correctly in a chilled glass, frosted with salt. Open Monday through Saturday till 10:30 p.m.

The **Cosy Home Coffee House,** 116 Melbourne St., doesn't look very much like either. It's a delicatessen festooned with Austrian travel posters plus movie star blow-ups. White garden tables and chairs inside and in front, plus bare tile floors, don't make for much atmosphere. But the place serves some of the best and cheapest German-Austrian specialties anywhere, and the service is what you'd expect in a vastly more deluxe eatery. Goulash with noodles comes at $4.20 and in copious quantities, Kassler (smoked pork) with sauerkraut for $4.90. Don't forget to leave room for a slice of the memorable Esterhazy torte in conclusion. The background music—a delightful melange of German folk and vintage jazz—keeps the meal happy. Open till 7 p.m. Monday through Wednesday, till midnight on weekends. You should also try the nonalcoholic "beer" that tastes, almost, like the real stuff.

The **Hungarian Restaurant,** while not especially cheap, maintains such high standards of quality that it shouldn't be left out. Located at 135 Cardwell

St. (just off Halifax) where its neon sign gleams like a beacon in an otherwise dark and dismal alley, it also provides gypsy music on Friday and Saturday nights. Otherwise—except for the cuisine—it has no distinctly Hungarian features, but looks blandly neutral with beige decor and oils as wall decorations. A smallish dinery with first-rate service, the food dished out here is as authentic as anything you'll get this side of Budapest. Stuffed cabbage rolls, paprika goulash, and beef Stroganoff all come for $6.50 and $7, and come *big*. But try and leave some room for a pancake, one of the finest desserts with which to wreck your diet. Open "until close"—meaning late.

Out in the beach suburb of Glenelg, the **Manchurin Restaurant,** 16 Jetty Rd., is the place to head for if you fancy Chinese cooking. Sedate and tastefully decorated, minus most of the pseudo-Oriental curlicues, the Manchurin instead provides soft lighting and thoughtful service at lower prices than most of Adelaide's Chinese eateries. I recommend either the curried chicken and fried rice at $5, or the Mandarin combination rice at $5.50. Open seven days a week, it closes at 9 p.m. weeknights, 8:30 p.m. on Sunday.

Coffee Breaks

Adelaide has a number of delightful coffee and snack retreats, most of which also serve light meals. Two we consider absolutely outstanding. **The Coffee Pot,** 27 Rundle Mall, is a wonderfully aromatic coffee store and lounge selling every conceivable kind of coffee-making utensil, including the beans. Try the hot apricot pie with whipped cream for $1.65 or the cream and fruit-smothered Pavlova for $1.80. Coffee comes at $1.45 per superb cup, but an extra cup is free—a rare gesture in Australia. **Café Boulevard,** Hindley St. at Gilbert Place, is rather elegantly European, with plushly upholstered seating to spoil your derrière and half-curtained windows to watch the streetlife amble by. There are Tiffany lamps over the window tables and in the rear a glass display case presenting tempting piles of Italian-style desserts. (We recommend the apricot and custard slices and Napoleons.) Open till midnight seven days a week.

Floaters

This aforementioned South Australian specialty is the main draw of the mobile pie carts that take up positions each night and stay until early morning. One is adjacent to the General Post Office, the other at the Railway Station. In a city not blessed with too many late-night eateries, they *are* a blessing. And luckily they also sell pies and pea soup separately if required. It's amazing how much better they taste apart. You can also get tea and coffee there, the former good and strong, the latter unmentionable.

DAYTIME ACTIVITIES: If you happen to hit Adelaide during the Festival of Arts (see "Special Events"), you'll have a difficult time deciding which of the avalanche of attractions to watch. But even in off years the **Festival Centre Complex** is the town's top tourist draw. Rising on the banks of the Torrens River, just north of tree-lined North Terrace, this dramatic yet wonderfully functional edifice to culture is the finest stage complex in Australia, both acoustically and in the facilities it provides. Completed in 1973 (within three years) it contains a main 2,000-seat auditorium, an astonishingly versatile smaller drama theater, and a revolutionary experimental showcase, the Space, as well as a tiered outdoor Amphitheatre, an art collection, restaurants, and a bar. Guided tours of the complex take place Monday to Friday on the hour from 10 a.m. to 4 p.m., on Saturday from 10:30 a.m. to 3 p.m., and cost $1.50.

One block away stands the **South Australian Museum,** North Terrace. This building contains one of the largest and most varied collections of Aboriginal artifacts in the world, a fascinating Melanesian display, and a huge range of New Guinea amphibia. The **Art Gallery,** right next door, displays some noted examples of Australian art as well as the country's greatest coin collection.

Ayers House, also on North Terrace (opposite the Royal Adelaide Hospital), is an elegant bluestone home that was once the residence of a state premier. Today it provides an enchanting reminder of 19th-century colonial-style graciousness—a study in wealth coupled with taste. It also houses a very posh restaurant and a bistro. Open daily except Monday. Admission is $2 for adults, 50¢ for children.

On the gently winding **Torrens River,** between Adelaide and North Adelaide, you can hire one of the sailing, rowing, or pedaling craft that form the **Popeye** fleet, based on a jetty in beautiful **Cresswell Gardens.** If you're feeling a bit more energetic you can climb Montefiore Hill (off Montefiore Road), to the splendid lookout called **Light's Vision,** stand under the statue of Col. William Light, and get a panoramic vista of the city he designed so well.

Built into a convenient bend of the Torrens River next to the Botanic Park is the **Adelaide Zoo.** Designed to reduce walking to a minimum, this compact collection of fauna includes a unique bunch of yellow-footed rock wallabies. The **Botanic Garden and Park** adjoining it enclose 16 hectares of native Australian and exotic imported plants, several lakes, and a multitude of majestic swans.

Adelaide's beaches are probably the safest in Australia. They stretch from **Seacliff** in the south to **Outer Harbor** in the north, offer miles of dazzling white sand and the virtual absence of that fierce undertow characteristic of the more open surfing beaches. The most popular beach suburb is **Glenelg** (take the tram for $1), with a roisterous amusement park and a first-rate shopping center. Also **Shell Land,** at the corner of Mary and Melbourne Streets, North Glenelg, displaying 1,800 sea shells from around the world. **West Beach** features **Marineland,** Military Road, which is Australia's largest undercover aquarium containing performing dolphins jumping through burning hoops, seals, and scores of other marine creatures. Also the only 360° circle-vision cinema outside Disneyland. Open 10:30 a.m. to 4 p.m. Closed Tuesday.

The Government Travel Centre runs half-day sightseeing tours that take in the city sights, the eastern suburbs, and terminate at the Festival Centre. Coaches depart from the Travel Centre office, 18 King William St., at 9:15 a.m. Monday to Saturday.

The biggest surprise in town is undoubtedly the **Constitutional Museum,** North Terrace. First, because it's housed in the state's old parliament building, and second, because it isn't a museum at all. It's an enthralling 100-minute audio-visual show titled *Bound for South Australia.* I've never seen anything like it dreamt up by a state government. The show, performed in three separate chambers, tells the story of South Australia. Opening in an Aboriginal rock shelter, it proceeds to take you aboard H.M.S. *Buffalo* on her voyage out, goes on to depict the early parliamentary struggles of the young colony (you actually sit in the chairs used by bygone members and are "called to order" by the Speaker). The show concludes with the development of South Australia in this century, brought alive by means of a 28-projector multiscreen presentation. Don't miss it. Adults pay $3; children, $1.50.

THE BAROSSA VALLEY: One of Adelaide's greatest attractions—and Australia's most celebrated wine region—lies 40 miles northeast of the city. The valley was named after a vaguely similar piece of terrain in Spain, but there the similarity ends. There is nothing Spanish whatever about the Barossa. The keynote is German, both in the namebrands of the wines and the physical appearance of the villages. If you've traversed Central Europe you'll recognize those houses, churches, and barns immediately: solid stones and slender steeples, lovingly regimented hedges and wine gardens in the shade of old trees. No trace of the colonial rawness and impermanence that marks so many Australian (and American) country towns. The first brick wall tells you that these people built things to last—not for decades but for centuries.

The people who settled the valley during the 1840s were strict Lutherans from Prussia, who had migrated in order to practice their religion without undue government interference. They knew little about wine, but plenty about orcharding and agriculture. It was only when a geologist drew their attention to the wine-growing potential of the soil they tilled that many of them switched to viticulture. The resulting combination of ideal earth and ideal climate, plus skill and hard work, produced a valley that looks like one vast garden. The place enraptures your eyes long before it gets to your palate.

Although the Barossa people are now staunchly Australian, the German influence is still strong. You drive along a road called Wein Strasse, past inns called Gasthaus, shops selling *Obst und Gemüse,* butchers displaying mettwurst, and a juvenile fashion store advertising *Kinderkleider.*

The valley's cuisine is a happy hodgepodge of Teutonic and Down Under— the same establishments serving sauerbraten, eisbein, and streuselkuchen cheek by jowl with hot meat pies and barramundi. But the wines are true native —the best the country produces. Here you'll find the essence of crisp Australian whites, full-bodied reds, smooth rosés, and party-spirited sparklers, as well as the more sedate ports and clarets. They blend well with the lush green hills, the weathered old Lutheran churches, and the little craft shops that dot the villages.

But here's a word of advice: pace yourself carefully. The valley has some 35 wineries, ranging from primitive iron sheds to huge combines with palatial châteaus and replicas of Rhineland castles. And nearly all of them invite you to drop in and taste, and pour generous measures. Unless you watch your intake you'll find yourself either incapable of driving or unable to enjoy the journey. The first eventuality would be dangerous, the second a pity. So sip with caution and travel proud.

This is particularly advisable if you're lucky enough to make your trip during the **Vintage Festival.** This is celebrated in the years of odd numbers (so as not to clash with the Adelaide Arts Festival), usually during the week after Easter— the Australian autumn. Well, the fountains don't gush wine, but half a million bottles do, and the valley goes into a whirl of parades, parties, dancing, feasting, and DRINKING, and to hell with the hangovers. Don't say you weren't warned.

The Barossa Valley proper (as distinct from the district) is a 20-mile strip running from Williamstown to the St. Kitts Hills, just north of Nuriootpa. Various companies run organized tours of the region (see end of chapter). If you're doing your own driving, here's a suggested route that takes in most of the highlights.

Take the Main North Road from Adelaide, turn right onto Sturt Highway (Route 20) and roll via Elizabeth and Gawler to . . .

Lyndoch

This is the gateway of the Barossa Valley, a pretty little hamlet, about 130 years old. By local standards that's antique. If you're economizing, stop at the **Lyndoch Hotel** for a counter lunch costing about $4.20. But if you're willing to splash a little, the spot for you is the **Postkutsche Restaurant.** Don't even try to pronounce it—it means Stagecoach Inn. (The stage actually used to stop there.) The restaurant looks exactly like a stagecoach inn should look, straight out of the Brothers Grimm or Dickens. The hostess is from Tanzania, of the gourmet tribe. And the house specialty is a filet steak with cheese, mushrooms, and smoked ham—and stuff dreams are made of.

At the **Château Yaldara** you'll get an idea of the magnificence of some of the wine establishments in the area. The main hall and upper halls are downright palatial, like the reception rooms of minor European royalty. The mansion itself is a superb hewn-stone structure, crammed with art objects, lit by impressive chandeliers, and hung with Persian carpets and gold-framed oil canvases. The wine-tasting is subtly regulated: starting with the driest and leading you slowly up to the sweeter table wines, thence to the liqueurs. It's free of charge—but with the fond hope that you'll buy a bottle or two or ten. Conducted tours are given five times daily from Monday to Friday. The cellars are open on Saturday and most holidays as well. There is also a picnic and barbecue area open to the public.

North along the Sturt Highway lies the unofficial capital of Barossa, a name so synonymous with wine that many Australians don't know whether this is a town or a bottle label:

Tanunda

Quite apart from its grape glory, Tanunda is one of the most captivating villages in the southern hemisphere. The gateway is flanked by green embankments, a decorated arch—crowned by a wine barrel—welcomes you, and you drive in among small white or weather-gray houses half-hidden behind trees and hedges, with music in the air mingling with the aroma of wine and country cooking. At first glance the whole place seems to have been cut out of a children's picture book.

Tanunda has a miniature **museum,** open seven days a week, where you can see the implements and the people who created the valley in its present form. Admission is $1 for adults, 50¢ for children. The **Art Shop** is another kind of museum: it sells art objects from copperware and pottery to elaborate home winepresses in front and dispenses coffee and cakes in the rear.

Almost opposite, designed for more serious eating, is **Die Galerie.** It's a genuine cellar restaurant, cool and dim, roofed with massive ridgum beams and lit by oil lamps, the whitewashed brick walls interlaced with wooden crossbars. On sunny afternoons or warm nights you can eat and drink in the vine-ranked courtyard in the shade of old trees. The entrance leads through an actual art gallery, where you can spend $50 for a small sketch or $500 for a large oil landscape.

Tanunda takes special pride in the **Langmeil Church,** which houses the burial ground and monument of Pastor Kavel—the man who emigrated here from Berlin in 1838, took his entire congregation with him, and founded the Evangelical Lutheran church in Australia.

The most impressive winery in the village is **Château Tanunda,** maker of the continent's no. 1 brandy. But, unfortunately, it's no longer open to the public.

The **Story Book Cottage** and **Whacky Wood,** Oak Street, Tanunda, are twin attractions with a distinct Aussie flavor and hard to resist for anyone below the age of 120. You can try the Sleepy Lizard Races, ride the whacky bronco, do the Wombat Wobble and Kangaroo Hop, or admire the miniature fairytale world behind the little green door. Live animals as well, down a rabbit hole. One admission covers both shows: $2.50 for adults, $1 for children. Open daily from 10 a.m. to 5 p.m.

Another portion of the Seppelt empire lies at **Dorrien,** just north of Tanunda. This is **Seppeltsfield,** a vast winery spreading over many acres surrounded by vineyards. All of it grew from a small patch of land on which Joseph Seppelt unsuccessfully tried to raise tobacco in the 1850s. When the soil proved unsuitable for smoking crops, he turned to the drinking variety instead and built his first wine cellar over and around his wife's dairy. The old cellar still exists, so well constructed that even after 110 years the heavy timbers haven't given an inch. The hospitality of the Seppelt family was proverbial and continues today. Visitors are welcome to gardens and picnic grounds, with tables, bench seats, and gas barbecues provided. Plus, of course, chilled wines and glasses to clink among the palms and date trees.

Nuriootpa

This township has been called the heart of the wine country, but that's purely geographical. In fact Nuriootpa is simply another delightful stop along the Sturt route through the valley, offering pleasures very much as before.

It does, however, boast the oldest house in the Barossa, built in 1840. Today the quaintly ramshackle little structure contains the **Barossa Gem Centre,** where you can browse among a collection of opals bought directly from Andamooka. Browse and hope—there's always a chance—a pretty faint one—that you'll make a "find," assuming that you know one when you spot it. The stones sell from about $10 upward.

On the lawn outside, **Coulthard House,** another museum, is the permanent parking place for the first caravan built in Australia, looking exactly like a cottage on wheels, complete with red tile roof. Any resemblance to contemporary trailer homes is purely coincidental.

The most imposing winery here is **Kaiser Stuhl,** an odd brand name meaning "Emperor's Chair," arousing visions of some bearded monarch squatting on a wine barrel. Kaiser Stuhl is a new outfit by valley standards, founded as a cooperative in the early 1930s. But its château—red brick with white facing—has all the regality of a century-old mansion, and the tasting room is among the most attractive in the area. The wine-making facilities offer a fascinating contrast to the old-world air of the château. The bottling plants (capacity of 12,000 per hour), the stainless-steel tanks storing 2,000,000 gallons of young wine, the laboratory where wines are tested and analyzed, are technological marvels. The winery offers six conducted tours six days a week. Closed on Sunday.

Nuriootpa (in case you've wondered, it's an Aboriginal word for "meeting place") has an outstanding German bakery, serving made-on-the-premises apple strudel, bienenstich, and other diet-killing delights. It's also a good place to spend the night if you're trying to preserve your energy for another day's tasting.

The **Vine Inn Hotel** (tel. 622-133) stands on Murray Street and serves grills and smörgåsbord salads (you help yourself). A new handsome hewn-stone building, the place somehow blends nicely with its surroundings, despite its obvious modernity. The hotel rooms have electric blankets and private showers, and cost $16 per single, $26 for doubles.

More economical is the **Caravan and Camping Park,** Centennial Park (tel. 085-62-1404). Nestling amid 40 acres of trees and lawns near the Para River, the park offers amenity blocks, washing machines, a kiosk selling milk, bread, etc., and ten on-site vans for hire. The vans, fully equipped, rent from $16.50 for two people, with additional persons paying $1.20 each. Near the van sites there's an enclosure with kangaroos nibbling the grass, waiting to have their heads scratched.

The valley stretches on . . . to **Angaston,** which has a wonderful boulevard restaurant called **Unter der Laterne,** with tables set beneath an arched street colonnade, exactly as you'd find in the Rhineland. Over Keyneton and Springton to Birdwood (watch for the interesting museum of old transport) to Cudlee Creek. If you're driving yourself you can take the winding Gorge Road back into Adelaide. But there are any number of tours, where the coach driver is the only one forced to stay sober, which, under the circumstances, might be the ideal form of locomotion.

Conducted Tours

Every touring company in Adelaide has a Barossa Valley excursion in its books. The tours quoted here are merely samples of the conditions and prices prevailing.

The **S.A. Government Travel Centre,** 18 King William St. (tel. 212-1644), sets out at 9:15 a.m. daily, the coaches leaving from the Centre. The rates are a uniform $24 for adults, $10.50 for children. The tasting stop (always the highlight) is at Seppelts. The buses return to Adelaide around 5 p.m.

Ansett Pioneer, 101 Franklin St. (tel. 51-2075) runs a full-day tour of Barossa Valley, departing at 9:30 a.m. and returning at 5 p.m. The trip includes lunch, a wine tasting, and visits to some of the Valley's most picturesque townships. Total cost is $26 for adults, half fare for children.

The same outfit also operates "City Sights" and "City Lights" tours—the former in daytime, the latter at night. Both last roughly 2½ hours, but the daylight trips costs $14 for adults, $7.50 for children, while the after-dark venture is $13 for adults, $6 for children.

If you prefer to sightsee independently, the ideal method is by the **Adelaide Explorer,** 101 Franklin St. (tel. 212-7344). This is a clearly marked bus that does the rounds of most of the city's tourist attractions. For a ticket costing $6 per adult, $4 per child, you can join or leave the bus at any of the eight stopping points as many times as you like for an entire day.

EVENING ACTIVITIES: Adelaide has a nightlife strip of sorts in the shape of Hindley Street. There, interspersed with excellent restaurants and cafés, you'll find some rather rheumatic bare skin establishments, porno peepshows, and a trickle of streetwalking ladies. (Also the nonporno **Third World bookstore,** which keeps night-owl hours). Also, at no. 94, there is the versatile **Jules Bar.** A disco from 9 p.m. on, it has a packed dance floor till dawn every night except Monday. Admission is free before midnight.

Farther out and usually higher in the price bracket is the **Hotel Enfield,** Hampstead Road, Clearview (tel. 262-3944). This establishment contains two of Adelaide's top night entertainments under one roof. The first is the Bull 'n Bush, an elaborate theater restaurant featuring tinseled, rollicking, song-studded oldtime vaudeville turns (no strip acts). You can enjoy it for $22 or $30, depending on the night, and including a three-course meal and liquor. The second is the Baron of Beef, an amusing mix of smörgåsbord and cabaret acts—the former including seafood, the latter lashings of singing, dancing, and comedy till 11 p.m., then dancing by the guests till midnight. It costs $22 a head Fridays and Saturdays, $30 including liquor.

There's more live entertainment at the **Tivoli Hotel,** 261 Pirie St., Tuesday through Thursday. The bands vary from hard rock to country rock, but admission remains at $2 a head with drinks at bar prices. On Friday and Saturday the hotel features live vaudeville, fast, bright, funny, and raunchy in spots, with prices ranging from $14 to $16 according to what manner of meal you choose to imbibe with the show.

The **Old Lion Hotel,** Melbourne Street, North Adelaide, sprawls over a series of discos, bars, and restaurants, and magnetizes the semigilded younger set. At times the management puts on grand-slam revues (including female impersonators) with lavish costumes, elaborate show suppers, and correspondingly gilt-edged prices.

Still on North Adelaide's trendy Melbourne Street, at no. 153 you'll find **Bogart's,** an intriguingly mixed-up cross between a wine bar and a disco with live entertainment. Bogie's is an institution with some locals and an irresistible magnet for suburbanites, and somehow manages to change its texture to please a preponderance of palates. A restaurant in daytime and early evening, it becomes a dance-drink-socialize melting pot after dark. A minuscule dance floor serviced by high-decibel disco and New Wave music by a resident DJ, a delightfully relaxed bar, and corners where you can talk/flirt/ogle—take your pick. Bar prices are among the lowest in town, the compulsory supper provided for patrons after 10 p.m. is surprisingly edible, the decor refreshingly simple, and the vibes mellow. Open all week.

Adelaide is the only city in the world that has turned its railroad station into a **Gambling Casino.** The suburban trains are still running in and out of the place, but where the administration offices used to be there is now a vast and very plush gaming palace. The casino features 105 gaming tables for roulette and blackjack, as well as a granite-floored ring for the traditional (and mostly illegal) Australian game of two-up. (For details on this fascinating obsession see our Tasmanian chapter.) The Casino also includes a superb wine bar, offering 400 brands of South Australian wines, and a suitably expensive restaurant, the Pullman, which has wandering minstrels competing with the resident band. The Casino hums seven days a week from noon to dawn. Well, I did mention that the "City of Churches" has changed somewhat.

SPECIAL EVENTS: Adelaide's **Festival of Arts** is by far the most important cultural event in Australia. It didn't start off that way back in 1960, but since then the affair has mushroomed wondrously—to the point where it gained its home base the title of Festival City, as if no other town had one. The festival takes place over three weeks in March of every even-numbered year. Its core, of course, is the magnificent Festival Centre, but the action spills over the entire city, into streets, parks, smaller theaters, sports arenas, and playgrounds. A list of the attractions could fill this entire chapter. They include traditional and experimental plays, classical ballet, and exotic folk dancing, mime troupes and marionettes, shadow puppets and Aboriginal ceremonies, symphony concerts, chamber music recitals, acid rock, and modern jazz. There are float parades and fashion parades, a special motion picture program, and a Fun Palace in an old Gothic mansion up on Montefiore Hill. There are the greats from overseas—Nureyev, Menuhin, Yevtushenko, Dave Brubeck, et al., and the pick of all-Australian talent. There is, above all, an air of shared joy in beauty that less fortunate cities might get once in a lifetime but Adelaide arranges biennially.

USEFUL INFORMATION: The **South Australian Government Travel Centre,** centrally located at 18 King William St. (tel. 212-1644), is open Monday through Friday from 8:15 a.m. to 5:30 p.m., on Saturday and Sunday morning from 9 a.m. to 2 p.m. Bookings made at no charge for tours and accommodation in South Australia. . . . For information on current activities in town, consult *This Week in Adelaide,* free from the Travel Centre. The *Advertiser* gives a good roundup of nighttime doings. . . . **City buses** depart from 111 Franklin St. (tel. 51-5891), as do most **country services** including **Greyhound Express** (tel. 212-1777). The **Pioneer Express** terminal is at 101 Franklin St. (tel. 51-2075). . . . The **train depot** is located at the corner of North Terrace and King William Street; phone 51-0231 for information. . . . There are **sea terminals** located at

Outer Harbour, approximately 15 miles from the city where larger overseas ships berth, and Port Adelaide, approximately eight miles from the city, which handles cargo vessels. Both can be easily reached by train, while Port Adelaide also has bus service. . . . The **Ansett Airlines** coach terminal is at 150 North Terrace (tel. 212-1111), and the **Trans-Australia Airlines** coach terminal is at 144 North Terrace (tel. 217-7711). . . . **The General Post Office** (GPO) is at 141 King William St. (tel. 216-2360). Open Monday through Friday from 8:15 a.m. to 5 p.m. There is Post Restante service and the telegraph counter is open Monday through Friday from 7:15 a.m. to 6:30 p.m. . . . There are no **24-hour petrol stations** in the city because of a city ordinance; however on South Road in the direction of Victor Harbour, approximately seven miles from the city, and on North Road in the direction of Gawler, approximately six miles from town, there are a number of petrol stations side by side. . . . **90-minute cleaning** can be obtained from Adelaide Valet Service, 120 Hindley St., open Monday through Friday from 8 a.m. to 5:30 p.m. and on Saturday from 8 a.m. to noon. If you arrive at the beginning of a load cycle you will have your garment after 90 minutes, but if the load cycle has already started, you will have to wait another 90 minutes after the cycle has finished. They also do quick alterations and repairs. . . . There are no **laundromats** in the city center. However, there are two on Hutt Street and two on O'Connell Street North Adelaide.

2. South Australia

This huge state (about 1½ times the size of Texas) occupies the central position on the map of Australia and has within its borders a portion of everything that makes up the continent—golden surfing beaches in the south and vast broiling deserts in the northwest; lush green wine-growing valleys and spectacularly rugged mountain ranges; rolling plains swarming with wild emus and kangaroos and carefully cultivated wheatlands; cattle stations, industrial complexes, and warm meandering rivers; regions of densely profuse forests and regions where nothing grows at all. It's all there in South Australia, so take your pick.

We'll start with a spot that is not only unique in Australia, but in the world—

COOBER PEDY: The name is Aboriginal and means "white man live underground." And that's precisely how the locals live. The reason is the climate. Coober Pedy lies in a lunar landscape of flat-topped sandstone ridges 590 miles northwest of Adelaide, where daytime temperatures soar to 130 degrees and nights are often freezing. By burrowing like human moles, the locals escape these drastic extremes of climate and achieve amazingly comfortable conditions.

But why would anyone live there at all? The answer is simple: Coober Pedy sits on the largest opal deposits in South Australia. And that's the reason for this town of over 2,000 people where the only structures above ground are the post office, school, police station, stores, and (air-conditioned) motels. And every morning the citizens emerge from their burrows to dig out about 90% of all the opals produced in the world!

Some of these cave homes are amazingly elaborate, complete with modern furniture, matching carpets, pictures on the walls, and record players on the liquor cabinets. The town even has a subterranean Catholic church, reminiscent of the Roman catacombs in which the earliest Christians held their services. You can join conducted tours of this "underworld," concluding with a visit to an opal mine in full operation.

Or—better still—do a bit of fossicking yourself. All it takes (in that order) is a pick and shovel, a strong back, and an eye for a dusty pebble emitting a strange fiery glitter. But take my advice and try it between May and August; it's cooler then. **Bull's Tourist Services** runs daily buses from Adelaide to Coober Pedy, a 15-hour trip. Or you can fly by **Opal Air** in about three hours.

KANGAROO ISLAND: A wildlife paradise lying just off the coast southwest of Adelaide, this is everything a holiday isle should be—cooler than the mainland in summer, balmier in winter, developed enough to offer every tourist comfort, primitive enough to harbor legions of furred and feathered beasties in their natural environment, small enough to be explored in a couple of days, large enough to keep you engrossed for a year.

Kangaroo Island has luxury hotels and budget hostelries, 50 species of wild orchids, hundreds of seals romping over salt-sprayed rocks, regiments of waddling fairy penguins, sheltered swimming pools, and some of the finest big-game fishing in Australia (including the legendary great white shark). Plus, of course, kangaroos. Officially they're "wild," but in reality they'll take your picnic apples right out of your hand. The dragon-like goanna lizards don't care for apples, but they'll gladly steal your ham sandwiches. Up in the trees the koalas stick to gum leaves, while the emus may even swallow your motel key if you're foolish enough to offer it. And if you're very discreet and quiet you may watch the shy duck-billed platypuses playing in the pools of Rocky River.

There's a daily (weekday) Kangaroo Island ferry connecting Port Adelaide with Kangaroo Island. The crossing takes 6½ hours. By air Ansett Airlines takes you over in 40 minutes.

CRUISING DOWN THE MURRAY: Three states share the wide, warm, leisurely Murray River, but South Australia makes the best use of its portion. This is a river to play on, to dream by, and to fish in, and South Australia facilitates all three pastimes with rare generosity—for instance, by not insisting on a fishing license.

Have you ever dreamt of cruising down a river in an air-conditioned steamer? Well, the *Proud Mary* is a luxury craft that you could imagine chugging along the Mississippi with Scarlett O'Hara mooning by the railing and Rhett Butler fanning a deck in the saloon. But this version has a modern heart. The cabins come with either hot and cold water or private showers, there are streamlined dining rooms and sundecks, excellent meals, and a well-stocked bar. The *Proud Mary* is based at Murray Bridge, east of Adelaide, and cruises for two days past glorious bush scenery, basking lizards, and multicolored birdlife. Plus deck games, parties, and barbecues on shore, unlimited fishing, and the chance to acquire a perfect suntan. The cruise costs from $190.

But perhaps you'd like to play skipper yourself? Preferably on a virtually unsinkable, "all mod. cons." craft that requires no more navigational knowhow than you need to drive a car. Well, there are more than 400 of these available at seven river towns along the Murray. They are drive-yourself houseboats equipped with paddlewheels or stern motors that push them along at an easy five miles an hour.

The fittings of these craft vary according to size and price. The deluxe mod els even have two-way radios with which to summon "room service"—which comes via a fast courtesy boat from the base. All of them boast cooking facilities, hot water, electricity, showers, gas refrigerators, and ample sleeping accommodations. Some also provide gratis fishing gear. You have 400 miles of picturesque river for a highway, scores of idyllic mooring spots beneath willow branches, or the choice of tying up at the wharf of a different little town each night. The riverbanks slide past, varying between sandstone cliffs, gum forests, irrigated orchards, and vast marshes alive with pelicans, ducks, cormorants, ibis, herons, and cranes.

These houseboats offer berths for four to ten people and can be rented at rates ranging from about $300 per off-season weekend. The South Australian Government Travel Centre has detailed literature and will arrange bookings for all of them.

THE FLINDERS RANGES: They rise abruptly near Crystal Brook, 120 miles north of Adelaide, and go on and on, one towering range after another, the stark bare grandeur of the peaks contrasting with the sun-drenched, multicolored gorges in between. This is the most ruggedly beautiful mountain country in South Australia, inspiration of dozens of landscape painters and millions of visitors. Despite good roads from Adelaide and clusters of motels in the townships, the ranges still have more wildlife than people: kangaroos and rock wallabies, earthbound emus, soaring wedge-tailed eagles, screeching parrots and cockatoos, and frilled mountain lizards that look like pocket dragons but are quite harmless. The core of this mountain glory is Wilpena Pound, just beyond Hawker, where the peaks form a complete circle around an emerald-hued valley.

You can explore the ranges by yourself or join one of the half-dozen tours offered by **Pioneer.** They take from four to eight days.

Chapter VI

BRISBANE

1. The City and Surroundings
2. The Gold Coast

THE MOMENT YOU ENTER BRISBANE you realize you're in holidayland—tourist territory—the capital of a state that counts tourism as a major industry. The subtropics start here, the sun shines with patriotic persistence, and the air is balmy when it isn't hot.

1. The City and Surroundings

Although Brisbane is now a metropolis of 926,000 people (bigger than Boston), the super-abundance of ultraviolet rays keeps the rat race down to a comfortable crawl, infused with a pleasant dash of mañana spirit. The shops are loaded with cheap tropical fruit and sugarcane, girls go habitually bare-armed and looking gorgeous, and everybody has a tan.

It's a condition that carries drawbacks as well as advantages. On the one hand there are few places in the world where visitors are made more welcome. The whole town seems to cater to them, woo them, seduce them to stay permanently (which they do in vast numbers, thus accounting for Brisbane's tremendous rate of growth). On the other hand certain penalties come attached to this semitropical langor. Queensland's politics and attitudes remain somewhat behind the times. Environmentalism is regarded with suspicion, and films and magazines are strictly censored.

And city planning is not exactly Brisbane's strong point. Traffic conditions resemble a Keystone Cops epic—hell on motorists and not so cozy for pedestrians either. The downtown portions are a jigsaw jungle of one-way streets, railroad tracks, and freeway entrances so badly marked that you find yourself zooming off to Sydney instead of your hotel. Adjoining **Fortitude Valley** has some fine restaurants and entertainment spots and the *potential* of becoming a nightlife center.

In the leap from small town somnolence to metropolitan dynamism Brisbane seems to have missed the mark. Although it boasts a number of handsome buildings, several striking vistas, superlative weather, and a relaxed atmosphere, it does not have a single genuinely attractive street. The parks and gardens and riverbanks glow in lush colors, but what lies in between is frankly blah. From the tourist point of view, Brisbane's main function is as a gateway to the scenic wonders of Queensland—perhaps the most spectacular, certainly the most controversial, state in the Commonwealth.

Like other Australian capitals, Brisbane was founded as a convict settlement in 1824. Unlike most others, however, it was established some 25 miles inland, on the banks of the winding **Brisbane River** that flows into Moreton Bay.

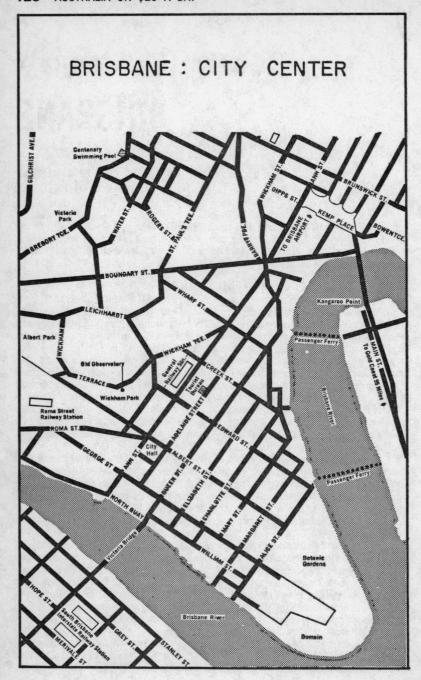

BRISBANE : CITY CENTER

The river links the city with the ocean and carries large vessels, but Brisbane was deprived of a harbor setting that might have enhanced its charms. The penal memories still linger—carefully preserved as tourist attractions. The meteorological station known as **Old Observatory,** for instance, was originally constructed in 1829 as a convict punishment treadmill and later became a signal post before mellowing into a popular landmark.

ORIENTATION: Read this section carefully because Brisbane is one of the worst (and least) signposted cities in Australia. Queenslanders have a deplorable habit of obliterating street names at important thoroughfares and not bothering to mark the less important ones at all. They figure that visitors can always ask the friendly natives for directions. The trouble is that frequently there's nary a native in sight—everyone you ask turns out to be another tourist!

The best spot for an overall view of the city is the lookout on the tower of the **City Hall,** a vaguely Florentine edifice on **King George Square** that backs the impressive **City Plaza** shopping center. From up there you get a real taste of the fabulous mishmash of Victorian, Edwardian, 1930s, and glass-walled contemporary architecture that characterizes the town.

If you look toward the huge **Central Railway Station** you're looking due north. Immediately below you run Brisbane's main commercial streets: Ann, Adelaide, Queen, Elizabeth, Charlotte, Mary, and Margaret Streets, running south to north, and George, Albert, Edward, and Creek Streets, running west to east. Northwest is the direction of **Brisbane Airport,** some six miles from where you're standing.

To your right (that's east) the **Brisbane River** makes an A-shaped bend. At the tip of this bend the beautiful **Story Bridge** crosses the water and farther to the left runs the ferry service across the river. Another ferry leaves from the foot of Edward Street, farther south. Behind you (southeast) the **Botanic Gardens,** containing the **State Parliament,** nestle in the opposite bend of the river. This is the direction of the **Gold Coast,** the sun-drenched chain of beach resorts we'll visit later in this chapter.

The second loop of the river (south of you) separates South Brisbane from the city. The southside embankment is delightfully landscaped and the site of a future cultural complex. Here the river is spanned by the **William Jolly, Victoria,** and **Captain Cook Bridges.** The Victoria Bridge serves as a landmark because nearby the spectacular **Elizabeth II Jubilee Fountain** throws a sparkling pillar of water high above the surface. Below this loop, fitted into yet another river curl, stretches the vast green pocket that surrounds the **Queensland University.**

Beyond the river, to the southwest, rises **Mt. Coot-tha Forest Park,** about four miles from the city, embracing the new Botanic Gardens and offering a panoramic view of the metropolis. Due west of you stands the **Roma Street Railway Station** and still farther west, **Government House.** Northwest stretches the huge green enclave of **Victoria Park,** next to **Bowen Park** and the **Exhibition Grounds.** The whole vast and beautiful complex contains the **Municipal Golf Links,** the **Queensland Museum,** and the **Centenary Pools** (at Gregory Terrace), among the finest swimming and diving facilities in the country. **Gregory Terrace,** which forms the borderline of these parks, is an important street to remember. It winds uphill and down from College Road to Fortitude Valley and has some of the best budget accommodations in town.

TRANSPORTATION: Public transport within the urban area consists of buses, trains, and river ferries. There is no central bus terminal, but most buses depart from points within a block of City Hall. For details regarding services, phone

225-4444, seven days a week. The Brisbane City Council provides multi-journey fare-savers: bus passengers may ride on a concession ticket allowing ten rides for the price of nine. That's a real bargain. You can buy these tickets from most news agents. For sightseeing the best buy is the **Day Rover.**

The Brisbane ferries are fast, cheap, clean, and great fun to ride on. And the river scene is one of the most colorful the city offers, with ocean freighters, tugs, and pleasure craft moored along the embankments. Try the **Golden Mile Ferries** (tel. 399-5054) for the fast commuter service from the City to East Brisbane.

Brisbane taxis are notoriously difficult to hail. Better get one from the various ranks or phone the following round-the-clock numbers: 831-3000, 229-1000, 391-0191.

You can rent bicycles at the **Brisbane City Cycle Hire,** at 214 Margaret St. (tel. 229-2592). Standard rates are $3.50 an hour, $7.50 per half day, $12 for a full day. You'll need some proof of identity.

For car rentals there's **Thrifty,** corner of Ann and Brookes Sts., Fortitude Valley (tel. 52-5994). They have a special weekend deal in which you get a car for two days for $99, including unlimited km and full insurance coverage.

Brisbane Airport

Brisbane Airport is located four miles northwest of the city center. Airport coach fare is $3 to downtown hotels, while a taxi would cost approximately $8.

At the airport you will find a **buffet** open from 6 a.m. to 6 p.m. (adjusted to meet special flight arrangements) and an à la carte restaurant open from noon to 2:30 p.m. and 6 to 8:30 p.m. In the terminal you will find the duty-free shop, open only for outgoing international flights, and car-hire facilities. There are no banking facilities.

There is no Tourist Information Office, however Ansett and TAA desks will give information and make bookings if requested.

Don't miss the glass-walled building, just inside the entrance, housing the *Southern Cross*—the celebrated aircraft that made the first air crossing of the Pacific Ocean in 1928. Commanded by Brisbane-born Sir Charles Kingsford Smith (known as "Smithy"), this antediluvian tri-motored Fokker monoplane did the trip from Oakland, California, to Brisbane—7,347 miles—in 83½ hours' flying time. Two of the four-man crew were Australians, two Americans. The plane they used was outdated even 50 years ago and affectionately dubbed "the Old Bus" by its crew. Smithy was killed in 1935, while trying to establish a new record for the England-Australia flight.

A NOTE ON PRICES: All prices in this guide are in Australian dollars (A$). As we go to press, US$1 = approximately A$1.40. Thus a room listed at $20 a night actually costs only about $14.50 in U.S. funds—good news indeed for budget travelers.

ACCOMMODATIONS: The economy lodgings scene in Brisbane has shrunk considerably since the last edition of this book. This is due partly to the on-again off-again perambulations of the local Y (which has entered the "no accommodations" phase once more), but chiefly, however, to the ongoing process of tearing down old, cheap, and comfortable dwellings and erecting expensive high-rises instead. By failing to replace budget-style habitats Brisbane is losing a large slice of the tourist trade, which is steadily drifting south to the Gold Coast where there's an abundance of low-cost digs. But just try explaining that to either city officials or developers, all wrapped in the delusion that visitors don't mind paying $40 a night for a small room as long as it's air-conditioned.

On the plus side remains the fact that nearly all our budget spots are located downtown or just a couple of bus stops out. And when it comes to finding rooms (as well as anything else) for weary travelers, you'll find the **Queensland Government Travel Centre** invaluable. They're at 196 Adelaide Street (tel. 31-2211) and bend over backward to be of service.

The Hostel

All advance bookings must be made at the Brisbane **YHA** office at 462 Queen St. (tel. 831-2022). The actual hostel is at 15 Mitchell St., Kedron, five miles from the center (tel. 57-1245). Catch the 172 Chermside bus on Adelaide Street and get off at stop 27A. A modern brick, glass, and veranda building, the hostel accommodates up to 80 people in real comfort. The place has a small food store, a community kitchen, reading and common rooms, automatic laundry, hot showers, and an outdoor barbecue area. Overall, one of the best of its breed in the country. The charges are $5.50 per night for seniors, $3 for juniors.

College Accommodations

Rooms at the **University of Queensland** are good but acquiring one is largely a matter of luck during the vacations. Students should contact **Union College** (tel. 371-1300) or **International House** (tel. 370-9593) and ask for the accommodations officer. The first charges $14 a day (no meals); the second, $10 for bed-and-breakfast.

Hotels

The **Atcherley Hotel,** 513 Queen St. (tel. 832-2591), welcomes you with a smart lobby, handsomely carpeted and decorated with a tropical fish tank. Apart from comfortable armchairs and vending machines, the public facilities include a TV lounge (private sets for hire), coin laundry, and a restaurant. The elevator for the four floors is elderly, but the corridors and bathrooms are immaculate, a sure sign of a well-run establishment. The 60 bedrooms face either the noisy street or the panoramic Brisbane River in the back. Rates are the same for both—so if you're lucky you'll get a rear location. The rooms vary considerably in decor, but all come with H&C washbasin, plug-in fan, fluorescent ceiling lights (some also with bedside lamps), combination dresser and mirror, and wall-to-wall carpet. Ceilings are lofty, wardrobes spacious, and furnishings ample. The Atcherley has special budget deals for genuine backpackers. Otherwise the standard tariffs are $20 for singles, $28 for doubles; family rooms go for $30.

Marrs Town House, 391 Wickham Terrace (tel. 831-5388), looks like a modern office building, and the ground floor actually *is*. The rest, however, comprises one of the newest and possibly finest budget establishments in Brisbane. The reception is up on the second floor. The whole place, kept in a delightfully soothing brown decor, breathes the restful quiet that comes from good carpeting and management. The lounge resembles a private club with pool table and TV; there's a restaurant, shopping kiosk, and a view of the park opposite, and even the elevator comes carpeted. Of the 65 bedrooms, 13 have private bathrooms; the rest are served by sparkling new public bathrooms. The four hotel floors are air-conditioned. All the rooms bear the stamp of comfortable good taste, kept in matching brown-whites, with ceiling fan, fluorescent lighting, H&C handbasin, large wardrobe, color TV, and radio (but no telephone). They also have coffee- and tea-making facilities, bedside lights, walnut cabinet fixtures. The house offers a guest laundry, lobby telephones, plus some truly thoughtful touches, such as special luggage trolleys to ease transport pains. (Other hotels, *please* copy.) Rates here start at $25 for singles, $36 for doubles.

Bed-and-Breakfast

Thanks to its tourist-mindedness, Brisbane has a much larger array of bed-and-breakfast facilities than most Australian cities. The culinary standard of the breakfasts is generally high, although the quantities served vary.

The **Yale Budget Tourist Hotel,** 413 Upper Edward St. (tel. 832-1663), is strictly economy lodging. A red-brick structure, made attractive by the greenery outside, this is a rather plain establishment charging among the lowest rates in town. No frills are wasted on the reception room and hallways. The small dining room serves breakfast only, but there's an upstairs TV lounge for the use of residents. The bedrooms are likewise small and fairly basic, but absolutely spotless. Some are equipped with hot and cold water basins, others not. All have wall-to-wall carpets and good-size wardrobes, but only a ceiling light. Each of the three floors has two bathrooms. Guests can use a communal laundry with ironing facilities. The charge is $18 for singles, $26 for doubles and the rates include continental breakfast.

Located opposite Brisbane's Exhibition Grounds, museum, and art gallery is the **Tourist Private Hotel-Motel,** 555 Gregory Terrace (tel. 52-4171). A pretty white weatherboard house with an inviting veranda, this hostelry consists of a bargain hotel portion and a costlier motel part. The hotel is a very relaxed and homey place, not elegant by a long shot, but delightfully friendly. The guest kitchen provides individual lockers for residents' cutlery and crockery. A full-menu breakfast is served—no other meals are served on the premises. The bedrooms are rather narrow and the furnishings old-fashioned. But they include H&C water, bedside lamps, ceiling fans, and wall-to-wall carpets. The motel units have their own toilet and shower, refrigerator, and tea- and coffee-making facilities. The management provides a TV lounge, laundry and ironing facilities, plus breakfast room service. The hotel tariff is $14.50 for singles, $13 per person for doubles. In the motel singles pay $21; doubles, $17.50 per person.

Right in the heart of the city, the **Canberra Hotel,** on Ann Street (tel. 32-0231), is big, busy, and usually swarming with the contents of touring coaches. The building has an old exterior, but surprisingly modern lobby and guest rooms. The lobby is decorated with copper sculptings, elevator service is fast, and the hotel provides a commendable range of guest facilities. There's a TV lounge, a laundry with irons, restaurant, snackbar, and a beautiful dining room. The 300 bedrooms vary considerably in their fittings. Those with private bathroom and TV are priced beyond the budget bracket. But, like its Sydney counterpart, the Brisbane Canberra offers singles at $23 per night and doubles for $32. If you're keen on a central corner location this might be well worth considering.

Serviced Apartments

Brisbane doesn't offer much in this bracket, worse luck. Most of Queensland's serviced flats are concentrated in the beach resort areas, where the tourist trade is thickest. But I did discover one real bargain establishment, the **Dorchester,** 484 Upper Edward St. (tel. 831-2967). The location is fine: within a few walking minutes of the main shopping streets, yet far enough to avoid the traffic noise. It's a small white building housing 12 apartments (flats), each completely private and self-contained. The hallways are quite plain, but the apartments are well maintained and equipped, although not luxurious. Each consists of a bed-sitter, bathroom, and surprisingly spacious kitchen. The management provides power, TV sets, cutlery, crockery, linen, towels, guest laundry, and a *weekly* floor cleaning service. The apartments have two beds (an extra bed or cot can be rented), and a dinette in the kitchen. Off-street parking is available with the accommodation. Furnishings are adequate—you get a dressing table, ward-robes, refrigerator, and a tub as well as shower. The tariff comes to $30 per night for two persons. The truly budget weekly rate is $26 per night for two.

Caravan (Trailer) Parks

Queensland is an ideal state for camping and caravaning and has a lot of facilities catering to both. Brisbane's caravan parks are mostly better situated than those in other capitals, at least as far as proximity is concerned. Those listed below are all within a ten-mile radius of the city center and all feature on-site vans for rent. The rates charged are between $10 and $20 for two people per day. Fees for parking your own van are between $4 and $8 per day. Unfortunately the Brisbane City Council has a ruling banning the erection of tents within a radius of roughly 15 miles around the General Post Office. This does not apply to "lean-tos" or canvas verandas attached to vans. For an excellent and comprehensive guide to Queensland camping grounds, ask for the brochure issued by the Government Tourist Bureau.

Aspley Acres, 1420 Gympie Rd., Aspley (tel. 263-2668).

Carina Caravan Park, 1497 Creek Rd., Carina (tel. 398-3081).

Sheldon Caravan Park, 27 Holmead Rd., Upper Mount Gravatt (tel. 341-6601).

Most of these parks are equipped with hot/cold showers and toilets, a kiosk or store, community laundry, barbecue, and ice dispensers. Some also feature TV lounges and games rooms. Some also provide linen and blankets as part of their van equipment, others charge extra for them. Find out by telephoning beforehand.

MEALS: Brisbane boasts far fewer quality restaurants than Adelaide—which is passing strange because Brisbane is the bigger of the two. Even stranger is the time schedule maintained by many eateries. All over the world the general rule applies that the warmer the climate, the later the dinner hour. But not in Brisbane. Here they've reversed the custom. Blessed with the balmiest weather of any Australian metropolis, they insist on eating *earlier*. Most Queenslanders seem to consider dining around 9 p.m. as vaguely decadent. And visitors willy-nilly must follow suit or risk finding a locked door and dark premises when they arrive for a meal.

While culinary standards are well below those of Melbourne, Sydney, or Adelaide, Brisbane does possess a number of good budget dineries and a couple of outstanding "big splurge" spots. Hotel lunches are mostly excellent as well as cheap. All in all, it's not a bad tucker town if only someone could persuade local restaurateurs to *keep open* longer hours.

Most restaurants are concentrated in two main areas—the city and Forti-tude Valley, just a little hill apart. Why eateries should cluster in a region as unprepossessing as the Valley, I cannot fathom. But this concentration certainly makes eating easier for the tourists. And as is the case throughout Australia today, the selection is lavishly cosmopolitan: from Spanish to Indonesian and points in between.

Lunch and Afternoon Tea

Our first two pubs are both in Fortitude Valley. The **Hacienda,** corner of Brunswick and McLachlan Streets, is a large complex styled à la Mexico which also provides night entertainment. Here we are only concerned with Maria's Room, where a very nice smörgåsbord luncheon can be had for just $5.50. The **Wickham Hotel,** Wickham Street, is an old colonial-style structure, also known for a spot of nightlife. From 11:30 a.m. to 2 p.m., however, you can get superior counter lunches ranging from $3.50 to $5, including rump steak, pork sausages and vegetables, and ham salad.

The ideal place to rest your weary sightseers' feet at a festive afternoon tea is the **Shingle Inn,** 254 Edward St., a beautiful English inn setting with Tudor-style beamed walls, sparkling chandeliers, rich red carpets, and lovely old pieces of pottery. Casement windows with boxes of flowers and greenery, and waitresses dressed like Ruritanian milkmaids enhance the illusion of rusticity in the midst of downtown. The atmosphere is genteel and soothing, the accent on desserts. The inn serves an exceptional lemon meringue pie and waffles with butterscotch sauce and ice cream, both $2.10. Tea comes in old silver pots. This could be a grand spot for after-theater snacks but, alas, closes its handsome doors at 7:30 p.m. sharp. Why?

The **Yorktown Coffee Inn,** 210 Edward St., has a window filled with goodies and a small, dark, handsomely carpeted dinery behind it. The atmosphere is calmly serene, aided by a large English village print on the wall, plus exceptionally comfortable seating facilities. Serves a daily roast joint lunch with vegetables for $5.50. Also very English cakes and scones, accompanied by very un-English (meaning good) coffee. Open Monday through Friday only and shuts at 5:30 p.m. (See what I told you about early closing hereabouts?)

Dinner

In Fortitude Valley, and solidly Italian, is **Giardinetto,** 366 Brunswick St. Popular with the locals, Giardinetto divides its fare between general Italian dishes and pizza, and it's hard to decide which category is better. A small hostelry with kitchen-type chairs, ceramic-topped tables, and latticework strung with bunches of plastic grapes and genuine chianti bottles, it provides a special touch by featuring original paintings by local artists for sale . . . in case you'd like a landscape along with your lasagne. Most of the dishes here come in "large" and "small" orders and you'll need a healthy appetite to polish off the biggies. The chicken milanese costs $8.40, cannelloni and ravioli come at $4.60, and the spaghetti carbonara (bacon-egg) in an immense portion. A dozen varieties of pizza —including a positively poetic combination of ham, salami, mushrooms, mozzarella, capsicum, and garlic covered in tomato sauce—are also offered. Open six nights a week until 10 p.m. Closed Monday.

In the city, the **Venice Restaurant,** 252 George St., must be one of the poshest pizza dispensaries ever built. The front part is highlighted by an illuminated aquarium housing giant gourami (imported from Timor). The rear is all azure carpets and gleaming white table linen. The whole establishment is air-conditioned and lit by soft amber lamps. The windows are decorated with a sterling-silver gondola and batteries of wine bottles. Even the sales counter is carpeted in blue. The Venice offers eight varieties of pizza at surprisingly economical prices—from $4 to $6. Try the calzone, a Neapolitan specialty stuffed with ham and cheese. Open till 9 p.m.

The plain, but very popular, **New Eastern,** 110 Elizabeth St., is a kind of Chinese milk bar with a little dining room two steps up in the rear. A few red lanterns are just about the only decorations inside this most functional of eateries. The fare, however, is both good and ample: for example, the chicken chow mein at $4.20 or an excellent stewed pork in garlic sauce for $5.50. Closed Sunday, but open from 11 a.m. to 9 p.m. other days.

You can have a splurge feast at not too splurgy prices at **Lennon's Hibiscus Room,** Queen Street. The dinery in question is 30 floors up in the sky at the huge Lennons Plaza hotel complex. The fabulous view alone is worth the elevator ride. It's a restaurant of ballroom proportions, tastefully decorated with hanging ferns and oil paintings of blossoms on the walls—hence the name. Thickly carpeted, with bright-red ceilings, the place has a wonderful banqueting air about it, reinforced by orange lights and candle flames. But the main decoration is provided by the food—one of the greatest smörgåsbord spreads in the country, a feast for the eyes as much as the palate. What's more, the people preparing the spread know that a real smörgåsbord isn't just a collection of dishes thrown together more or less at random. They cater to the correct nuances that make it a feast. So start—sparingly—with the cold shrimps and sardines and graduate to the varieties of salami, then to the cold ham, and chicken. Leave plenty of space for the hearty roast beef, the juicy slices of pork (lots of crackling on the plates), baked ham, baked potatoes, corn, carrots, and peas. It won't matter if you can't make it to the desserts, which are rather indifferent. And you can spare yourself the coffee. But the wine list is extensive and you face a choice of 15 brands of beer, including Danish, Irish, and German. During the week the smörgåsbord is strictly a lunchtime treat, from noon till 2 p.m. But on Sunday it's on from 5:30 to 8 p.m. The inclusive price is $15, with children paying $7.

Jimmy's on the Mall. There may be some confusion here because there are actually *two* Jimmy's, at opposite ends of the beautiful and brand-spanking-new City Mall (Queen Street). The second specializes in crêpes and other light victuals. It's the first we're talking about. An outdoor-indoor dinery with smart marble-topped tables sheltered by (purely ornamental) umbrellas, Jimmy's is a patch of transplanted Paris set amid Brisbane's busiest shopping bustle. Potted plants sprinkled among the tables make for greenery. Apart from the shopping throngs, you can watch live crabs wandering around their tanks before they make the menu. The atmosphere is delightful and the fare amazingly varied and cheap: fettuccine carbonara for $4.40 or Chinese roast duck for $7.90, as well as lasagne, spring rolls, or seafood. The place is licensed for wines and liqueurs, and stays open till midnight seven nights a week.

The **Cathay,** 222 Wickham St., Fortitude Valley, is divided into an economy downstairs and a considerably pricier upstairs portion. This is one of the local favorites and mostly packed. The menu features about 100 dishes, a quarter Australian, the rest Chinese. The restaurant is air-conditioned and fully licensed and stays open until after 11 p.m. weeknights and 10 p.m. on Sunday. You eat in intimate little booths, listen to unobtrusive piped-in music and admire the gold wallpaper. I had a tasty pork and sweet corn soup, followed by soya chicken—total, $7.90. The steak dishes on the Australian menu are among the best in town.

Another late closer—and one of the most charming eateries in the state—is the **Tortilla,** 26 Elizabeth Arcade, off Charlotte Street, and right opposite the Festival Hall. An altogether delightful melange of Spanish and Mexican decor as well as cuisine, the Tortilla has whitewashed walls decorated with bullfight posters, bull's horns, and matador swords. Wagon wheels serve as chandeliers, tables and chairs are heavy darkwood, and there's a dining alcove upstairs from which to view the scene below. For once even the music is right—Spanish and

Latin American themes instead of the irrelevant pop most restaurants insist on regaling you with. A bustling, happy place, especially late in the evening after the theaters close—this being one of the very few spots where you can eat after a show at reasonable prices. Tacos cost $1.95, enchiladas (a kind of Mexican minimeal), $6.95; and the pollo, toro, or pesedos (chicken, beef, or seafood), $4.95. Do leave room for a luscious dessert called Fiesta—a concoction of grilled bananas, walnuts, and maple syrup rolled inside a pancake. Open till midnight.

DAYTIME ACTIVITIES: The **City Hall,** King George Square, is one of Brisbane's showpieces. It contains art collections as well as the Tower Lookout (above the clock) which you reach by elevator. Conducted tours for groups can be arranged by phoning 225-4360.

Just across Victoria Bridge rises the **Performing Arts Complex,** Brisbane's new and most impressive theatrical edifice. The gleaming cultural giant contains three world standard theaters, each one designed for excellent accoustics and maximum audience comfort. The vast foyers fulfill a dual role as art galleries, decorated with changing exhibitions and also offering magnificent views of the Brisbane River and the city. If you can't see a performance there, do take one of the conducted tours of the place proceeding hourly from 10 a.m. to 4 p.m. Monday through Saturday. They cost $2.50 for adults, $1.50 for children.

Queensland Aboriginal Creations, 135 George St., is the curio section of the Department of Aboriginal and Islanders Advancement. It offers a fascinating display of tribal masks, weapons, fire sticks, and the strange musical instruments known as "bullroarers." Also bark paintings, oils, and pencil sketches, some of them outstanding. The artworks shown are for sale. Hours are 9 a.m. to 4:30 p.m. Monday to Friday.

The **Observatory,** Wickham Terrace, was originally built by convicts as a windmill. But the sails couldn't be made to operate, so the structure was converted into a (man-propelled) treadmill. Later it became a meteorological station and still later a test lab for television experiments. In 1934, the first picture ever televised in Australia was the image of the Observatory, transmitted to Ipswich over 20 miles away.

A must for American visitors is the memorial titled *They Passed This Way.* Located at Lyndon B. Johnson Place, Newstead Park, it was erected by the people of Queensland as a tribute to the U.S.A. During the Pacific crisis stage of World War II, General MacArthur made his headquarters in Brisbane.

The **Queensland Art Gallery,** South Bank, South Brisbane, houses a good collection of Australian contemporary painters and an excellent Picasso. Open seven days a week till 5 p.m. **Newstead House,** Newstead Park, Breakfast Creek Road, is Brisbane's oldest historical building. On display are relics from the early colonial settlers' days and the residence itself is a museum. Open Monday to Thursday from 11 a.m. to 3 p.m., on Sunday from 2 to 5 p.m. Closed Saturday. Admission is by donation.

The Tourist Bureau has compiled an informative brochure, "Travel Through History," which you can use as a guide to historic sites and buildings throughout Queensland.

Mount Coot-tha Forest Park is a miniature nature reserve right in the center of a metropolis (the entrance on Mount Coot-tha Road lies only about four miles from the GPO), a wonderful lofty oasis of towering eucalyptus, tropical shrubs, and millions of birds. Within this complex stretch the new landscaped Botanical Gardens, plus an adjoining park with picnic grounds, barbecues, and a series of cascades. Carefully graded walking tracks snake through the entire area and strategically placed gaps in the timber provide constantly changing views of the city, suburbs, distant mountains, and the sea.

Also at Mount Coot-tha is the **Sir Thomas Brisbane Planetarium,** largest of its kind in Australia, seating 144 people and featuring a regular observatory. General programs dealing with the enthralling movements of the cosmos are staged at the Star Theatre Wednesday through Sunday twice or three times daily. The observatory houses an excellent 150-millimeter refracting telescope available for public use on a booking basis. Visitors should phone 377-5896 for bookings.

Metropolitan Brisbane has no beaches, but a string of superlative swimming pools instead. For anyone accustomed to the dreary municipal pools of America, these are eye-openers. The Centenary Pool, Gregory Terrace, the Oasis, and the Acacia Tourist Garden at Sunnybank are deep blue, fringed with palms and shrubs, and surrounded by vast lawns and flower beds.

Two of Brisbane's top attractions lie a short way out of town. **Lone Pine Sanctuary,** Fig Tree Pocket, is a 15-minute drive west of the city. This was the first koala sanctuary established in Australia and now has a colony of around 100 of these cuddlies. The welcoming committee consists of a koala named Jockey riding on the back of a patient German shepherd. There's a photographer on the grounds to snap you and yours with one of the live teddy bears in your arm. But koalas are merely part of Lone Pine's charms. The sanctuary on the banks of the Brisbane River houses a large cross section of Australian fauna, including kangaroos and emus you can feed by hand. Others you certainly can't— Queensland pythons, Tasmanian devils, and dingoes, or the freshwater crocodiles from the Northern Territory, for instance. The platypus can be seen guzzling its enormous meals of worms and tadpoles daily from 3 to 4 p.m. The layout is beautiful and includes barbecue and picnic areas, and there's a special lecture spot where you can learn a lot about koalas from someone who knows.

You can ride the seven miles to Lone Pine by bus. Catch it on Adelaide Street. But it's more fun to take the 14-mile route by river ferry. The launch leaves **Hayles Wharf,** at North Quay, daily at 1:30 p.m. Chugging leisurely down the Brisbane you get a running commentary on the various features of the river and developments on the banks. The return trip leaves 2¼ hours later. Round-trip tickets cost $9 for adults, $4 for children.

Bunya Park, Bunya Park Drive, about ten miles from the city, is another outstanding sanctuary for wildlife, consisting of natural bushland surrounding an artificial lake. You can move freely among the birds and animals. The park is designed around a "bush walk" leading through various reserves where the inhabitants live as similarly as possible to their natural habitats. Kangaroos to koalas, wedgetailed eagles to wombats—all ready for your camera. For the kids (all ages) there's a Fairy Tale Mini Zoo, featuring swarms of small pettables. Bunya Park also boasts a highly ingenious maze (or labyrinth) which pits a tricky design against your scouting skill. The object is to find the mythical monster of Aboriginal folklore, the "Bunyip," and it takes considerable figuring before you finally confront it. You can score your rating in maze travel and compare your points to others. The park is open seven days a week, 9 a.m. to 5 p.m. Admission is $7 for adults, half price for children.

Sightseeing Tours

Ansett Pioneer, 16 Ann St. (tel. 226-1184), operates a coach tour of the city and surroundings, departing at 9 a.m. and returning at 12:30 p.m. The jaunt takes in most of the municipal sights, then goes out to Mount Coot-tha lookout and on to the Lone Pine Koala Sanctuary. The tour runs Monday and Thursday, and costs $12 for adults, half price for children. Entry fee not included.

Boomerang Tours, 186 Ann St. (tel. 221-9922), offers a full-day excursion to the subtropical beauties of Mount Tamborine, including jungle walks, waterfalls, and panoramic views of the Gold Coast. It departs at 9:30 a.m. and returns at 5:30 p.m. Cost is $17.

Scenic Tours, 72 Newmarket Rd., Windsor (tel. 57-5610), has a Jungle Day Tour going to Lamington National Park, 72 miles from Brisbane. You visit a magnificent rain forest with hanging gardens of orchids and ferns, hand-feed tropical birds, watch whip-tail kangaroos in their mountain habitat, and walk through an orchid sanctuary with thousands of native orchids. Tours leave 9:30 a.m. every Tuesday, Thursday, and Sunday from the Greyhound Coach Terminal, returning at 6 p.m. Cost is $22.

City Explorer Tours (tel. 341-4866) operates an hourly coach that stops at most of Brisbane's tourist attractions. For $8, half for children, you can ride it all day, getting off at whatever point holds your interest, then boarding the next coach arriving an hour later. You can buy the tickets on the coach or from the Government Travel Centre.

Bay and River Cruises

The Brisbane Paddlewheeler is a 62-ton sternwheeler with twin funnels, built like a Mississippi showboat and filling much the same function. Every Sunday it goes on a Jazz Cruise, when the throb of the giant paddles mingles with the blare of New Orleans brass. The cruise costs $14.50. Alternatively there are Party Nights, with disco dancing on a large floor in the moonlight, costing $18.50. For information ring 246-1713.

Golden Miles Ferry Service, Creek Street Ferry Terminal (tel. 399-5054), lets you see Brisbane from the river, chugging past parks, stately homes, and the naval base. Trips depart daily (except Sunday) from the Creek Street Terminal opposite the A.M.P. Building, and cost $1.40 for adults, half for children.

AFTER DARK: Brisbane's movie scene is rather handicapped by a frenetic local censorship, snipping cutting shears with far more enthusiasm than finesse. But the city has good live theater, both professional and amateur. The best is probably the **S.G.I.O. Theatre,** Turbot Street, the luxuriously appointed home of the Queensland State Theatre Company, which puts on anything from Broadway comedies to contemporary Australian drama. The **Brisbane Art Theatre,** 210 Petrie Terrace, and **La Boîte,** 57 Hale St., are fine amateur stages and cheaper than their professional brethren. The **Festival Hall,** Charlotte Street, while modest compared to its Adelaide counterpart, presents leading imported and local talent. During my visit the guest stars were the London Festival Ballet with Rudolph Nureyev; also featured are gymnastics, ballroom dancing, boxing, etc. Check the newspapers for who's appearing in what and where.

Nightlife is decidedly limited, but not as severely as scoffers from other states like to pretend. Brisbane has several pleasant theater restaurants. One of them, **Dirty Dick's,** at the corner of Judge and Weetman Streets, is another of the wonderful chain of Elizabethan spoof spots you'll find represented in most Australian capitals. It puts on medieval (sort of) fun, food, and drollery six nights a week and charges $20 per reveler, lavish feast included.

There's quite a healthy crop of discos in town, several of them stomping till one or three in the morning. One of the late-closers is **Pip's,** 74 Elizabeth St., which goes from Tuesday to Saturday. **General Jackson's,** at the Crest International Hotel, King George Square, runs Wednesday to Saturday till 3 a.m.

Wilson's 1870, 103 Queen St., is a gorgeous subterranean vault of Victoriana and triples as a restaurant, cocktail bar, and dance spot. The whole sumptuous conglomeration is a study in scarlet plush, gold fittings, and black leather. Bands and entertainment vary, but there's always a pianist tinkling the keys while patrons tinkle their glasses, and dancing nightly.

Henry Africa's, part of the vast Melbourne Hotel, Browning Street, South Brisbane, doubles as a self-service steakhouse and entertainment center. The steaks are excellent, serving yourself keeps the cost moderate, and the entertainment caters to virtually all tastes, depending which night you pick. It's jazz rock on Wednesday, Dixieland jazz on Friday, and country and western on Saturday. On *some* Thursdays there's an Adult Disco in action as well. The same complex also houses an intimate and elegant little piano bar called **Clancy's,** in case you want to slip away from the madding throngs of the steakery.

There's quite a lot doing in the rock, jazz, and folk fields. The **Hacienda Hotel,** at the corner of Brunswick and McLachlan Streets (see lunch section), features rock six nights a week, as does the **Sunnybank Hotel,** Mains Road, Sunnybank. The **Majestic Hotel,** 382 George St., reserves the acid blasts for Friday and Saturday nights. On Wednesday and Thursday the attraction is a folk singer. The hotel's Bull & Bear bar, incidentally, is a beautiful English pub-style watering hole, with old horse brasses hung on wood pillars and an atmosphere as mellow as dark ale. None of these rock pubs has a cover charge and drinks come at bar prices. And there's more jazz Thursday and Saturday night at the **Adventurers Club,** 1 Annie St., Kangaroo Point, currently the stomping ground of the Brisbane Jazz Club. Also folk music, parties, films, etc., five nights a week. The Adventurers is a genuine club, organizing hikes, climbs, campouts, and safaris for its members. But these night events are open to all comers.

Sibyl's, 383 Adelaide St., is another entertainment center providing a happy melange of dineries, drinkeries, and danceries. You get a locally celebrated DJ in one room, a piano bar cum restaurant in a second, and a bar with musical entertainment in the third. Supper and dancing till 3 a.m. Wednesday through Saturday. There's also an "adult disco"—meaning for over-25s.

Finally we have **Lennon's Hotel,** 66 Queen St. (see the dining section), featuring a changing lineup of guitarists, pianists, vocalists, and combos in its Hibiscus Room and Matilda's Restaurant Monday through Saturday.

SPECIAL EVENTS: Warana is an Aboriginal word meaning "blue skies" and

has been given to the annual spring festival held late September/early October. Although Brisbane's sky is blue most of the year anyway, the town takes on a carnival hue for the occasion. Huge street processions with floats and clowns, dancing in the squares, a riverside Mardi Gras, beauty competitions, pop bands, symphony concerts, art exhibitions, an international pageant . . . it all happens in the week of "Warana." If you're lucky enough to be in town then, you'll find the people at their happiest—the hotels at their fullest.

USEFUL INFORMATION: The Queensland Government Travel Centre, cen-

trally located at the corner of Adelaide and Edward Streets (tel. 31-2211), has full free-of-charge travel, accommodation, and tour-booking service. . . . For information on current activities in town, consult *This Week in Brisbane,* free from the Travel Centre. The *Courier Mail* and *Telegraph* give a good roundup of nighttime doings. . . . **Central Railway Station** is on Ann Street, near Anzac Square. Phone 225-0211 for information.

Heading south toward the Gold Coast, some 15 miles down the main highway, you reach **Pioneer Valley Park,** Beenleigh Road, Kuraby, which has the world's largest collection of horse-drawn vehicles on display, plus an awesome array of old coach lanterns, bridles, harnesses, and pioneer tools. You can also go on steam train rides, buggy rides, hay rides, horse rides, and canoe rides.

On Pacific Highway, 23 miles south of Brisbane, lies **Bullens Lion Safari.** An Australian bushland setting rather incongruously contains swarms of live lions, strolling, snoozing, and inspecting visitors (through the car windows).

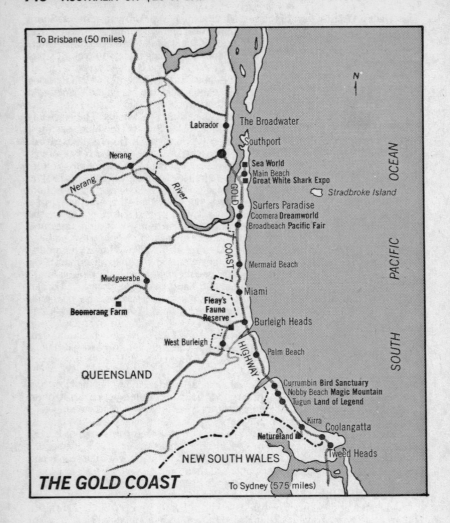

To Brisbane (50 miles)

N

Labrador

The Broadwater

Southport

Nerang

Sea World
Main Beach
Great White Shark Expo

Nerang River

Stradbroke Island

GOLD

Surfers Paradise
Coomera Dreamworld
Broadbeach Pacific Fair

OCEAN

PACIFIC

COAST

Mermaid Beach

Mudgeeraba

Miami

Boomerang Farm

Fleay's
Fauna
Reserve

Burleigh Heads

West Burleigh

SOUTH

HIGHWAY

Palm Beach

QUEENSLAND

Currumbin Bird Sanctuary
Nobby Beach Magic Mountain
Tugun Land of Legend

Kirra
Coolangatta

Natureland

Tweed Heads

NEW SOUTH WALES

THE GOLD COAST

To Sydney (575 miles)

You drive right among them, after being firmly advised *not* to roll down a window. An enclosure houses leopards, bears, and tigers. There's also an animal nursery and a delightful pet corner. Feeding time for the big 'uns is 1:30 p.m. weekdays, 11:30 a.m. and 2:30 p.m. weekends. Admission for adults is $6, half price for children.

2. The Gold Coast

Southeast of Brisbane, along the surf-wreathed beaches of the warm Pacific, lies Australia's premier tourist resort: the **Gold Coast.** I use the singular sense deliberately because the entire 20-mile chain of beach resorts is technically *one* town, with one mayor—even though it keeps changing its name every few miles.

The Gold Coast starts at **Southport** and runs all the way past **Coolangatta** and across the New South Wales state border to **Tweed Heads.**

In practice the resort consists of a dozen or so small townships, with **Surfers Paradise** as unofficial capital. But because of its status as a single entity, I'll treat it as such in this chapter.

The native population of the Gold Coast is only around 220,000, but during holiday seasons this swells to well over two million and "natives" become as hard to find as the proverbial needles in haystacks. The reasons are obvious: idyllic climate, perfect beaches, warm water, magnificent surf, and, as a backdrop, some of the most spectacular mountain scenery in Australia, the **Mac-Pherson Ranges.** A bunch of very astute entrepreneurs have wrapped all these natural advantages into one big glittering tourist package, expertly gauged for mass appeal, backed by a year-round publicity campaign that generates ever-bigger throngs of visitors and a permanent air of expansion.

The Gold Coast is such a perfect replica of Miami Beach that you couldn't tell the two apart until you heard the prevailing accents. The same high-rise hotels and apartment blocks fronting the ocean, the same aromatic melange of saltwater air, gasoline fumes, frying hamburgers, and sizzling suntan lotion; the same din of car engines, outboard motors, screeching transistors, and whooping beach crowds; the same dazzle of neons when velvety darkness descends. If you like Miami, you'll love the Gold Coast. If you don't . . . well, skip the rest of this chapter.

There are, of course, variations within the area. Surfers Paradise is simultaneously the largest, flashiest, noisiest, and liveliest resort. Coolangatta comes on like a poorer and more subdued relative. And in between you can find some fairly peaceful and serene ocean spots (although peace and serenity are *not* what the tourists come here for). There are also decided advantages for the budget traveler. Because local competition is fierce, the region offers an astonishing number of economy lodgings, eateries, and entertainment spots, most of them giving very good value for their prices. Nightlife, furthermore, is plentiful and not expensive. And the glorious beaches are free—the Gold Coast has not copied the pernicious Riviera custom of allocating choice strips of sand to the luxury hotels. But why, oh why, are they studded with loudspeakers pouring an incessant barrage of pop music and godawful commercials over their captive audience?

More serious than this sound pollution is the threat of an increasingly solid row of high-rises blocking off the Surfers Paradise beach. The shadows they cast over the sand by mid-afternoon are forcing sunbathers to keep moving in order to catch whatever rays manage to streak between the buildings. When the gaps are filled by new constructions, there won't *be* any sun patches from, say, 4 p.m. on. A very effective method of killing the goose that's been laying a lot of golden eggs.

GETTING AROUND: Gold Coast transportation is generally first rate: direct air service from Sydney to Coolangatta; direct bus service from Brisbane, and regular service between all points along the coast and to most of the attractions. (Miami, please copy.) On top of that all Brisbane touring companies feature a Gold Coast excursion on their agendas. **Greyhound** buses (tel. 44-7144) operate from Brisbane ten times a day. The trip costs $8.10 to Southport, Surfers Paradise, or Coolangatta. **Surfside** provides local bus service on the coast. For information on schedules, phone 36-2449.

You can rent bicycles (solo or tandems) all over the coast. **Holiday Car Rental,** at the corner of Cavill Avenue and the Esplanade, Surfers, has them from $2.50 an hour upward. There's also a local specialty called **Silly Sycles,** rentable at **Tony McDonald,** 3102 Gold Coast Hwy., Surfers. These contraptions—three-wheel affairs with two sets of pedals and a sunshade overhead—do indeed look rather silly, but they're great for rolling around and will hold three people.

ACCOMMODATIONS: This is the gilt on the Gold Coast gingerbread, the benefit you get from overcommercialization. The coast lives and breathes tourists and has the facilities to put them up and bed them down in every notch of the price scale. Let's start with the most central and busiest hostelry of the entire region, the **Hub,** Cavill Avenue, Surfers (tel. 31-5559). These are serviced motel apartments built into a shopping arcade, which puts everything you may need within arm's reach, so to speak: stores, cafés, and restaurants right, left, and below, plus the crowds that go with them. The beach runs a few yards from your apartment. The units are small, ultramodern, done out in standard motel style, but with every facility. Your own balcony, bathroom, and refrigerator, food-cocktail bar, TV, electric toaster and jug, cutlery, crockery, plus a laundry on the premises. Fluorescent lights on the ceiling, individual bedside lamps, and wall-to-wall carpeting . . . this is utility plus. The rate structure has the typical resort pattern. There's a general rate of $24 for single, $15 per person for multiple occupancy; a holiday rate of $24 per person for multiples, and a still higher rate for extra-special holidays like Christmas and Easter. My advice is to stay away from the Gold Coast during the latter periods.

There's nothing either Hawaiian or villagey about the **Hawaiian Village,** 11 Cavill Ave. (tel. 31-7126). Located in a bustling shopping mall (no motor traffic), this place boasts its own 50-foot swimming pool although the beach is within shouting distance. It's a pretty pastel-hued building, the hallway hung with ferns and tropical plants, a sundeck with colored umbrellas running along both floors. The 19 units are self-contained, each with fridge, TV, compact bathroom, tea- and coffee-making facilities, and fluorescent lights. The fittings are standard, the rooms medium-size, wallpapered in an attractive art nouveau theme, the carpeting deep blue. Fair-size wardrobes and extra luggage shelves help to create elbow space. Singles cost $22, doubles run $28, and if you book for seven nights or over the rates drop by $2 per night.

It's easy to miss the **Paradise Springs Motel,** 3204 Gold Coast Hwy. (tel. 31-5004), which would be a pity because it's one of the nicest spots in its price range. The entrance is a narrow driveway next to the Commonwealth Bank, but once you get in you're in a secluded tropical garden, away from traffic sounds. Most of the 18 units are on level ground and have sliding glass doors leading to the garden, sundeck, and pool. (The beach is only a couple of blocks away.) The rooms are quite charming, quite large, and very modern. All have private bathroom, kitchen sink, dining table and chairs, refrigerator, full kitchen utensils, TV, and ceiling fans, plus fluorescent lights as well as individual bedside lamps and delightfully spacious wardrobes. The daily tariff runs $28 single and $42 double in season; $20 single and $26 double off-season.

Coral Sun Motel, 3360 Gold Coast Highway (tel. 39-9414) is an oddly Alpine-looking building with a lemon-hued frontage and two swimming pools. All of the 25 units come with fridge, color TV, shower and toilet, but no telephone. The rooms are fairly large, bright, airy and nicely carpeted, though sparsely furnished and illuminated only by ceiling lights. Breakfast (the only meal served) arrives at your room. Guest laundry available. The tariff is a uniform $20 for singles or doubles, rising slightly during school holidays.

Chelsea Motor Inn, 2990 Gold Coast Hwy. (tel. 38-9333). A low-slung beige structure with a small pool in front, flanked by young palm trees plus several umbrella-shaded tables. Has 17 nicely furnished and well-equipped units, nine air-conditioned, the others with ceiling fans. All with private bathroom, large sliding-door wardrobes, fridge, writing desk, color TV, and telephone. Heavy blinds ward off the sun, there's plenty of drawer space and the bathrooms have large enough sink surfaces for *all* your toilet utensils. You get tea/coffee making equipment, a laundry on the premises, and breakfast in your room if desired. For singles and one-nighters the Chelsea is above our budget bracket at $30 per night. But it's a bargain for two persons staying a minimum of a week, for then the tariff drops to $30 for *two*.

Heading south along the Gold Coast Highway you come into the "frontier region" between Queensland and New South Wales. The state border, in fact, runs through the highway, dividing what is practically the same town into Coolangatta, Queensland, and **Tweed Heads**, N.S.W. Luckily you don't need a passport to walk across the road. These resorts are considerably quieter than Surfers Paradise, boasting neither the bustle nor the nightlife of their hedonistic sister. They are also cheaper, both in the food and the lodging department. You get a few old-style bed-and-breakfast places, a commodity that seems to have become extinct in the flashier north.

The Coolangatta budget market is dominated by the **Pacific Village Hotel**, 88 Marine Parade (tel. 36-2733). A huge, cut-price fun factory, this attractive three-wing complex has its own entertainment and touring organization and provides maximum facilities at minimum rates on a conveyor-belt system, a definite budget bonanza for those who don't mind a little regimentation. While overlooking the ocean, the hotel has a 50-foot swimming pool with tiers of sun-decks arranged around it. The units are simple, small, and marvels of compactness. Each has a private balcony overlooking pool and beach, also shower and toilet, ceiling fan, piped music, refrigerator, tea- and coffee-making facilities, and a radio. The hotel puts on gala dances with a house band, costume parties, and sightseeing trips. There's a licensed bar and disco on the premises as well as a games room, color TVs in all units, restaurant, sauna, and a charcoal grill. Notice boards in the lobby announce the welter of activities, and special photo boards display the snaps taken of the participants. It's go-go-go all the way, from Hawaiian nights to Change of Sex nights to Western nights to cruises, tropical tours, disco dances, cabaret visits, and what-have-you. The tariff structure is unusual, insofar as all rates include *full board*—simple fare, but plenty of it. Normal rates run at $32 a night, rising to $36 during the Christmas/January period.

Overlooking Greenmount Beach, the **Bahamas**, 7 Hill St. (tel. 36-1824), is a tropical two-story structure with a sheltering two-level veranda partly hidden behind lush greenery. The rooms are suitably large and airy, equipped with shower and toilet, fridge, fan, toaster, color TV, and electric jug. Breakfast, included in the tariff, is "tropical" and served in the rooms. Wall-to-wall carpeting, individual reading lamps, ample wardrobe space, and first-class foam mattresses provide comfort. Rates are $30 for singles, $40 for double rooms.

The **Queensland Hotel**, Boundary Street (tel. 362-600), is a modern two-story brick affair with lots of bar facilities and 23 bedrooms. Also one of the best and cheapest eateries in town (see our food section). There are two bars, a very attractive TV lounge with ultra-comfortable armchairs, a restaurant, pool tables, and a weekend disco with live entertainers. Most of the rooms come with H&C handbasin only. But all of them are neatly compact, nicely furnished in lightwood, and equipped with bedside mirror tables, wall-to-wall carpeting, fluorescent lighting, good-size wardrobes, and springy new beds. Rates here include a full breakfast (nothing "continental" about it) and are a standard $20 per person.

The **Bombora Holiday Lodge**, Marine Parade (tel. 36-1888), is a brightly modern and very lively place—an excellent budget bet for *two* persons. Entertainment laid on: swimming pool, a games room with pinball machine, jukebox and pool table, color TV in the lounge, and a round of organized social activities. Monday night it's a get-together poolside barbecue; in daytime, scenic outings in the "Bombora Buzzabout" (a small white bus)—visits to cabarets and social clubs and a tropical tour of the hinterland. The 45 units have showers and toilets, wide beds, radios, fans, tea-making equipment, overhead and bedside lights—everything in utilitarian motel style. There's a separate pavilion housing the restaurant and a wonderful abundance of patios, balconies, deck-chairs, awnings, and sun umbrellas. The tariff is full board—meaning a large Australian breakfast and three-course dinner—and a free breakfast for all backpack travelers. All meals are served in the extremely comfortable restaurant. The rate comes to $27 a day in shared accommodations, rising to $32 at Christmas and Easter. The Bombora also offers a ten-day holiday package (including three days of scenic touring and two nights out in the local fun spots) for $28 a day.

Also in Coolangatta is the atmospheric **Grand Hotel,** 107 Griffith St. (tel. 36-3477), a lovely old white building, vaguely Spanish in design, with a beer garden, beautiful old trees, lawns, and a fountain. The setting is rather old-fashioned, but charmingly Mediterranean, and the hotel counter lunches are famous: half a chicken with salad and chips for just $3. The dining room is sumptuous and the tariff here includes breakfast: singles pay $20; doubles, $34.

Across the border in Tweed Heads lies the **Whitehall Lodge,** Stuart Street (tel. 36-3233), a quiet little hotel on the fringe of the Gold Coast, but only a few blocks away from the ocean. The lodge is a modern beige brick structure fronted by a small garden with shrubs and multicolored umbrellas. If you don't care about a private shower or toilet, this is one of the best bargains in the area. There's a bright and airy guest lounge with color TV and an adjoining games room with a dart board. Also nine immaculately kept public bathrooms. The bedrooms have tea- and coffee-making facilities, good carpets, and excellent beds. Above all, they're quiet. Rates here include either breakfast or full board—that is, dinner as well. All meals are taken in the adjacent restaurant, the **Cartwheel** (see our dining section). Bed and breakfast are $17 a head.

Serviced Apartments

Holiday apartments on the Gold Coast may be either completely independent units or parts of a motel. Either way they're usually superior to their big-city equivalents (newer furniture and better facilities) and can be ideal, pricewise, for two or more people, but not so hot for singles.

The **Jolimont,** 8 View Ave., Surfers Paradise (tel. 31-7812), is a small block of four flats, with a pool and sundecks in front and a shaded veranda upstairs. A modern yellow-brick building (the flats are soundproof), it lies 150 yards from the surf, surrounded by a lush lawn setting, one street away from the main shopping area. Two of the apartments have two bedrooms, two have one. All come with screened windows, sliding drapes opening on balconies, tiled bathroom, and fully equipped electric kitchen (cutlery and crockery for four persons). Carpeting and furnishings are good and quite ample for four. And you'll appreciate the ironing board that's part of the household gear. Lettings are for a minimum of one week and start at $150 per week for the smaller apartments.

The **Rex Motel,** 106 Marine Parade, Coolangatta (tel. 36-2175), is an attractively modern place with a front veranda and large sheltering eaves. The owners offer accommodations by the day as well as for longer periods. The 12 units have ample breathing space for three or four persons—the balconies with tables and chairs provide something like an extra room. Although the apartments are completely self-contained you also have the option of having break-fast (hot) served to your doorstep. Each apartment has shower and toilet, color TV, fair wardrobe space, refrigerator, ceiling fan, and kitchen with electric frying pan, jug, toaster, stainless-steel sink, etc. Full sets of linen, cutlery, and crockery are supplied. The rates, which include continental breakfast, are $25 a day for singles, $30 for doubles.

A Hostel

Although quite unconnected with the official AYHA chain, the **Back-packers Inn,** 45 McLean St., Coolangatta (tel. 36-2422), is among the best of its breed. At least it's the only hostel I've ever found that has a licensed restaurant and bar on the premises. Located in a beautiful mansion-like building atop a slight hill, surrounded by lawns and two minutes from downtown and the beach, the inn/hostel has 65 beds in twin or double rooms (no dormitories), an excellent music system, TV lounge and barbecue facilities. The rooms are airy and rather nicely furnished, the restaurant provides economy-priced breakfasts and dinners seven days a week, and the obligatory bed sheets can be hired. Rates run to $6.75 per person, and for that you get international telephone service as well.

Caravan (Trailer) Parks

With an ideal camping climate, it's not surprising that the Gold Coast abounds in caravan parks. Not all of them, however, rent on-site vans (known as fixed vans hereabouts) and only some offer tent facilities. All the places listed below provide on-site vans at about $15 to $19 per night for two persons, but you'd better call to inquire about tenting, since that situation seems to change rather rapidly.

Florida Car-O-Tel, Redondo Avenue, Miami (tel. 35-3111). H&C showers, laundry facilities, restaurant, two swimming pools, TV rooms, squash court.

Gold Coast, Gold Coast Highway, Palm Beach (tel. 34-2290). H&C showers and baths, laundry facilities.

Border Caravan Park, Boundary Street, Tweed Heads (tel. 36-3134). H&C showers, laundry and ironing facilities, store opposite.

MEALS: The Gold Coast culinary scene has been described as "wall-to-wall junk food," which is reasonably accurate but only partly so. There is, indeed, such a super-abundance of "snackeries" that at first glance you get the impression that they've muscled out every other form of nourishment. Luckily t'ain't so. In between and behind and around the serried ranks of hot dogs, hamburgers, pies, and french fries you'll find a goodly sprinkling of restaurants serving food fit for folks who have not had their taste buds lobotomized. Some, in fact, are downright excellent, although they take a bit of tracking. The following survey is aimed at easing that task.

In Surfers Paradise the **Billabong,** Gold Coast Highway, opposite Cypress Avenue, has an unusual layout: a small kitchen kiosk in the center with garden tables or sheltered booths all around. You collect your meal at the kiosk and take it to whichever open or enclosed eating spot you choose in the palm- and gumtree-shaded garden. You can spot this hostelry by the flaring gas torches flanking the iron gateway. Hitching posts for your horses are provided inside. (What, you *walked* in? Never heard of anything so outlandish.) T-bone steak and chips is $4.90. Open daily from noon to midnight.

The **Springfield,** 44 Cavill Ave., looks like a whitewashed cellar on level ground, with the entire decor kept in red and white to produce a candy-cane effect—white brick walls and arches, white ceilings with red beams. The place consists of two small, brightly lit rooms filled with white garden tables and wrought-iron chairs against a background of red curtains. The only Chinese touches are supplied by tassled lanterns. This is a BYO that also serves good cappuccino. Sweet-and-sour pork goes for $5.60, braised chicken and almonds for $6.50. Open seven nights a week till 10 p.m.

The **Crêperie,** St. Tropez, Orchid Avenue, cooks French crêpes while you watch. Take them away or eat them there—but you must BYO if you want the appropriate liquid with them. There are 39 fillings to choose from, from chicken and mushroom to Tia Maria. These are genuine Brittany crêpes, not the leathery imitations you get at so many places. The menu obligingly tells you the proper pronunciation of crêpes—it's "crayp." They cost from $4.50 to $6.90.

Cherry's, 4 Orchid Ave., specializes in chicken dinners at the bargain rate of $4.50 each. A small, plastic, spotless place, appealingly colored black and red, with a rose on each plastic tabletop as a touch of charm. One wall has a huge mirror in which you can watch yourself gnawing drumsticks. The chicken portions come with roast potatoes, vegetables and bread. If you don't fancy roast fowl you can order it "paradise," meaning crumbed. Open till 9 p.m., all week.

Schnitzel House, 23 Elkhorn Ave. Another specialty spot, specializing in guess what. Small and very cozy, with three rows of highly polished wooden peasant chairs and tables, village-style windows with white lace curtains, ornamental brasses on the walls and potted creepers on the ceiling. The decor is just rustic enough without being intrusive and the menu wishes you a polite "Guten Appetit." All dishes here cost $8.95, and the schnitzels come in eight varieties; from Hunter (with mushrooms) to paprika (in paprika sauce). There's a separate blackboard on which the going desserts are chalked—actually called that instead of the indigenous term "sweets." These include a quite un-Germanic and outstanding banana crêpe. Likewise outstanding is the homemade chicken liver pâté. Open till 9:30 six nights a week. Closed Sundays.

La Rustica, 3118 Gold Coast Hwy., comes as close to Italian rusticality as a relatively new establishment can. With cool tile floors, bare lightwood tables, wood-paneled walls decorated with prints, guitars, and wine bottles, and charmingly personalized service, the place is a leisurely haven in the fast-food hurricane raging all around. Although it doubles as a pizzeria, the accent is on the Italian main courses, most of them outstanding. You can't go wrong with the scaloppine al vino or marsala, tenderly cooked in wine sauce, concluded with superb homemade gelati. The meal will cost you $11, but if you stick to the pasta plates you'll get by on $8. Open till 10 p.m. all week.

Down in Coolangatta gastronomics are less varied but cheaper. The **Queensland Hotel,** Boundary Street, is *the* economy eating spot hereabouts. Servings are divided into "full" and "half"—a full serving of roast beef, fish, or goulash costs $3.30, and the half costs half that. And the halves, believe me, make a full meal.

Higher up on the atmosphere and price scale is **Markwells,** 64 Griffith St. The downstairs portion (upstairs it's costlier) resembles a fisherman's shack (or should it be fisherperson?). Anyway, it has a low beamed roof, wooden tables and chairs, and fishing nets hanging from the ceiling. The centerpiece is a huge sea aquarium with a moray eel. The establishment slogan runs "Straight from the Sea to You," and you can taste the truth of it. Ordering is a wee bit complicated: you give your order at one end, sit down until your number is called, then collect your victuals together with cutlery and condiments. But the place is air-conditioned and licensed *or* BYO, so you can choose. The menu, chalked on a blackboard, requires a lot of chalk. For starters try the tangy seafood mini rolls with plum sauce for $3.90. As a main course, try the catch of the day. In my case it was filets of flathead, which came with french fries and salad, plus tea or coffee —the whole for $8.80. The place is open seven days a week till 9:30 p.m.

Over to the **Cartwheel Restaurant,** Stuart Street, Tweed Heads. Good, cozy, and inexpensive but slightly out of the way, at least by Coolangatta standards. The place is dressed up as a country barn, the walls hung with wagon wheels, horse bridles, plows, and other items agricultural. The orange-hued tables and chairs look incongruously urban alongside all these rustic decorations. The fare is simple and solid: grilled pork sausages with french fries and salad for $3.70, crumbed whiting for $5.50. Closed Sunday and open other days only from 11:30 a.m. to 2:30 p.m.

DAYTIME ACTIVITIES: The entire Gold Coast is geared to keeping tourists happy—meaning busy. Consequently it offers a dazzling array of attractions over and above its principal ones: sun, sea, and sand.

Two of the tops are situated at the Spit, between Southport and Surfers Paradise. The first is **Sea World,** which ranks among the greatest aquatic show spots found anywhere. It is, as the name implies, almost a world by itself, a miniature Disneyland of 50 acres, packed with land, sea, and sky rides, viewing pools, fun parlors, bars, restaurants, and gift shops. There are dolphins and sea lion shows, waterski acrobatics, divers feeding sharks underwater, a climbable replica of Captain Cook's ship *Endeavour,* an Adventure Island cruise, and live marine exhibits including turtles, rays, and little fairy penguins. Also Australia's first flume ride, a kind of roller-coaster ride on water. Open daily till 5 p.m. Admission is $14 for adults, $9 for children.

Pacific Fair, on Pacific Highway, Broadbeach, is easily Australia's most unusual shopping center. Built around a central lake, complete with waterfall and tropical fish, the complex is divided into half a dozen distinct national and period styles selling more or less appropriate merchandise. Children can ride a special train while their elders stroll from one section to another. From a charmingly incongruous English Tudor village to a colonial frontier boardwalk with wooden verandas, through an Indian village with shops housed in teepees to Basin Street in the French Quarter with cast-iron balcony lace, from the Place de la Concorde through the Lindenstrasse (with transparent roof) into what resembles a sliver of picture-postcard Hawaii. It's all entertainingly cute and corny— particularly Fisherman's Wharf and the Cottswold Cottage beside a stone bridge and a waterwheel churning up a goldfish pond—and makes for a great fun shopping spree even if you don't buy a thing.

Barry's Art Gallery, 34 Orchid Ave., Surfers Paradise, is a large wooden cottage structure, but vastly superior to the average run of resort gallery where the paintings frequently look as if they'd been churned out by computer. The exhibits here are in excellent taste, mostly by contemporary Australian artists, but with a sprinkling of European masters like Picasso and Chagall. They're all for sale, prices range from $50 to $30,000, but you can admire them gratis. Open Monday to Saturday from 11 a.m. to 6 p.m.

Dreamworld, Coomera, the Gold Coast's latest playpen, opened in December 1981. It's the biggest, liveliest, most gee-whizzing theme park in the southern hemisphere, a happy melange of Disneyland and Coney Island, with a few authentic Aussie touches thrown in. You can chug around it in antique model cars, scream your lungs out on a looping roller coaster, take a log ride through a dizzying flume, bounce on an old-fashioned merry-go-round, explore pioneer cabins, run riot in penny arcades, let out your aggressions in bumper cars, and gorge yourself in a dozen eateries. There's a magic shop, an antique car museum, theaters, craft shops, shooting galleries, and realistic lions and crocodiles lurking on the lawns. The "theme" is kind of vague, the fun absolutely genuine, the number of souvenirs for sale overwhelming. Admission is $15 for adults, $9.50 for children, but this includes all the rides. Open till 6:30 p.m. every day.

The **Great White Shark Expo,** 211 Seaworld Dr., Main Beach, stars the marine menace forever imprinted in the memories of those who've seen *Jaws.* It also stars Ron and Valerie Taylor, the world-famous Australian diving couple who have kept closer company with these monsters than anyone else alive to tell about it. You see some of their absolutely breathtaking underwater films and marvel at their survival powers. Even more amazing is their message: the two erstwhile spearfishing champions are now firmly *against* the wholesale killing of sharks. Open daily till 5:30 p.m. Admission is $5 for adults, $3 for children.

The **Palms,** Coomera, about 15 minutes by bus from Surfers, is a stud farm and a magnet for horse-lovers from every part of the globe. The magnificent 50-acre spread displays studies in horse contrasts: from Argentinian Fallabellas, the smallest breed in the world, to mighty Clydesdales, probably the biggest and certainly the gentlest of their kind. Also a foal nursery, training exercises, a horse parade, and a performance of dancing stallions. Performances are twice daily; admission is $6 for adults, $2.50 for children.

The **Land of Legend,** Gold Coast Highway, Tugun, features an array of lavish tableaux including Sleeping Beauty (who actually breathes), a ferocious Pirates Den and a life-size (and very demure) Harem. Colorful and superb lighting effects. Admission is $2.50. The **Fairytale Castle** on David Low Highway, Bli Bli, is a replica of an 11th-century Norman fort with moat, draw-bridge, and portcullis. Inside are 30 fairytale dioramas and an interesting display of medieval armor, broadswords, halberds, maces, and shields. Open daily till 5 p.m.

The **Wax Museum,** Gold Coast Highway, Surfers, has the usual collection of the famous and infamous in wax, plus an unusual cluster of historical documents, such as Adolf Hitler's testament and the death warrant of King Charles I. Also a large and varied Chamber of Horrors demonstrating the delights of the Scottish Maiden, the Disemboweler, the Rat Torture, the Flesh Tearer, the Rack, and sundry others. The museum costs $3 for adults and $1.50 for children. Open every day and night.

Traintasia, 2480 Gold Coast Hwy., is the greatest display of model railroads, toy houses, cars, and machinery I've ever seen under one roof. There's an entire operating city covering an area of 500 square feet and more than 600 feet of railroad tracks. The trains stop and go, load and unload, cranes hoist heavy loads while a carnival is going full blast and a miniature fire brigade is fighting to save a burning house. They had to drag me out of the place. Open Monday to Saturday till 5 p.m.

Magic Mountain, Gold Coast Highway at Nobby Beach, is a highly imaginative entertainment complex built around the craggy rock outcrop, high above the surf, that holds a Magic Castle. You can reach the castle by way of a spectacular ride that swings you 1,000 feet up in open fiberglass chairs—or by more conventional means. The castle presents magic, housing a museum devoted to the art plus a cavalcade of stage wizards. Around and about the complex you'll find some of the most ingenious thrill contraptions in Australia. These include a (eminently safe) Parachute Tower, a (literally) breathtaking wave swinger, and gentler items like a two-tiered carousel, dodge-'em cars, and kiddie trains. The whole package contains 12 rides and three daily magic shows, and costs $9 for adults, $7 for children.

Natureland, on the New South Wales side of the border at Kirra, Coolangatta, is Australia's third-largest zoo, with a big collection of lions, giraffes, American and Himalayan bears, ostriches, apes, emus, and lots more. Admission is $4 and the zoo is open all day, every day. The **Sea Shell Museum,** 31

Millers Dr., Currumbin, shows thousands of beautiful shells, plus specimens of sea snakes, giant clams, and poisonous cone shells. Admission costs $3 for adults, $1 for children.

The Boomerang Farm, Springbrook Road, Mudgeeraba, sells, displays, and makes boomerangs and teaches visitors the art of throwing them. Also shows a collection of Aussie oddities labeled "Hysterical Historicals" beside a unique boomerang museum. The admission charge includes instructions in throwing. Open seven days a week.

Fleay's Fauna Reserve, one mile outside Burleigh on West Burleigh Road, is the largest wildlife sanctuary on the Gold Coast. It contains beautiful lyrebirds, eagles, cassowaries, plus tree kangaroos, dragon-like goannas, deadly taipan snakes, and a platypus family. You can watch the platypus (platypuses? platypi?) feed daily at 3 p.m.

The **Bird Sanctuary,** half a mile south of Currumbin Creek, is the site to which hundreds of wild tropical birds flock every morning and afternoon to feed on plates of bread and honey. The birds, mostly multicolored little lorikeets, are quite unafraid and can be fed by visitors when they come down from their bushland habitat. The sanctuary also has koalas, kangaroos, emus, and water birds. Admission is $7 for adults, half price for children.

And for sheer stark contrast to the above there's the **War Museum** (filled with World War weaponry) and a collectors' armoury on Springbrook Road, three miles past Mudgeeraba. Open every day till 5 p.m.

TOURS AND EXCURSIONS: If you only have time for one jaunt, make it the full-day trip to **Stradbroke Island,** a patch of (almost) unspoiled paradise just off the coast. **Jetaway Cruises** (tel. 38-3400) operates a truly memorable and economy-geared outing to the place. They use a specially built craft, 60 feet long and shiny white all over, and you're welcomed aboard by the friendliest bunch of bearded T-shirts you've ever met. Lunch is T-bone steak and tropical salad—and it's free. At the island, 14 miles of virgin beach await you. You can swim or loaf around, and if that's too tame the tour has a speedboat for waterskiing or toboggan rides. Dinner comes from a wood barbecue . . . more steak, and again free. The entire outing costs $24, half price for children.

A vehicle named "Love Bus" offers a tour of the Gold Coast at night, bookable at 31-5447. You get a whirl through the tropical bright lights four times weekly, visiting assorted niteries, revues, and discos. The all-inclusive price is $25, and the double-decker delivers you back to your hotel at around 12:30 a.m.

Ansett-Pioneer, Hanlan St., Surfers (tel. 50-2966), has a tour of the Gold Coast down to Coolangatta. This includes a scenic drive to the Terranora Country Club, with time enough to try your luck at the poker machines there, as well as imbibing a spectacular view. Departs at 1:30 p.m., lasts four hours, and costs $8 for adults, half that for children.

EET, 45A Cavill Ave., Surfers Paradise (tel. 38-0000), has a full-day tour (except Sunday) to the Sunshine Coast and Noosa. You drive through Brisbane, stop for lunch and a ride on a sugarcane train at the Big Pineapple, and return leisurely via the Sunshine Coast. Coaches leave at 7 a.m. and the tour (not including lunch) costs $25. Another day-tour covers Mt. Tamborine and a visit to the new Beenleigh Rum Distillery (yes, you get free samples), followed by a panoramic picnic lunch atop Mt. Tamborine and a stroll through rain forest. The $20 price includes lunch, but not the distillery admission price.

"M.V. Neptune" (tel. 32-5031) is a sleek white little motor cruiser that will take you on a two-hour canal and harbor tour. The boat leaves from the river end of Cavill Ave. (Surfers) at 10:30 a.m. and 2 p.m., sailing past the Gold Coast's most sumptuous luxury homes, the flotillas of private yachts, and the fishing fleet, past Sea World and the heliport, into the expanse of Broadwater, then back to Surfers. Morning or afternoon tea included in the price of $9 for adults, half for children.

Holiday Services, Griffith Street, Coolangatta (tel. 36-1635), offers a full-day road-and-sea tour to North Stradbroke Island. You ride to Wellington Point by luxury coach, then embark on a vehicular ferry for the one-hour cruise across gentle Moreton Bay to the playground island, most of which is still in its beautiful natural state. Superb scenery on the return trip. The tour runs every Friday, departing at 6 a.m. from Coolangatta, at 7 a.m. from Surfers. Cost: $30 for adults, half price for children.

AFTER DARK: The small strip of Gold Coast offers more nightlife than the rest of Queensland taken together. The variety is quite remarkable, but sophistication is *not* exactly the keynote. Most of the attractions are geared to the holiday-makers' market whose tastes run to costume musicals in one form or another. Still, there are exceptions.

One of them is the surprising entertainment complex housed under one roof at the Penthouse, Orchid Avenue, Surfers Paradise. The fourth floor features the **Old Place,** a nostalgia den, furnished speakeasy style, where you can enjoy a truly deluxe piano bar till 2 a.m. with a first-rate jazz ivory tickler providing atmosphere and the most attractive Gold Coast ladies adding glamor vibes. One floor down is **Club 3,** with a live band plus cabaret. The first and second stories contain a disco each, **Mad Mary's,** on the ground floor, being the hoppingest along the coast. In action Monday through Saturday. For reasons best known to themselves they charge $6 admission just to get into the building.

At the other end of the scale stands the **Music Hall,** at the corner of the Esplanade and Hanlan Street. A variety theater for family consumption, the place puts on brightly costumed and undemanding musicalia, two hours of it, combined with a three-course dinner and an M.C. (called "chairman") whose patter is as mellow as the lilt of the sing-along tunes on stage. Total cost is $22.50 per adult diner, with children paying $12.50, Tuesday to Saturday.

The **Broadbeach International,** Victoria Avenue, Broadbeach, has the famed Celebrity Room, most fashionable nightspot in the region. The cabaret performers here are top-class imported or Aussie talent, costumes and setting suitably sumptuous, and the clientele on the well-heeled side. The choice is between an excellent four-course dinner plus show or the show only.

Jupiters Casino, Conrad International Hotel, Gold Coast Hwy., Broadbeach, is a deluxe glamor establishment devoted to roulette, blackjack, baccarat, Big Six, craps, Sie Bo, and two-up in the most velvety of settings. The hotel also has a multi-tiered showroom featuring some of the finest Australian stage and TV talent. The whole place is a stomping ground for celebrities and a lot of people go there just to spot them.

The Gold Coast's budget bonanza, however, stems from a legal technicality. Queensland does not permit poker machines. New South Wales does—and it so happens that the border between the two states runs along Boundary Street, which divides the twin towns of Coolangatta and Tweed Heads. On the New South Wales side there's a cluster of clubs whose revenues depend on the one-armed bandits. They gladly subsidize meals, transportation, drinks, and lavish entertainment to entice tourists over from Queensland to feed those insatiable slots.

Ostensibly these clubs are "private," i.e., for the use of members only. But in practice they'll admit "bona fide" visitors. Simply call them up beforehand, then show some identity proof (passport or drivers license) to the doorman, and the gates fly open for you. You're welcome to partake of some of the best—and cheapest—victuals on the coast, and watch top-class floor shows at no extra charge. And nobody forces you to gamble.

There are direct daily "pokey buses" running from Brisbane and every Gold Coast town. If you're in Coolangatta, you just walk across the border street.

The **Twin Towns Services Club** (tel. 36-2277; show bookings, 36-1977) puts on a galaxy of Australian and overseas "superstars" every afternoon and evening in its Anchor Lounge, overlooking the water. The lineup changes, but the plush cocktail bar, smörgåsbord bistro, sports room, and air-conditioned lounges are permanent fixtures. Dinner at the bistro or the restaurant will cost you from $3.50 up.

Terranora Lakes Country Club (tel. 54-9223) has a gratis bus service leaving thrice daily from Coolangatta Post Office. The club features a show band, plus selected solo performers. In the Bistro dining room, roast beef, roast pork, or chicken go for very little.

The **Tweed Heads Bowls Club** (tel. 36-3800) does indeed offer bowling, but also a gorgeous gals revue show, famous stage and television comedians, plus 300 slot machines and six bars. No cover charges, and bistro meal prices hover around the $5 mark.

TIME WARP: All Australian states—except Queensland—go on Daylight Saving Time in summer. Which means that during the hot season Queensland lags one hour behind the rest of the country. If you happen to be in Coolangatta, you have to adjust your watch every time you cross Boundary Street into Tweed Heads. And vice versa on the way back. I told you this was a controversial state.

Chapter VII

CAIRNS AND THE GREAT BARRIER REEF

1. The City and Surroundings
2. Queensland

WE'RE STILL IN QUEENSLAND here—locals, in fact, call this the *real* Queensland—but now we've entered the Far North, the Australian tropics. The landscape has become incredibly green in different shadings: light emerald in the pasturelands; deep, dark, and sated in the jungle portions. Human habitations fade into insignificance amid the sprawling immensity of the vegetation. From the air it seems as if the lush wilderness could engulf man's settlements at any given moment.

1. The City and Surroundings

Cairns is the northernmost city in Queensland, a bustling, thriving, humid harbor town just over a century old. The metropolitan population is now around 48,000 but appears much smaller because the streets are so wide that they give an impression of emptiness. This is one of the very few tourist haunts where you never feel jostled or crowded; there's always plenty of elbow room.

The town has a spectacular setting. Overlooking the radiantly blue waters of Trinity Bay, Cairns lies enclosed in a ring of green sugarcane fields which form a natural boundary. Farther inland the mountains rise in steep slopes, covered in thick rain forest. During the crushing season—from June to December—the cane fires blaze every night to clean the stalks for the next day's harvest, licking against the dark sky like the campfires of a race of jungle giants. In daytime the fields are noisy with the whistles of miniature trains chugging to the district crushing mills with loads of sweet cane stalks.

Cairns is a friendly, easy-going town, with streets broad enough to resemble squares, palms swaying in the ocean breezes, and the kind of tropical architecture that always looks like an outdoor movie set—ornate but slightly ramshackle. It's a town of tropical sea delicacies rarely served elsewhere and of wonderful exotic fruits like mangoes, pawpaws, lychees, and tiny sweet fairy bananas. It has a fascinating oceanfront where the island traders dock and the great seagoing luxury yachts ride at anchor, and you can feel like a Joseph Conrad character by just strolling alongside.

But Cairn's claims to tourist fame are its proximity to the Great Barrier

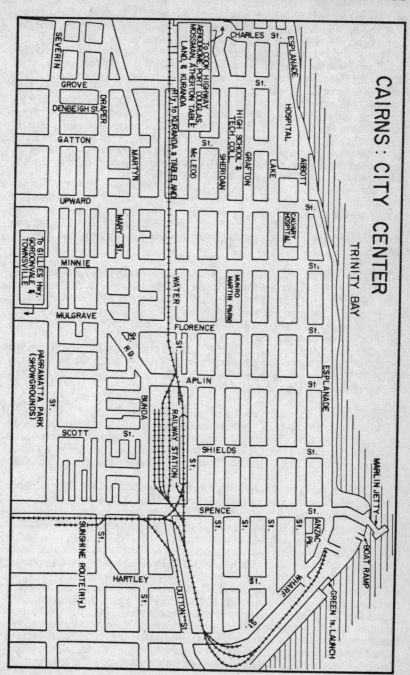

CAIRNS : CITY CENTER

Reef (Green Island lies a 75-minute launch ride away) and marlin fishing. Black marlin—no good for eating—are probably the world's foremost game fish, fabulous fighters which, even when hooked, are not caught by a long shot. Every year around September these giant bullfish migrate with the south-bound current from New Guinea. They cruise and hunt in the deep waters on the ocean side of the Great Barrier Reef, leaping high above the surface of the Coral Sea as if challenging the big-game fishermen to come and get them. And these fishermen come out of Cairns, home port for the famous "Marlin Meet," that attracts the international set of sea hunters out to break the world black marlin record. The very rich come in their own craft from across the ocean. The merely prosperous hire them on the spot—the Cairns harborfront has rows of sleek and powerful game-fishing boats for charter. The rest of us watch or go fishing for grouper or coral trout. Marlin fishing is decidedly for the well-heeled: charters for the specialized launches *start* at over $300 a day.

Strangely enough, despite its bay location Cairns has no beaches. All the swimming in town takes place in pools. The harbor is only for boat and bird watching—you can see flocks of pelicans, white egrets, and herons while lying on the lawns along the Esplanade. But a few minutes away, up and down the coast, lie some of the most splendid beaches on earth. We'll visit them in due course.

GETTING THERE: Cairns's brand spanking new **International Airport** lies about three miles from downtown. It was built primarily because Qantas now flies here directly from San Francisco. The airport has—well, nearly—everything an international terminal should have, including banking facilities, self-opening doors, and good air conditioning. The airport bus to the city costs $3, a cab comes to around $5.

Otherwise, the best way to reach Cairns is from Brisbane, and you can do it by plane, train, or bus. The air trip (Ansett or TAA) takes 2¾ hours and costs $228.40. The train is the leisurely *Sunlander* which arrives the next day. The bus (Greyhound or Pioneer) costs $75.

ORIENTATION: Cairns is a small town and requires a minimum of orientation. If you stand in Shields Street outside the Government Tourist Bureau and look toward the oceanfront Esplanade, you're facing northeast. The **bus terminal** is just across the road, and in the same direction a bit farther on lie the boat ramps, the ocean jetty, and the departure points for the **Green Island** launches. Also the "fun part" of the harbor.

Directly behind you stands the **railway station** and to your right stretches the wharf section once known as the **Barbary Coast,** still housing some of the city's oldest hotels but grown considerably tamer since its wild and colorful days 50 years ago. To your left (northwest) the road goes to the **airport** and—farther out—to the chain of superlative beaches.

The direction of the railway station is also the way to the **Parramatta Park Showground** and eventually leads to the **Great Dividing Range,** the magnificent, densely forested tableland that forms the backdrop of Cairns.

Cairns has a new pedestrian mall, the **City Place,** at the corner of Shields and Lake Streets, a quite charming affair with lawns, palms, benches and small fountains, ideally suited to the town's languid ambling tempo. (The only rapid motions occur when raising elbows to down beers.) The mall even boasts a couple of outdoor cafés, which are bliss. Unfortunately they're infected with the Queensland bug of early closing. They shut shop between 8 and 9 p.m., precisely when the cool of the evening makes you *want* to drink or eat in the open.

A NOTE ON PRICES: All prices in this guide are in Australian dollars (A$). As we go to press, US$1 = approximately A$1.40. Thus a room listed at $20 a night actually costs only about $14.50 in U.S. funds—good news indeed for budget travelers.

ACCOMMODATIONS: The Y's of Cairns are, sadly, nonexistent. But their places are amply filled by an abundance of hostels, which make this tropical port one of the best budget propositions in the country. The largest is operated by the Young Australia League, a somewhat misleading title since you have to be neither young nor Australian to stay in their holiday center. This is the **Tropicana Lodge,** 158c Martyn St. (tel. 51-1729). The YAL is affiliated with the Youth Hostel Association and accepts YHA membership for discounts. The Tropicana, less than two miles from the post office, has an attractive layout embracing one acre of lawns and gardens surrounded by low white bungalow structures containing the 126 bedrooms. The complex houses a TV lounge, laundry, swimming pool, and dining room (ample lines to hang out washing and the right climate for drying), and the downtown bus stops right outside. The rooms are pleasantly furnished—even the dormitories have wall-to-wall carpets—and each one comes with H&C water, individual bed-lights, large wardrobes, and tea-making facilities. The management is very friendly and the entire place beautifully kept and run. The tariff includes breakfast (at 7 a.m., unfortunately), but you have to make special bookings for lunch and dinner. Rates are $16 for singles, $13.50 per person for doubles, half price for children.

The seafront Esplanade is lined with rows of lodging places in most price levels and degrees of comfort. **Caravella's Hostel,** at no. 77 (tel. 51-2159), is a real economy establishment, small and red brick with a nice upstairs balcony. The 40 rooms (all but four are singles) have bare floors, large ceiling fans, and small wardrobes. Furnishing is somewhat sparse, but you get bedside lamps and all of the rooms come with H&C water and ceiling fans. The house has four modern bathrooms, a swimming pool, and a fully equipped communal kitchen for the use of guests. No meals are served on the premises. The tariff is a modest $6 in shared rooms, $13 in doubles.

The **Old Lido,** no. 147 (tel. 51-3267), is a tropical bungalow with corrugated iron roof and 16 rooms of varying dimensions, half of them singles. The house is well maintained but slightly cramped for space, offering a TV lounge, a laundry, plus a fully equipped communal kitchen. The bedroom floors are linoleum, the ceiling fans large and efficient, the rates uncomplicated. Guests pay $10 a night per person, $6 in the dormitory.

The **Linga Longa,** no. 223 (tel. 51-3013), displays a garish sign above a rather weatherbeaten front, but this negative façade is deceptive. This is an excellently run establishment, proudly groomed by the management, and an exceptional holiday bargain to boot. There are six holiday apartments, all tucked away in the rear so they get no traffic noise from the Esplanade in front. Laundry facilities on the premises. The apartments accommodate from one to three people in goodly comfort. They consist of bedroom, bathroom, and kitchen, and come fully equipped with linen, and cooking and eating utensils, plus fair-size wardrobes, ceiling and bedside lights, and TV. Public telephone in the house. The daily rate is $20 for two people.

There are at least a dozen more accommodation places along the Esplanade, a lawn-fringed, palm-lined promenade that runs the entire length of the

Cairns waterfront as far as the wharves. The above are merely a few samples. Farther inland we have the—

Parkview Tourist Hostel, 176 Grafton St. (tel. 51-3573), overlooking the park. This is actually a set of four separate houses, which makes for a diversity of accommodations: you get a choice of rooms or dormitories. Also printed cards saying "Welcome" in five languages, a courtesy pickup bus, free video movies, and a swimming pool. All the houses are nicely maintained and the management lives up to its welcome cards. The park lies in front, more green lawns in the rear, and palms sway all around. The eight double rooms are fairly small and minus H&C water. But the buildings contain eight bathrooms, plus three large white community kitchens for the seven dorms (each housing 4 to 8 persons.) You can cook your own meals with all necessary utensils supplied. Singles pay $12 a night, doubles $15 and dorm inhabitants $6. Travelers arriving with this book get a 50¢ discount.

Central House, 88 Abbott St. (tel. 51-2869), is an elderly but nicely renovated guesthouse. The establishment has seven apartments and 17 rooms, neither completely self-contained. The house offers a lot of guest facilities: a backyard garden with an exceptionally large swimming pool, barbecue grill, deckchairs, and laundry. Also a spacious communal kitchen and a small dining room. The bedrooms have ample wardrobe space and good carpeting, but fluorescent ceiling lights only—no bedside illumination. The flats come with dining kitchens (gas stoves) and bed-sitting rooms, and have complete kitchen equipment. Bathrooms—all large and spotless—are shared. The rates are $10 per person per night.

The **Cairns Girls Hostel,** 147 Lake St. (tel. 512-767), takes only ladies (of any age) and keeps males out of bounds with several stern notices saying exactly that. With space for 35 persons, the hostel is excellently maintained, but rather hard to spot: the entrance is a narrow passage, easily overlooked. There are three bathrooms, a TV lounge, laundry facilities, and communal kitchens. Bedrooms have bedside tables for one or two occupants. Rates are either $10 per night or $35 per week.

Pacific Coast Budget Accommodation, 100 Sheridan St. (tel. 51-1264), sounds like a generic caption but is actually part of a chain that stretches through Queensland to N.S.W. This particular one is an elderly tropical structure with a vast veranda and a second story that forms an awning. There is no elevator and the stairs are fairly steep, but the building has a communal kitchen with refrigerator, a TV lounge, and a coin laundry. The 65 bedrooms are of medium size, all with ceiling fans and ample wardrobe space but no bedside lamps or handbasins. Breakfast, included in the tariff, is served in the dining room, where you also get hefty three-course meals for $6.50. Singles pay $15; doubles, $24. No strangers are allowed in the guest rooms.

Caravan Parks

There are 13 caravan parks in or around Cairns, most of them renting onsite vans, the majority equipped with swimming pools. As a sample, there's the **White Rock Cabins & Trailer Court,** at Skull Road, White Rock, about six miles from Cairns (tel. 54-1523). On-site vans, hot and cold showers, TV room, self-service store on the grounds, swimming pool, and a community laundry with washing machines.

MEALS: For a town of its size Cairns has a remarkable number of good eateries, plus a couple of really great ones. The selection is surprisingly cosmopolitan as well—a far cry from the days when the only foreign cuisine found in

Northern Queensland was the local chop suey joint. The price range is the same as in Brisbane, an unusual aspect in a tourist center.

But why couldn't the Queenslanders import Mediterranean dining hours along with the fare? Mealtimes in this tropical haven remain geared to the old Anglo-Saxon cold-climate clock, as ludicrously out of place here as rolled umbrellas, galoshes, or woolen mittens. Also, with balmy skies above and wide streets below, Cairns is a natural setting for outdoor café life. If this town stood in France, Italy, Spain, or Latin America, the entire Esplanade would be blossoming with striped sunshades and little tables. So why not a few more ventures in that direction?

The **Pancake House,** 43 Spence St., functions in one of the first permanent structures built in colonial Cairns—first occupied by a Chinese vegetable store. Today the place leads a lucrative double life: pancake parlor in front, a steakhouse in the rear. The colonial aura still lingers in the copper lamps hanging from the ceiling. Each table is set with maple syrup dispenser, coffee crystals, and handsome wooden pepper and salt shakers. The pancakes come fast and filling, divided into equal numbers of savory or sweet selections. In the former the sausage and egg on pancake costs $5.10; in the latter the chocolate pancake $4.80. It's a meal or a dessert, depending on what you fancy. The place also serves excellent steaks. Open seven days a week until 11 p.m.

The **Kowloon,** 102 Lake St., is probably Cairns's most popular Chinese establishment, and with good reason. The place is lovely, large, and ornate enough to keep you interested while you're waiting for a table (at the elegant bar and seating facilities provided in front). Illumination comes from traditional Chinese lanterns, casting their glow over Oriental statues in glass cases and a gorgeous tropical aquarium. Bar and kitchen quarters are separated from the dining area by a dragon-decorated screen. The overall effect is surprisingly pleasant and the cuisine better than the average Aussie-Oriental standard. I'd favor the chicken and mushroom soup at $2.20 and the steak in black bean sauce at $7.80. Open till 10 p.m. six nights a week, till 9 on Sunday.

The **Little Gringo,** 95 Grafton St., is a Mexican surprise package tucked away in a small passage facing the local squash center. It's petite, intimate, and wonderfully atmospheric, complete with inn shingle over the doorway. Petite describes the place—there are only five tables of varying dimensions. Which means a full house most of the time. No meal costs more than $8. The menu is displayed on two blackboards, French style, but the establishment is a quite un-Gallic BYO. Open from six to 10 p.m. six nights a week. Closed Wednesday.

Riccardo's, 89 Grafton St., is a small, wonderfully relaxed Italian eatery with tables and umbrellas on the pavement outside and a genial host named Riccardo who welcomes patrons personally. The walls are decorated with travel posters plus hundreds of little snapshots of people dining here. The menu features a lengthy and very interesting discourse on Italian cuisine. The best things here are "of the day"—the "zuppa del giorno" (subject to chef's mood) for $3, and the fresh fish of the day (subject to fisherman's luck) for $10. This BYO charges 50¢ corkage for folks who bring their own. The large servings of jovial atmosphere come free. Open till 9:30 p.m. six nights. Closed Sunday.

For your splurge meal I'd recommend **Fathoms,** 6 Grove St., which is simply too good to miss. This is a seafood place par excellence and one of the most tastefully furnished restaurants in the entire state. The decor is kept in cool aqua colors and gives the impression of a deluxe tropical bungalow. You can eat in the raised main dining area or on a beautiful white veranda overlooking lush greenery. Lights are mellow, the table linen gleaming white, the service downright diplomatic. Fathoms has some of the freshest and finest barramundi and coral trout extant. For starters you should try the cold avocado soup or the barbecued prawns. Meals come complemented with the best and crispest homemade rolls we've ever eaten. The establishment is air-conditioned, so the ceiling fans have purely decorative value. Dinner here—without liquor—would cost around $18. Getting a table may be difficult, so you'd better book by calling 51-2305. Opens nightly at six and stays open "till late."

Now we have a trio of lunch suggestions, picked for culinary contrast, each excellent in its own fashion:

Life in the Raw, 44 Spence St., a vegetarian spot that permits no smoking. Simple but very attractive, with wooden tables and chairs and a cool tile floor. Serves tangy but mild vegetable curries for $2.50, huge salad platters for the same price, and for dessert delicious "fruit smoothies" with natural ice cream and tropical fruits.

Oscar's Carvery, in the Great Northern Hotel, Abbott St. This vast and handsome room changes its functions according to the time of day. At lunchtime it's very much a businessman's rendezvous air-conditioned, expensively decorated, buzzing with shoptalk, and redolent with the aroma of good eats. Heavy red carpets underfoot, it's lit by Spanish chandeliers, guarded by nail-studded castle doors, and hung with copper bulls, toreador gear, and genuine banderilleros. The large bar is separated from the dining area by screens that form intimate nooks—ideal for contract negotiations. Although the place holds over 100 people the sound level is pleasantly muffled. Service is fast, but the eating leisurely—just the way it should be. I had a very tasty grilled sole for $4.95, followed by rich French cheesecake at $1.50. We'll come back to the Great Northern in the nightlife section, for in Cairns this versatile establishment is all things to all men—or very nearly so.

American Coffee House, 68 Abbott St., may not resemble any American coffee dispensary I've ever seen but is a fine snack spot nevertheless. Located on the ground floor of a new shopping arcade, this cool, ultramodern refreshment parlor serves far better coffee than you usually get in the States. At $1 a cup, it's cheaper as well. A quiet, peaceful little haven with a coffee-flavored air, it also serves outstanding ham, salami, or pork sandwiches for $1.50, and dainty plates of cold cuts. Open from 8 a.m. to 4 p.m. Monday to Friday.

While we're at the luncheon scene, let me point out a few places that sell the ingredients for splendid outdoor eating. All you have to do is find a nice shady spot and plop down on the lawn. Preferably where you can watch the boats and the birds.

Cairns is remarkably well supplied with "hot bread kitchens"—bakeries offering vast varieties of fresh crusty loafs and rolls, seasoned or sweet, from the darkest Russian rye to the whitest of Vienna poppyseed twists. Plus freshly baked apple pies, custard tarts, and raisin buns—the kind of goodies you simply don't expect in the tropics.

You get them at **Congo's,** Civic Shopping Centre, at the corner of McLeod and Florence Streets. Open seven days a week. Or at **Monte's Drive-In Bakery,** 136 Anderson St. Open seven days a week.

For the fillings you can turn to **Andre's Deli,** 70 Grafton St., a chalet-style gourmet stronghold. Andre's stocks 100 brands of cheeses from around the globe, a couple of dozen types of salami and wurst, Mexican tortillas, Mid-Eastern savories, and an entire section of Chinese delicacies.

DAYTIME ACTIVITIES: Not surprisingly nearly all daylight action in and around Cairns is the outdoor kind. It's hard to find anything with a roof overhead except shopping. One of the exceptions is the **House of 10,000 Shells,** 32 Abbott St., a shell museum displaying specimens from every part of the world. Open daily.

Two others are situated at the waterfront. **Windows on the Reef,** Wharf St., is a small theater that takes patrons on a cleverly simulated dive to the Great Barrier Reef. A turning deck and a sophisticated audio-visual arrangement give the illusion of actually being under water as you see and hear the 460-million-year history of the coral reef in shows lasting 45 minutes. Open seven days a week, from 10 a.m. to 5:30 p.m.

Reef World, Marlin Parade, shows you the reef animals and plants alive. These include giant groupers, turtles, sharks, huge clams, and the deadly poisonous stone fish. Also a remarkably friendly stingray named Pirate who is fed by hand. Open seven days a week, from 10 a.m. to 5:30 p.m.

Some 17 miles north on the Captain Cook Highway stands the **Wild World** (take the bus that goes up the coast to the beaches or join one of the many tours heading there). This is a combination reptile-animal-bird park, containing 150 Queensland crocodiles, both fresh and saltwater species. They range from babies looking like clockwork toys with needle teeth to monsters like Sarge—14 feet long and a century old. Sarge was so christened because she lunged out of Cowal Creek and gobbled up a local police sergeant's dog. After being netted she had to spend a night in jail before the zoo people transported her to her present enclosure. She's now the only croc extant with a hoosegow record. The park also shows Australia's deadliest snakes, the taipans, plus birds, kangaroos, and giant pythons. You can watch the crocs being handfed, the snakes being "milked," and do some bird and wallaby feeding yourself. Admission is $8 for adults, half for children. Open daily, from 10 a.m. to 5:30 p.m.

For one of the best showplaces you have to go some 25 miles north on the Captain Cook Highway to **Hartley's Creek Zoo.** This is far more than a menagerie, it's a variety act run with terrific flair, humor, affection and knowledgeability. The setting is pleasant, with shady walks, little pools, and miniature bridges. But the fascinating part is that all the zoo's denizens can be found, wild, within five miles of the location. They include cassowaries, tree kangaroos, dragon lizards, and innocuous-looking taipans, mud-brown and unspectacular but actually the world's most lethal snakes. Also flying foxes, the giant Queensland fruit bats with heads like small dogs. You see them fed with apples and they manage to look very appealing while munching them—upside down. The array of 163 crocodiles includes Charlie, a veteran weighing a solid three-quarters of a ton. The snakes are milked and the crocs fed by a jolly keeper, who maintains a wonderful patter while avoiding getting his hands chewed off. He has Charlie perform the crocodile "death roll"—an acrobatic feat designed to knock prey off its legs—and slam his jaws with a *wham* that can be heard for a mile. Adults pay $4; children, half price. Open daily till 5 p.m.

The **Cairns Botanical Gardens** are located on Collins Avenue, Edge Hill, about two miles from the center but easily reached by bus. Planted back in 1886, they are now wonderfully luxuriant—a kind of harnessed tropical jungle plus parkland, featuring more than 10,000 trees, shrubs, and flowers, among them 200 different species of palms. Also magnificent orchids, a beautiful fernery, and a collection of exotic flowering trees. Open daily from sunrise to sunset. Admission is free.

Marlin Wharf can be the most envy-arousing experience of your life if you're into fishing. During the big-game season, from August to November, the black marlin hunters head there to weigh—and show off—their catches. They dock toward evening and some of the whoppers hoisted up on the scales go well over the 1,000-pound mark. This is a fine place for celebrity spotting as well. I saw movie hero Lee Marvin bring in a monster marlin about twice as long as he is.

The Waterworks, Lake Street, is the town's newest attraction and one of the greatest fun contraptions I've seen outside Disneyland. It's a kind of water complex: four giant waterslides, each different, where you go belly-down head-first through a winding enclosed tube that finally spits you gently into a pool. They range from exciting to scary—take your pick—and I'd have slid them all day if duty hadn't called. The works also include the world's largest bubbling spa pool with its own waterfall and hundreds of tingling jets, private hot spa huts for aquatic massages, and a coffeeshop. Open seven days a week from 10 a.m.

The Beaches

Captain Cook Highway winds, undulates, and meanders from Cairns northwest to Mossman. It leads through some of the most picturesque country you'll ever see: fields of sugarcane, palm and gum forests, sleepy tropical townships against a backdrop of steep jungle hills that look absolutely magical when partly shrouded by morning or evening mists.

Most of the signposts point to the right, where the beach resorts lie like a string of pearls. They're all beautiful; some are exquisite. Everybody has a different favorite, so take your pick:

Machans Beach, about ten driving minutes up the highway, is the closest beach to Cairns. Apart from fine swimming it offers the **Fish and Reef Museum,** 189 Esplanade, which shows about 600 different breeds of fish, plus corals, sea stars, and crustaceans.

Holloway Beach is divided from Machans by a tidal lagoon and a creek, popular with the fishing and netting crowd. The township has a mini-market that sells everything you may need for a beach barbecue.

Yorkey's Knob is the only resort beach I've ever seen that looks even lovelier in reality than on picture postcards. There's a beachfront caravan park and a nine-hole golf club that welcomes visitors.

Trinity Waters is about 12 miles from Cairns and my personal favorite. A rather narrow beach, flanked by green hills and backed by rows of shady trees, it has rocks at one end for fishermen to meditate on and kids to climb over. There's a shopping area right on the waterfront, plus a hotel with outdoor tables. You can rent catamarans at $6 an hour and the gentle surf provides just enough chop to make sailing them interesting. It's difficult to turn over in these superbly stable craft, but even if you do it doesn't matter unduly. You can right them again with one good heave.

Clifton Beach, next in line, very quiet and serene, is fringed by the permanent homes of people who like serenity. **Palm Cove** is the base of the Cairns Life Saving Club and aglow with vivid bougainvillea, the foreshore lined with slender palms. It's much livelier than its neighbor, due to the presence of the Reef House, an international luxury pad with a magnificent garden restaurant.

Ellis Beach is the most popular spot for family groups and picnic parties. It has a motel and beachside restaurant and a large caravan park right by the water —well sheltered and gorgeously panoramic against a backdrop of jungled hills.

The beaches go on all the way to Mossman, which lies about 50 miles from Cairns. A tranquil and sunbaked little town at the foot of towering Mount Demy, Mossman is the center of the local cane industry. During the crushing season—June to December—you can visit the sugar mill.

Timetables for the buses serving the northern beaches are posted at the bus shelter at Anzac Park, opposite the Oceanarium on the Cairns Esplanade.

Tours and Excursions

One of the best, cheapest, and most enchanting outings in all of Australia is the scenic rail trip from Cairns to **Kuranda.** The motor train tracks run for 28 miles through spectacular vistas—and the train obligingly stops at the greatest for the benefit of the camera hounds. The mountains of the Atherton Tableland rise green, steep, and majestic before you, waterfalls cascade like silver curtains beside the track, and the air breathes sweet and cool. There are 15 tunnels en route, each opening up on some new panoramic splendor. At **Barron Gorge** the roaring waters of the Barron Falls have been harnessed to a hydroelectric complex, but the trip through the gorge, on high iron girders, is almost as scary as it is dramatic. Kuranda lies on the rim of the Great Plateau and boasts what may be the prettiest railroad station in the world—a cross between tropical bungalow and flower garden. The round trip costs $10.20 for adults, half price for children.

The town has a wildlife park, a pioneer cottage museum, and the **Mountain Groves** hostelry, Kennedy Highway, where you get Devonshire tea and delicious scones, fresh orange juice from the orchard, and a ride on an amphibious army duck through citrus plantations and rain forests. You'll agree with the local authorities who raised **Robb's Monument,** a stone memorial to the engineer who built this fabulous track.

From mountain railroad to **paddlewheeler.** This quaint little craft departs from Marlin Jetty daily at 10 a.m., and 12:30 and 3 p.m. for a leisurely two-hour cruise through the Cairns **Everglades.** That's the name bestowed on the maze of creeks, inlets, and waterways branching out of Trinity Bay. They were originally explored by Captain Cook personally, in a ship's whaleboat on Trinity Sunday (hence the label). The shallow-draft paddlewheeler follows in his wake.

The shorescape is green, wild, and swampy, and some of the creeks wind like giant snakes through the mangrove forests. They harbor strange marine life, and many species have not yet been fully classified. One of the strangest is the very common "mud skipper," a fish with huge goggle eyes that can breathe out of water and climbs up mangrove trees. Occasionally you see crocodiles sunning on the mud flats at low tide. And you always see the large colony of flying foxes, hanging upside down like clusters of black pears. Clouds of butterflies hover over the greenery. Hunting for prey are night herons, blue cranes, egrets, and sometimes a lone giant sea eagle. The water is mirror-calm, the air hot and sleepy. Cost of the jaunt is $8 for adults, $4 for children.

Cooktown has been called "Australia's living museum." No other place on the continent remains as tangibly linked with its past as this idyllic semi-ghost town—mainly because there's not much present to interfere with the memories. Cooktown was actually the *first* British settlement in Australia, but quite involuntarily so. In June 1770, Captain Cook's little *Endeavour* ran aground on a coral reef while exploring the Queensland coastline. By jettisoning his cannons, the captain managed to sail the tiny craft up the mouth of a river, then settled down to a seven-week repair job. This was the historical foundation of Cooktown. The river was duly christened Endeavour, after the ship.

There was no "settlement" to speak of until 103 years later, when gold was discovered on the banks of the Endeavour River. Almost overnight the resultant rush boomed Cooktown into the colony's major seaport: a brawling, sweating, gambling gold metropolis with 94 hotels and 50,000 people, of whom 18,000 were Chinese. The glory lasted only as long as the gold. When the strikes petered out, Diggers and those who lived on them decamped for the south. Today Cooktown is left with a populace of just 550 and a lot of memories.

It's those memories that make the township fascinating. Most of them are on show in the **James Cook Museum,** a beautiful old building surrounded by a botanical garden, which contains the world's greatest collection of Cook memorabilia. There is a Chinese shrine, a graveyard for the thousands of Cantonese who labored and died here during the boom, the old colonial bank building, the ruins of once rip-roaring taverns, and Grassy Hill lookout, where Cook stood and peered for a passage through the mass of reefs. Cooktown lies some 250 miles north of Cairns and the best way of visiting it is by bus—an eight-hour trip costing $30. (The dirt road leading inland from Port Douglas is so lousy that there's no point in risking the springs of *your* car.)

Cairns-Starliner, 10 Shields St. (tel. 51-3444), runs a tour of Cairns city sights, picking you up at your hotel at 1:30 p.m. daily, returning at 5:30 p.m. You inspect a coral jewelry factory, drive to Lake Placid for morning tea, visit the Flying Doctor base, and take time off for a stroll through the Botanical Gardens. Adults pay $7; children, half price.

Cairns Travel, 5 Shields St. (tel. 51-8811), offers a scenic drive to a crocodile farm, a visit to Mossman, and afternoon tea at the Hartley Creek Zoo. En route you see historic Port Douglas. Departs at 8:30 a.m. on Thursday, and costs $18.50 for adults, half that for children. The same outfit also takes you to Cape Tribulation every day. You cross the Daintree River on an old-world cable-operated ferry, drive through jungle areas on real bush tracks, and get a chance to photograph some of the manifold birds and animals in the region. Make sure to inquire first, since this remote region isn't always accessible. When it is, adults get there for $29, children for half price.

For a real taste of the tropics in all their raw splendor you should go on the **Daintree Wildlife Safari.** This is a one-day coach and boat journey cruising along the creeks and backwaters of the Daintree rainforest River. You see giant moths and butterflies, wonderful wild orchids, clouds of rainbow-hued birds and crocodiles basking on the mangrove mud flats. The coach departs Cairns at 7:45 a.m. and brings you back after 5 p.m. Morning tea and lunch included in the price of $45 for adults, $22 for children. Book at the Cairns Convention and Visitors Bureau, 41 Shields St. (tel. 51-7366).

A Word on Crocodiles: Northern Queensland is crocodile country and if you intend seeing it outside the organized tours you'd better become aware of a few basic facts. There are two types of Queensland crocs: the small, harmless freshwater breed, growing to a maximum size of five feet, and the saltwater or estuarine species, which can reach 16 feet, weigh a ton, and become extremely dangerous. At some rivers or ponds you'll see unmistakable warning signs showing open crocodile jaws. They're not put there for decoration—you'll disregard them at the risk of your life. But even where no such warnings are posted you should take some elementary precautions: don't go swimming alone, camp at least 30 feet from the water's edge, don't stand on logs overhanging deep pools, don't dangle your foot in the water when boating, don't clean fish or prepare food on the water's edge, and don't approach *any* croc you happen to see. They're ordinarily sluggish but can move like reptilian lightning when they want to.

Air Queensland

This unique airline, now a subsidiary of TAA, headquartered in Cairns at 62 Abbott St. (tel. 504-222), deserves a section to itself. AQ—affectionately known as "Bushies"—is an outback institution, the large blue Q on the tails of its aircraft the most welcome letter on earth to thousands of isolated homesteaders throughout the vast and rugged Australian North.

AQ, originally christened "Bush Pilots Airways," traces its birth to a single dramatic hour in January 1951. It happened during the incredible northern "Wet," the season when the rain comes down like a lukewarm deluge, turning dry creek beds into roaring rivers, washing out roads in minutes, and pounding grasslands into swamps. At Cargoon Station, up on the wild Basalt Tableland, a critically ill woman had to be taken to a hospital. The roads all around were bogs, the swollen creeks uncrossable. A plane was the only means of rescue.

Capt. Bob Norman, piloting a tiny machine, managed to set it down on a sodden hillside landing strip, specially built for the mission. He got the patient on board, lurched back into the air, and flew her to Hughenden hospital in the barest nick of time.

This incident drove home a point to a number of stock farmers—called graziers in Australia. Ten of them got together and chipped in $600 each for the purchase of a brand-new Auster plane, which Norman would fly for them at an hourly rate. One aircraft, one pilot, and ten shareholders were the ultramodest beginnings of AQ.

Today the airline's staff has grown to 300, its fleet to 22 craft, and its fame into legend. The pilots are bush veterans with a kind of ESP for torrid-zone aviation. They'll fly and land in conditions that would send ordinary commercial crews on instant strike. And they'll carry anything: mail, beer and newspapers, breeding rams, parties of geologists, movie makers and police patrols, women in the ultimate stages of pregnancy, school classes, wedding parties, hockey teams, fishermen with their sodden catches, hunters with their game, live snakes, Aboriginal tribal elders, stretcher cases, high explosives, and—yes— tourists. Especially tourists. First because they'll fly to where normal airlines won't venture. Also because they have acquired an enviable safety record, largely due to the awesome know-how of the pilots and the mother-hen fussiness of their mechanics.

The AQ network now covers Queensland and the Pacific Islands around. They'll fly VIP luxury charters and regular "milk runs" to dots on the landscape. It's the only airline that will land you on a strip beside a single isolated homestead—past a curious kangaroo twitching its ears as you taxi in. And I can say that I've never felt more confidence than I had in those bronzed and breezy pilots whose standard response was, "Upper Wompa-Wompa? Too right I know where that is. Old Charlie Whatshisname owns it, doesn't he. No trouble, sir."

AQ offers some outstanding travel bargains which enable you to see more of Northern Australia in a shorter time for less money than by any other means of conveyance.

Cooktown Day Trip operates biweekly from Cairns (except January and February, the rainy season), and includes a guided tour of the historic sites. Inclusive fare is $120.

Lizard Island Day Trip. Lizard Island, adjacent to the outer Great Barrier Reef, is a deserted patch of paradise that has been transformed into a national park. It contains a magical Blue Lagoon for skinny-dipping or scuba diving, plus a dozen shaded beaches you have virtually to yourselves. The Australian Museum conducts a marine research station on the island. Inclusive cost of the trip is $190.

Great Barrier Reef Islands

The Great Barrier Reef is the largest structure ever built by living creatures —to wit, by corals. It stretches from the New Guinea region all the way south to the Tropic of Capricorn, a length of more than 1,200 miles. The term "reef" is rather misleading. Actually it's a series of reefs, coral cays, islands, and tiny islets lapped by a warm, wonderfully clear blue-green sea rarely more than 100 feet deep. This strip of shallow ocean harbors the most varied and colorful marine life found anywhere on the globe: some 1,400 varieties of fish and amphibians and reptiles including sea turtles, sharks, giant rays, marine snakes, jellyfish, octopi, starfish, mollusks, and sea urchins.

At low tide vast stretches of the reef lie exposed. You can wander over them and explore some of the marvels left behind by the retreating water. But you *must* observe a few elementary precautions. Put on tennis sneakers or similar footwear since some of the coral is razor sharp. Don't pick up anything unless you know what it is—even tiny creatures can have poison stings or needle teeth. And don't disturb the delicate balance of nature that keeps the reef alive. Always replace rocks you overturn and don't throw away garbage. A hundred thousand careless visitors can wreck the ecology of this wonderland.

Many of the reef islands are tourist resorts, several offering luxury-style accommodations. But even the simpler ones aren't exactly in the economy bracket. If you're planning overnight stops on any of them, it'll run you into money. The budget method of seeing them is to take one of the day excursions from Cairns and return the same evening. You have a lot of choice there.

Green Island is a small coral cay rising about two feet above sea level, densely wooded and lapped by crystal-clear water. This is the most popular of the Barrier Reef islands, offers the most fun facilities, and draws the biggest crowds.

Anchored on the seabed offshore stands the **Underwater Coral Observatory,** where you actually walk on the oceanbed and gaze at the submarine scenery through viewing windows. You see the fantastic coral gardens, the clouds of darting rainbow-colored fish, the clams and starfish and ribbon-like water snakes. (They're quite timid and unaggressive, but their poison is as lethal as a cobra's.) For a view from above you can take a ride in the **Glassbottom Boats,** among the island's top attractions. Or you can go down by yourselves. Right beside the boat pier there's a stand renting out flippers, masks, and snorkels at $1 per set.

On shore there's **Marineland Melanesia,** a sunlit arcade of tanks displaying fabulous fish, live corals, and possibly the most spectacular collection of crocodiles on view anywhere—monsters up to 18 feet long, whose terrifying jaw power you can observe, safely, when they lunge for dangling chunks of meat. Next door you'll find the **Castaway Theatre,** showing color movies of underwater reef scenes.

There are several ways of visiting Green Island. The fastest is by seaplane (flying time: nine minutes) with the shuttle service operating from Cairns Airport. Or you can take the "Big Cat," a specially designed twin-hulled double-decker launch equipped as a luxury cruiser, with its own bar and glass-bottom boat. The powered catamaran leaves from Marlin Jetty at 8:30 and 10:30 a.m. daily. The round-trip fare is $21 (children, half that) and this includes afternoon tea on the way back. Or you can do the 90-minute hop by ordinary launch. The boats leave daily at 9 a.m. from Hayle's Terminal at the wharf end of Abbott Street. The fare is $12.

Dunk Island is a rather plain name for a dazzling beauty patch, developed to the tune of $2.5 million to make it luxurious as well. Dunk has everything you'd expect from the proverbial tropical paradise: unspoiled vegetation and home-grown produce; delicate reef fish and top-grade chefs to cook them; vast lonely stretches of sandy beach and a hectic nightlife that breaks loose when the sun dips below the horizon; clear, warm coral waters, landscaped gardens, and cool streamlined cabana units; mangos, figs, and coconuts on the one hand, imported wines on the other.

Dunk is obviously not an economy haven to spend time on, but TAA runs one of its **Take 7** holiday packages to Dunk, comprising seven days there, plus transportation and all meals. Total price is from $1,009.

Low Isles is a small coral cay and a striking contrast to the above—the only residents are a lighthouse-keeper's family. The lighthouse is over a century old, the corals can be viewed from a glass-bottomed boat, the low tide on the reef flat exposes some of the most gorgeous shells in creation (no, you can't collect them, they're protected), and the water is so crystal clear that you can almost count the pebbles many feet below you while you're floating on top.

AFTER DARK: Nobody could call Cairns a hotbed of nightlife. With the exception of one quite beautiful restaurant-cabaret (in the upper price region) all the nocturnal action centers on pubs. The hub is the Great Northern Hotel, which caters to a variety of tastes. The establishment's **Galahad's Bar** packs in a very young, very volatile crowd—and *pack* is the word. On weekends it's an acrobatic feat just to get change out of your own pocket. The Galahad features live rock bands from 8 p.m. to midnight and has a (Friday and Saturday only) admission charge of $2. The **Marlin Bar** offers an immensely popular jazz pianist, whose instrument seems specially designed to hold the rows of beer glasses placed on it by foot-tapping customers. A great mingling spot, particularly around the piano. **Oscars,** by way of contrast, features live jazz to 2 a.m. nightly. You do get breathing space and the bar is ideal for a quiet drink and/or conversation.

Hides Hotel, at the corner of Lake and Shields Streets, has a lounge given over to a changing parade of entertainers. When I dropped in they had the "Working Class Band," an absolutely terrific outfit including one lass with a box fiddle. The numbers, mostly Irish-Aussie folk stuff à la Clancy Brothers, got the audience clapping and stamping, and a rollicking sentimental time was enjoyed by all, including yours truly.

SHOPPING: There's an intriguing influx of Asian and Pacific Island goods on the Cairns market, such as Indonesian batik dresses, shell necklaces from the Philippines, and carvings from Thailand, Tahiti, and Papua. Most of them sell cheaper here than in the large cities of the south and you can—if you have a keen eye—pick up some good bargains in that line. The **Papua New Guinea Emporium,** 32 Abbott St., sells Indonesian art, basketware, and coral necklaces, and carries a large array of ornaments, weapons, carvings, and masks from New Guinea. Also has an extensive boutique for tropical clothing.

SPECIAL EVENTS: Each October Cairns celebrates its **Fun in the Sun Festival.** This marks the official start of summer, if you can use that term here. The city is decked with flowers and the air perfumed with frangipani. The festival is a carnival affair of float processions, public dancing, and watersport competitions.

USEFUL INFORMATION: The **Queensland Government Travel Centre** centrally located at 12 Shields St. (tel. 51-4066), is open Monday through Friday from 9 a.m. to 5 p.m. Bookings are made for tours and accommodation throughout Queensland at no charge. Their after-hours emergency number is 51-8615. There is also a **Visitor Information Centre** centrally located at 44 McLeod St. (tel. 51-3588), open Monday through Friday from 9 a.m. to 5 p.m. They do not make bookings, but are very helpful in providing information on the far north of Queensland from Innisfail to Cooktown, including the tablelands. . . . For information on current activities in town, consult the *Cairns Post,* printed daily. . . . **Bus** services from the city terminal located at the back of Anzac Park on Esplanade to the beaches and suburbs are very good and cheap. All buses circuit the main shopping area. . . . Interstate buses are operated by **Pioneer,** 58 Shield St. (tel. 51-2411), and **Greyhound,** 78 Grafton St. (tel. 51-3131). . . . **The railway station** is on McLeod Street; phone 51-1111 for information. . . . **Sea Terminal** is located on Wharf Street, about a quarter of a mile from the city center, within easy walk of the city. The Wharf is basically used for freight and fishing vessels, and occasional cruise ships. . . . **Ansett Airlines** terminal is at 84 Lake St. (tel. 51-3361) and **Trans-Australian Airlines** terminal is at the corner of Lake and Shields Streets (tel. 503-777). . . . The **General Post Office** is at the corner of Spence and Abbott Streets. Telegrams can be sent from there and Post Restante service is available. . . . **Same-day service** cleaning can be obtained from Nu Tone Dry Cleaners, 149 Lake St. . . . There are **laundromats** at 49 Grafton St., on Lake Street, and on Sheridan Street. One load of wash costs 80¢.

2. Queensland

Color Queensland gold like the sun, beach sands, and ripe oranges, red like coral reefs and tropical sunsets, blue like the South Pacific, green like waving palm forests, lush cattle grass, and—if you like—tourist dollars. For this is the **Sunshine State,** the national playground, a region so bursting with Technicolor that it looks as if God had spilled all His paint pots over the landscape.

Queensland comes closest to looking the way some foreigners imagine *all* Australia looks. This is the youngest state of the Commonwealth, the second-largest, and the most rapidly expanding. By a benevolent freak of geography, Queensland's 667,000 square miles are split exactly in two by the Tropic of Capricorn. Which means that the northern half has tropical climate, the southern portion Mediterranean temperatures—adding up to an absolutely ideal holiday environment.

The two million Queenslanders—perhaps the healthiest bunch of people on earth—live in the usual lopsided Australian pattern: over 900,000 in the capital of Brisbane, the rest thinly scattered over the enormous bulk of the state. Nature has treated them like a fairy godfather; they have one of the natural wonders of the world—the Great Barrier Reef—as well as some of the juiciest pastureland, richest agricultural soil, and greatest mineral resources on the continent. What more do you want—oil? Yes, they have that too!

Queensland is Australia's tropical fruit basket, the nation's sugar bowl, her principal beef producer, her greatest copper and silver miner, and looks like she's developing into her top coal producer as well. But, above all, Queensland manufactures holiday happiness in fabulous quantities.

Most of that joyous commodity is concentrated along the gently curving coastline lapped by the warm Coral Sea, which, among other pleasures, provides superb year-round fishing. Depending on where you are and how far out you want to go, you can hook anything from estuary whiting, bream, salmon, and barramundi to deep-sea fighting game like tuna, dolphin, marlin, barracuda, and shark. Even giant groupers that come truly gigantic—eight feet long, with cavernous mouths large enough to swallow a man whole.

Queensland's second-greatest magnet for tourists, the **Gold Coast,** is covered in the chapter on Brisbane. Her top attraction, however, is undoubtedly the scenic wonder known as the—

GREAT BARRIER REEF: The reef is the world's largest coral creation—an irregular chain of reefs, lagoons, and islands stretching 1,250 miles along the coast. It covers a total area of 80,000 square miles, and lies between 10 and 200 miles offshore. Close to shore the reef is splintered into a labyrinth of lagoons and pools, up to 200 feet deep and as clearly transparent as fish bowls. And as the tide recedes these pools become showcases of living coral in a hundred rainbow colors and of the thousands of plants, fishes, and mollusks that swim, crawl, hunt, and hide around them.

There are shells ranging from the tiny cowrie to the giant clam—the size of a bathtub and strong enough to trap a careless diver. There are minute coral fishes, looking like multihued drops of paint flicked from a palette. There are octopi and razor-toothed eels, starfish and flat wing-flapping rays, ribbon-like sea snakes and fluorescent sea anemones, flower-like but deadly poisonous to their prey.

The most wondrous creature of all may be the coral itself, although it's only the size of pinheads. Corals are animals, of the polyp species, and the reef harbors more than 350 varieties of them. They are the architects of the reef. Living together in dense colonies, the corals secrete a protective limestone substance which hardens into formations with a thousand different shapes—hands, organ pipes, fans, snails—and scores of color shadings. Infinitely slowly, over millions of years, they formed the Great Barrier Reef, and are still at it . . . building.

Recently the coral polyps seemed in danger of extermination. Something went haywire in nature's balance of feeder and food. There was a sudden mass incursion of the coral's worst enemy, the crown-of-thorns starfish, which wiped out entire coral communities. But government skindivers fought the spiny invaders and destroyed about 50,000 of them. And—as far as the eye can see—they haven't made much of a dent in the reef.

There are many different ways of viewing this marine paradise from every conceivable angle. One is reefing—simply wandering along the exposed portions of the barrier at low tide and peering at the teeming life in the pools. The entire area is also dotted with underwater observatories and coral museums, enabling you to watch through glass portholes. Then there are cruises, in glass-bottom boats, low-level flights for a bird's-eye view, and—for the more energetic—skindiving and snorkeling.

The best time to explore the reef is from May through November, when the tides are lowest. And by far the best method is to stay on one of the resort islands, where accommodation ranges from ultra-plush to economy.

We have already visited a few of them, **Green Island** and **Low Isles,** in the Cairns section. But the choice is vast, and your selection depends entirely on your tastes and your pocketbook.

For the fairly flush there's **Hayman Island,** 35 minutes by helicopter from Mackay. Hayman swings and has become at least as famous for its sultry night-life as for picturesque mountain scenery and the fascination of the reefs.

At the southern tip of the reef lies **Heron Island,** a wonderfully unspoiled haven for nature lovers, birdwatchers, fossickers, photographers, and swimmers. Accommodation here offers few frills, but very reasonable rates.

Brampton Island, although it lies some distance from the heart of the Barrier Reef, may be the most paradisical patch of them all. A Twin Otter aircraft flies you over from Mackay in 15 minutes and when you land you think you've been whisked to one of those South Sea Edens they used to create specially for Hollywood sarong epics.

The island has forest-shrouded hills with near-tame kangaroos, groves of coconut palms, romantic little bays, ribbons of dazzling white beaches, some of the finest fishing on the Reef, clouds of rainbow lorikeets that will peck from your hand, plus all the champagne-bubble nightlife you can cope with. At low tide you can wade over to neighboring Carlisle Island, a National Park that contains herds of brumbies—wild horses introduced by early settlers and now roaming free, unsaddled, and very far from tame.

Brampton is a resort par excellence, offering plush and semiplush accommodation, every conceivable brand of watersport, plus a few you may never have heard of . . . like boom netting and water tobeganing. It's not exactly cheap, but TAA offers a package deal that cuts the cost considerably. You get transportation and seven nights in a twin-share Palm Unit (a double-story bungalow) for $835 per person, including all meals and most activities.

These are merely a few of the island resorts at your disposal. And remember, the reef is so huge and so varied that the only way to get an overall view of its beauties is to settle in for a few days and take several cruises. No shortage of cruise vessels—they come in all sizes and price ranges, from mass excursion launches to semiprivate charter yachts.

Getting back to the mainland, let's head for the—

SUNSHINE COAST: A chain of splendid surfing beaches 40 miles north of Brisbane (take a bus), this is a relatively less developed region, although it boasts one of Australia's swankest resort hotels, the **Surfair International.** But as a whole the Sunshine Coast is the antidote to the honky-tonk sand circus atmosphere of the Gold Coast (farther south) described in the Brisbane section.

Here the golden sands lie uncrowded, the skyline free of neon jitters, the sea breezes blow unpermeated by hot-dog smells. The rolling breakers that fringe the sands stretch on and on endlessly, interspersed with bays and inlets equally ideal for swimming or fishing. The backdrop consists of green mountains and forests, little rivers, and warm quiet lakes. The region grows pineapples, bananas, and paw paws and their scent flavors the air, their gold and russet hues gleam through the tropical foliage. (Once you've tasted the little Queensland fairy bananas you'll find other brands pretty dull.)

At **Kondalilla National Park** you can catch glimpses of a weird living fossil that inhabits the deep pools there—the "lung fish," a genuine fish with the ability to survive out of water, in mud. And four miles south of Nambour lies the **Sunshine Plantation,** a vast expanse of sugarcane fields through which you can ride on a miniature train.

Great Keppel Island is a tiny fun-filled dot lying some 45 miles off Rockhampton in the blue Pacific, about four flying hours from Sydney and Melbourne. The island has 17 superb beaches, some thronged, some for solitude, all fringed with deep-green tropical vegetation. It also has a disco with resident band, sporting facilities, a bar, a café, a restaurant, and a hairdressing salon—and a young, immensely enthusiastic clientele. Aside from deluxe accommodation in carpeted holiday units, there's a caravan and camping ground for the budget-conscious. The on-site vans come with electricity, linen, cutlery, gas stoves, and refrigerators (but no towels).

You reach Great Keppel by taking a coach leaving from the Rockhampton post office every morning except Thursday, which connects with a speedy hydrofoil whizzing across to the island. Round-trip fare is $12 for adults, half price for children.

You can also buy a TAA holiday package, containing seven days on the island, including transportation, bed, all meals, and a welcome drink on arrival. (Your liquor consumption over and above that reception drink costs you extra.) Prices vary according to *when* you go, *where* you come from, and *how* you want your accommodation. The price of standard living quarters in the low-cost season starts at $743.

MOUNT ISA: A thousand miles northwest of Brisbane lies what is—by definition—the largest city in the world. The Mount Isa City Council administers a "municipality" much bigger than the entire Netherlands, but housing only about 22,000 people. "The Isa," as the locals call their phenomenon, also has several other claims to fame. It's the biggest copper producer in Australia and one of the greatest silver-lead-zinc miners in the world. And it enjoys the longest milk run on earth—milk deliveries come from Townsville, 600 miles by rail, every morning.

Mount Isa (take a plane from Brisbane or Cairns) lies surrounded by an immense loneliness studded with ochre red rock ramparts, astonishingly green valleys and blue lakes, forests of ghost gums and natural springs. Here dingoes prowl and wild camels nibble the scrub while eagles draw slow circles in the deep blue inland sky. The contrast between the timeless empty solitude of the land and the booming hustle of "The Isa" is almost unreal—a miracle wrought by copper.

WHITSUNDAY COAST AND ISLANDS: A sun-drenched, mountain-fringed stretch of seashore some 120 miles north of Mackay, with 100 or so tropical islands sprinkled offshore, and as lush as (but rather more isolated than) the Barrier Reef, this area can give you at least the illusion of "getting away from it all"—whatever "it" may be. A whole armada of big and little pleasure boats start engines or hoist canvas every morning in **Shute Harbour** to cruise the Whitsunday waters, which have a picture-postcard blue most of the year.

There's a wildlife sanctuary at **Airlie Beach** with glass reptile pens, crocodile enclosures, plus kangaroos, emus, and swarms of exotic birds roaming free. Also a holiday resort called **Wanderer's Paradise** renting two-person tents, sleeping bags, etc., with showers, laundry facilities, restaurant, and club bar. A TAA package gives you seven days of romping there, plus two-way transportation for $538 from Sydney staying in their Melanesian units.

The offshore islands bear a close resemblance to Robinson Crusoe's involuntary retreat—except that some of them boast swimming pools, tennis courts, golf courses, and air-conditioned beach units. You reach them either by launch or seaplane from Shute Harbour.

Daydream Island is somewhat less stylish but at least as attractive. Secluded beaches and superb waterskiing are the main joys here, apart from a Polynesian-style restaurant specializing in local reef seafood.

Daydream houses tourists in the **Polynesian Village,** either in standard units or suites, each equipped with private facilities, radio, and piped-in music (air conditioning, refrigerators, and color TV in the VIP suites only). Social life revolves around a huge, free-form, and rather redundant swimming pool with a bar on a tiny islet in the middle.

South Molle Island lies in the heart of the panoramic **Whitsunday Passage,** fringed with sand and coral beaches and rising to a pyramidal mountain peak that might have served our friend Crusoe as a lookout post.

The fleet of motor and sailing cruisers setting out from Shute Harbour every balmy morning serve a delightfully wide range of purposes. Some simply take you fishing, snorkeling, and diving. Others have glass bottoms for coral viewing. Others visit the islands, including several of the uninhabited ones. Still others act purely as fishing craft, with lines and bait included in the price. All these cruises include your lunch and take children up to 12 years of age for half price. A TAA holiday package lets you stay seven nights on the island for $748—including all meals. Book through any tourist bureau in Queensland.

Long Island, about five miles southeast of Shute Harbour, is a tranquil little patch of green roughly a million miles removed from the rat race. The place has a budget settlement in the shape of small cabins at **Palm Bay**—not to be confused with the much pricier resort at Happy Bay. At Palm Bay you get cooking facilities and refrigerators, but share the showers; meals are not included in your rates. No frills or entertainment, but complete relaxation and all the sand, surf, and sunshine you've ever dreamed about. For information, consult the Queensland Tourist Office in Brisbane.

Moreton Island is a genuine hideaway some 20 miles from Brisbane. The island only has one resort, Tangalooma, but several fascinating features. There's the world's largest sandhill to toboggan from, a mystery desert to explore, an antique lighthouse, wild horses, pigs, and goats, plus some of tropical Australia's finest fishing. Tangalooma has a beautiful bushland setting right by the beach and offers cocktail bars, tennis courts, waterskiing, and aquaplaning. All units—standard or deluxe—are completely self-contained.

TOWNSVILLE: With a population nudging 100,000, Townsville is Australia's largest tropical city as well as the southern gateway to the Great Barrier Reef. Its lifestyle could be said to offer the best of both worlds: lots of city action combined with enough tropical lassitude to suggest the ambience of an eternal vacation.

The misnamed **Town Common,** for instance, is actually a wondrous bird sanctuary, flapping ground of the unique dancing brolga. **Flinders Mall,** palm shaded and modernistic, is the hub of a pretty sophisticated shopping and restaurant strip. The **Strand,** which follows the curve of Cleveland Bay, is an elegant boulevard created for strolling, cooled by fountains and waterfalls, lined with some of the lushest garden landscapes in the land. And in case you crave an industrial touch, there's Victoria Mill, the biggest sugar mill in the southern hemisphere, where you can inspect operations during the crushing season from June to November.

Five miles offshore—35 minutes as the ferry chugs—lies **Magnetic Island.** This is possibly the most idyllic of the Barrier Reef islets, with tall hoop pines, rugged headlands, brilliant coral formations, a fernery, sealife aquarium, and some very velvety resorts. Daily passenger ferries will get you there and back, and let you enjoy the Koala Park Oasis, walking trails, and 25 beaches for a round-trip fare of $5. TAA offers a package deal that includes seven nights at the Alma Den beach resort (bed and breakfast) for $462.

Chapter VIII

PERTH AND THE FAR WEST

1. The City and Surroundings
2. Western Australia

TO TELL YOU THAT PERTH is the world's most isolated major city means to risk evoking a completely false picture of the place. So I'll start by saying that Perth is one of the prettiest cities on earth and probably the most all-around charming town in Australia. Isolated she certainly is—not merely from the Australian mainstream but from everybody else's as well. But somehow this has worked in her favor. From her remote vantage point, Perth was able to watch other centers grow, then follow suit and avoid most of their mistakes.

Thus she acquired liveliness without garishness, beauty without pomposity, modernity without frigidity. Helped along by an ideal Mediterranean climate, an amiable population, and the enormous mineral wealth of her state, Perth developed into the nearest facsimile of an ideal metropolis. How long she will remain so—given her rate of growth—is another question.

1. The City and Surroundings

Her main commercial street, St. George's Terrace, ranks among the most elegant thoroughfares in the world. Instead of shopping streets, Perth has shopping arcades and malls, some on two and three levels connected by escalators and elevators. In the City Arcade the elevator emerges from a fountain that surrounds passengers on three sides without splashing them. The shopping areas abound in patios, trees, flowers, benches, and delightful little boutiques. Almost constant glittering sunshine and vast areas of parkland give the city a wonderful *open* look usually reserved for small resorts.

It's a modern town created for pedestrians, not motorists. The core is formed by arcades radiating from a central mall, encircled counterclockwise by one-way streets. This arrangement is tough on drivers, but pampers them the moment they climb out of their vehicles and start strolling. If you rent a car, don't drive it downtown. In Perth the infantry gets there faster.

The first white settlers arrived here in 1829, but it wasn't until the gold rush of the 1890s that Perth became a city of sorts. The mineral rush that followed World War II then transformed her from a drowsy backwater into a metropolis. Today the capital of Western Australia has over 800,000 people (more than San Francisco) and is expanding rapidly, but according to a masterplan that matches new building developments with equivalent parks and gardens.

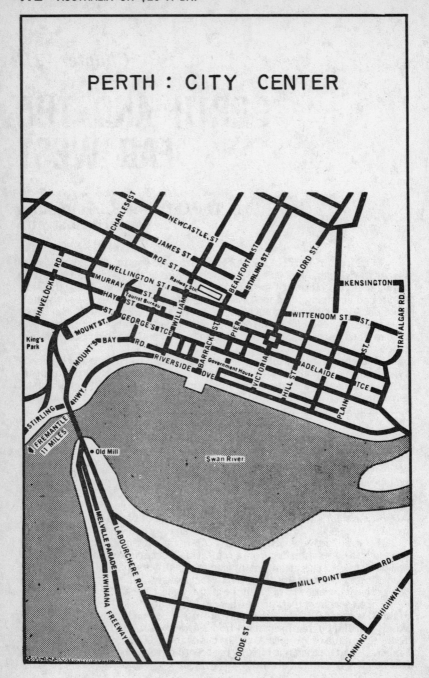

PERTH : CITY CENTER

Perth lies astride the **Swan River,** some 12 miles inland from her seaport of **Fremantle.** This is one of her special characteristics: Perth faces the Indian Ocean while every other Australian capital faces the Pacific. The location gives Perth the advantage of a beautiful riverfront, yet with half a dozen great ocean beaches just a suburban train ride away. On warm evenings, when the cooling breezes fail to arrive, tens of thousands of people flock to the beaches to swim under the stars. And while the suburbs are relentlessly spreading north and south along the coast and inland toward the Darling Ranges, Perth can boast that she still has thriving vineyards, producing quality wines, within ten miles of her General Post Office.

Perth is billed as the "Sunshine City," and can prove the title statistically. She gets more radiance than any other Australian capital—averaging eight hours of sunshine daily throughout the year, a possible world record. The local temperament reflects the weather—the aptest term for it is "sunny." And perhaps her climate will save Perth from the urban What-Makes-Sammy-Run blight for which she seems destined by the rate of her expansion.

GETTING THERE: Nothing drives home the sense of Perth's remoteness like the process of getting there. If you want the full taste of it, try the rail trip from Sydney: the "Indian-Pacific" takes three days for the continental crossing. It's shorter and cheaper from Adelaide (Port Pirie), but still a mighty haul across the tabletop-flat Nullarbor Plain. You can also do it by Greyhound or Ansett Pioneer bus, two days riding from Adelaide for $95.

The Eyre Highway that crosses the Nullarbor was only completely surfaced in 1976. Since then driving or hitching across has become quite popular, although this can be a pretty wearing experience for all parties concerned. An enterprising outfit called **Travel Mates,** 496 Newcastle St., West Perth (tel. 328-6685), operates a "Share-A-Car" service. They introduce one to the other and passengers pay a share of the costs, plus a $10 office fee. Rental cars are also available at the airport.

Both TAA and Ansett run daily air services to Perth from all other capitals. The flight from Sydney takes four hours and 20 minutes and costs $383.40.

GETTING AROUND: Perth city buses are probably the best in Australia in regard to comfort, frequency, and punctuality. The downtown area also has a wonderful *free* bus service for shoppers—the **City Clippers.** Red Clippers go east, Yellow Clippers do a circuit of the inner shopping area. Blue Clippers do the "cultural" round of museums and art galleries. The inquiries office at 125 St. George's Terrace is open six days a week (tel. 325-8511). Wellington Street Ferries to South Perth leave from the **Barrack Street Jetty.**

To call a cab, phone **Swan Taxis** at 22-0111 or **Black and White** at 25-5555. For car rentals **Thrifty** has a desk at Perth Airport and a main office at 73 Bennett St. (tel. 325-4700). One of the local companies, **Sydney Andersons,** 216 Stirling St. (tel. 328-1477), offers a Honda at $8 a day plus 10¢ per kilometer.

However, despite (or because) of its modernistic layout Perth is not an easy city to drive in—leastwise not for unwary visitors. It's bisected by rail lines with far too few crossings. These handsome road bridges, overflights, and underpasses make for a pleasing variety of vistas but also for traffic snarls where none need be. One-way streets are poorly marked and street signs are scarce, often hidden behind decorative trees. And once you get out of the main streets, the illumination frequently resembles Tombstone in the days of Wyatt Earp. The brand-new freeways look beautiful, but their entry and exit system doesn't match their appearance. Some intersections must be navigated by a mixture of cunning, instinct, and faith in one's guardian angel. Put it all down to growing pains. . . .

Perth International Air Terminal lies about five miles northeast of the city. By airline coach it's $3; by cab, about $7.50. The airport is new, smallish, and cozy. The cafeteria stays open around the clock and sells, among other edibles, sandwiches that are infinitely superior to those retailed at U.S., British, or New Zealand airports. The two bars, though, are understaffed and overworked, and the banking facilities operate only on arrival of international flights. There's a duty-free shop and a 24-hour gas station. And a charming welcome touch in the shape of a little stone pond on which black swans sail majestically in circles—black swans are the symbols of Westralia.

ORIENTATION: The **Holiday W.A. Centre** is at 772 Hay St. (tel. 321-2471) and makes a good orientation point. This is the commercial core of the city, the so-called central block. Hay Street runs parallel to the other main thoroughfares: Murray and Wellington Streets, and St. George's Terrace (which becomes Adelaide Terrace farther east). In this central section you'll find all the large retail stores and company offices, government departments, and theaters as well as the shopping arcades and malls mentioned earlier. At the head of St. George's Terrace stands the venerable **Barracks Arch,** one of Perth's landmarks. The other is the **Town Hall,** corner of Hay and Barrack Streets, built in the style of the English Jacobean market hall—but with convict labor.

St. George's Terrace runs west to east. To the north of where you're standing lies the **General Post Office** (GPO) and the **railway station.** To the south is the **Esplanade** and adjoining it **Barrack Street Jetty,** from which the ferries cross the river to South Perth. The **Swan River** makes a curving bulge around the city, separating the downtown section from the vast suburban sprawl to the south. The two main bridges linking the portions are the **Causeway** (east of Barrack Street Jetty) and the **Narrows** (west of it).

West of your position stretches the Indian Ocean with the popular beaches at Leighton, Cottesloe, Swanbourne, City, and Scarborough. And southwest, at the mouth of the Swan River, stands **Fremantle,** which deserves a section of its own. Northeast, alongside the Great Eastern Highway, lies the airport and farther out in the same direction the magnificent **John Forrest National Park.**

A NOTE ON PRICES: All prices in this guide are in Australian dollars (A$). As we go to press, US$1 = approximately A$1.40. Thus a room listed at $20 a night actually costs only about $14.50 in U.S. funds—good news indeed for budget travelers.

ACCOMMODATIONS: Perth is well—almost lavishly—equipped with budget beds, both in the downtown area and the inner suburbs. But it lacks any kind of motel strip where hostelries stand in rows and you can go from door to door and do comparison shopping. It does, however, boast a larger than average share of hostel-type places (possibly due to its geographical position) which helps to keep accommodation costs down, since most of them offer comfortable alternatives to the standard hotels.

Hostels

Jewell House, 180 Goderich St. (tel. 325-1085), a former nurses quarters converted into a private hotel, stands in a central position in a blessedly quiet street—which is still a hospital zone. A trim building, kept absolutely spick and span, the Jewell accommodates 250 guests in rooms ranging from single to family size (two adults, three children). The free City Clipper to take you shopping stops right outside. The hotel has laundry and ironing facilities, a TV lounge, and a dining room. The double rooms come with coffee- and tea-making facilities, and the shared bathrooms positively sparkle. Bedrooms are small but comfortable and airy, with overhead and bedside lamps, wall-to-wall carpets, writing shelves, and good-size wardrobes. They don't, however, have washbasins. Singles cost $18, doubles are $24, and the family rooms run $45.

Next we come to the **Leederville Lodge,** 193 Oxford St., Leederville (tel. 444-7359). The lodge is a curious whitewashed brick building in a relatively quiet part of Leederville's main shopping street. City transport stops at the door. The house has a sundeck, a big clean and plastic dining room looking rather like a gym hall, an upstairs laundry, a TV lounge, and 34 bedrooms, all but six of them doubles. Wall-to-wall carpeting, big wardrobes, writing desks, and handy shelves make for simple but neat furnishings. The rooms have no basins, but the public bathrooms are well fitted and absolutely spotless. The tariff here includes breakfast and dinner, both ample. Singles pay $20; doubles, $18 per person. Considering that this pays for board as well, you're not likely to find lower rates anywhere.

Beatty Lodge, 235 Vincent St., North Perth (tel. 328-1288), is a quite charming hacienda affair, red-roofed and palm-fringed, standing opposite the beautiful Aquatic Centre in Beatty Park. (The front, unfortunately, faces a pretty noisy main road.) The lodge has its own swimming pool and sundeck and a bus stop at the door, also three separate recreation lounges (color TV), snack kiosk, laundromat, seven bathrooms, and 80 bedrooms. The units are of medium size and very nicely appointed: green wall-to-wall carpets, refrigerator, lots of wardrobe space, and two mirrors with individual illumination. But no handbasin or bedside lights. You can have either bed and breakfast or dinner as well included in the tariff. Room only costs $15 for singles, $24 for doubles. The family rooms go for $40 for four persons.

I have already mentioned **Travel Mates** in the "Getting There" section, but this remarkable outfit has extensive lodging functions as well. For basic comforts, rock-bottom rates, and a hang-loose atmosphere, this is it. Headquarters stands at 496 Newcastle St., West Perth (tel. 328-6685), and has two adjoining hostels operating dorm style on a casual daily basis. You can't miss "H.Q.'s" turn-of-the-century house with a huge sign on the front lawn showing a bearded swagman doffing his hat to you. Not exactly luxurious, but it exudes cozy vibes and runs minus any petty regulations. You get the drift of things when you meet Del Little, the manager. Del isn't little, but a tall and striking lady as efficient as she is charming. Mates also supervise their own chain of "share houses" located in the suburbs. All these houses are shared by small groups on a communal basis. The "share houses" host only two persons per bedroom, while the hostels sleep you in dormitories with basic facilities. Share houses cost $30 weekly, hostels come to $6 daily. No wardens or lockup times, and sociability is on the house.

There are two official **Youth Hostels** in Perth, both situated less than a mile from downtown. The first is at 60 Newcastle St. (tel. 328-1135), the overflow hostel at 46 Francis St. (tel. 328-7794). Both are erstwhile guesthouses, now renovated, with laundries and full kitchen facilities. They total 98 beds and charge $5.50 per night.

A third Youth Hostel operates in Perth's adjoining harbor town of Fremantle. Located at 96 Hampton Road (tel. 335-3467) and charging the same rates, this is a historic building—an erstwhile family home that became a maternity hospital, then a nurses' home before its present function. A charming traditional Colonial-style building, it's situated close to the America's Cup marinas (yachting fans please note) and within walking distance of downtown.

The Y

Perth's **YMCA,** 119 Murray St., (tel. 325-2744) takes men, women, and couples, offering very basic accommodations at very basic prices. The Y stands in central downtown, but has no elevator and rather steep stairs. Laundry facilities and a TV lounge are on the premises, but no restaurant, although there are plenty nearby. The 56 bedrooms have no handbasins and ceiling lights only. Furnishings are fairly Spartan, except for ample hanging space in the wardrobes. The staff is exceptionally friendly, even by Westralian standards. Singles here cost $9 to $11, doubles $8 to $9 and triple rooms $9.

Hotels

First choice here is above our budget range, but such an exceptional find for couples or family groups that I felt compelled to include it. The **Airways Hotel Apartments,** 195 Adelaide Terrace (tel. 323-7799), is part hotel, part office building, and an equal mixture of comfort, convenience, and stylishness. Opened in 1981, the Airways has 156 self-contained units with ultramodern kitchens, plus a grocery and delicatessen to keep them stocked. It has a central downtown location, plus a doctor, dentist, dry cleaner, restaurant, coffeeshop, newspaper kiosk, and souvenir store on the premises. The units, kept in matching shades of brown and white, have little balconies, wide beds with bedside radio, multitudes of drawers, vast hanging space, color TV, and handy writing desks. The kitchens are equipped with gas range (a rarity), refrigerator, and ample sink, plus cooking utensils complete down to salt and pepper shakers, trays, bread knives, and corkscrews. The compact bathrooms, fluorescently lit, are supplied with shower caps and thick towels. As a crowning touch the Airways also boasts one of the fastest elevator (pardon me—"lift") services in town. Double units cost from $48; family units (two adults, two children), from $72.

The **Criterion Hotel,** 560 Hay St. (tel. 325-5155), opposite Perth's Town Hall, is a picturesque old Victorian complex containing four bars done out magnificently in scarlet and walnut, a restaurant, and 60 bedrooms. The lobby welcomes you with ornate vintage splendor, though the bedrooms are smallish, fittings very old-fashioned. You get overhead and bedside lights, lofty ceilings, a tiny dressing table with mirror, and tea- and coffee-making equipment. The Criterion dining room is locally famous for its five-course Roast of the Day dinners costing only $8.95. Standard single rooms cost $20; standard doubles, $40, including breakfast.

Both of the following establishments stand opposite the railway station, facing the new W.A. Trade Centre. The **Imperial,** 413 Wellington St. (tel. 325-8877), is one of those biggish old railroad hotels from the time when architects believed in elbow space for hotel guests. The facade doesn't look like much, but don't be deceived by the frontage, which includes the lobby. The public rooms are spacious and very comfortable, and the bedrooms large and excellently maintained. Some of them come with private facilities. The dining room is vast and lit by chandeliers and the guest lounge cozily wood-paneled in a rich shade of walnut brown. The 69 bedrooms have high old-fashioned beds, dressers with good mirrors, bedside lamps, and generous hanging space. About half are singles. The tariff is from $17 for singles, from $28 for doubles, and includes breakfast..With private bathroom it's an extra $7 per day.

The **Grand Central,** 379 Wellington St. (tel. 325-5638), is cheaper and more basic. The majority of the 60 rooms are singles, but there are also several family rooms. Wall-to-wall carpeting, large wardrobes, but only one ceiling light and the furniture is pretty archaic. The hotel has laundry facilities and an elevator as well as a dining room. There are two public bathrooms on each floor. Singles here pay $10; doubles, $17. No food is served on the premises.

The **Hotel Britannia,** 253 William St. (tel. 328-6121), blends well with its cosmopolitan surroundings despite its regal title. A quaintly antique structure with a small corner tower, the Britannia greets you with a lobby studded with potted plants and settees, plus a mysterious separate door marked "Nite Entrance." The 80 bedrooms have basic fittings—no handbasins—but with carpeting and bedside lamps. Wardrobes are a mite tiny, the beds old-fashioned, but all rooms are spotless. There's an excellent restaurant, the **Casa Latina,** on the premises. Also vending machines and a perfect labyrinth of corridors. Rooms rent for $10 and up.

Serviced Apartments

Our first selection occupies one of the choicest locations in the city. The **City Waters Lodge,** 118 Terrace Rd. (tel. 325-5020), overlooks Langley Park and the Swan River, right in the heart of Perth. A brand-new motel-style apartment block, it comprises 32 self-contained units ranging from single to family size, all charmingly and quite lavishly furnished, all with kitchen, modern bathroom, and all necessary utensils, linen, crockery, cutlery, and color TV and air conditioning (but neither radio nor telephone). There's lots of wardrobe space, plus excellent refrigerator and a gas range in the kitchens. Laundrette on the premises. Singles cost $32 a day; doubles, $35.

The **Canning Bridge Auto Lodge,** at 891 Canning Hwy., Applecross (tel. 364-2511). The suites accommodate from two to five persons and the block has a private pool and a children's playground. Every apartment is air-conditioned and self-contained. Appliances include all kitchen equipment, linen, refrigerator, telephone, TV, and radio. The beds have inner-spring mattresses and individual reading lights. Rents range from $30 a day for one-bedroomers to $50 for the two-bedroom units for four people. But there is also a 10% discount for weekly rentals.

The third selection is at one of Perth's most popular beach resorts. **Westhaven House,** 150 Marine Parade, Cottesloe (tel. 384-4738), offers typical seaside holiday accommodations in a large building right beside a delightful beach, with the Indian Ocean at your door, a shopping block across the road, and a reasonably quiet environment. The Westhaven has two types of units: two-bedroom flats, fully equipped and self-contained, renting from $30 a day, and bed-sitters, which have only a cooker, shared bathroom, but also refrigerator and all utensils and cost from $15 a day.

College Accommodations

The University of Western Australia is at Crawley, next to Kings Park, beautifully placed amid the greenery facing a small bay of the Swan River which widens to lake dimensions at this point. The various colleges have rooms available for overseas students during the holidays over Christmas, May, and August. Booking, however, is heavy. The rates are around $15 a day with full board. Check the following numbers: St. Columba College, 386-7177; St. Thomas More College, 386-5080; Currie Hall, 380-2772; St. George's College, 386-1425.

Caravan (Trailer) Parks

Perth is as well supplied with caravan parks as with all other types of accommodations. There are 31 of these parks within and around the city area: 27 of them have on-site vans for hire and the majority permit camping. For a complete list of these facilities get the guide brochure at the Holiday W.A. Travel Centre, 772 Hay St. Herewith a few samples:

Perth Caravan Park, Hale Road, Forrestfield (tel. 453-6677), 9½ miles from the city, has on-site luxury vans and supplies cooking utensils and crockery. Guests are advised to bring their own linen or rent it at $7 a week. Rates range from $20 a day, $75 a week, for two persons.

Combo Beach Caravan Park, 4 Ednah St. (tel. 367-1286), three miles from the city. Close to the beach with bus terminus at the entrance. It has vans with four to six berths and all cooking equipment. Rates from $100 a week for four to six persons.

MEALS: One reason why the word "isolated" conveys such a false image of Perth is the culinary scene. It happens to be among the best in Australia. Perth boasts a happy profusion of eateries running the scale from Arabian to Yugoslav, many of them in the economy bracket. What's more, they are heavily concentrated in a distinct area, which makes it delightfully easy to track them down. The region is James Street/William Street, the latter lying across the railroad tracks, a somewhat seedy neighborhood chock-a-block with small, cheap, ethnic family restaurants providing delicious fare.

Lunches and Snacks

Hotel counter lunches have the usual high Australian standard, sometimes coupled with a lot of atmosphere. The **Grosvenor Hotel** in Hay Street, corner of Hill Street, offers both. This is an intriguingly schizoid place: the older portion —white, colonial, and absolutely beautiful—has one of the most pleasant wine gardens in Perth. The new part—tacked on as if by absent-minded afterthought —possesses all the subtle charm of an airport passenger lounge. The two halves are shoved together like immobile railroad cars, turning the interior into a maze of bars, lounges, dining rooms, and saloons in which you can get lost for hours. But the plastic new portion puts on outstanding counter lunches, particularly braised beef for $4.

An excellent coffeeshop opens early for breakfast and unfortunately closes early as well. **Rubens,** on the ground floor of the Wesley Arcade, corner of Hay and William Streets, serves the only filtered coffee with individual dripolators in Perth, as well as sweet and savory dishes. It opens at 7:45 a.m. and closes at 6 p.m. weekdays, 1 p.m. on Saturday.

Seek out **Miss Maud's** sandwich shop, at the corner of Murray and Pier Streets, where the sandwiches have a downright poetic quality. (The adjoining restaurant, however, while excellent, is also expensive.) In Cinecentre Arcade, 96 Barrack St., is the **Trade Winds,** a delightful coffee lounge combined with an art gallery. The paintings on the wall range from pleasant to mediocre, but decidedly give the place atmosphere. You can buy them on the spot from $50 to $300, and occasionally someone does. Also small objets d'art that go from $2.50

each. Otherwise it's a restful and comfortable snackery that serves artistic sandwiches, piles of fluffy European pastries, and Vienna coffee.

Dinner

The **Pancake Kitchen,** 92 Barrack St., is somewhat gaudy and plastic, but surprisingly versatile and very handy, since it opens its portals seven days a week. It's a large, bright, comfortable eatery with revolving chairs and wagonwheel lights, and the fare covers the entire range from porterhouse steak to potato pancakes. The pancakes come in 21 guises—pineapple to prawns—and cost between $3.85 and $8.60. The menu also offers pork, chicken, or beef schnitzels (curiously enough, no veal) and several makes of steak. Your coffee or tea cup is refilled free of charge, and the service is outstandingly courteous. Open till 11 p.m. weeknights, till 1 a.m. on Saturday and Sunday.

Another all-weeker is the **Canton,** 532 Hay St., a softly lit and carpeted Chinese dinery, with excellent food and leisurely service. It provides an odd contrast between ornately tassled chandeliers and severely functional metal tables. I had dim sum for starters, followed by a vegetarian combination with nuts, both highly commendable. The meal came to $7.70. Open every night till 11 p.m. or midnight, on Sunday till 9:30 p.m.

Franco's, 323 Hay St., is an attractive corner building with two small dining rooms. The establishment has a dual personality—Anglo-Spanish—which even flavors the decor. Walls and ceiling, with oak beams, wagon wheels, and ornate lanterns represent the Iberian touch. Tables and chairs are strictly Anglo-utilitarian. The menu and cuisine are split as well. The rice that accompanies the dishes is saffron, but the chips, peas, and carrots taste very Aussie indeed. The fine paella is unfortunately served only on Tuesday (for two or more diners, at $8.95 per mouth). On other days I'd recommend the pepper steak or the chicken español ($7.95 and $7), with the flan con nata as dessert. This is a BYO—so do. Open, except Sunday, until around 10 p.m.

All the following places are along or just off **William Street,** which stretches north to the unfashionable side of the tracks. There are plenty more besides those mentioned, for this is *the* budget eating strip of Perth. Most of them are European mom-and-pop establishments, which usually guarantees quality, if not decor. The turnover, though, is rather rapid. So if you find that a particular hostelry has disappeared or changed names or turned into a hardware store, simply wander on to the next.

Agostino, at no. 287, is a small, cluttered food bar with counter and stools—far from stylish but both cheap and excellent. Meals are take-out or eat there, and every dish comes with a choice of seasonal vegetables or salad or spaghetti. Scaloppini al vino blanco costs $7.50; half a roast chicken, the same; and the homemade minestrone, 80¢. Open seven days a week: Monday to Thursday till 11 p.m., Friday and Saturday till 1 a.m., Sunday till 10 p.m.

The **Bohemian,** at no. 309, despite its name is more Balkan than Czech. It's a large, handsome two-room eating house, lit by orange lanterns, with old city prints adorning the walls and a palate-tingling aroma of charcoal-grilled goodies in the air. There are two bars, one for each room, candles flickering in wine bottles, salt-shakers shaped like Grecian urns, and nightly entertainment consisting of bouzouki and guitar music. The food is as tangy as the atmosphere. Stuffed paprika or smoked pork and beans come at $8.50. The Turkish coffee is a *must,* and it's served with a small plate of Turkish delight. And each order arrives accompanied by superb salads of lettuce, tomatoes, onions, and black olives.

The **Los Gallos Mexican Restaurant,** across the road at no. 276, is a small Latino charmer holding its own in the surrounding throng of Italian, Greek, and

Yugoslav hostelries. And as a rule it's packed. Inside it's candles on the ceiling, more candles at the tables, and—by way of contrast—an air-conditioned dining room. The average three-course meal costs $10. Open five days a week; closed Monday and Tuesday.

At **Romany,** no. 188, you're back in the Italian fold. The place has the plainest of white tile fronts, but remarkable atmosphere engendered by home-style cooking, patrons who all seem to know each other, and soul-saturating portions. The only jarring note comes from the constant blare of rock and pop tapes, loud enough to melt the pasta. The two small dining rooms are divided by a curtain. And each meal is preceded by a heaped basket of crisp white Italian bread. The ravioli soup is outstanding at $2, as is the chicken parmigiana for $9.

Just off William Street, at the corner of Lake and Aberdeen Streets, stands the cottage-style **Mamma Maria's,** the most famous Italian eating house in town. The fame is well earned. Not only does "Mamma" (actually owner Harry Ferrante) put on glorious grub, but he adds complimentary plates of cheese and greens at the beginning and muscat or vintage port at the conclusion of your meal. On top of that you get remarkable decor (including a village hand pump attached to the stairway), pretty waitresses in peasant frocks, truly powerful black coffee, and a menu that unrolls like a royal proclamation. The menu is worth studying. The fine print contains quotes from Cicero and informative snippets like, "Dishes marked thus * we have run out of." Soup, main course, and coffee sets you back around $12.50. Mamma's is air-conditioned and most nights there's a wandering and singing guitar player to reinforce the atmosphere. Open seven days a week "till late."

Haus Tirol (that's the correct spelling) is located in the Imperial Hotel, 413 Wellington St. Setting and cuisine are both Tyrolese, including the Alpine zither and yodeling strains that accompany your meal. A large establishment that resembles a hunting lodge, the Tirol has a central bar with an (indoor) shingled roof, very comfortable peasant-style chairs with carved backs, walls full of antlers, bridles, sickles, and silver plates and a general air of rustic hospitality. Tables are beautifully set and the fare complemented with superb rye bread and pats of butter served on wooden platters. We had tomato salad for starters, followed by aromatic zwiebel rostbraten (beef with fried onions) accompanied by some of the finest homemade potato salad we've ever eaten. Total cost $12. The Tirol closes on Sundays.

DAYTIME ACTIVITIES: Perth is one of the few cities in which the shopping areas can rank as sights. The **Hay Street Pedestrian Mall** is tremendous fun and **London Court,** linking Hay Street to St. George's Terrace, a real museum piece. This arcade, built in delightfully ridiculous mock-Tudor, actually opened in 1937 but pretends to be a kind of medieval fortress. Guarded by iron portcullises, which are lowered at night, it contains two "dungeon towers," the statues of Sir Walter Raleigh and Dick Whittington (plus cat), and moving clockworks showing St. George perpetually slaying the poor dragon and tilting knights having at each other.

Just across the Narrows Bridge stands the **Old Mill,** a relic from 1835 which was once used to grind flour but now houses a collection of early colonial tools, artifacts, and mementos. For some even older relics, go to the **Western Australian Museum** on Francis Street and admire a 30-foot whale skeleton and a meteorite weighing 11 tons. There's a better museum in Fremantle, which we'll visit further on.

The small modern **zoo** is in the South Perth on the other side of the river, interesting because it contains many animals unique to Western Australia. You can take bus 36 from St. George's Terrace or the ferry from Barrack Street Jetty.

For more Westralian fauna there's **Lake Monger** in suburban Wembley. This is a haven for the state's famous black swans (and hundreds of other waterfowl), and if you bring a bag of buns the swans will eat out of your hand. Take bus 90, 91, or 92 from the Central Bus Station and get off at the corner of Harbourne and Grantham Streets.

The pride of Perth is **Kings Park,** a 1,000-acre reserve of natural and culti-vated bushland at the top of Mount Eliza. The park is not only magically beauti-ful but also offers a panoramic view of the entire city below. Within the area there is the joyously spurting and bubbling fountain dedicated to the Pioneer Women, a floral clock, some ancient cannon, and a tragic row of gumtrees, each one planted by the family of a fallen "Digger" as a living memorial marked with his battalion colors. Also an excellent and expensive restaurant with a dining patio and next to it a pleasant snack terrace (little tables and self-service) that sells very good sandwiches and afternoon tea.

Perth's most celebrated sight, unfortunately, is not so readily viewable. This is the ornately beautiful **America's Cup.** Ever since the *Australia II* cap-tured the world's prime yachting trophy it has been exhibited throughout the continent like a prize scalp. At the time of writing, however, the Cup is cloistered within the private portals of the Royal Perth Yacht Club at Pelican Point, Crawley. In order to see it you must be taken in by a member, a privilege not available to the majority of tourists.

The **Art Gallery,** 47 James St., opened its gates in October 1979 and is the newest, and in some respects the most magnificent, of Australia's art museums. The building cost $10 million and looks every cent's worth. The pièce de rési-stance is the superb Thyssen collection of modern masters, including works by Picasso, Cézanne, Monet, Renoir, and Van Gogh. Other artistic magnets in-clude paintings by Whistler and Rembrandt, some of the finest contemporary Australian canvases, and a wonderfully displayed section of "Art of the West-ern Desert" by the Aboriginal Panunya tribe. Watch for the changing traveling exhibitions announced in the newspapers. And reserve several hours of sight-seeing time to give this palace its due. Open Monday through Sunday from 10 a.m. to 5 p.m.

One of the nicest ways of seeing the city and environs is by water. Daily (except Saturday) between September and May the Metropolitan Transport Trust operates **Swan River Ferry Cruises** up- and downstream. The trip starts from Barrack Street Jetty at 2 p.m., daily except Saturday, takes about three hours, and costs $7 for adults, $3 for children. The glass-enclosed boat follows the course taken by the exploring Capt. James Stirling and goes past islands, racecourses, and riverside garden suburbs, accompanied by a learned commen-tary from the ferry master. Afternoon tea is served on board.

The longer run to Fremantle Harbor and back leaves Sunday from the same jetty at 2 p.m. This is by larger craft that carries a salon bar and snackbar, and offers "cruising music" as well.

FREMANTLE: Perth's seaport on the Indian Ocean is an astonishing place. Founded as the original Swan River Colony by Captain Fremantle in 1829, the town is only a few years older than Perth, but looks centuries her senior. Fre-mantle had a curiously reversed history. It was the first voluntary settlement; that is, the settlers were free immigrants. But they found themselves so desper-ately short of labor that the infant colony *requested* the government to send them convicts. The authorities obliged and dispatched nearly 10,000 "gentle-men of the broad arrows" to the Swan River, where they constructed most of the fine old buildings that today give the port its quaintly archaic air.

Over the past few years Fremantle has undergone an astonishing transformation, mainly because as the site of the 1987 America's Cup challenge race she has been spreading the welcome mat for a very cosmopolitan clientele. Her port facilities have always been modern and streamlined, capable of handling 15 million tons of cargo annually. But suddenly the brooding atmosphere of her old-world streets and squares was rejuvenated by a crop of smart shops, "in" restaurants and sophisticated cafés. They provide some much-needed glitter and make the place a fun spot to stroll around in, but don't change the basic character of the town. The contemporary touches still appear like a superficial graft. Fremantle's soul remains Victorian—a century removed from Perth, which lies only 12 miles away. It is this oddly appealing schizophrenia, the contrasts that strike you at every corner, that gives Fremantle a unique charm found nowhere else on the continent.

The town had the first bridge ever built across the Swan River and its official opening—in 1866—ranks as the most hilarious episode in the annals of the colony. For the man who cut the ribbon was not a local dignitary but Moondyne Joe, a notorious bushranger who had just escaped from prison! Fremantle Gaol, built in 1851 by convicts to house convicts, still stands grimly gray and formidable and still functions as a jail. (You can admire it from the outside.) Despite its Dickensian appearance, however, it is reputedly the most comfortable lockup in Australia. Another jail, the **Round House** on Arthur's Head, is no longer used in that capacity but represents the oldest building in the state and can be inspected daily.

Fremantle is narrow streets, old churches and warehouses, Dutch gables and Gothic cloisters, and a pub at every corner, as befits a harbor town. Most of the watering holes are steeped in seafaring tradition, like the **P & O Hotel** on High Street, looking as if it might have been frequented by the Ancient Mariner. It also puts on excellent counter lunches: chicken soup, grilled snapper for $2.50, supplemented by a big help-yourself salad bar.

The most famous building in town began as the colony's first lunatic asylum in the 1860s—a stark but beautiful showpiece of convict colonial architecture. Due for demolition in 1900, it was saved by the taste and foresight of the then mayor and duly converted into the—

Fremantle Museum. Standing at 1 Finnerty St., this is one of the truly fascinating museums Australia has to offer. To make things even better, it's free. The place is actually more than a museum: one of the wings is given over to local artists as work and exhibition space. And the courtyard becomes a star-lit stage on summer nights. The museum proper is an enchanting melange of relics, maps, photographs, artifacts, weapons, paintings, documents, clothes, and utensils that tell the story of Western Australia. There's a raised cannon from a 17th-century Dutch East India Co. ship and the jewelry worn by fashionable colonial ladies. There are century-old newspaper ads and the harpoons used by Fremantle whalers. There are muskets, pistols, swords, and clubs used by Victorian garrison troops and bushrangers alike. There are evocative old photographs, ancient maps, fashion plates, official proclamations, ladies' sunshades, lighthouse equipment, diving gear, carved whales' teeth, and superb early ships models. There are. . . . but see for yourself. Open seven days a week till 5 p.m.

The **Fremantle Markets** have been operating since 1897, when they were established as exact replicas of the European models. Situated on the corner of Henderson Street and South Terrace they consist of over 100 variegated stalls selling fresh local seafood and exotic herbs and spices, antiques (genuine and phony), jewelry, gem stones, finery, bric-a-brac, and handmade craft items. The background is an ornate 19th-century colonnade, the air is full of music and tangy smells, and the whole scene delightful. In action all day on Friday and half of Saturday.

You can get to Fremantle from Perth by catching bus 101 or 103 in St. George's Terrace.

OUT OF TOWN: As I mentioned earlier, the nearest **ocean beaches** are all outside Perth, but very easy to get to. The Indian Ocean surf is quite heavy and you'd better gauge your capabilities before joining the surfboard brigade. But the golden sands offer glorious lounging and the boys and gals on the boards can be as much fun to watch as to join. Among the most popular ocean resorts are **Scarborough**—catch bus 260 at the Central Bus Station, then change to 268 to reach the foreshore. **City Beach** can be reached directly by bus 84 from the Central Station. **Cottesloe** is a large resort with extensive shopping centers, hotels, restaurants, etc. Get there by bus 72 or 207 from St. George's Terrace.

El Caballo Blanco is an absolute must for anyone with a horsey bent. This is a wonderful Spanish-Moorish hotel at Wooroloo, combined with a stud farm for Andalusian horses. The stallions, mares, and foals are magnificent and the attached **Carriage Museum** has rows of rare, lovingly restored vehicles. The amazingly trained "dancing horses" perform daily except Monday. Every Saturday night is "Fiesta"—a weekly carnival affair amid roses and bougainvillea with music, dancing, and a lot of hilarity. The stud farm lies about 45 miles from Perth along the Great Eastern Highway. There's a special Saturday night Fiesta tour that includes coach transport both ways, a four-course Spanish dinner with wine, the horse show, dancing, and entertainment for $27.50 per person. For inquiries phone 321-9728.

The Darling Range. Once the wild stomping ground of Moondyne Joe and dozens of other bushrangers, the Darling today is Perth's favorite excursion goal. Several small townships nestling in the hills, the area has breathtaking panoramas and—in springtime—immense carpets of wildflowers. One of the villages, **Kalamunda,** has a **Folk Museum** with early steam trains and historic photos. Take bus 297 or 302 from Hay Street. Those sitting on the left-hand side of the bus get the best views. **Yanchep Park,** a 6,000-acre bushland reserve 34 miles north of Perth, offers wildlife, boating, and swimming, and also some spectacular caves in the limestone cliffs rising 270 feet above Loch McNess. **Crystal Cave** contains an enchanting grotto with an underground stream that reflects the images of stalactites and stalagmites in its crystal-clear water.

Rottnest Island was unflatteringly (and wrongly) named by the early Dutch explorers who thought the place was swarming with rats. What they actually saw were cute, pint-sized marsupials called quokkas, which were indigenous to the island and still hop around there in furry bunches. Now affectionately known as "Rotto," the island is a patch of tranquil beauty in the deep blue of the Indian Ocean, 12 miles offshore from Fremantle.

"Tranquil" is the word. There are no motor cars and no mechanical noises on Rottnest. Hardly anyone wears shoes. The air is absolutely pure and mostly balmy, the beach sand like talcum powder, the only means of transport across its seven-mile length are bicycles whirring softly over smooth roads. Tons of fun, though. There are peacocks and quokkas on land, herring and skipjack leaping in the water, a big and beautiful pub, fishing from boats or rocks, golf, tennis, bowling, and of course swimming. "Rotto" is more than a resort, it's a solidified tonic for frayed city souls, although that deep enfolding silence takes a bit of getting used to. You can reach the island in two hours by ferry from Perth's Barrack Street Jetty ($17 round-trip ticket) or whiz over in 65 minutes by hydrofoil.

ORGANIZED TOURS: The **Holiday W.A. Centre,** 772 Hay St. (tel. 322-2999), organizes a day tour to one of the most spectacular—and least known—natural wonders of Australia. This is **Wave Rock,** a solid granite formation that looks like a titanic wave breaking over the flat countryside, dwarfing the tiny humans standing at its base. Wave Rock is perhaps even more awesome to behold than the much-publicized Ayers Rock. Coaches depart at 7:45 a.m. from the corner of Hay and William Streets and arrive back at 8 p.m. You get a picnic lunch at Wave Rock and also view other rock formations aptly called Hippo's Yawn and The Humps. The tour costs $45 for adults, $25 for children.

The **M.V. Captain Cook,** No. 2 Pier, Barrack St., (tel. 325-3341) offers a scenic harbor cruise daily, chugging downriver, then through Fremantle harbor and into the Fishing Harbour, where the America's Cup yachts prepare for the great race. After the return at 4:45 p.m., a wine-tasting takes place at the Cook's private cellar. The cruise costs $10 for adults, half for children.

Australian Pacific Tours, 25 Barrack St., (tel. 325-9377) has a variety of full-day tours through and around Perth. One of them includes the city highlights and country hills, taking in Lake Monger, the watershed where the unique black swans of Westralia abound, going out to the restored pioneer village of Armadale and on to the crest of the Darling Range. Leaves at 9:10 a.m. and returns in the evening. Adults pay $25, children half.

AFTER DARK: Perth is a surprise package, and that includes her nightlife as well. It's as varied and jumping as it is unexpected. For a start there's a very active live theater movement, both amateur and professional, with prices generally cheaper than in the eastern capitals. The **Playhouse,** 3 Pier St., puts on a full range of professional theater, from musicals to the classics. The **Hole in the Wall Theatre,** 180 Hamersley Rd., Subiaco, goes in for more avant-garde and unusual—at least 50% Australian—material. **Her Majesty's,** Hay Street, gets the tried and proven successes. The **Old Mill,** Mends Street, South Perth, puts on amateur rep in charming surroundings. There are half a dozen more companies and you can find their programs in the daily papers or the current issue of *This Week in Perth.*

Perth has two main auditoriums for musical presentations—in the broadest sense of the word. The **Concert Hall,** 5 St. George's Terrace, presents international ballet companies and musicians, all the way from pop to classical. The **Entertainment Centre,** Wellington Street, is a vast and lavishly modern air-conditioned complex, seating 8,000 people, where you can see the cream of visiting celebrities and listen to some of the finest concerts performed in the country. The Centre also has a bar and restaurant. Check *This Week in Perth* for current offerings.

Other action abounds. The **Sheraton-Perth Hotel,** 207 Adelaide Terrace, has a dual attraction in the shape of a lobby that can pass as a visual feast and an adjoining disco. The lobby is possibly the most grandiose example of interior decorating in the southern hemisphere . . . a subtly perfect blending of sumptuousness and functionalism, palatial and simultaneously supremely comfortable, like the antechamber of a middling oil king. The foyer contains, among other delights, the smartest cocktail bar in town—perhaps in the country. The **Clouds Disco** is in action Tuesday to Saturday till 3:30 a.m., featuring a very smooth DJ, elegant decor, and good vibes. Males pay $8 admission, depending on the night, while ladies get in free Tuesday through Thursday.

Disco and Other

Largest of local disco palaces is **Pinocchio's,** 393 Murray Street, a high-volume, garishly decorated gyration grove that features imported talent along with the native fare. It vibrates until 3:30 a.m., and charges $3 admission weeknights, $6 on weekends.

The Closet, 240 West Coast Hwy., Scarborough, has a famous jazz combo, the Perth City Stompers, every Wednesday blowing until midnight. **Crazy Cats,** 434 William St., is the prime strippery of Perth. Apart from the actual bareskin performers, the place features "See Thru Waitresses" every night except Sunday till 3:30 a.m. There's also an excellent dance floor in use between the floor shows. **Gobbles,** at 613 Wellington St., is decked out like a tropical island and has appropriate entertainment six nights a week. The $3 admission on week nights doubles to $6 weekends. **Muso's,** 418 Murray St., jumps from 8 p.m. till 3:30 a.m. six nights a week, featuring a changing lineup of rock groups.

But the best development in Perth's impressive nightlife is the blossoming of a regular entertainment region in William Street (across the railroad bridge) and the adjoining James and Lake Streets. This has become a glittering ribbon of bars, cafés, restaurants, and stripperies, thronged with pedestrians, where you can stroll along and drop in on whatever appeals to you.

A few random samples will have to suffice: **Milligan's Piano Bar,** at the corner of James and Milligan Streets, is large, brassy, and atmospheric and charges $6 admission. **Hannibal's,** 69 Lake St., comprises a downstairs disco and upstairs piano bar, enabling you to swing from one to the other as your mood dictates. **Café 215,** 215 William St., has a novel catering concept—you sit at balcony tables equipped with telephones and phone your order inside (which, by the way, doesn't always guarantee its prompt arrival). The strip joints aren't numerous or blatant enough to spoil the laid-back atmosphere of the region, and the abundance of good cheap eating places keeps down the costs of a night out. (Several are described in our dining section.)

Theater Restaurants

Perth has quite a collection in that line, with offerings much the same and tabs slightly lower than in other capitals. The most elaborate of them is **Dirty Dick's Elizabethan Rooms,** 194 Cambridge St., Wembley. You get an Elizabethan banquet handed out by buxom and comely serving wenches, presided over by a king and queen, and kept lively by court jesters, jugglers, musicians, etc. The tab is $23 per glutton. Open every night.

The **Civic,** 380 Beaufort St., has name entertainers and a bevvy of chorus belles, a four-course meal and dancing to follow, with drinks at bar prices. The package costs $19.95 weeknights, $3 more on weekends. **Romano's,** 187 Stirling St., imports singers, dancers, and comedians, and has an excellent resident band.

Fun Bars and Taverns

The **Cine-Cellars Tavern,** at the corner of Murray and Barrack Streets, has a rock duo playing Thursday through Saturday till midnight. But the main attraction here is the decor. The walls are decked with large photos of screen immortals, Garbo to Gable. Interspersed are authentically archaic movie cameras, projectors, and film spools dating back to the 1920s, plus scenes from positively primeval "cine" performances, with bearded gents and corseted ladies gaping at the latest thing in "living pictures."

Sassella's Tavern, up a winding flight of stairs in City Arcade, has an agreeably Olde English decor—but without the obligatory drafts of the real thing. Cellar walls, lantern light, horse brasses, and huge Breughel paintings for decorations. The music that accompanies the clink of glasses is traditional folk on Thursday through Saturday. The **Golden Rail Tavern,** National Mutual Arcade in the Hay Street Mall, features an excellent pop trio Thursday through Sunday. This is a good spot on Sunday—a problem day throughout Australia—since it has a late Sunday license.

SHOPPING: An undiluted delight in this city of arcades. Along the Hay Street promenade you can rest your legs on seats beneath umbrella shades amid little potted trees, undisturbed by traffic. Within ambling distance lie the shopping walkways of Plaza Arcade, City Arcade, Piccadilly Arcade, Terrace Arcade, and London Court, each with a distinct—sometimes contrasting—style, each filled with elegant, quaint, intimate, or brash little stores. After a shopping tour of Perth you'll find it hard to understand why more cities don't follow suit. Well . . . it does mean confining His Sacred Majesty, the automobile, to underground dungeons or forcing him—horrors—to make a detour so that people on two legs can enjoy walking.

At several **Duty-Free Shops** you can take advantage of your tourist status to pick up bargains for later use. The **Downtown** is in Wanamba Arcade, Hay Street, the **International** at 55 St. George's Terrace. At the **Sapphire & Opal Centre,** St. Martins Arcade (off London Court), you get a 32½% sales-tax exemption on production of your passport and airline ticket.

The **Aboriginal Traditional Arts,** 224 St. George's Terrace, is the authorized marketing outlet for authentic Aboriginal artwork. The place operates on behalf of the native craftsmen of Western Australia. The items on sale span the entire range of artistic expression: painting, carving, incising, and fiberwork, and some of these supposedly "primitive" works have a haunting beauty entirely of their own.

2. Western Australia

Gigantic is the only word that describes Westralia, the biggest, emptiest state of the Commonwealth. With its million square miles the state could comfortably engulf all of Western Europe or swallow up Texas four times over. It boasts one square mile of elbow room for every inhabitant—if they were evenly spread. Actually, with 800,000 living in the capital of Perth, only 300,000 are left to sprinkle the enormous remainder.

Westralia has a distinct air of separateness, of thriving apart from the other states. It looks north toward Asia rather than eastward. As the jet flies it's as far from Perth to Sydney as to Singapore and Indonesia. Between Western Australia and the country's main population centers stretches the dizzying vastness of the Nullarbor Plain, flat as a kitchen floor and crossed by the longest straight railroad track on earth.

And "thrive" is what Westralia does. As one of the globe's mineral treasure chests it harbors, among other riches, enough iron ore to supply mankind's industrial needs single-handed. The West is an immense boom territory, wide open and barely tapped, sprawling from the tropical Timor Sea in the north to the temperate Southern Ocean more than 1,500 miles away.

Western Australia lies off the usual tourist routes, but offers some of the most grandiose sights in the hemisphere to those who tackle the distances involved. It also grants the rare thrill of seeing Tomorrowland, of viewing an awakening young titan flexing mammoth muscles.

The climate of the state spans the spectrum from heavenly to hellish. Perth enjoys the balmiest Mediterranean weather on the continent. Marble Bar, on the other hand, is the hottest town in Australia, sizzling in an average daily temperature of 96 degrees!

The sights beckoning in Westralia cover as wide a range as the climate—from wildflower fields stretching into infinity to mysterious cave paintings allegedly daubed by Aboriginal tribal "spirits" 2,000 years ago. On our blitz tour of the highlights we'll start with—

NEW NORCIA: A slice of Spain, cool, ancient, and secluded, rising on the Victoria Plains 82 miles north of Perth, this is perhaps the most unexpected attraction you'll find in Australia; you feel like rubbing your eyes to make sure it's really there. Nova Norcia was founded by Spanish Benedictine monks, driven from their homeland in 1846, and created in the exact image of the medieval monasteries they had inhabited in Compostela.

The purpose of the monastery is the same today as it was then—to care for the local Aborigines. But today you'll find it difficult to believe the grinding poverty and backbreaking struggles of the early monks that went into the making of this palm-shaded oasis. The Benedictine fathers proudly show you around, beaming over the orphanage, the gardens and orchards, the library with its medieval manuscripts, and the art gallery boasting some rare religious paintings.

WAGR buses leave Perth every weekday morning for the two-hour trip to New Norcia and return the same afternoon.

GOLD AND GHOSTS: In the desert east of Perth lie the once fabulous Westralian gold fields. During the great gold rush of the 1890s, some 200,000 prospectors tried their luck there, battling nature and each other for the yellow metal. The town of **Kalgoorlie** sprang up almost overnight, boasting two stock exchanges, seven newspapers, and the swinging rip-roaring "Golden Mile"—reputedly the richest square mile of real estate in history. The glory lasted until the gold dwindled. Kalgoorlie still mines gold—you can see the 4,000-foot-deep mine shafts in action—but no longer in legendary quantities. The town has calmed down considerably, but the unique atmosphere of a desert mining community remains strong; the "smell of gold" still lingers.

Twenty-six miles southwest stands haunted **Coolgardie,** once the Queen of the Goldfields, now Australia's most famous ghost town. Of the 15,000 Diggers who brawled in the city's 29 hotels and bars, not a soul remains. But the old covered wagons still stand on the main street, and the Goldfields Exhibition in Bayley Street preserves the relics of the town's wild past. The greatest chunk of gold dug out here weighed 2,000 ounces! And all around the area, now studded with motels and caravan parks, there are the glittering remnants of wealth—flecks of gold and gemstones. These gemstones find their way into the oddest places. A Coolgardie garage has tiled walls sprinkled with them, turning the place into a kind of Aladdin's Cave when the light strikes them.

You can tour the gold fields by MacRobertson-Miller Airlines (MMA) or in the air-conditioned parlor coaches operating from Perth by **Ghost Town Safaris.** They even supply prospecting equipment as part of the tour. Book through the Government Tourist Bureau.

WILDFLOWER TOURS: Westralia's wildflowers have to be seen to be believed—they look like multicolored oceans rolling to the horizon in exquisite shades of light blue, deep azure, bright scarlet, and golden orange. From August through October some 7,000 native species of blossoms carpet immense areas of the southwest. Most of these plants are unique, found nowhere else on earth, a phenomenon due to Western Australia's long isolation that allowed hundreds of primeval forms to survive and bloom every year in an unchanged habitat.

The most celebrated wildflower fields stretch around Albany on the southern coast, and Geraldton, about 300 miles north of Perth. You can choose one of several special wildflower tours traveling from Perth during the three-month blossom season. Both **Pioneer** (26 St. George's Terrace, Perth, tel. 325-8855) and **Parlorcars** use air-conditioned coaches with wide windows and reclining seats.

THE MIGHTY KIMBERLEY: Rising from the northern corner of Western Australia is the colossal Kimberley Plateau—a region larger than California, but housing only 6,000 people. All the Kimberley is spectacular, some parts are stunning. At Wolf Creek there's a meteorite crater measuring 2,800 feet in diameter; the Ord River Scheme culminates in Australia's largest man-made lake, a miniature ocean of 286 square miles; in the gorge country at Geikie the green Fitzroy River carves its way through towering limestone cliffs, the warm water alive with stingrays, sharks, and freshwater crocodiles; at Windjana the cliff caves were once used as Aboriginal burial grounds and are still decorated with wonderful primitive cave paintings.

Although the Kimberley has developed into a popular tourist region it's too vast to become crowded. MMA flies regular jet services up from Perth, doing the hop in less than four hours.

Chapter IX

CANBERRA—THE NATIONAL CAPITAL

1. The City and Surroundings
2. Australian Capital Territory

CANBERRA IS AN "ARTIFICIAL" CITY, an attribute she shares with some other capitals like Washington, D.C., Brasilia, and Ankara. Like them, she was designed with the express purpose of housing a central government under the best possible conditions. Unlike the others, however, Canberra succeeded completely in that aim.

1. The City and Surroundings

Canberra is a "model capital" in every conceivable respect: a city without slums, no ugly industrial areas, no traffic congestion, clean air, minimal crime, beautiful surroundings, good public transport, and the nation's two largest centers within easy driving distance. Her layout is an urban planner's dream come true (literally) and all her government departments are comfortably accessible for foot sloggers as well as motorists.

In the past 15 years Canberra has even overcome her sole major drawback —a paralyzing dullness, enlivened only by periodic political brawls. In the early 1950s a famous local journalist cracked, "You can pronounce Canberra the same way you yawn." He certainly won't be saying this today. Now the place is sparking on all plugs, generously helped by the fact that the Capital Territory has unlimited licensing laws, with every watering hole open for business as long as it chooses.

Yet Canberra had a remarkably slow start. Her site wasn't even selected until 1908 (diplomatically midway between the archrivals Sydney and Melbourne) and not until 1927 did Parliament actually convene there. For the next 30 years the capital developed with the tempo of a handicapped snail. The entire grandiose experiment seemed stillborn, throttled by bickering politicians, financial crises, and World Wars. Someone compared Canberra's image to her coat-of-arms: supposedly representing two graceful swans supporting a crowned fortress, it actually looks like two angry ducks kicking down a toy castle.

But suddenly, in the late 1950s, the city took off like a rocket. The capital heaved, churned, vibrated, and began to expand at a positively dazzling rate. Today Canberra has a population of more than 230,000 and her annual growth rate of 9½% makes her the fastest growing city in the Commonwealth. Yet so perfect was the masterplan under which she was conceived that the immense population increase has flowed smoothly into prepared channels, causing neither chaos nor social problems nor congestion nor even clashing architectural designs. Canberra is full of avant-garde buildings and has the highest ratio of cars to people in the country. But all her structures blend beautifully into the city pattern and the countryside around. And the cars neither clog the roads nor foul the atmosphere. Thanks to a wonderfully ingenious network of freeways, underpasses, and parking areas, they hardly intrude at all.

Like the Sydney Opera House, the design of the national capital was set up as an international competition. The winner was a Chicago landscape architect and former associate of the great Frank Lloyd Wright named Walter Burley Griffin. He came to Canberra in 1913 and nearly went out of his mind with frustration at the slow growth of his brainchild. But today the city mirrors his dream: classical public buildings overlooking a huge artificial lake and a core of central circles with broad tree-lined avenues radiating out to landscaped garden suburbs.

The balance between parklands and built-up areas is weighted in favor of greenery. From the air Canberra looks like a vast park sprinkled with patches of city. Wherever you go you're in sight of trees and grass. Native birds and animals live and breed in the vicinity of the city's landmarks. And the real bush lies only a few minutes' drive away. Canberra has no actual shopping streets but a pattern of shopping centers, malls, arcades, and complexes, free of traffic and ablaze with colorful shrubs and flowers. Instead of allowing real estate developers to build up the core of the metropolis at the expense of open space, Canberra opted for satellite cities farther out, linked with the center by the finest freeway system in Australia.

The capital is unique among large Australian cities by lying 90 miles inland, 1,900 feet above sea level, and having no port. But she has her own private lake, right at the core, created artificially and strictly for decoration and entertainment. It bears the name of the American who didn't live long enough to see his drawing-board infant grow up—Lake Burley Griffin.

No such memorial exists for the other American who helped to birth Canberra, a highly controversial character named King O'Malley. A former Kansas realtor, O'Malley took advantage of tax concessions granted to religious bodies by founding his own—the "Waterlily Rock-bound Church of the Redskin Temple in the Chickasaw Nation." In Australia he described himself as a bishop of the church. And in order to run for Parliament he claimed to be Canadian born, therefore a British citizen. O'Malley not only won a seat but became Australia's minister for home affairs at the time of Canberra's foundation. A rabid teetotaller, he pushed through an ordinance prohibiting the sale of alcoholic drinks in the Federal Capital Territory. His handiwork lingered long after Mr. O'Malley had left the scene, keeping Canberra in a state of social retardation. On weekends half the population fled their dry kindergarten and made for Queanbeyan, across the New South Wales border, to get a drink. Queanbeyan prospered while Canberra parched. Gossip had it that this was O'Malley's revenge on the wicked journalists who had voiced doubts about his birthplace.

The shades of "Bishop" O'Malley have been happily banished. Canberra now ranks among the best eating *and* drinking spots in the country. And because the inhabitants are predominantly young, single, and prosperous, the place radiates *joie de vivre* to a degree rarely found among civil service cities.

Finally, unlike most Australian cities, Canberra has distinct seasons: gold and red autumn leaves, blossoming spring flowers, broiling dry summers, and genuinely icy winters with occasional snow flurries.

GETTING THERE: Canberra lies within a 934-square-mile area known as the

Australian Capital Territory (ACT). The city is 150 miles southwest of Sydney, 300 miles northeast of Melbourne and has good traffic connections with both.

By train the journey costs $20.50 from Sydney; but the Melbourne choo-choo only goes to Yass and you have to take a bus the rest of the way. The bus trip from Sydney (Pioneer or Greyhound) takes 4¼ hours and costs $22. From Melbourne it's $32. By air (TAA or Ansett) it's a 30-minute hop from Sydney at $83.10, an hour from Melbourne at $116.40.

ORIENTATION: The core of Canberra is sliced into two roughly equal portions by Lake Burley Griffin and the two halves connected by the **Commonwealth Avenue** and **Kings Avenue** Bridges. Right beside the Commonwealth Avenue Bridge is an ideal orientation landmark: the **Captain Cook Memorial Water Jet** which flings six tons of water 450 feet into the air and can be spotted for miles. (On windy days it can also be *felt* from an amazing distance.)

Each of the two portions has its own central core from which all the important avenues of the area radiate. In the northern half this is **City Hill,** in the southern **Capital Hill.** The northern part contains the facilities of city life: shops, restaurants, post office, hotels, university, churches, and theaters. The southern half is the political and administrative territory, housing Parliament, the prime minister's residence, foreign embassies, the governor-general's mansion, etc. All around these central portions lie the suburbs and satellite towns, interspersed with enormous parks and recreation grounds. Farther out to the east lies **Canberra Airport,** to the west and south **Kosciusko National Park** and the **Snowy Mountains,** and to the northeast **Lake George** and the New South Wales city of Goulburn.

Although **Parliament House** is the official center of Canberra, for practical purposes the core is **London Circuit** on the north side, which encloses City Hill, adjoins **Civic Square,** and into which run all the main thoroughfares of interest to tourists. The **ACT Government Tourist Bureau** is at the corner of London Circuit and West Row, the **City Information Centre** on Northbourne Avenue.

GETTING AROUND: Canberra sprawls over an enormous area for its population. Luckily most of the sights, accommodations, eateries, and shopping are concentrated in a relatively small space north of the lake. But if you want to play the poker machines you'll have to cross the New South Wales border into adjacent Queanbeyan (known as "Queen bean"). The one-armed bandits are banned within the Capital Territory.

Apart from sightseeing cruises around the lake, the only transportation in Canberra is by road. Bus services are frequent and the vehicles new and comfortable; fares run to 60¢. There is a *free* service in operation around the inner-city shopping areas. For bus information ask one of the green uniformed inspectors or call the **Department of Territories** at 47-7052.

Canberra can also be seen by bicycle, but it's advisable to stick to the bike tracks. You can rent a bike at the Youth Hostel (see "Accommodations").

A NOTE ON PRICES: All prices in this guide are in Australian dollars (A$). As we go to press, US$1 = approximately A$1.40. Thus a room listed at $20 a night actually costs only about $14.50 in U.S. funds—good news indeed for budget travelers.

CANBERRA: CITY CENTER

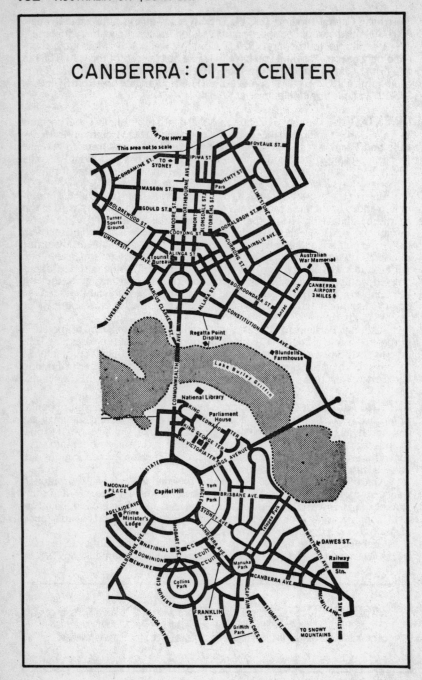

ACCOMMODATIONS: One of Australia's main tourist attractions as well as administrative center, Canberra is amply supplied with accommodations, although not particularly cheap ones. Among the best bets are the various government hostels, first rate and not in the least hostelish. The only trouble is getting into them, booking tends to be heavy.

Canberra boasts a real accommodation row—it's **Northbourne Avenue,** an endless ruler-straight boulevard that runs all the way from the Federal Highway to London Circuit. But the street is so long and buildings so generously spaced that you can't talk about lodging houses nestling cheek by jowl . . . within shouting distance of each other would be a more appropriate term. If you have difficulties getting a bed, contact the **Canberra Tourist Bureau,** in the Jolimont Centre, Northbourne Avenue (tel. 45-6464), and rest assured that they'll find you one. There's also a local specialty called accommodation complexes, places that simultaneously provide motel, caravan, and camping facilities. We'll look at a couple at the end of this section.

The **YWCA,** 2 Mort St. (tel. 47-3033), is very centrally housed in a massive concrete slab that bears a certain resemblance to Hitler's bunker retreat. The place takes only women. The building has a comfortable TV lounge, a dining room, elevator, and a laundry. Also a guest kitchen, but you have to supply your own cooking utensils. No private baths, but an ample supply of showers. The 20 bedrooms are fairly well furnished, every one with H&C water and fair-size wardrobes. Rates here run to $15 a night for singles, $26 for doubles, $10 in dormitory.

The Canberra Youth Hostel is the **National Memorial Hostel,** Dryandra Street, O'Connor (tel. 48-9759), about five miles from the city. Bus 380 goes every half hour from the London Circuit Post Office. Get off at Scrivener Street, then follow the YHA finger posts. A one-story brick building, the place has four dormitories, a fully equipped communal kitchen, hot showers, a small food store, and imposes a staying limit of five days. It charges $6.50 per night and closes between 9:30 a.m. and 5 p.m.

The **Macquarie,** 18 National Circuit, Barton (tel. 73-2325). Located south of the lake (one of the few hostelries that is), this is a modern four-story brick structure, about three miles from the city and adjacent to the National Press Club. The Macquarie offers a lot of facilities: color TV in the lounge, special billiard and table-tennis rooms, book and magazine kiosk, a cafeteria-style dining room, and outdoor barbecue service where you can cook your own meat. The bedrooms are pastel bright, with colorful floor rugs, built-in wardrobes, wonderfully handy writing tables, excellent lighting, and hot and cold water, plus a guest laundry with irons. The tariff, including breakfast, is $19.50 for singles, $15.60 each for doubles.

The **Gowrie,** 210 Northbourne Ave. (tel. 49-6033), towers huge and massive on the main Sydney-Melbourne highway, about a mile from the city. Consisting of twin ten-story buildings, this private hotel can accommodate 569 guests in single rooms. While big, the Gowrie is also very comfortable, with a vast cafeteria-style dining room, a music room on the ground floor, and recreation rooms (billiards, table tennis, and color TV). Each floor has an automatic coin-in-slot washing machine and a special drying room. The bedrooms are bright and airy, furnishings simple but modern, all rooms with H&C water, bathrooms on each floor. All rates include a full cooked breakfast: singles pay $19.50 daily, doubles cost $31.20.

Bed-and-Breakfast

The following places are all in one section at the northern end of Northbourne Avenue, and very prominently signposted. **Chelsea Lodge,** no. 526 (tel. 48-0655), is a villa-like building with a pleasant veranda porch and a tiny potted palm. It has a plain little breakfast room (no other meals served) and 12 bedrooms, all with TV. Two of the rooms have private shower. They also have built-in wardrobes and electric blankets. The cooked breakfast is exceptionally good. You pay $13 per person without shower, $16 with.

The **Blue & White** and **Sky Blue Lodges,** no. 524 (tel. 48-0498), are double hostelries under one management with a total of 17 bedrooms. The place has a breakfast room, plus attractive bathrooms with colored tiles. There is TV in the bedrooms, some of which also have tea-making facilities, but no water taps. Singles pay $20; doubles, $24. **Platon Lodge,** at no. 522 (tel. 47-9139), has ten bedrooms and two bathrooms. A charming beige brick building with colored lights beneath the roof, the Platon offers a TV set in every room, tea-making equipment, bedside lamps, and electric blankets. The tariff is $16 for singles, $20 for doubles.

A Motel

The **Motel 7,** Cooma Road, Narrabundah (tel. 95-1111), is a remarkable economy establishment offering full facilities at amazingly low rates. This is done by using automation to the greatest possible extent, and cutting out frills but none of the standard modern comforts. A solid two-story brick building, the motel operates 63 units, each with private bathroom, TV, and bed-sitting room. The motel has a guest laundry, a swimming pool, a licensed restaurant next door, and a vending machine room on the premises. The rooms are not exactly spacious but equipped with good beds, fans, and blow heaters, plus blackout curtains for late risers. You can get all this for $23.50 per person (two people sharing a unit with a double bed). About five miles from the city.

Motel-Caravan Complexes

The **Canberra Motor Village,** Kunzea Street, O'Connor (tel. 47-5466), stands in a beautiful tree-shaded setting five minutes from the city center on the slopes of Black Mountain. The complex consists of the Cedar Lodge motel, mobile homes, stationary caravans, and caravan sites. It forms a world of its own, with every facility provided. The village has a swimming pool, mini-markets, restaurant, a lounge with color TV, children's playground, car wash, dry-cleaning service, coin-operated laundry, tennis court, gratis bicycles, and a gas-fired barbecue. The 38 motel units are paneled in wonderfully aromatic cedar wood, each with private bathroom, thermostat heating, and refrigerator. Family units have their own kitchenette. Rates at the lodge are $53 for doubles. Caravans rent for $25.50 for two persons.

The **Canberra Lakes Carotel,** Federal Highway, Watson (tel. 41-1377), lies four miles north of the city, just off the highway from Sydney. An unusually versatile complex, it has motel units with private facilities, two-room holiday flats, stationary caravans, caravan sites, and camping sites. The rows of little red-brick units form a regular street and have the facilities of a village. A fast-food bar, general store, playground, car wash, swimming pool, and recreation lounge with pool tables and piped-in music are available. Accommodations vary accordingly. The brick lodges and chalets have both cooking facilities and bathrooms. The on-site caravans (four-berth) come with stoves and refrigerators, but not with blankets, crockery, and cooking utensils. Chalets rent at $23 for one, $27 for two persons per night; lodges at $28 for one, $34 for two.

Hotel

Tall Trees, 21 Stephen St. [...] want to draw fine distinctions. [...] building in a quiet side street abou[...] fully kept, as is the central garden. A[...] overlook the greenery outside, and the [...] las. The rooms are bright and sunny, equ[...] wall carpeting, bedside tables and lamps, [...] There's a laundrette, a charming breakfast roo[...] lounge with color TV, and tea-making facilities. [...] for doubles.

Campus Accommodations

The Australian National University has a vast and vari[...] of residential places, but the situation is rather confusing. Some colle[...] [...]e only students, others accept nonstudents as well; some prefer groups, ot[...]rs don't. The accommodation is excellent and cheap—when you can get it. One of the best is **Toad Hall,** Kingsley Street (tel. 49-4722), which has single study-bedrooms grouped around lounge, kitchen, and bathroom areas. The residents cook for themselves and the accommodation is available during the vacation periods from mid-August to early September and November through February. Tariffs are $13.50 a day for students, $18 a day for nonstudents.

For other possibilities check Bruce Hall (tel. 49-2784), Ursula College (tel. 48-0770), or Burgmann College (tel. 47-9811).

MEALS: The eating scene is as cosmopolitan as you would expect in a city housing a score of foreign embassies and hundreds of overseas students. Prices are generally high, but there's a fair sprinkling of budget dineries, most of them in and around Civic Square.

Lunches and Snacks

High Court Cafe, King Edward Terrace, Parkes. You don't expect a cozy hostelry in a High Court building, but here is one. With a nice view of Lake Burley Griffin and a generally beautiful setting, this café caters to an awesome array of legal eagles who traditionally know where to find a good bite. The quiches are excellent (made on the premises) and served with salad at $4.95. For the same price you can get a grilled perch with french fries and salad. A stubbie of beer sets you back $1.10. The café is open seven days a week (unlike the Court) but unfortunately only until 4:15 p.m.

The **Corner Coffee Shop,** at the corner of London Circuit and East Row, is a tiny European-style snackery with French staff. The place only holds five tables and is simple, bright, and charming, and there are more tables outside. The walls are hung with original paintings by local artists. Open-faced Danish sandwiches—salami, cheese, liverwurst—at $1 to $1.25. Superlative chocolate cake and excellent espresso and cappuccino for $1. Closes at 6 p.m.

The **Dubbl Dekka**—no, this isn't a misprint—stands in the City Walk shopping mall. A big yellow Sydney double-decker bus, decorated with tropical plants, it now doubles as a rather unique snackery. You can either eat inside the monster, refurbished with little tables instead of leather seats, or in the tent-like extension that has been patched on sideways. It's quite charming in a vehicular way, but open on weekdays until 5:30 p.m., on Saturday until 12:30 p.m., specializing in pancakes, sweet or savory, starting at $1.80.

...es at 17 Lonsdale St., a thoroughfare otherwise given
...n camps for secondhand cars. The Stockade is a very large,
...y bar-restaurant, decked out like a cross between a stable and a
...oosegow. The bar in front is festooned with framed prison regulations
...m the colonial days, some of them pretty scary. The patrons happily ignore
the strict "No Speaking" rule, because the problem here is to make yourself
heard at all. The dining room in the rear contains lots of rustic gadgetry, plus a
huge open electric grill. You select your victuals from glass cases filled with
meats, sweets, and salads, then take them to the center grill and cook them
according to your fancy. The meat is top grade; ham steak goes for $5.50,
and it's $5 for either rump or T-bone steak. That grandiose dessert import
from New Zealand—Pavlova—costs 80¢. Open six days until 11 p.m.; closed
Sunday.

Mario's, Petrie Plaza, is our splurge place in Canberra, a quite gorgeous
establishment with piano bar, low ceilings hung with fishnets cunningly draped
around boat lanterns, the walls highlighted by stained-glass windows depicting
classical Greek pastorales. There's an immense array of pigeonholed wine bottles extending over acres, and red-bloused, black-skirted waitresses dispensing
fast, efficient, and very amiable service. Near the entrance you'll find a portrait
gallery of Australian prime ministers, some of whom have presumably eaten
here. The cuisine leans toward seafood and steak and is impeccable, but the
establishment has an unfortunate habit of serving everything—including
wienerschnitzel—with dressed potatoes. Meals come to around $13. Open till
midnight every night, but closed Sunday.

The Pancake Parlor, at the corner of East Row and Alinga Street, is the
local link in a chain that benevolently girdles Australia. This particular link lies
tucked beneath the Canberra City Pharmacy. The decor is early colonial and
features the chain's trademark: a soulful Victorian damsel holding up a fork and
exclaiming, "Lovely." The great thing about all the Pancake Parlors is the trading hours—round the clock, seven days a week. The pancakes they dish up are
hefty, the crêpes somewhat lighter; but neither is designed for weightwatchers'
banquets. You can get them meaty and savory or sweet; they make solid meals
in both shapes at prices ranging from $4.20 to $5.80. The place has a pleasantly
relaxed atmosphere and cheerful staff, even in the wee gray hours.

The Woodstock, Alinga St., is a comfortable and highly congenial eatery,
but minus any trace of Woodstock flavor. A long room with brown on brown
decor, dimly lit and featuring wooden eating nooks, it has a huge counter selection of edibles for your perusal. Table service, very fast and efficient. Lasagne or
spaghetti bolognese costs $4.60, and the place stays open seven days a week till
10 p.m.

Garema Place is a shopping area between Mort and Petrie Streets, and it's
dotted with good, fairly economical dineries. The **Pizzeria,** in the arcade, has
the reputation of serving the best pizzas in the territory, which you can take out
or eat there. Small, modern, and functional, with a window facing the square
and a permanent throng inside, it offers 12 varieties of pizza—small for $3, me-
dium for $1.50 more. Open seven days a week till 9 p.m.

Gus's Café, in adjacent Bunda Street, is a tiny restaurant with a much larger outdoor dining terrace, partly glassed in and wholly delightful. One tree is in
the middle, flower boxes all around gaily multicolored tables. It offers a gratis
selection of newspapers and magazines to read at your table—a European custom that has been s-l-o-w-l-y catching on elsewhere. Interior decoration is devoted mainly to dozens of framed mottos, slogans, and extracts dealing with
pollution—moral and physical—the evils of drug abuse and the virtue of things

small as opposed to things big. Gus's serves indubitably the finest cheesecake in Canberra—in Australia—perhaps the world, at $1.50 a slice. The heartier dishes are likewise excellent and heartwarmingly cheap, like beef goulash for $3. Open seven days a week from 7 a.m. till midnight.

The Private Bin, 50 Northbourne Ave., preserves its "privacy" by hiding in the back of a very noisy bar. The surprise, once you pass through the rambunctious front, is all the greater: a charming little bistro, air-conditioned and green-carpeted with—biggest surprise—economy prices. You can choose from the buffet spread in the center or order a steak. The buffet always features one roast plus a vast array of side dishes and trimmings. These peripheral salads, soups, and vegetables vary in quality, but the roast is superb. Your total meal— and you can help yourself to any amount of trimmings—comes to $9. Open till 10 p.m. six nights a week. Closed Sunday.

If you're out and hungry late at night, watch for the **Tuckerbuses.** These are old Sydney double-decker monsters that park "anywhere we can make a buck," and dispense hot dogs, hamburgers, etc., till all hours. Last time I spied them they were in Belconnen Way.

A final and glorious Canberra specialty: Lake Burley Griffin is stocked every year with 25,000 trout. Fishing is free and you don't need a license. So rent a boat and catch your own lunch. Then take it to one of the numerous picnic grounds and grill it over the coin-in-slot gas barbecues you'll find in all of them. You'll have a memorable al fresco feast. There are picnic areas all around the lakeshore. But my own favorite is in **Weston Park,** Yarralumla, south of the lake. It has treehouses, a mini-railroad, and an area specially developed for kids to climb, hide, paddle, and run.

DAYTIME ACTIVITIES: Canberra is a city of "sights"—so many of them that it's difficult to decide where to start.

So let's begin with **Parliament House,** designed as the focal point and centerpiece of the capital. It was meant to be considerably more majestic than it turned out—in fact, monumental. But World War I interrupted construction and when the House finally assembled in 1927 it was in a "provisional" structure hurriedly completed for the occasion. Which is how it has remained ever since. Parliament is a handsome, classically simple complex of white buildings fronted by beautiful lawns and fountains. But monumental it ain't.

The interior has a restrained beauty and dignity of its own, as well as many touches copied from the "Mother of Parliaments" in London. King's Hall, the entrance lobby, is a spacious colonnaded reception area decorated with statues and portraits of notables. It features a prize exhibit in the form of one of the only three surviving exemplars of Magna Carta, issued in 1297. (The original Charter, arm-twisted from King John at Runnymede, was annulled after only nine weeks.)

On either side of King's Hall lie the engine rooms of the Australian Commonwealth so to speak—the **Senate** on the right and the **House of Representatives** on the left. Together they form what is termed Parliament. They have a total membership of 127 and normally meet on Tuesday, Wednesday, and Thursday. You can see either of the chambers in action from the visitors' galleries. You don't need an admission ticket to the Senate, but for the House of Representatives it's advisable to apply in person a couple of days in advance for admission tickets at the Inquiry Desk in King's Hall.

Tours of inspection take place when only one chamber is sitting—then the other one gets inspected. Inspection hours are Monday to Saturday from 9 a.m. to 5 p.m., on Sunday from 9:30 a.m. The only day of the year Parliament closes is Christmas Day.

Currently, a new and truly monumental Parliament Building is under construction, but don't hold your breath.

Canberra's biggest tourist attraction is the **Australian War Memorial** on Anzac Parade, at the corner of Limestone and Fairbairn Avenues. It stands at the foot of Mount Ainslie, an absolutely splendid edifice in honor and memory of the 100,000 men and women who died for the Commonwealth in two World Wars. The memorial contains exhibition galleries and one of the finest libraries in the country.

It's hard to say which exhibits are more fascinating: the vast dioramas of combat or the mechanical relics of it. The former show the gruesome slogging trench warfare of the First World War and the African desert struggles of the Second in minute detail and brutal realism. The latter include **Aeroplane Hall** with the strutted biplanes, sleek Spitfires, and hulking bombers flown by Australian airmen in both wars; the artillery pieces, tanks, and landing barges, the shells, bombs, and torpedoes used by the men from Down Under. And by their enemies: among the relics is the colossal German Amiens gun (the barrel weighs 45 tons) and the toy-like Japanese midget submarine, reconstructed from the two sunk in the attack on Sydney Harbour in 1942. And then the cost of it all—the bronze panels inscribed with the awesome roll of names of the fallen, covering two huge walls. The memorial is open to visitors every day from 9 a.m. to 4:45 p.m. Admission is free.

The **Canberra Carillon,** one of the largest musical instruments in the world, was a gift from Britain to Australia to mark Canberra's jubilee. A tall white pillar, it stands at the northern end of the Kings Avenue Bridge and is played in regular Sunday and Wednesday recitals. A carillon is an instrument in which tiers of bells are played from a "clavier"—an organ-like keyboard. The Canberra version has 53 bells, the largest weighing more than six tons, the smallest only 15 pounds. Playing them requires considerable strength and tremendous skill: the performing artists have to wear padding on their little finger which strikes the hand batons that sound the bells by means of a long steel wire connected to a soft metal hammer. Inspections on Saturday from 1 to 4 p.m., on Sunday from 9 a.m. to 2 p.m.

The **Australian National University** covers an area of 320 acres of north of the Civic Centre and enrolls more than 6,000 students. The campus is beautifully landscaped, sprinkled with modernistic fountains and sculptures. One of the top attractions is the **Institute of Anatomy,** containing one museum of Australian fauna and another on the culture of Aborigines and the natives of New Guinea.

Australian National Gallery. Rising on the shores of Lake Burley Griffin, this edifice houses permanent exhibitions chosen from the various Australian collections and overseas galleries. The selections are mostly outstanding—the last one I saw came from New York's Metropolitan Museum of Art, and offered a chance to see the works of such artists as Monet, Marin, and Cézanne, together with American modernists like Sheeler, O'Keeffe and Hartley. The Gallery is a surprise package, not least because of its excellent restaurant facilities overlooking the lake. Open daily 10 a.m. to 5 p.m. Admission is $2, but students and children get in gratis.

The **Captain Cook Memorial** jet operates from 10 a.m. to midday and from 2 to 4 p.m. daily, hurling six tons of water into the air at any one time. Part of the memorial is a nine-foot terrestrial globe on the shoreline, showing and describing the routes of exploration followed by the illustrious navigator. The **Royal Australian Mint,** off Kent Street, Deakin, is the place where they make the filthy lucre. You can watch the operation of the production floor through plate-glass windows in the visitors gallery. No, they don't hand out free samples. In the foyer there's a large coin exhibition. The machines can be seen in action Monday to Friday from 9 a.m. to 4 p.m.

The **Botanic Gardens** are situated on the lower slope of Black Mountain, entry from Clunies Ross Street. Devoted entirely to native Australian flora, the gardens are crisscrossed by beautifully designed walks through green and shady glens over bridges and small ponds, with no playgrounds or picnic areas to disturb the hushed peace. **Blundell's Farmhouse** was built in 1858 as a ploughman's cottage, located on Wendouree Drive. Three rooms are furnished in the old pioneer style and you can visit them from 2 to 4 p.m., 10 a.m. to noon on Wednesday. The **Royal Military College,** in suburban Duntroon, is the training establishment of Australia's Regular Army officers. Conducted tours are held at 2:30 p.m. Monday to Friday (starting from Starkey Park) March through October.

The **Embassies:** Over 50 countries maintain diplomatic representatives in Canberra and their mission buildings form a tourist attraction all their own. The architectural styles range from tasteful to terrible (the Thai embassy looks like Fu-Manchu's castle dipped in whitewash), but a glimpse of them is an established part of "doing" the capital. It can be surprising. Thus the British High Commission is housed in a depressingly functional building, resembling an upper-class college dorm, while the U.S. ambassador dwells in an enchanting Virginia mansion, the site of which, incidentally, was leased on the day Pearl Harbor was bombed. Most of the embassies are in the suburbs of Red Hill, Forrest, and Yarralumla, and you can't inspect them from the inside unless you wish to cause a diplomatic incident. But the **Indonesian Embassy,** Darwin Avenue, Yarralumla, has a charming pavilion housing a display of artifacts, puppets, and musical instruments and is open daily from 9 a.m. to noon and 2 to 4 p.m.

The **National Library** in Parkes Place, near the Commonwealth Bridge, is the newest and most beautiful of Canberra's public buildings. Based on the Greek Parthenon style, it's a clean and subtly dramatic structure in the neoclassic tradition, fronted by two gushing fountains. The library houses two million books, over 300,000 maps, 390,000 photographs, 65,000 moving films, including the earliest ever shot in Australia, and 440,000 sound recordings. Only the foyer and exhibition areas are open to visitors, but guided tours of the building are available.

Artworks and Fountains: Canberra is dotted with artistic sculptings and statuary, sometimes combined with fountains or acting as children's fantasy implements. All are modernistic and most are symbolic. The National Capital Development Commission authorizes and buys major works of sculpture, paintings, stained glass, tapestry, and ceramics from local or overseas artists and distributes them around the city. Because of this central guiding body (and because that body has excellent taste) there's a sense of unity, of theme and purpose linking all these objects that make a special tour of them worthwhile. The only other city I have seen make equally splendid use of public ornamentation is Rotterdam in Holland. Among the really great works are Henry Moore's *Reclining Figure,* Tom Bass's *Ethos* (in Civic Square), and the fountain of *Thespis* by the American Robert Cook, at the Theatre Centre. Get hold of the excellent folder "Artworks in Canberra," produced by the Development Commission and use it as a guide. It is available from the Canberra Tourist Bureau.

Out-of-Town Activities

The **Mount Stromlo Observatory** lies ten miles west of Canberra, along Cotter Road. The large science-fictionish silver domes house the telescopes and measuring instruments of the Department of Astronomy of the National University. The observatory is one of the biggest and best equipped in the southern hemisphere. A visitor center at the 74-inch telescope is open daily from 9:30 a.m. to 4 p.m.

Tidbinbilla Nature Reserve. Stretching over a valley by the same name, some 25 miles southwest of Canberra, this embraces 12,000 acres of unspoiled bushland. Offering scenic walks and picnic sites (but no gas stations) in a region that sometimes wears a light snow mantle during winter, it has lots of native flora and fauna and an opportunity to hand-feed kangaroos kept in a special enclosure. The kangaroos are gentle muzzlers, but their companion emus have mighty sharp beaks and aren't above pecking the hand that's feeding them—so you're warned against it. The whole reserve stays open from 9 a.m. to 6 p.m.; the fur and feather enclosure can be visited the same hours. Admission is free.

Lanyon, a gracious colonial homestead (built in 1859) stands on the east bank of the Murrumbidgee River on the road to Tharwa off the Monaro Highway. Now a National Trust building, Lanyon has the original kitchen, stables, and furnishings of the period. On the grounds you'll find the **Nolan Gallery,** showing the works of that superb Australian artist Sir Sidney Nolan, whose bush scenes imprint themselves on your visual memory like very few other paintings. Open from 10 a.m. to 4 p.m. Tuesday to Sunday. Admission is $1.20 for adults, half price for children.

Telecommunications Tower, Black Mountain. This is the capital's brand-new landmark, stabbing skyward like an immense fine-pointed needle encrusted with electronic doodads. The purpose of the tower is to centralize TV and radio transmitters and radiotelephone communications, but it also makes a superb viewing platform. There are three levels of technical equipment plus two enclosed and two open levels for public pleasure. They contain a revolving restaurant, a (stationary) snackbar, a glassed-in viewing gallery, and two floors for open viewing. The panorama below is absolutely spectacular—you think you can see the entire continent and a bit of next week as well.

Canberra Space Centre. Located at Tidbinbilla, some 32 miles from the capital, the Centre contains a fascinating array of model spacecraft, space photos, and space research equipment. Also self-operated audio-visual displays and "talking chairs" giving you a chatty insight into the mysteries of deep space tracking while you sit in them. Open daily from 9 a.m. to 5 p.m. Admission is free.

Cockington Green, Gold Creek Road, Gungahlin. About five miles northwest of the city, this is a miniature patch of Britain set into the green-brown Australian landscape—an entire Olde English village, studded with historical buildings, lovingly handcrafted on a scale of 1 : 12. Thatched cottages and a forbidding gray castle, country inns and a scale-model speed train, every tiny brick and tile, wheel and window, wrought individually, as are the teensy clay model people and animals. Open daily from 10 a.m. to 5 p.m.

Organized Tours

Ansett Pioneer, corner of Northbourne Ave. and Ipima St. (tel. 45-6624), runs a variety of excursions including half-day City Sights Tours, visiting different attractions on each. The afternoon round, starting at 1 p.m., takes in the university, War Memorial, Carillon, Parliament, Telecom Tower, Captain Cook fountain, and a scenic drive, costing $11 for adults, $7.50 for children.

Another half-day tour by the same company starts at 1:20 p.m., Monday, Wednesday, Friday, and Saturday. This embraces highlights not visited in the other tours, then goes out into the suburbs and countryside. You see Duntroon Military College, Mount Ainslie, an animal sanctuary, and another portion of diplomatic embassies. Costs $11 for adults, $7.50 for children.

Canberra Cruises (tel. 95-3544) offers a selection of cruises on Lake Burley

Griffin, as informative as they are fun. You can choose between morning and afternoon cruises, both on lovely snow-white launches serving light refreshments, both viewing city sights from the water, the afternoon cruise costing $9 for adults, half for children, both departing from the Acton Ferry Terminal. There is also a "floating restaurant" tour, held on board an air-conditioned and luxurious dinner-boat that serves à la carte meals while the shoreline glides by. Departs Tuesday to Sunday at 1 p.m., and costs $24 for adults, $18 for children.

The most economical method of touring is by bus. You can get a day-tripper ticket for $1.30, which entitles you to ride city buses all day.

Another method (for which you need a rental car) is to join a **Radio Motorcade.** These depart daily from the Visitor Information Centre at 9:30 a.m. and 2 p.m. A guide car leads the convoy past the sights and delivers a running commentary relayed to the participants' vehicles by means of a radio receiver placed in each. Each convoy has a maximum of six cars and each tour lasts two hours. The cost is $12 per car.

AFTER DARK: Canberra has what most cities sorely lack: a performing arts complex in a central position. It couldn't be more central, because the Civic Square, off London Circuit, is the geographical core of the capital. The **Canberra Theatre Centre** contains the Theatre, the Playhouse, the Centre Gallery, and the Rehearsal Room (for lunchtime performances), which can (and do) put on anything from Shakespeare to rock festivals. Usually there's a visiting professional group, and various amateur theatrical and musical units. You get modern and classical dramas, grand opera, symphony and pop concerts, ballet, modern dance, choral works, chamber music, and operettas. (There's also an adjoining restaurant.) Consult the daily press or *This Week in Canberra* for current offerings. Ticket prices vary but lean toward expensive. For a production by a visiting professional theater group you'll pay around $10.

Most of the standard movie theaters are around the Civic Square area too. Special screenings of foreign-language films and others classed as not standard commercial fare are held at various cultural centers: the National Library (free), the Maison de France, and the Goethe Centre.

Other kinds of nightlife are concentrated mainly in the large hotels, like the sumptuous Lakeside International, and they tend to be costly. Also somewhat more formal than the usual Down Under style. This is probably due to the heavy diplomatic influx into the capital's nightlife. Another oddity, probably based on the same reason, is the super-abundance of hired escort agencies. You find more paid-date bureaus in Canberra than anywhere in the country, advertising "warm and carefree company" or "dates for business executives."

Canberra now boasts some fairly swinging discos, swarming with young and medium-done government functionaries of all sexes.

SHOPPING: Canberra's commercial center consists of a series of shopping complexes either adjoining or close to Civic Square. They house large department stores as well as scores of little boutiques, cafés, and gift shops, and I can't think of any other form of retail design that spoils shoppers so thoroughly: no parking worries, no chance of getting wet when it rains, and no distances to tire your feet. The only drawback is that the range of goods isn't quite as great as in Sydney or Melbourne.

The largest complex is **Monaro Mall,** between Petrie Street and Alinga Street. Fully enclosed and air-conditioned, the mall is built on three levels and contains two separate department stores and dozens of specialty shops. Others are **Garema Place** and **Petrie Plaza,** which occupies a special niche in the hearts of Canberra kids. It boasts a wonderful big old merry-go-round that twirls during business hours to the strains of the real traditional tweedle-zing-oompa-pa orchestreon music, guaranteed to awaken nostalgia in most hearts. Ticket prices, unfortunately, no longer reflect the music. One spin now costs 20¢. The **Boulevard** is an open plaza, beautifully landscaped and facing Akuna Street. Strongly cosmopolitan, as the name indicates, the Boulevard has three ultra-modern levels filled with international boutiques, a couple of movie theaters, and several gourmet-oriented food stores.

Canberra also has an entertaining commercial throwback in shape of the **Trash and Treasure** market. This is an open-air, open-ended market held on Sunday mornings at the Jamison shopping center car park, organized by the local Rotary club. It offers exactly what the name promises—you can buy or sell virtually anything there. Heaps of trash and an occasional treasure, and half the fun is hunting for it.

CANBERRA AIRPORT: Although one of the busiest in the nation, Canberra Airport is rather small and unimpressive; you might say cozy. Located four miles northeast of the city, it's easy to get to, easy to park in, and impossible to get lost in. There are the Big Four car-rental desks, a cocktail bar, and a bistro. No banking facilities, no tourist information counter. It does have a weighing machine, though.

USEFUL INFORMATION: The **Canberra Tourist Bureau,** in the Jolimont Centre, Northbourne Avenue (tel. 45-6464), is open during business hours and on long weekends, and provides information, brochures, and a free booking service for accommodations and tours. The **Visitor Information Centre,** Northbourne Avenue, Dickson, is open every day from 9 a.m. to 5 p.m. . . . For current activities in town consult *This Week in Canberra,* free from hotels and the Tourist Bureau. . . . The morning *Canberra Times* gives the best roundup of evening doings. . . . For the addresses and phone numbers of foreign embassies call the **Tourist Bureau.**

2. Australian Capital Territory

This is a 939-square-mile enclave in N.S.W., carved out for the specific purpose of holding the Commonwealth capital—and to prevent New South Wales and Victoria from fighting a war over which was to house the seat of government!

From the tourist point of view Canberra *is* the A.C.T., although the city covers only a fraction of the territory. But to the southwest lies one of the most grandiose showpieces of the entire hemisphere, the—

SNOWY MOUNTAINS HYDROELECTRIC SCHEME: The "Snowy Scheme," as the Aussies call it, was named by the American Society of Civil Engineers as one of the "Seven Wonders of the Engineering World." It is the mightiest technological task ever accomplished in Australia and has become an almost mystical focal point of national pride. For sheer magnitude the "Snowy" can only be compared with America's Tennessee Valley Authority water scheme.

The significance of the S.M.A. (Snowy Mountain Authority) stems from the fact that Australia is the driest of all continents, mainly because it has few massive mountain ranges to precipitate rain and give rise to rivers. The basic idea of the scheme was to divert the Snowy River from its original path into three rivers that would flow west into water-needy country. And in so doing not only provide irrigation and thus fertility, but also a colossal amount of water-generated electricity for power and light for homes, industries, and transport in the plains below.

Begun in 1949, the project took 25 years to complete and cost $800 million, the labor of 6,000 men, and the lives of 54 killed by rockfalls and misfiring tunnel blasts. This was the price paid for the astonishing speed of the tunneling operations, which frequently reached a rate of 541 feet per week. (The previous world record, set up by the Swiss, was 362 feet of tunneling a week.)

The S.M.A. boasts a mass of dazzling statistics. Ninety miles of tunnels hewn through the mountains, 80 miles of aqueducts constructed, 1,000 miles of road laid down, seven power stations in operation, producing 4,000,000 kilowatts of electricity! The entire scheme involves an area of over 2,000 square miles and has created a chain of huge artificial lakes, the largest of them, Eucumbene, containing nine times the volume of water in Sydney Harbour!

But better than all these figures is the loving care with which the whole undertaking has been blended into the scenery. Far from marring the beauty of the mountain ranges, the "Snowy Scheme" has enhanced them. Many of the power plants are underground and invisible until you reach the entrance. The immense silvery-white dams blend with the snow-capped peaks like natural waterfalls. The lakes, cold, blue, and crystal clear, have been stocked with rainbow trout and provide some of the finest game fishing in the country. And somehow, even the masses of sightseers attracted by the project are absorbed with a minimum of blatantly commercial tourism.

COOMA: Gateway and launching pad for a tour of the Snowy, this formerly drowsy little mountain hamlet burst into new cosmopolitan life when it became Snowy Scheme headquarters. Today it proudly flies the flags of 27 nations—one for each country whose sons took part in the project.

Cooma lies 30 minutes by air from Canberra, about an hour from Melbourne or Sydney, and can also be easily reached by bus, train, or car. I would advise you to take one of the conducted tours of the Scheme—it's impossible to view the magnitude of the project without expert guidance.

Tours lasting one to three days leave Canberra and Cooma several times a week. Typical of the budget range is the one-day jaunt run three times a week from Canberra by **Boomerang Tours,** 92 Sharp St., Cooma, N.S.W. (tel. Cooma 21111). This includes a fascinating film show of the S.M.A., visits to Lake Eucumbene, a dam, an underground power station, and lunch at Cabramurra, the highest township in Australia.

Chapter X

ALICE SPRINGS—
THE "RED HEART"

1. The Town and Surroundings
2. The Northern Territory

THE "TOWN CALLED ALICE" lies at almost the exact geographical center of Australia—a long way from *anywhere*. The Alice is movieland, picture-book Australia: streets sprinkled with reddish desert dust leading nowhere in all directions; sunbaked pubs propped up by tall men in khaki shirts; drifting groups of Aborigines; an infinity of blue-hazed sky with wedge-tailed eagles floating motionless on the air currents; and all around an endless expanse of surrealistic wilderness—harsh, primeval, barely touched by man, wrinkled and split, churned and clefted by cataclysmic upheavals in ages before human imagining . . . the landscape of Dreamtime.

1. The Town and Surroundings

Alice Springs is all that, but a few other things as well: a modern desert town of 14,000 people, a tourist resort with elegant hotels and surprisingly sleek restaurants, a rapidly growing government center that expects to quadruple its population in the next 20 years. Perhaps the oddest detail about the Alice is that while foreigners find it completely in accordance with their image of Australia, the Aussies consider it quaintly "different."

The Alice is an incredibly young city. In 1911 the area was still being supplied by camel caravans driven by Afghans. In 1929, when the railroad reached the town, it numbered 200 inhabitants. The passenger train from Adelaide was promptly christened "The Ghan" in tribute to the Afghan camel drivers. The railroad terminates here. It can't go anywhere else. Alice Springs is the only sizable community in Central Australia. Darwin, the territorial capital, lies 954 miles to the north.

The center forms the southern portion of the **Northern Territory** (not a state), a region of over half a million square miles with under 100,000 people—of whom 22,000 are Aborigines. After the polar caps, this is the most sparsely settled patch of land on earth. There's a saying that "One Territorian is a village. Two Territorians are a town. Three Territorians are a population explosion."

In 1860 explorer John McDouall Stuart became the first white man to set foot on the present town site. In 1871 a surveyor came upon a large waterhole

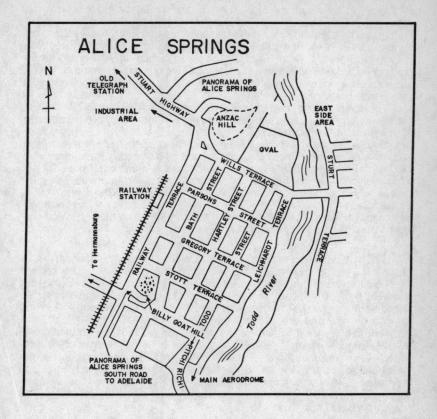

and christened it the Alice Springs, after the name of his employer's wife. This occurred during the building of the Overland Telegraph Line, linking Port Augusta with Darwin. A telegraph repeater station was built at the site, followed by a settlement of sorts about two miles south. The settlement, then called Stuart, numbered exactly 40 souls by 1926. It was renamed Alice Springs when the railroad went into operation.

The old telegraph station is now a museum, preserved exactly as it looked when the telegraph wire represented the territory's only link with the civilized south and the world beyond. But Alice Springs has meanwhile shed its shantytown image, at least in parts. Yet you're always conscious of the fact that this is an oasis in the midst of the "Never Never." The wilderness laps on all sides, there's an unmistakable whiff of desert in the air, and you only have to drive a few blocks to find yourself alone with the limitless horizon.

Once the wide red land all around belonged to the Arunta, the Pintjantjarra, and the Gurindji, and their descendants are still there. You see them in little bands drifting through the alien streets, always moving, always going somewhere and from there to somewhere else, as if searching in circles for some destination that eternally eludes them. The ancient nomadic urge still flickers, even though their water and food supply is now stationary and they wear the white man's clothing, receive medical treatment, and know how to drive trucks. Perhaps beer and automobiles and brick shelters are no substitute for the harsh majesty of the bush, and canned meat doesn't taste like the kangaroo you tracked and speared. Or perhaps it's just a fading memory of a time with no roads or houses or fences, when you walked as far as your feet would carry you and slept in the open with your woman under stars as ageless and unchanging as the earth beneath you.

The desert climate is a reminder too. There is a kind of brute violence in its extremes that no amount of air conditioning can tame. From November to March the town sizzles, the landscape glimmers with heat. From April to October the days are sunny—sometimes hot—but the temperature drops steeply as soon as darkness falls. Overnight frosts are common and early in the morning it can be several degrees below freezing! When a heavy rainstorm strikes, dry riverbeds become foaming torrents and the first touch of wet brings out an explosion of flowers and shrubs in the arid hills. Then the landscape turns into a scene of magic beauty, of colors so vivid and contrasts so pure and clear that you begin to understand what Territorians mean when they say about their grim and gorgeous land: "There's no place like her."

CLOTHING: Sunglasses are an essential in the Alice any time of the year, and a shady hat if you're sensitive to ultraviolet exposure. Also *sturdy* walking shoes if you plan to visit scenic attractions. Elastic-sided boots are ideal for keeping out sand and burrs. If you come in winter, bring at least one warm sweater or coat. Alice Springs men usually wear short-sleeved shirts, shorts, long socks, and shoes in daytime, the women light cotton frocks or pants. In the evening "Territory Formal" means long-sleeved shirts, long slacks, and a tie for men (coats optional, depending on the season), for women anything from caftans to pantsuits, worn with either shoes or sandals. "Out bush" the most common outfit is jeans and long-sleeved shirts. Going bare-armed and bare-legged leaves you unprotected against insects and prickles—and the territory has a superabundance of both. The one garb you'll hardly ever see is tropical whites. Red dust plays havoc with them.

GETTING THERE: Alice Springs lies 820 miles north of Adelaide, the closest big city. Flying time is nearly two hours and the trip costs $218.50. By bus it's an overnight 16-hour haul costing $95. If you're a railroad buff, you've missed a historical moment—the demise of the legendary "Ghan."

This was the train that first connected the Alice with civilization in 1929 by starting a fortnightly freight and passenger service to Adelaide. Until then goods and people were hauled back and forth in camel caravans by Afghan camel drivers. The train was nicknamed Ghan after those hardy cameleers. Riding the Ghan was liable to be more of an adventure than the passengers bargained for. The builders of the track had figured that this was desert country, permanently dry, and consequently laid rails and sleepers flat on the ground without the ballast considered essential in wetter climes. They didn't realize until too late that they had laid the track through one of the most flood-prone regions in Australia. The result was that the entire train was frequently marooned for several weeks in a flood in the middle of a desert! The passengers, it was said, got to know each other pretty well during those castaway periods.

Otherwise the old Ghan was a comfortable affair, air-conditioned and slow enough to give you plenty of opportunity to admire the wild horses, buffalo, and camels often seen through the windows. The journey from Adelaide took nearly 48 hours northward, but a good 10 hours less going back—it's downhill then, because Alice Springs lies 2,000 feet above sea level.

A new train started service late in 1980, running on a line built about 100 miles west of the former track, immune to lightning, floods, and washouts, considerably faster and much less exciting. Already veteran travelers are murmuring, "Nothing like the old Ghan." And with a little bit of luck they'll be right. But the wild desert animals are still there to provide entertainment. The fare from Adelaide is $116 for adults, half price for children. The new train runs twice a week and takes 24 hours.

ORIENTATION: On the map you'll see that Alice Springs is divided into two sections by the **Todd River.** Most of the year, however, this is merely a dry sandy riverbed. The locals go wild with excitement when rains momentarily transform this gully into a genuine torrent, which can be pretty strong while the water lasts. The town has one main street: **Todd Street,** starting off as **Gap Road** and changing its name about halfway down its length. The square formed by **Stuart** and **Wills Terrace** in the south and north, and **Todd Street** and **Railway Terrace** in the east and west is the city center. Nearly every hostelry, eatery, and office can be found in this small area.

The **Stuart Highway,** called "The Track" by Territorians, branches off Railway Terrace and runs northward out of town, all the way to Darwin. Also at the northern end of town lies the **Alice Springs Telegraph Station National Park,** the site of the original telegraph post. The Stuart Highway actually enters the city from the south, running alongside the railroad line, but becomes Railway Terrace before regaining its identity at the exit point. At the southern tip lies the **Alice Springs Airport** and the **Pitchi Ritchi Sanctuary.** On both sides stretch the **MacDonnell Ranges,** whose fantastic red rock formations leap into view wherever you go.

Possibly the most important address in town is the **Northern Territory Government Tourist Bureau,** 51 Todd Mall (tel. 52-1299). They not only arrange accommodations and tours, but Brian Price, the man in charge, is a living encyclopedia of territorial know-how and lore, which he dispenses with wit, erudition, and unflagging amiability.

GETTING AROUND: The Alice has as yet no public transport and doesn't need it—as yet. Bus services are confined to schoolchildren. But there are plenty of taxis. Also several car-rental firms: **Thrifty** has a desk at the airport and an office at 113 Todd St. (tel. 52-1303). You can rent mopeds at the **Thrifty** address for $8 a day. The **Alice Springs Airport** is a miniature affair—but it takes jets. It doesn't boast much by way of facilities. No bar or information booth. Just a little snack counter and the car-rental desks. But it's delightfully easy to get to, from, and around in. The cab fare from the city comes to about $9. Or you can take the airport shuttle for $4.

A NOTE ON PRICES: All prices in this guide are in Australian dollars (A$). As we go to press, US$1 = approximately A$1.40. Thus a room listed at $20 a night actually costs only about $14.50 in U.S. funds—good news indeed for budget travelers.

ACCOMMODATIONS: Alice Spring's economy depends heavily on tourism and there's no shortage of guest rooms in a variety of price ranges. The peak tourist season runs from March to October—the winter months—and during that period it may be wise to book ahead through the Tourist Bureau. Standards are generally good (not great) and *most* hostelries provide air conditioning. In the guesthouse and hostel category the rates are pretty reasonable, but once you get into the hotel and motel range they climb steeply.

Stuart Lodge, Stuart Terrace (tel. 52-1894), is a nice, cool, modern building, completely air-conditioned, ten walking minutes from the town center. The place has spacious grounds, a TV lounge, guest laundry, and tea-making facilities. Accommodations are in single, double, and triple rooms. The bedrooms are bright, nicely furnished, and cheerful, with good wardrobe space and individual bedlamps as well as ceiling lights. No H&C water in the rooms, but plenty of bathrooms on the premises. The tariff comes to a modest $15 per night per person in twins, $22 in single rooms, and families get a reduced rate for children.

Hostels

The **Youth Hostel,** corner of Todd Street and Stott Terrace (tel. 52-5016), is located in the somewhat picturesque former meeting hall of the Country Women's Association, which gets rather crowded. The 62-bed establishment comprises six dormitories and provides full kitchen facilities. Also a piano in the main hall and bicycles for hire—a very handy touch since Alice possesses no public transport and you can get to most of the popular attractions by bike. The tariff is $6 per night, and you're strongly advised to book ahead.

Guesthouses

My favorite in this bracket, and one of the prime hostelries in town, is the **Melanka,** Todd Street (tel. 52-2233). The front looks like a modernistic high school, but the interior is set in its own large and beautiful grounds, a pattern of handsome brown and white stone structures surrounded by tall trees, tropical shrubs, and a very photogenic rose garden, centered by two fair-size swimming pools. The Melanka accommodates 237 guests in fine style: lounges with TV and pool tables, a special recreation room with table tennis and other indoor games, two spacious and airy dining rooms overlooking the garden area (all meals are self-service). The entire complex is air-conditioned and tastefully decorated. The bedrooms are small, compact, and spanking modern, all with H&C water, private refrigerator, tea- and coffee-making equipment, built-in wardrobes, writing desk, bookshelves, bedside lamps, and such extra touches as divan beds and shaving cabinets. No private showers, but every room has a shower room, toilet, and laundry just a few steps away. On top of all this the Melanka offers poolside barbecues, a same-day dry cleaning service, ironing facilities, and a tour-booking service. The tariff comes to $27 for singles, $35 for doubles.

The **Sandrifter Safari Lodge,** 6 Kharlic St. (tel. 52-4859), stands on the left bank of the Todd River just across Todd Bridge. All rooms open onto a garden, a nice feature. It offers cooking and laundry facilities, but no TV or telephones. Accommodation ranges from single and double rooms to self-contained flats and a (very cheap) bunkhouse—all quite simple, clean, and pleasantly homey. Singles go for $14, doubles for $6 per person, while the bunkhouse costs a mere $6.

Somewhat more luxurious is the **Alice Lodge,** 4 Mueller St. (tel. 52-7805). An old outback home converted into a modern lodging house, the Alice is fully carpeted and air-conditioned, all rooms fitted with private refrigerator. There's a good communal kitchen, a little pool, shady garden, and barbecue facilities. Also a house rule forbodding smoking in the dormitory. No H&C handbasins in the rooms, but attractive wood-paneling, tiny cupboards with drawers, and hanging rails for clothes. Singles here cost $15, doubles run $10 per person, while the 11-bed dorm charges $6.

A Motel

The relatively new **Outback Motor Lodge,** South Terrace (tel. 52-3888), is a genuine bargain for *two persons*, offering a whole range of deluxe facilities, including private bathrooms, fully equipped kitchenettes, air conditioning, and color TV. A large rectangle of brick units about a mile from town, the Outback is fronted by lovely strips of lawn with chairs, tables, and sunshades, and has a fair-size swimming pool. Fittings are very modern, including comfortable armchairs, bar stools at the kitchen counter, double wardrobes, and all necessary cooking and eating utensils. The management is exceptionally attentive and helpful. All the units can easily sleep up to six persons, and cost $45 for two, $6 for each additional person.

Tourist Cabins

Toddy's Cabins, 41 Gap Rd. (tel. 52-1233), consists of 28 modern rooms and a dormitory "bunkhouse," all air-conditioned but fairly basic in their furnishings. The establishment maintains excellent and spotless bathrooms and two large well-equipped community kitchens. The cabins have handbasin, refrigerator, and bedside lamps, but come with matted floors and with open hanging cupboards for your clothes. The rates are $25 per night for singles, $35 for doubles. In the bunkhouse it's $8.

Caravan (Trailer) Parks

There are half a dozen caravan parks in the Alice Springs area, all of them very close to town. You can camp at every one and the majority have both tourist cottages and on-site caravans for hire.

Wintersun Gardens (tel. 52-4080) is about 1½ miles north on the Stuart Highway. On-site vans, fully equipped with kitchen utensils and air-cooled, hold a maximum of seven people. H&C water and three laundries in the park.

Carmichael Motel and Caravan Park on Larapinta Drive, about 2½ miles west (tel. 521-200), has cabins for two to six persons. Kitchens on the site as well as a laundry and swimming pool.

MEALS: As stated earlier, the Alice boasts several surprisingly sophisticated

eateries. Less surprising is the fact that they aren't exactly cheap. In the economy range (which is only slightly dearer than the equivalent down south) you have a fairly extensive choice. The food generally is at least as good as the fare offered by American, English, Canadian, or New Zealand cities of similar size, although nowhere near the quality encountered in Sydney or Melbourne. Some of the swankier restaurants strike a formal note and insist that gentlemen wear ties at the table—although not necessarily coats.

For your Sunday lunch (which can be a bit of a problem in this town) try the **Shell Todd,** behind the Shell service station in Todd Street, divided into two parts: take-out counter in one, restaurant with table service in the other. The restaurant resembles a small bright gym hall, glassed in on two sides, airy and spacious all over. There are colored territory prints on the walls and a well-stocked little bar in the corner, brown carpets underfoot. Few frills, but good and attentive service. Half a roast chicken costs $7; an ice cream sundae comes to $2.50. Open till 10 p.m.

The Todd Tavern at 1 Todd Mall has several eating and imbibing nooks on its charming colonial premises. Among them is **The Other Place** (also known as Tops) serving the only counter meals in town. The setting is decidedly casual, the fare Anglo-Aussie, the prices around the $5 mark for a meal. Open all week from 11 a.m. to 11 p.m. Try the casserole dishes for excellence.

Likewise good for lunch (but not on Sunday) is the dining room of the **Stuart Arms Hotel,** Todd Street, from midday till 2 p.m. The room is large, low-ceilinged, and cool, barefloored and looking rather like an airport hangar with travel posters decorating the walls. The fare, however, is hearty, lamb chops for $6 and ham steak the same.

For your splurge dinner I'd recommend the **Overlanders,** 72 Hartley St. It's one of those plush steakhouses masquerading as a rustic barn, but with every curlicue of comfort thrown in: a large and stately fireplace for crisp nights, pretty, polite, and attentive waitresses in long scarlet skirts, an extensive wine list to browse over. The establishment has few windows, and the barn atmosphere is maintained by massive oaken rafters, whitewashed walls hung with cattle hides, antique telephones, rifles, pistols, branding irons, and several oil portraits depicting what you're eating. Succulent filet steak costs $12 and there's also the territorial classic—"buffalo à la witchetty." Open seven nights a week, and reservations are advisable.

Ermonde Arcade, Hartley Street, houses two restaurants with contrasting flavors. One is **Chopsticks,** Chinese, of course, and the only one of its kind in town. Surprisingly elegant and astonishingly formal, it welcomes you with a tuxedoed receptionist. There's a small and smart bar in front, plus an illuminated aquarium with tropical fish. Dimly lit by globular lamps, deeply carpeted floors and beautifully paneled walls, the place is a picture of stylish repose, with soft background music blending into your sweet-and-sour pork. Menu and wine list impressively leatherbound and red serviettes pyramided on gold tabletops make a very attractive showing. The cuisine is superior by Aussie-Oriental standards. I can highly recommend the braised beef in garlic sauce for $11.50. Chinese tea costs $1. Open seven days a week "till closed," as the menu puts it with suitable inscrutability.

The other arcade establishment is the dual-natured **Mia Pizza Bar.** The front is indeed a pizza parlor and rather utilitarian, featuring 16 breeds of pizza to take out or consume on the premises. But the back section is a charming restaurant, pricier than the front, serving authentic Italian cuisine, decorated with nostalgic Italian scenery prints. The Mia also sports outside tables and chairs beneath shady umbrellas. Open all week till 1 a.m.

The **Ghost Gum Bistro,** Gregory Terrace, is the dinery of the Telford Alice Motel (not to be mistaken for the Telford Territory), a sparkling modern buffet affair with bar attached. It's bright with large quantities of plastic (including the tablecloths), comfortable lightwood chairs, and large striking outback landscapes. The air conditioning ranks among the best in town and makes up for the overbright ceiling lights. The buffet selection is not extensive, but the quality very good. The main course—roast beef, lamb, or pork—comes with potatoes and three kinds of vegetables for around $8. You also get a small array of cold cuts, salads, and fruit salads. Drinks are served separately at the adjoining bar. Open till 9:30 p.m.

The **Telford Territory Restaurant,** Leichardt Terrace, is the dining room of one of the best hostelries in the Alice. The decor has elegant simplicity, with the accent on comfort. No ostentatious doodads and no canned elevator music, the management be blessed. Instead you get softly glowing lights, cushioned bamboo chairs, caressing carpets, and first-rate service. On the walls are illuminated oil paintings of dusty red outback scenes—to stimulate thirst maybe? Well, there's a chic little bar to take care of that. A meal here adds up to about $19.

DAYTIME ACTIVITIES: The most celebrated establishment in Alice Springs has premises at Stuart Terrace, between Todd and Simpson Streets. This is the **Royal Flying Doctor Service (RFDS).**

Books, movies, and a television series have turned the Flying Doctor into an almost legendary institution, its founder—the Rev. John Flynn—into a kind of outback saint. The reality is both more mundane and more impressive. Instead of daily heroics and hairbreadth adventures there's daily grind and an organization that depends on meticulous planning and maintenance far more than on daredevilry. The adventures are taken in stride—part of the routine. You'll only appreciate them after you've seen some of the so-called airstrips on which those little prop planes land in order to take patients to emergency treatment. And hope that you'll never experience the flying conditions under which some of those evacuations take place.

The main thing at the RFDS base is to keep the radio network going on which the whole service depends. And the chief function of the network is to facilitate the 6,000-or-so medical consultations given each year over the air between the sophisticated equipment at the base and the far more primitive transceivers out in the bush. Without those transceivers—and the painstaking routine devotion that keeps them operational—the aerial medicos would be useless stuntmen.

The base you see has come a long way from the pedal generator sets and moth-like DH50 biplanes used by the pioneer flying doctors of Flynn's Australian Inland Mission back in 1929, when the service started. Today the bases in Alice and Port Augusta fly dentists to bush clinic centers as well and conduct air search and rescue operations when requested by the Department of Civil Aviation. You can see the whole fascinating works in conducted tours held every half hour Monday to Saturday from 9 a.m. to 3:30 p.m. Admission is $1.50 for adults, 50¢ for children.

The **School of the Air** is actually a service conducted from Head Street. It's run from studios in which teachers help and advise unseen pupils whose homes are widely scattered and spread over thousands of square miles of the outback. The school supplements the grades these children are taught in correspondence classes—the only means of educating them as long as they live at home. Their parents are supplied with loan transceivers at a nominal charge that covers their maintenance as well. Visiting hours are 1:30 to 3:30 p.m. weekdays, and there's no charge.

The **John Flynn Memorial** is a beautiful simple modern church on Todd Mall. Dedicated to the founder of the Royal Flying Doctor Service, the building is a shrine and museum at the same time. Erected by the Australian Inland Mission, it commemorates the great, gentle, and wonderfully stubborn padre with the twangy voice, round spectacles, and a dream in his heart. The dream was to spread "the mantle of safety over inland Australia," and it took an awful lot of scrapping and flying and crashing before that dream came true. Flynn died in 1951, but in a way he flies with the little bush buzzers every time they take off on another mercy mission. The western annex of the church is devoted to the actual relics of John Flynn's life and work: the first pedal generator set used with the first transceiver, the old Morse keyboard, a scale model of the biplane that inaugurated the service, Flynn's maps, some of his writings, and the smoky, battered old billy in which he brewed his tea when out "on the wallaby."

Pitchi Richi—an Aboriginal term meaning "break in the range"—is an outdoor museum and bird sanctuary just across Heavitree Gap on the southern fringe of Alice. The museum part, blending with the open bushland all around, is a delightful mixture of art and artifacts. The art is that of sculptor Bill Ricketts, who carved his dreamlike Aboriginal faces and figures into trees and rocks so that they seem to be *growing* out of nature and become integral portions of the landscape. The sheer melancholy yet serene beauty of his *Emu Spirit Children* and *Arunta Men* would lose their haunting quality if they were placed indoors, surrounded by walls.

The folk museum features the implements used by the territorial pioneers —tools, weapons, and vehicles, including an antique Minerva car converted into a camel wagon. Open daily 9 a.m. to 5 p.m. Admission is $1.50 for adults, 50¢ for children.

Panorama "Guth," 65 Hartley St., is a museum built around the colossal work of Dutch artist Henk Guth, who came to Alice Springs in 1966. He conceived the idea of a panoramic painting of his new home from a similar project existing in The Hague, Holland. The Alice Springs panorama is a canvas 20 feet high and 200 feet around, with a foreground of natural sand and shrubs that give the painting an uncanny air of realism. You view it from a platform with special lighting effects that could make you swear you're gazing at a real sunlit landscape all around you. The rest of the museum features artistically arranged showcases with pewterware, coins, and watercolors by native Arunta painters, and Aboriginal weapons and tools. Admission is $1.50.

For a real panorama of the town you can climb **Anzac Hill,** at the northern end, off Stuart Highway. There's a war memorial on top and a superb view of the entire city and the desert beyond at your feet. "Climb" is rather hyperbolic, it's more of a gentle uphill stroll. And it doesn't cost a cent.

Australia's one and only **Camel Farm** lies at Emily Gap, just south of the city. Camels were originally imported as domesticated beasts of burden to Australia. But a number escaped into the desert, where they adapted, survived, and multiplied, and became a very *wild* part of the native fauna. There have even been cases of "killer camels" terrorizing outback settlements.

Noel Fullarton got the idea of reversing the process. He began capturing wild camels, breaking them in—a grueling task that takes three to four months —and utilizing them again as riding animals. Today his camel farm not only breeds the animals, but actually exports them to Iran and Saudi Arabia! The reason for this is the uniquely tough and sturdy species produced by the Australian desert strain. Fullarton himself is a Kiplingesque graybeard who occasionally stars in movie roles requiring camel drivers. He also supplies the necessary camels. Visitors get a fascinating lecture of camel lore (they aren't as strictly vegetarian as the textbooks have it) and a tour of the farm, which has a small museum of camel-riding implements. They can also go on **Camel Safari,** a one-day jaunt, with all camping gear supplied. On safari the camels travel in tethered string, so you need no riding skills. The farm is open for visitors from sunrise to sunset.

The **Old Telegraph Station,** about two miles north of the town off the Stuart Highway, was the birthplace of Alice Springs. The original spring is still there and so are the simple but attractive little station buildings. The whole area is now a national park. The first message on the newly completed overland telegraph line—spanning the continent from Darwin in the north to Port Augusta in the south—was sent in January 1872. It was a momentous day for Australia, because the wire—linked to submarine cables—connected the colony with the Dutch East Indies as well as Europe. The Northern Territory National Trust now displays some interesting oldtime photographs and documents in glass cases in the station buildings. Just across the railroad track lies the Alice's first cemetery, with the graves of the earliest pioneers who settled the region—and mostly died young. The station is open daily from 8 a.m. to 8 p.m. Admission and building inspection costs 50¢.

Araluen Arts Centre, Larapinta Drive, is a multi-arts complex in the widest sense. The building houses an Exhibition Gallery for touring exhibits of every kind, a permanent gallery for art and crafts objects, an art and crafts studio where the objects are created, and a large air-conditioned theater for stage and film showings, plus a restaurant. It all adds up to a highly stimulating showpiece, deserving far more publicity than it's getting. Open daily from 11 a.m. to 4 p.m.

Also on Larapinta Drive is the **Diarama Village,** a combination of Aboriginal art exhibits and native legendry. You can see how, according to mythology, the kangaroo got its tail, how the Milky Way and Southern Cross were created, how the deserts were made, and how the first waterhole appeared. Open seven days a week from 10 a.m. to 5 p.m.

The **Stuart Auto Museum,** Emily Gap Road, houses a collection of beautifully restored "horseless carriages," the types and makes used to open Central Australia in the early days—although how they ever managed to run along the roads then in existence remains a mystery. (A lot of these roads prove impossible for *today's* vehicles, unless they have four-wheel drive.) Also on view are some antediluvian stationary engines used for pumping water on cattle stations (steam-driven) and a collection of early "talking machines." Open daily from 9 a.m. to 5 p.m. Admission is $2 for adults, free for children. Fully air-conditioned, the place also features a licensed restaurant.

The **Aviation Museum,** Memorial Drive, is housed in an erstwhile hangar, next to the Kookaburra memorial. You can view photographs of the adventurous pioneering era of desert flying and some of the planes and engines that took part in it, including one recovered after a crash landing. Open Monday to Saturday, 2:30 to 4:30 p.m. Admission is free but donations are welcome.

EXCURSIONS FROM ALICE: There are organized tours to every one of the attractions described here. But should you decide to strike out on your own, you *must* observe a few simple rules. By and large the territory in general and Central Australia in particular are considerably safer than, say, the streets of New York. But just as you automatically look both ways when crossing a city street, you have to take some elementary precautions when heading into an enormous empty desert land. As I said, the territory is pretty safe country, but it's *not* rural Iowa or Sussex. You can be made to pay dearly for ignoring this.

First you must check your vehicle for mechanical defects. Take a tool kit along: there are few service stations where you're going. Make sure, by asking, that your destination doesn't require a four-wheel-drive vehicle. In any case, you'll need a spare tire (two are better), fan belt, coil, and condenser. If you intend to leave the main roads, take an extra jack, a gallon of engine oil, and a shovel. Also some reserve gas, but only in a proper container. Plastic containers are likely to expand and burst through heat.

The most important item is water. Apply the rule of always taking twice as much as you think you'll need. This goes even for a day trip. One gallon per person per day is regarded as a minimum for survival in summer, and a child needs as much water as an adult.

The territory is renowned for kangaroos, wild camels, horses (brumbies), and buffalo. Watch out for them on the roads. A collision with a buffalo is no joke. Above all, watch out for road floodings. In a predominantly arid country even a little rain can have devastating effects on road conditions. *Never* try to drive through a washaway—if your car gets stalled you're in real trouble.

The Northern Territory Tourist Bureau has an excellent pamphlet, "Driving in the Northern Territory." Get it and read it before setting out.

Most of the animals you may encounter are completely harmless to man, although snakes are always best left alone. Dingoes—the wild yellow dogs of the territory—will give you a wide berth. Even the giant perentie lizard—a species of goanna that grows to seven feet in length—is shy and unaggressive unless cornered. The so-called mountain devil or horned dragon is a seven-inch lizard covered with sharp spines that give it a rather ferocious appearance. Actually it's a gentle critter that makes quite a good pet. Plants are much more likely to be dangerous, so don't chew any. Two or three seeds of the castor-oil plant, for instance, can kill you.

Since you'll probably get very hot and dusty on the road, a swim in a waterhole or gorge looks tempting. It can also be very risky. Desert water is often *freezing cold* and can induce sudden fatal cramps. The water on top is usually the warmest—so check the temperature *below* the surface before plunging in. These holes are often much deeper than they look, so check the depth as well. Also check for hidden snags in the water.

The main rule to remember at all times: Treat the territory with respect. It's no jungle—but it's not your backyard either.

Château Hornsby

Something to make you blink with disbelief—a winery in the middle of the desert! Spreading green vines over the red soil some 12 miles from Alice, this desert miracle is the creation of Dennis and Miranda Hornsby, who also own the region's largest pharmacy. The Hornsbys refused to believe the ancient dictum that you *can't* grow grapes in a summer temperature of 125 degrees. They do just that, using irrigation water pumped from beneath the desert sand and refrigerating the grapes as soon as they're harvested so they won't shrivel into raisins. The vinery started in 1972 and today produces some 1,000 cases of wine annually. The Château also has an air-conditioned restaurant where you can sample the "miracle vintage" along with specialties like braised buffalo steaks and homemade beer bread.

Amoonguna Aboriginal Settlement

This is the closest of its kind to Alice Springs. It lies near Emily Gap, six miles from town. You can join other visitors for a tour of the settlement's activities, and there's an Aboriginal guide to explain them to you. Also a Social Club that operates a canteen and sells artifacts made in the settlement. Not particularly "primitive," but interesting and about as near as you'll get to Aboriginal life.

Kings Canyon

The largest and most spectacular in Central Australia, this is a mighty cleft in the George Gill Ranges, about 140 miles southwest of Alice. Until recently it was quite inaccessible to tourists, but now it forms one of the territory's top attractions. Immense walls of pink sandstone reflect in hundreds of rock pools, creating fantastic color combinations from cream to deep purple. This is an oasis of wildlife—birds, huge lizards, and rock kangaroos hunting and feeding in the lush vegetation. And all around the cliff walls rise to 700 feet and more.

Hermannsburg Mission

The oldest Aboriginal mission station in the territory, some 175 miles southwest of Alice, this is a typical outback mission, run by the Lutheran church. It is a famous training ground for Aboriginal painters and craftsmen, some of whom you can watch at work. Across the Finke River, 15 miles to the south, lies **Palm Valley.** The track leading there, going through the sandy river-bed, can be a stretch of sheer hell, so be sure to inquire about its current condition at Hermannsburg. The valley is a flora and fauna reserve and perhaps the most beautiful oasis of the center, all the more striking because of the arid wilderness surrounding it. The vegetation includes some of the oldest plant forms on earth—tall palms, ferns, and cyads, sheltered by towering cliffs, casting their reflections into mysterious rock pools. Despite its beauty, the place has a strange eeriness, like a patch of another planet grafted into the desert. It won't surprise you to learn that the valley is a focal point of Aboriginal tribal myths, populated by phantom creatures and supernatural totem animals.

Stanley Chasm

Thirty-six miles west of Alice Springs, this cleft in the MacDonnell Ranges, 15 feet wide and more than 250 feet high, that glows dark red under the midday sun, draws camera buffs from every part of Australia. You can walk through the entire fissure and feel those soaring ochre-red walls closing above you. Local Aborigines run a refreshment stall and the site is quite touristy—toilets and all. Also a 50¢ admission fee. The Aborigines come from the nearby **Jay Creek Settlement** and also organize trail rides through the surrounding countryside. The trail boss is a mine of information about tribal legends and the rides are fascinating if you're an average horseperson.

Ross River Resort

About 48 miles east of Alice, this old territory homestead, white-fenced and tree-shaded, has been restored and gussied up for tourist accommodation: each guest cabin with its own air conditioner. Horse riding and swimming are the main pleasures, and the resort acts as springboard for jaunts to various beauty spots in the vicinity. **N'Dahla Gorge** has native rock carvings estimated to be 30,000 years old. **Arltunga** is a crumbling little ghost town that was once a gold-mining center, until the stuff petered out around 1912. Almost as many prospectors perished getting *to* the place as eventually worked there. **Trephina Gorge** and the **Valley of the Eagles** are a region of tranquil waterholes forming chains, edged by sandy white "beaches" and giant river gums. You can watch the mighty wedge-tail eagles circling high in the sky, occasionally pouncing on rabbits or lizards they spot with their bomb-aimers' eyes.

Ayers Rock

This is *the* landmark of the territory and one of the most stunning natural marvels in the world. It is the summit of a buried mountain, the largest monolith on earth, rising unbelievably huge and abrupt from the flat scrub desert that surrounds it. Towering 1,143 feet above the plain and measuring 5½ miles in circumference, the rock is twice the size of central London. The wind playing around its titanic flanks gives the monolith a strange moaning "song" that the Aborigines—who venerated it for centuries—believed were spirit voices. They called the rock Uluru.

Ayers Rock lies amid **Mount Olga National Park,** about 280 road miles southwest of Alice. The sight takes your breath away—the suddenness with which this monster looms before you, the sheer silent immensity of its bulk catches your throat before you become aware of its colors. The colors change with the time of day: from deep scarlet to molten gold to delicate lilac, presenting entirely new vistas with every hue. The rock is honeycombed with caves, many of them still unexplored, some used for tribal ceremonies and burial chambers. There is an aura of ageless mystery about the rock that no amount of camera-clicking, no tourist buses and airplane roars can dispel. As if the stone was aware that it will still be there, unchanged and eternal, when all of us have vanished.

You can climb all the way up, but I wouldn't advise it unless you're in reasonably good physical condition. The desert sun beats down, it's steep, and for the first 280 feet there are no handholds. At the top you sign your name in the park ranger's book and get your reward in the form of a fabulous view—the crystal clarity of the air shrinks distances in an amazing fashion.

Twenty miles west of the rock stands a cluster of striking blue domes called the **Olgas.** These are huge round monoliths topped by Mount Olga, rearing 1,800 feet and encircling some of the most beautiful bushland in the center. These rocks too change their coloring and glow like red-hot iron in the morning. Ayers Rock and the Olgas are parts of the same national park and most visitors combine these sights in one trip. There's a $1.50 entry fee.

The park has a large variety of wildlife, from big goannas to tiny marsupial mice. Unfortunately it also has flies—millions of 'em. These flies are the curse of the Australian bush, for they seek body contact with a persistency that borders on the maniacal. Veterans like the park rangers have learned to ignore them, more or less, but they keep the rest of us slapping away at our arms and faces. The park rangers are a philosophical lot. I asked one of them how often he'd climbed the rock. His smile wrinkles deepened. "Me? Never. D'you think I'm crazy? I work here."

Ayers Rock ranks almost with the Great Barrier Reef as a tourist attraction. In order to accommodate the swelling tide of visitors the Northern Territory government, together with private developers, has constructed the $160 million **Yulara International Tourist Resort.** A desert oasis of inspiring proportions, Yulara is entirely self-contained, offering swimming pools, a shopping mall, supermarket, tavern, bars, banks, a spectacular multi-level Information and Display Centre, an 800-seat amphitheater, and a miniature theatrette. Also accommodations for 5,000 persons a day. Although somewhat top-heavy on the luxury side, the available berths do span the entire range from economy to plush. In the former you get space in the camping ground (with power, showers, toilets, hot and cold water, on-site caravans, and barbecue facilities) for $3.50. In the latter you can pay $150 a night at the five-star Sheraton Hotel. In between these extremes there are cabins for rent at $7 a night per person or $28 per night in four-bed family units.

The resort has been thoughtfully planted just outside the national park so as not to spoil the Rock's grandiose wilderness effect. It's located about 4½ driving hours from Alice Springs on a fair road and some 13 miles from the Rock itself.

ORGANIZED TOURS: For a town its size, Alice Springs offers a larger choice of jaunts, trips, and organized excursions than any place in the hemisphere—partly because the territory depends on tourism for the jam on its bread, partly because it's not an easy country to cover on your own. For the remoter points, at least, you'd do better to join one of the group tours and leave the driving to the guides.

Cata Tours, Todd Street (tel. 52-1700), has a 5-hour excursion to the Stanley Chasm. You drive through the Western MacDonnell Ranges, wander through the Chasm, and continue to Simpsons Gap. See if you can spot the rock wallabies (it's easy). Price includes lunch and entrance fees. Adults are charged $26; children, $18. The same company runs a road trip to Ayers Rock five days a week that lasts two days. This takes in the Olgas as well and includes all meals and overnight accommodations. Adults pay $184.

Ansett Pioneer, corner of Todd and Parsons Streets (tel. 52-2422), features an Alice Springs town tour that departs at 2 p.m., returns at 5 p.m., and takes in the Old Telegraph Station, camel ranch, Flying Doctor Service, and Panorama Gath. Tickets cost $10 for adults, $5 for children. Also a two-day road excursion to Ayers Rock seven times a week with an overnight stay at the motel, where they wake you early enough to admire the fabulous sunrise. You get to climb to the top of the Rock or explore the many caves, according to inclination or energy. Adults pay from $90.

Frontier Tours, P.O. Box 2836, Alice Springs (tel. 52-3448) offers several interesting jaunts on camelback. These riding camels *don't* bite, spit, or kick (only ill-treated camels do), make more comfortable mounts than horses and kneel—more or less—on command. The economy ride is a trot along the sandy course of the Todd River, costing $15 per hour per person. But the greatest fun is to "Take a Camel out to Dinner," a 1½-hour sway to dinner and wine tasting at Château Hornsby. The dinner is excellent, the wine likewise and both are included in the price of $38 per person.

Outback Experience, P.O. Box 688, Alice Springs (tel. 52-3389) has a fleet of four-wheel-drive vehicles for tours to "out bush" places not easily accessible for tourists. Their rates are budget, their knowledge of the landscape is impressive. Being a small family outfit they can dispense with rigid timetables and large crowds of trippers. One of their tours, the "Waterhole Wanderer," depends on seasonal water conditions and takes you to some of the most beautiful local desert pools for swimming, wildlife watching, and exploring. This one-day jaunt costs $45 for adults, $25 for children.

Dreamtime Tours, 51 Todd St., (tel. 52-1299) takes you on a half-day visit to an Aboriginal encampment. You watch the making of weapons and implements, sample some genuine "bush tucker" caught in the wild, and learn a little about the original Australians' lore, religion, and lifestyle. Adults pay $46, children $24.

A further word concerning Ayers Rock: Bring a sweater along; desert mornings can be quite nippy and nothing can ruin a sunrise better than goosebumps. If you want to climb up you *must* wear rubber-soled shoes. Even then it's pretty tough going, so don't play Edmund Hillary unless you're physically fit.

NIGHTLIFE: Let's face it, there isn't much. Alice Springs boasts two movie houses—the **Pioneer Theatre,** an open-air cinema in town, and a drive-in on the Airport Road. There's also an amateur live theater group that puts on performances irregularly. For these and all other after-dark activities, check the weekly *Centralian Advocate* or *This Fortnight in Alice,* available free at hotels and the Tourist Bureau.

Most of the action takes place at the **Old Riverside Hotel,** a kind of local entertainment complex at the river end of Todd Street. A vast rambling old inn, charming in some parts, plastic in others, the Riverside caters to a clientele that ranges from jukebox jackeroos to what passes as the local jet set, with prices and decor that vary accordingly, depending on what portion of the place you pick.

Thus the **Hitching Rail Bar,** open till 11:30 p.m. Monday to Saturday, caters to a very young, extremely noisy, and totally relaxed crowd that favors strident canned rock, a vaguely western setting, and budget bar prices. **The Other Place** is a smartly decorated dinery, with soft lighting effects, a low arched roof, and huge photo blowups showing oldtime territorial vistas. Friday and Saturday nights it features a sing-along piano bar: excellent pianist or organist, but most of the sing-alongers sing in skeleton key. The pièce de résistance of the complex is **Ida's Disco,** which features a dance floor with revolving lights.

The **Casino.** Alice Springs, of all places, now glories in one of Australia's legitimate gambling casinos. Opened in 1981, this $12-million playground resort has the most spectacular setting of any such institution on the globe. Ringed by granite hills that change color every hour with the movements of the sun, this is a superbly adapted scattering of low, white, red-roofed safari-style buildings, modestly concealing their splendiferous interior.

Apart from a luxury hotel, the resort features an around-the-clock coffee-shop (the gourmet restaurant is a mite costly for budget bedouins), swimming pool, an open-air amphitheater concert bowl, and of course the gaming rooms. You can test your lucky streaks at American roulette, mini dice, blackjack, punto banco, or keno, or get a spinning acquaintance with the Australian ritual of two-up.

The Casino, incidently, is the only such enterprise anywhere run by a lady—a tall, supremely chic, and rather gorgeous blonde from Birmingham, England, name of Rosemary Nin, with a lifelong background of hotel business. So much for Australia's alleged macho fixation.

ABORIGINAL ART: Australia's original inhabitants have been producing art-work for over 40,000 years, but it's only quite recently that the white man has deigned to take more than condescending notice of it. Aboriginal art became fashionable with the advent of Albert Namatjira, an Arunta water-colorist trained at the Hermannsburg Mission, whose landscapes won a string of awards and focused international attention on Australian "primitives." Namatjira died young and lies buried in the city cemetery. He founded a specific school of paint-ing that is being followed by scores of imitators, most of them way below his class.

But although the Europeanized Namatjira-style bushscapes sell best, they form only a very small portion of Aboriginal art output. Most Aboriginal visual arts expression is religious and deals with the myths and totemic beliefs con-nected with their spirit ancestors. Traditionally the tribes had no professional artists. Everybody participated in the work, which—together with ceremonial dancing, music, and song cycles—was inextricably linked with daily life. Thus only those works expressing a tribal *theme* can be called genuinely Aboriginal. Everything else is a copy of the white man's art. Which isn't so bad, considering that American painters, for instance, spent centuries copying the styles of Euro-pean masters.

Alice Springs is a major market for Aboriginal artwork in all its forms. A dozen or more shops and galleries retail the output or what passes as such. If you're interested in the genuine article you can't do better than browse around the **Centre for Aboriginal Artists & Craftsmen** at 86 Todd St. This was the first gallery in Australia designed and built solely for the display of Aboriginal handi-work. It's a government enterprise, operated on behalf of Central Australia's native artists.

The exhibits—all for sale—are divided into "Authentic Traditional" and "Adapted and Contemporary." The former embrace bark paintings, weapons, carvings, musical instruments, burial poles, and string bags. The latter include woven rugs, pottery, leathercrafts, sand paintings, wall hangings, watercolors, and screen prints. All are interesting, some outstandingly beautiful. No one will hassle you to buy, but you can get baskets from $20 upward, paintings from $15, and carvings from $1.50 to $30.

SPECIAL EVENTS: **Henley-on-Todd,** held annually on August 27, is possibly Australia's most famous aquatic event—but with the aqua left out. It's a boat race on dry land, actually in the dry riverbed of the Todd. The competing yachts are propelled by the sturdy legs of their crews—they have no bottoms. To watch these "12-metre craft" puffing and panting along the river, always in danger of being capsized by a strong gust of wind, is a sight that'll keep you laughing for days.

The **Bangtail Muster** was named after an old practice of cutting the tails of horses as they were counted before shipment. Today the name applies to a fun event staged early in May for which the whole town and half the countryside turns out. The high point is a parade of hilarious floats depicting current events and public figures in a most unflattering style.

The **Apex Rodeo,** staged August 20–21, draws top competitors from all over the continent to compete in roughriding, bull riding, calf roping, and bareback contests. Some of the horses used are genuine brumbies—freshly caught and totally wild—which adds a lot of excitement to the proceedings.

2. The Northern Territory

The road running north from Alice Springs to Darwin is officially named Stuart Highway. The Territorians never call it that. For them it's either "The Bitumen" or "The Track." But whatever label you give it, this is the high road to adventure, the path through the "Never Never," the 954-mile-long spear of civilization stabbing into one of the remotest, least known, and most exciting frontierlands on the globe.

The Northern Territory hasn't achieved statehood yet. With fewer than 100,000 people inhabiting an area twice as large as Texas, the process may take a good many years. But meanwhile the territory is surging ahead at a pace that seems dizzying after its 150 years of Rip van Winkle sleep.

Until the construction of the Overland Telegraph Line in the 1870s, the north slumbered undisturbed, isolated and mysterious as the valleys of the moon. With the telegraph wire—stretching from Port Augusta in South Australia to Darwin, clear across the continent—came a track. Then a road of sorts, trodden mainly by adventurers and gold seekers hardy enough to brave it. But during World War II, with the tide of Japanese conquests surging toward Australia's northern shores, "The Track" suddenly became a lifeline, a vital military artery. Hundreds of thousands of Australian and American soldiers passed up and down that sun-scorched bitumen ribbon, and at last Australia learned that it was neglecting the north at its peril.

One of the few blessings of the war was the tremendous improvements it brought to "The Track." And these, in turn, resulted in a steady flow of tourists, lured by hunting thrills, nomadic tribes of Aborigines, and the wild surrealistic grandeur of the landscape.

In places the scenery resembles a canvas by Salvador Dali. Gigantic meteor boulders, some as perfectly round as cosmic marbles; magnetic anthills towering 20 feet high; white ghost gums reflected in lagoons of incredibly clear blue water; rice grass that closes over a horseman's head; rust-brown deserts, darkly mysterious rock chasms, immense lushly green mangrove swamps . . . all this is the North.

WILDLIFE: Regardless of whether you go armed with gun, rod, or camera, the territory provides action. Flocks of emus race through the mulga, wild buffalos muster you warily, dingoes howl around the campfires at night, huge pythons slither over the rocks, while rivers and sea harbor catfish and sharks, harmless freshwater crocodiles, and the dangerous saltwater kind. Kangaroos and wallabies—from little dwarf hoppers to "big red" six footers—flee in fantastic leaps. And in the air teeming swarms of parakeets, ducks, geese, tiny wrens, and occasionally a mighty wedge-tailed eagle.

The territory knows only two seasons, "wet" or "dry"—and only the dry is suited to tourist activities. It lasts from early April through October, and comes close to being ideal. Cloudless skies day after day, the average daytime temperatures hovering around 80 degrees, the nights pleasantly cool, sometimes even chilly.

DARWIN: This small tropical port on the Timor Sea is the territorial capital and something of a phoenix among cities. In its brief history Darwin has risen twice from almost total destruction. Before World War II, Darwin was a sleepy little outpost, drowsily uninterested in becoming anything else. But the Japanese bombers that virtually flattened the place also gave it the spark of new life. Darwin was reborn as a model of town planning, blossoming out in tree-lined streets, shady parks, and cool ultramodern public buildings. Then—at Christmas 1974—came Cyclone Tracy and did as thorough a destruction job as the Japanese. And for the second time Darwin rose from the debris, picked up the pieces left by the hurricane, and built anew.

The city now contains nearly half the entire population of the north and today boasts one of the fastest expansion rates of any Australian community. It currently houses over a dozen air-conditioned hotels and at least six first-rate restaurants. Also a Chinese temple, a superb Botanic Garden, and a string of silver sand beaches on its doorstep.

In 1982 it got an additional magnet in shape of the **Diamond Beach Hotel-Casino.** Looking somewhat like an architect's dream from the *Arabian Nights*, this gleaming white edifice is set in acres of tropical gardens, right on the coast so as to provide a panoramic view across the ocean. Most of the clientele, however, are less interested in views that in the roulette, blackjack, mini dice, punto banco, and keno action in the gaming rooms. The hotel also houses a top-ranking cabaret (big-name performers only), two topline restaurants, and a 24-hour coffeeshop, which Darwin can do with very nicely.

The "top end" of Australia is not exactly a cheap place to get to or stay at. But it does have budget accommodation once you get there. One of the best bets is the **YWCA Hostel,** 119 Mitchell St., which is spotless and well-furnished, with communal bathrooms and ceiling fans. Singles pay $14; doubles, $12 per person.

For a home on wheels, go for one of the camper-vans rented out by **Thrifty,** 131 Stuart Hwy. Darwin (tel. 81-8555). A four-berth van costs you $600 per week, with unlimited kilometers, plus $5 per person for cooking utensils and bedding.

SAFARIS: From Darwin a variety of organized safari tours head for the creeks, lagoons, and nature parks east and south of the city. These jaunts cater to a wide range of interests, purses, time schedules, and stamina. Meaning that you can shoot, fish, film, watch, stalk, or just laze around, according to fancy. Ducks and geese can be hunted all year, and your safari guide can arrange permits to shoot red kangaroos and buffalo. For fishermen there's the giant barramundi—one of the finest table delicacies on earth, apart from saratago, mullet, and saw fish. But for most tourists the thrill lies in observing the wildlife, flora as much as fauna, and in seeing a slice of nature still very much in the raw.

Safari accommodations run from elaborate cabins with electricity, showers, and septic-tank toilets to simple tents for bush camping. And the time involved, from one morning to four days and nights.

Greyhound (tel. 81-8510) runs an economical two-day jaunt to Katherine Gorge—one of the territory's top beauty spots—daily except Monday. You drive to historic Springvale Homestead, take a swim in the famous thermal pool, stay overnight, then proceed to Katherine. There you get a launch ride on the gorge waters before returning to Darwin. The cost is $104 per person on a shared-accommodation basis.

For the real Top End experience you have to venture into **Kakadu National Park,** the most wildly exotic of Australia's nature reserves. Densely forested, swarming with scaled, furred, and feathered wildlife (100 species of reptiles live in the rivers), sprinkled with Aboriginal rock paintings, Kakadu represents the untamed essence of the tropical North. **TAA** has a three-day coach and launch tour through the park, starting and finishing in Darwin. This includes meals of buffalo steak and barramundi, visits to sites of native rock paintings, and a couple of engrossing river journeys. One of them takes you down the South Alligator River, within sight of basking crocs (there are *no* alligators anywhere in Australia). The tour (twin shared accommodations) costs $229 per person.

Chapter XI

TASMANIA—THE ISLAND STATE

1. Orientation
2. A Tour of the Island

TASMANIA HANGS LIKE A heart-shaped pendant 150 miles south of the Australian mainland coast, separated by a very turbulent stretch of water called the Bass Strait. On some world maps the island gets left off altogether, and it certainly is the state foreign visitors know the least about. Yet in some respects it is the most fascinating component of the Commonwealth.

There is something oddly un-Australian about Tasmania, a sense of not belonging where it's at. You get the feeling that during the immemorial past it had been towed from the northern hemisphere and left anchored here by mistake. Tasmania's climate, vegetation, topography, and general appearance don't belong in the Antipodes. But historically this is part of Australia's cradle—the grimmest and most tragic part.

1. Orientation

The smallest and, with fewer than half a million inhabitants, least populous Australian state, the island is affectionately known as Tassie among mainlanders, and the diminutive denotes its status in the political pecking order. As a tourist attraction, however, Tassie enjoys big advantages. Her size—with 26,383 square miles she's a bit smaller than Ireland—brings everything within easy reach. Her scenic beauty is fabulous in parts and well-watered, green, and lush everywhere. Her climate is mildly European, without extremes in either direction. And she has preserved her historical heritage so well that the island is a treasure trove for those interested in the white man's "fatal impact" on the region.

Most of that heritage is brutal, some of it hideously so. The island was discovered by the Dutch seafarer Abel Tasman in 1642, who named it Van Diemen's Land. (Eventually it was renamed after *him*.) But the British under Captain Cook were the first to explore and take possession of the place in 1777. Lt. William Bligh of the *Bounty* (who later achieved fame of sorts as captain of the same ship) planted the first apple tree on the island—forerunner of her major export crop today.

Hobart, the capital, was founded in 1803—some 15 years after Sydney—and ranks as Australia's second-oldest city. But the island's chief role was a dumping ground for "unmanageable" convicts from the mainland, a kind of penal settlement within a penal colony. The treatment meted out to these men and women was reflected in the name the convicts bestowed on the Bass Strait: "The passage between earth and hell on earth." Today the ruins of the old penal stronghold of Port Arthur are a top tourist attraction. Then they meant a living death for thousands of human beings in chains, driven to work by the constant cracking of rawhide whips across their backs.

If the treatment of whites was gruesome, that of blacks was unspeakable. For the Aborigines of Van Diemen's Land weren't merely decimated. They were exterminated in what must pass as a 19th-century experiment in genocide. After repeated clashes with the natives, the administration decided to get rid of them all. The original Tasmanians were even more primitive than the mainlanders and therefore even more helpless. After a concerted drive across the entire island failed, they were captured or coaxed out in little groups and either killed or deported. The last pure-blooded Tasmanian Aborigine died in 1876. There is *not one* left.

The convicts left their marks in the form of carefully preserved buildings and bridges. The Aborigines left nothing except a memory, fading fast.

For many visitors, however, the real interest of Tasmania does not lie in historical mementos but in the scenery. The island is one of the most mountainous on earth and much of the southwest is a barely mapped, hardly explored wilderness of towering peaks and dense forests broken by roaring streams—a wonderful challenge for mountaineers and bushwalkers, but a rugged one. Sir Edmund Hillary, the conqueror of Mount Everest, used to come here to sharpen his skills. It's also a paradise for fishermen who flock from all over Australia to tackle the river and lake trout.

The wilderness also harbors animals which have become extinct on the mainland. One is the Tasmanian Devil, a carnivore about the size of a fox terrier with huge teeth and an extremely ugly disposition. The other is probably the rarest known beast in the world today. The marsupial wolf—or tiger—is built like a German shepherd, with blackish-brown stripes across the hindquarters. A lone nocturnal hunter, it captures its prey by outrunning it, loping along tirelessly until the victim drops with exhaustion. These wolves are now so rare that none has been sighted in recent years.

Around the well-trodden tourist trails (the ones we will tread) the landscape is rolling and gentle, redolent with fruit trees, and sprinkled with tranquil villages that call themselves towns. Tassie only has one real city, Hobart, but that packs a real surprise. It boasts one of Australia's legal gambling establishments, the **Wrest Point Casino**—as distinct from hundreds of illicit ones flourishing on the mainland.

GETTING THERE: Tasmania is connected to the mainland by air and sea transport. All the TAA and Ansett flights go via Melbourne, the closest mainland city. By jet from Melbourne it's a bit under an hour to Launceston, a bit over an hour to Hobart. The fares are respectively $117.20 and $136.30.

Going by sea may be more fun, and it can save you some money. But if you're prone to seasickness you may not take kindly to the Bass Strait, or vice versa. It can, however, be a delightful and relaxing experience, particularly if you've been doing a lot of jetting. The **Abel Tasman** operates three times a week between Melbourne and Devonport, a handsome vessel with a bar, shop, restaurant, and cafeteria on board. You leave Melbourne at 6 p.m. and land in Tasmania at 8 next morning. Breakfast is included in your fare. A bunk in a four-berth cabin costs $56 in low season. For further details contact the **Tasmanian Tourist Bureau,** 256 Collins St., Melbourne (tel. 636-351).

GETTING AROUND: Public transportation on the island is first class, giving

you a choice of road, or air hops, although the last is no way of seeing the country. But because of Tasmania's mountainous personality, surface travel always takes considerably longer than the mileage on the map would indicate.

Several years ago Tasmania scrapped her wonderful rail service—for the usual demand "economy reasons." (The Railway Department would rent you an entire railroad train, just in case you happened to need one.) So let's all heave a concerted sigh for the snows of yesteryear.

However, the island has a nice little airline specializing in the grasshopper leaps required. **Airlines of Tasmania** (tel. 918-422) connects all the major and some of the minor population points. Sample airfares from Hobart: to Launceston, $46; to Queenstown, $60; to Wynyard, $60.

All main centers are connected by bus services operated by **Redline Coaches,** 96 Harrington St., Hobart (tel. 34-4577), and 112 George St., Launceston (tel. 31-9177). Sample fares: Hobart–Launceston, $11.40; Launceston–Devonport, $7.60; Burnie–Queenstown, $17.30. You can, in fact, make the complete loop of the island for about $70. There is also the Redline **Tassie Pass,** costing $53, which gives you unlimited bus travel around the island for a week.

Best of all, if you can swing it, is to rent a car. Here you benefit by Tasmania's small size. Unlike their mainland colleagues, who have to contend with enormous distances, the local drive-yourself firms usually offer one-way rentals, enabling you to drop your vehicle wherever your trip terminates. For absolute rock-bottom rates on four wheels, try **Rent-A-Bug,** 105 Murray St., Hobart (tel. 34-9435). They have a fleet of Volkswagens, not exactly new but reasonably well maintained, that rent out at $15 a day, $90 a week, including unlimited kilometers. For more modern transportation, it's **Thrifty,** Launceston Airport and 156 Harrington St., Hobart (tel. 23-2741). Thrifty also rents camper-vans, fully equipped, which enable you to use the excellent caravan parks that dot the island.

Theoretically you can also bicycle around Tasmania. However, after looking over those steep, winding mountain roads I'd suggest you let it remain a theory. On the other hand the island is probably the safest and easiest place for hitchhiking in Australia.

Keep in mind, though, that many of the townships are very small indeed and tend to go into semihibernation outside the peak tourist season, i.e., from around May to September. When I got to Bridport, billed as a resort town, I found that all my traveler's checks wouldn't buy me a meal. The one restaurant was booked for a private wedding reception. The manager of my hotel wouldn't hear of cooking dinner "for just one guest." And the local snackbar served only take-out food—and I had no place to take it to and nought to eat it with. I went to bed hungry that night, thinking that this would make an ideal headquarters for the weight-watchers association.

2. A Tour of the Island

Now follow me on a tour of the island, traveling clockwise and stopping at *some* of the highlights as we go. There are lots of packaged or organized tours for the same route, which we'll study at the end of this chapter. To help you choose, get a current copy of *Tasmanian Travelways,* a bimonthly newspaper published by the **Department of Tourism** and the finest periodical of its kind I've ever perused. It's invaluable, but they hand it out gratis at every Tourist Bureau.

LAUNCESTON: Looking at the north coast of Tasmania from the air you might well think that you're approaching rural England or Ireland instead of an island in the South Pacific. Below you stretch green velvet hills broken by brown rectangles of plowed land, ribboned with winding country lanes, little fishing villages along the seashore, white stone farmhouses among the fields, and a cooling mist hanging over the scene.

Launceston is Tasmania's second-largest city, although with 65,000 people it can hardly be called a city. It lies 35 miles inland at the head of the **River Tamar,** a small commercial and industrial complex surrounded by immense garden tracts. The Tamar and South Esk Rivers join right in the heart of the city. The short trip from the airport costs $2.50 by Redline coach.

The downtown section consists of a few blocks between Bathurst and Tamar Streets, east of the river junction, although the **Railway Terminal** lies on the west side, across **Victoria Bridge.** Your best orientation point is the **Government Tourist Bureau,** corner of Paterson and St. John Streets (tel. 300-211). It's not only a convenient starting base for all excursions but—like the others throughout the island—an unfailing fount of information, helpfulness, and courtesy. If Tasmania makes it on the international tourist map it'll be largely due to the men and women who staff these government offices. The **Post Office** is at the corner of Cameron and St. John Streets, one block away. Both **TAA** and **Ansett** have their terminals at the corner of Brisbane and George Streets.

Launceston and its scenic surroundings are served by modern buses of the

Metropolitan Transport Trust (MTT). The drivers will sell you unlimited travel tickets (all MTT routes) for $1.20.

A NOTE ON PRICES: All prices in this guide are in Australian dollars (A$). As we go to press, US$1 = approximately A$1.40. Thus a room listed at $20 a night actually costs only about $14.50 in U.S. funds—good news indeed for budget travelers.

Accommodations

The **Motel Maldon,** 32 Brisbane St. (tel. 31-3979), is a white colonial charmer with lace-iron grillwork, an upstairs balcony, and bay windows. It's also slightly beyond our price range in single accommodation, but right in for doubles. The 12 units, all with private facilities, are surprisingly modern, not in the plastic sense but beautifully so: pastel-colored, bright and airy, with TV set, refrigerator, springy carpeting, and bedside lamps. Bathrooms come with shower and toilet and marble sink tops. Continental breakfast is included in the rates. No other meals on the premises. Singles cost $28, doubles, $36.

The **Royal Hotel,** 90 George St. (tel. 31-2526), stands in the heart of the town's shopping district and runs a very lively bar trade. Also serves good budget-priced counter lunches. A small white, spick-and-span structure, the hotel has 14 rooms, all with H&C water but without private facilities. The rooms are neat as pins, not modern but comfortable. You get a nice dressing table with mirrors, indirect bedside lamps, and wall-to-wall carpeting. The place has six impeccable public bathrooms and a downstairs guest lounge with TV. The tariff includes a *big* breakfast and comes to $16 per single, $32 per double.

There are several other economy-priced hotels and guesthouses in the downtown area, including the **Crown,** 152 Elizabeth St. (tel. 31-4137), which has bed-and-breakfast for $15, and the **Riverview,** 43 Lower Charles St. (tel. 31-4857).

Tasmania has 20 **Youth Hostels** strategically placed at beauty spots all over the island. You can do the entire round trip hostel hopping from one hostel to another. But a lot of other folks have the same idea and in summer accommodation in that field gets pretty tight. If you're planning a hosteling tour in peak tourist season it would be wise to work out your itinerary beforehand and book your lodgings. Contact the Tasmanian YHA office, 28 Criterion Street, Hobart (tel. 34-9617).

Launceston House Hostel, 36 Thistle St. (tel. 449-779) is an erstwhile woolen mills canteen set in park-like grounds about 1½ miles from the city center. The place is well equipped and comfortable and charges $5 per night for members of the YHA, $8 for nonmembers. The hostel also rents out bicycles with lower than normal gearing (for Tasmania's hilly roads) at $5 a day.

Windmill Hill Tourist Lodge, 22 High St. (tel. 31-9337), a special charmer deserving of a special mention. A converted two-story home built in 1880 (it was never a windmill, merely built on the site of one) the hotel still retains the style and ambience of its colonial origins. Modern additions include tea-making facilities, TV, and electric blankets in all rooms, a laundry, excellent public bathrooms, and a pleasant little dining room serving home-cooked meals. Singles pay $19; doubles, $27.

The **Treasure Island Caravan Parks** form a chain with links in Launceston, Burnie, Bicheno, Queenstown, and Hobart. These parks are uniformly first class and supply standardized facilities at standard rates. All of them rent on-site vans and permit camping. Some offer self-contained units and one (at Burnie) has a luxurious swimming pool. All of them also feature laundromats. The vans come equipped with thermostatic heating, cooking facilities, eating utensils, TV sets, refrigerators, double beds, and bunks. Linen is supplied for $2 per person. The rates are $24 a night for two people plus $3 per extra person. In Launceston the Treasure Island park is on Glen Dhu Street, at the corner of Melbourne Street and Glen Dhu (tel. 44-2600).

Meals

By and large the culinary scene in Tasmania ranks several notches below the mainland—chiefly because the island is less cosmopolitan and still cooks happily in the old bland Anglo-Aussie tradition. With the exception of a few splurge restaurants in the bigger towns, the hostelries dish out solid, wholesome, and very dull fare, unmarred by either imagination or skill. Tasmanians get the freshest and tastiest fish in the country, but all they can think of doing with it is to fry it Cockney-style, a process guaranteed to eliminate every trace of flavor. With it they usually serve "chips," fried potatoes limp and greasy enough to hang across a clothesline.

In this chapter I've tried to pick out the eateries that combine economy prices with a degree of culinary finesse. I haven't always succeeded because that combination is somewhat rare in these here parts, particularly in the small resort towns. It makes the joy all the greater when you find one.

Such a one is **Dicky White's Bistro,** 107 Brisbane St., in the Launceston Hotel, reputedly the oldest operational pub in Australia. Dicky White, incidentally, was a notorious highwayman who served his time in Van Diemen's Land, reformed, and founded the hotel in 1814. The bistro is beautifully decorated à la rustic inn, with whitewashed walls, milky oil lamps, carved wooden chairs, and stained-glass windows overlooking the street. On the wall a framed Reward Notice promising "Fifty Sovereigns and Unconditional Pardon" to anyone helping in recapturing three escaped convicts. You get your own wine from a small bar. The food is brought to your table, always preceded by warm sesame rolls. The place is famous for steaks—a small filet steak in mushroom sauce costs $9.50— and you can help yourself copiously from the salad bar. But don't miss out on the Tasmanian deep-dish apple pie with cream for $1.60—the best there is. Open till 9 p.m. all week.

The **Royal Oak Hotel,** corner of Tamar and Brisbane Streets, is famed for its counter lunches. The dining room doubles as a nostalgia nook—all the walls carry portraits of bygone movie greats and antique film posters. At the counter you get excellent grilled flounder and roast lamb in impressive quantities for $4.

Claytons Coffee Shop, situated in the charming Quadrant Arcade, is a small modern eatery, featuring outside tables that give you a view of the mall fountains within screeching distance of the parrots inhabiting the miniature aviary. The interior is bright and smart with lightwood furniture and contemporary prints. The quiche Lorraine costs $4 and is worth it, and don't forget the quite outstanding chocolate marble tarte to go with your coffee. Unfortunately the place closes at 5:30 p.m. sharp, a fairly ludicrous curtain hour for a café.

Sights

Launceston's **City Park,** stretching east of Tamar Street, is the most centrally located of the town's parklands. A beautiful oasis, it harbors a miniature zoo and a conservatory with a display of begonias, cyclamens, and other hothouse blooms. On the park fringe, in Tamar Street, corner of Brisbane Street, stands the **Design Centre.** This is a display of the work produced by contemporary Tasmanian artists and craftsmen, some of whom you can watch in action. Anything from oil painting and pottery to weaving and wood turning, housed in an elegant building where you can also sit, drink coffee, and listen to music. Open Monday to Friday till 6 p.m., on Saturday till 1 p.m., on Sunday till 5 p.m.

The **Queen Victoria Museum and Art Gallery,** Wellington Street, houses a unique collection of Tasmanian fauna, Aboriginal relics, colonial period paintings, and historical weapons and artifacts. The vintage firearms, crude, heavy, but devastatingly effective, are particularly interesting. The museum also has a Zeiss planetarium. Admission is free (except to the planetarium) and the hours are 10 a.m. to 5 p.m. weekdays, from 2 p.m. on Sunday. **Franklin House,** Franklin Village, South Launceston five miles from town on the Hobart road, was erected in 1838, originally as a schoolhouse. The interior has been restored and now contains the furniture and fittings of the period. Open daily 9 a.m. to 5 p.m. Admission is $2 for adults, 50¢ for children.

The **Wildlife Sanctuary,** located along Punch Bowl Road, south of the city, contains a large variety of native birds, beasts, and reptiles, all living in their natural surroundings. Also a famous rhododendron garden. Admission is 50¢. **Red Feather Inn,** at Hadspen, was built in 1845 and now stages Australia's first "Sound and Sight" theatrical presentation, a dramatized history of the inn told in music, fascinating light effects, and voices. The building itself is completely restored to its Victorian glory. Performances take place five nights a week at 8:30 p.m. Admission is charged.

Cataract Gorge, a few minutes by bus from the city center, ranks as one of Australia's foremost beauty spots. A long pathway on the face of a towering cliff leads to the First Basin in the Cataract Cliff Grounds, a scene of gardens, picnic areas, and panoramic vantage points, with an Olympic-size swimming pool across the river and peacocks strutting conceitedly around the lawns. The gorge is spanned by a scenic **chair lift,** which gives you a dizzy, exciting, but eminently safe six-minute ride over 1,450 feet, linking the two sections of the reserve. The chair-lift ride costs $2 for adults, $1.20 for children.

Launceston Casino, the smaller, younger, more country-clubish sibling of the big edifice in Hobart. Sitting in 85 hectares of landscaped grounds with a golf course and ornamental lake, the casino forms part of the ultra-plush Federal Hotel, about four miles outside Launceston. The place has a distinct southern-mansion air, but a foyer that Scarlett O'Hara could only have dreamed about. It houses a disco, 24-hour coffeeshop, sumptuous dining room, a health spa, eight bars, a cabaret, and the gaming room. You can play American roulette, blackjack, mini dice, and the great Australian game of two-up (about which more later). Instead of zooming skyward, this establishment spreads along the ground in stylish two-story structures containing some of the most velvety bedroom suites in Australia. Even if you don't gamble yourself, the action is exciting to watch and the setting a scenic delight.

Penny Royal World, Paterson Street, is a remarkable showpiece—or rather half a dozen combined in one complex. The "world" consists of antique but working gunpowder mills, a cannon foundry, a gun emplacement, and artificial lakes on which a ten-gun sloop fights daily sea battles with a six-gun privateer. The setting is an old quarry converted into gardens with waterfalls, windmills, and watermills, and housing an excellent restaurant as well. You can take barge rides around the complex or simply stroll from one attraction to another. Open daily from 9:30 a.m. to 5:30 p.m. The combined lot costs $10.50 for adults, $5.50 for children.

Organized Tours

The Tourist Bureau runs a series of tours in and around Launceston. Some sample excursions: **City Sights,** a half-day jaunt that includes Cataract Gorge and Franklin House. You also get trips to **Mount Barrow,** the historic **Clarendon House,** and a **Tamar Round Trip** offering some superb views of the river.

FROM LAUNCESTON TO PORT ARTHUR: Traveling east (clockwise) from Launceston we reach the coast at **St. Helens.** A pretty holiday center by the calm waters of George Bay, the township offers safe swimming, sailing, fishing, and bushwalking for visitors.

If you drive (or are driven) south, you pass through some of the loveliest countryside on the island. The excellent road winds through dark-green mountain forests, rising high and skirting the seashore, the ring of distant breakers shimmering through the treetops. Lone farms and little villages dance by and small flocks of sheep or cattle graze in the emerald-green pastures.

Bicheno (accent on the first syllable) was once a whaling station where lookouts, posted in the trees, scanned the Tasman Sea for the telltale spouts of whale herds, and signaled to the waiting boats in the cove below. It's an old place by Australian standards and an enchanting one by any standards. Bicheno looks like a Swiss mountain village, except that the cottages are rustic-luxurious and the children's playground is equipped with a genuine fishing boat resting on blocks.

The **Sea Life Centre** on the Tasman Highway is Bicheno's newest tourist attraction—and quite possibly the only place extant that combines a fish zoo with a seafood restaurant. Some of the menu items are the same as those floating behind the plate-glass windows. Others are rare and only found in Tasmanian waters. You can see giant crabs and miniature crayfish, seahorses of every size, eels big and little, small school sharks, sea slugs, barracuda, and dozens of other denizens of the deep. Open every day until 5:30 p.m. Admission is $3.50 for adults, $1 for children.

Farther south, but inland, lies the 130-year-old former stagecoach stop of **Buckland.** The village nestles in the green valley of the Prosser River and has a wonderfully weathered stone church with a magnificent window that supposedly dates from the 14th century.

Directly south of Buckland lies the **Tasman Peninsula,** which would be a separate island off the coast except for a narrow strip of connecting land called **Eaglehawk Neck.** This is the cradle of Tasmania's history. It was here that Abel Tasman landed in 1642 (the village of Dunalley marks the spot) and christened the island Van Diemen's Land, after the then governor of the Netherlands Indies.

The narrow neck of land was the reason why the peninsula served as top-security holding bag for the entire penal colony. A line of savage guard dogs was chained across the center from shore to shore, and the area patrolled by mounted soldiers. Not a single convict ever pierced that line which rendered escape from the Tasman virtually impossible. The water is rough there and few of the prisoners could swim. Many tried that route and all of them drowned.

The strongbox of the peninsula lay near the southern tip—the penitentiary settlement of **Port Arthur.** This was Australia's Alcatraz, a stone and iron complex that housed some 12,500 of the 120,000 men and women deported from England between 1803 and 1854. A large town grew around the central prison, its inhabitants living on the business of imprisoning people. The settlement operated until 1877, when the penitentiary was closed and the last of its inmates transferred to the new Hobart Gaol.

Today Port Arthur is a semi–ghost town, haunted by its past but simultaneously living on it. For this is one of Australia's chief tourist draws, visited by hundreds of thousands of mainlanders for the same reasons that U.S. tourists flock to Alcatraz. They learn about the unspeakable "dumb cells" where difficult convicts were broken and frequently driven mad by confinement in total darkness and total silence. And about the "model prison" whose inmates had to wear masks during chapel services so that their solitary confinement would continue even there. About desperation that reached such a pitch that some convicts murdered their mates simply in order to be taken to **Hobart** and hanged "among real people."

The main building still in use today is the old **Lunatic Asylum,** now housing an audio-visual theater, a museum, and a scale model of the original Port Arthur. You can also see the ruins of the Penitentiary, the convict-designed and built church, the model prison (considered remarkably advanced and humane in its period), the commandant's residence (now a private home), the guard house, and the hospital. And no matter how warm the day you'll feel a slight shiver as you walk among those stone reminders of man's inhumanity to man.

Port Arthur is a national park, so you can't bring dogs, cats, or firearms into the area. The Park Service operates the **Garden Point Caravan & Camping Park,** located about a mile from the historic site, off the Arthur Highway (for bookings, phone 502-340). The park has toilets and showers, laundry facilities, and powered sites, and a basic food store. Shopping facilities are at Port Arthur. Charges for camper vans are $7 per night for two persons; for tent sites it's $6 for two persons, half price for children.

From the Tasman Peninsula you travel 68 miles northwest to the island capital of—

HOBART: Tasmania's capital is a city for which the term "picturesque" might have been specially invented. It lies between towering Mount Wellington and the serene Derwent River, about 15 miles upstream from the river mouth which forms one of the world's finest deep-water harbors. Few cities have been so blessed with their scenic setting—green wooded mountain ranges on one side, shimmering blue water on the other.

Hobart is small enough (164,000 people) not to blot out the surrounding landscape. And she is dotted with beautiful old Georgian buildings, constructed by convicts of solid freestone, that permeate her with old-world charm, particularly around the waterfront. Even the new steel and concrete monstrosities mushrooming all over haven't been able to destroy the town's colonial image—yet. Her river estuary is still guarded by the eight-inch muzzle-loaders mounted at Kangaroo Bluff Battery on the eastern shore of the Derwent—placed there after Russian warships showed the czar's flag in the Pacific in 1873.

Hobart's airport is located about ten miles out of the city and offers only bus station amenities. There's a snackbar and a newsstand, but no banking or any other facilities, and the plastic seats are designed for minimum comfort. The coach to town costs $3, and you'll be glad when you get there.

The actual city lies on the west bank of the Derwent, linked to the suburbs on the eastern shore by the new **Tasman Bridge,** rebuilt since the old one was rammed by a runaway tanker. The downtown section adjoins the magically antique waterfront, a patch of colonial warehouses and colorful street markets, of small squares and tall masts irresistible to photographers. However, the patina that gives Old Hobart charm also makes her a devil of a place to drive or park in. Her traffic operates under the slogan "You can't get there from here." So don't try. Walk. There seem to be only three types of parking facilities—illegal, impossible, or someone else's.

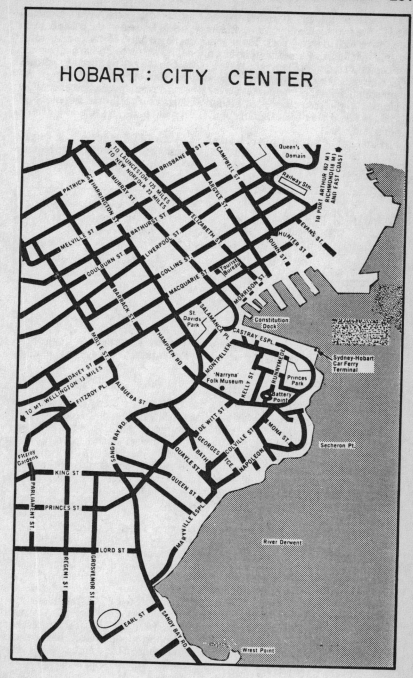

HOBART : CITY CENTER

North of the city stretches the vast parkland called **Queen's Domain.** Across the river, linked by bridge and ferry, lie **Bellerive** and the other eastern suburbs as well as the **airport.** To the south lies **Sandy Bay,** Hobart's main tourist area that houses **Wrest Point Casino,** the stubby white tower that has become the capital's landmark. This suburb is connected to the city by **Sandy Bay Road,** which crosses **Davey Street,** and then becomes **Harrington Street,** one of the main commercial thoroughfares. Davey Street runs southwest and eventually takes you to the scenic slopes of **Mount Wellington.** The **Tourist Bureau** is on **Elizabeth Street** (between Bathurst and Liverpool) and can serve as a central orientation point.

Public transport in Hobart is supplied by the MTT buses, which run by sections, fares ranging from 40¢ to $1.20 according to the number of sections. The Tourist Bureau will sell you all-day all-route concession tickets costing $1.

A NOTE ON PRICES: All prices in this guide are in Australian dollars (A$). As we go to press, US$1 = approximately A$1.40. Thus a room listed at $20 a night actually costs only about $14.50 in U.S. funds—good news indeed for budget travelers.

Accommodations

Hobart is not well supplied with budget hostelries, miserably so compared to most mainland capitals. What there is belongs mainly to the pub variety, places that usually care more about the bar trade than house guests. In the higher rate brackets, however, the accommodation picture changes to middling rosy.

The best territory for tourist lodgings is Sandy Bay, where our first selection is located:

Number 27, 27 Red Chapel Ave. (tel. 25-2273), is a pretty red-brick structure on a quiet street with a lovely garden outside and an air of old-fashioned coziness throughout the house—nothing cubistic about *this* place. The dining room, with ship models and a vintage gramophone, looks like an ad from a 1920s home magazine. The house is proudly maintained, the bedrooms simple, well groomed, and amply furnished. Large wardrobes, wall-to-wall carpets, bedside lamps, plus electric blankets. No H&C water, but four bathrooms are on the premises as well as a TV lounge, refrigerator, laundry, and a coffee bar. Breakfast (large) is included in the rates. Singles pay $20; doubles, $30.

In the downtown area there is the **Alabama Hotel,** 72 Liverpool St. (tel. 34-3737). A three-story establishment in a busy street with a busy bar, the Alabama has ten bedrooms and four public bathrooms. The bedroom fittings are pretty basic, but include carpeting, bedside lamps, color TV, H&C handbasins, and good wardrobe space. The rates include a full breakfast and come to $20 per person.

Also downtown, the **Globe Hotel,** 178 Davey St. (tel. 23-5800), is a red-brick corner pub with a splendid mural depicting a globe of the world as visualized in Shakespeare's time. The 12 bedrooms are small but nicely furnished: bedside lamps, good carpeting, ample wardrobes, modern H&C handbasins, and electric blankets, but no radio, TV, or telephone. The hotel, which is very well maintained, serves no breakfast; counter lunches and counter "teas" (meaning dinner) only on weekdays. Weekends, you have to go out. The standard rate is $15 for singles, $27 for doubles.

Dr. Syntax, 139 Sandy Bay Rd. (tel. 23-6258). This oddly named establishment dates back to colonial times—a little white-fronted hostelry on an elegant street, housing all of four bedrooms. The furnishings are new and all rooms have private shower, TV, coffee- and tea-making facilities, radio, and excellent beds. The downstairs bar is very busy indeed, and the rates out of our range in singles, but fine for doubles: $35 for two persons.

Good Woman Inn, 186 Argyle St. (tel. 34-9091). The "good woman" in question is a Tudor maiden carrying her head under one arm. The hotel exterior and guest rooms are appropriately decorated in Olde English style, and there is a very attractive dining room and a comfortable TV lounge with lounging facilities. The bedrooms have cheerfully patterned wallpaper, wall-to-wall carpets, electric blankets, bedside lamps, and tea- and coffee-making equipment. Rates include a good solid breakfast and come to $20 for singles, $36 for doubles.

The **Astor Hotel,** 157 Macquarie St. (tel. 34-6384), has the advantage of being centrally located, yet remarkably quiet. The hotel has a distinct 1930s look, with 25 rather old-fashioned bedrooms. There's a very popular restaurant on the premises as well as a cocktail bar and TV lounge. Some of the rooms come with private shower, all with H&C water, small wardrobes, individual bedside lamps, electric jugs for tea making. There are four bathrooms for the benefit of the showerless guests. Rates include breakfast: $22 for singles, $35 for doubles.

The **Youth Hostel** is at 52 King St., Bellerive, across the river (tel. 44-2552), an atmospheric old stone building, erected as a school in 1859, with enough space to house a regiment. You take the ferry across from the city. The hostel has coin-operated showers, refrigerator, and washing machine; it charges $4 per night for seniors, half price for juniors. A second hostel operates at 7 Woodland Ave., New Town (tel. 28-6720), charging $4.50 for seniors, half price for juniors.

Customs House Hotel, 1 Murray St. (tel. 346-645). A small, white, picturesque waterfront structure in an ideal position: overlooking Hobart harbor as well as Tasmania's Parliament. The hotel is rather old-fashioned and a bit cramped, but so atmospheric that you forget about lack of elbow space. It's a historic pub in a historic setting that conjures up the vision of windjammers anchored at the front door. The bedrooms are upstairs and the stairs pretty steep. The rooms are smallish, wardrobe space limited, though you get plenty of drawers. There's wall-to-wall carpeting, bedside and ceiling lamps and—from some windows—entrancing views of the busy waterfront. The downstairs bar and restaurant serve meals six days a week (never on Sundays). The straight rate of $20 per person includes breakfast.

Meals

The capital has, logically, the best and most varied eating scene in Tasmania. Most of the food dispensaries are concentrated in three areas: downtown, Sandy Bay, and Battery Point, a romantic little spot near the waterfront, between De Witt and Colville Streets. For some arcane reason, it's not marked on most city maps—perhaps they don't want the czar's fleet to know that there's no battery there.

Lunches and Snacks: The pubs are the best bets here—some of the older and shabbier ones putting on amazingly good counter lunches, possibly to compensate for their appearance. Elegance, however, doesn't mean inferior food, as shown by the **Old Hobart Bar,** Elizabeth Street. This is a beautiful cellar establishment, brick vaulted and red carpeted, with an imposing figure-eight bar as the centerpiece. You can wander around with a beer in your hands, studying the hundreds of enthralling photos of 19th-century Tasmania that decorate the walls. The food counter is on one side, serving fried bream for $3.80 or chicken satay for $3.50 until 7 p.m.

Even classier is **Anthonys,** on the first floor of the Town House Hotel, 167 Macquarie St. Decor and atmosphere are that of a rather fashionable London West End club, a soft brown on brown with masterly marine sketches on the walls and an air of quiet enjoyment permeating the entire room. From Monday to Friday you get a really first-rate, low-cost single-course lunch here: grills for $5.50. The establishment's Charcoal Grill, open seven days a week, is considerably more pricy.

The **Domino,** 55 Elizabeth St., specializes in bargain lunches, possibly the most bargainy in town. A snackbar in front, restaurant in the rear. Although it has tiled floors, narrow counters, bar stools, plastic everywhere, and no atmosphere to speak of, it dishes out surprisingly good fare at reasonable prices: lamb chops for $5.15, top-grade apple strudel for $1, and excellent espresso. Closes at 6 p.m.

Chequers, 53-A Murray St., is another downtown quickie with a coffee lounge in front and a restaurant in the back section. A pleasant modernistic eatery with plastic tabletops and swivel chairs, one wall lined with mirrors, the place is brightly lit and decorated with potted plants. The dessert shelves in front are tempting—and meant to be. It offers a large variety of economy meals, plus very fast, very cheerful service: fried flounder for $5.50, fisherman's platter for $6. Cappuccino comes at $1. Open till 8 p.m. five days a week, but closed half the weekend.

Conveniently placed right opposite the Tasmanian Tourist Bureau is **Banjo's,** 103 Elizabeth St. A bright and cheery coffeeshop, redolent with the wonderful smell of baking bread, Banjo's has become a focal point for tourists of every age and monetary group. The place actually operates seven days a week, though only until 6:15 p.m. (Why 15?) Not many frills here and lights that are downright merciless, but excellent coffee and very tasty economy snacks like quiches for $1.35, steak and mushroom pie for 99¢, and large breakfasts for $2.50.

Dinner: Early closing and a tendency to shut on weekends is the bane of Tasmania's dining scene. The places listed here have been chosen not only for economy and quality but also because they keep reasonable eating hours.

The **Old Vienna,** 112 Liverpool St., is quite a sumptuous establishment, featuring flowers on every table, deep blue carpeting, gleaming table linen and silverware, and service that matches the decor. The Vienna has a pleasantly festive air, aided by the soft illumination supplied by candle-shaped lamps. The only Austrian touches (apart from the authentic menu) are the music tapes and a cuckoo clock whose occupant intones "oo-oo" at the appropriate moments. The meals are both hefty and tasty: bauernschmaus (a concoction of smoked pork, dumplings, sauerkraut, and vegetables) for $9.60, paprika chicken for the same, and very rich Austrian rolled pancakes called palatschinken for $3.50. Closed Sunday.

The **Black Prince,** at the corner of Elizabeth and Melville Streets, is an ultramodern little hotel that belies its Shakespearean label. It has an ambience of its own, though. The flanks of the dining room are entirely covered by mirrors, giving the illusion that it is the size of a banquet hall (it's actually quite small and intimate). You sit in very comfortable leather chairs, get flowers on your table, and admire the political cartoons, horse pictures, and panoramic views hung up for your enjoyment. The lighting is soothingly amber, the taped music toned down to conversation pitch. Nothing pub-like about this place except the prices. A fine T-bone steak with onions costs $5.50. Meals, unfortunately, are served only till 8 p.m.

Back to the Nuclear Age at the **Carlton,** corner of Liverpool and Argyle Streets, opposite Qantas Airways. Here functionality reigns. Most of the premises are occupied by a milk bar with curved windows overlooking the busy street corner. At the rear there's a small, equally functional restaurant. A large wall mirror and scarlet curtains provide the ornaments. The roast chicken and bacon costs $5, and I can recommend the apple pie dessert. Open all week, thank Neptune, till 9 p.m.

Don Camillo is a small, chic eatery in the small, fashionable Magnet Court shopping center, off Sandy Bay Road—a little bright coffee bar out front and a more lavish (and expensive) restaurant in the rear. The food is very good in both sections, although understandably pricier in the licensed back quarters. In front risotto comes at $3, lasagne for $4, and the coffee is outstanding. Open till 11:30 six nights a week; closed Sunday.

The **Mandarin,** 177 Liverpool St., is a nice and cozy Chinese restaurant, well carpeted and lit by Chinese lanterns in various inoffensive hues. Otherwise there's a minimum of pseudo-Oriental knickknackery. The tables are bare and plastic, the chairs steel, the fare a pleasant mixture of Cantonese and Mandarin. Prawn crackers cost $2, the sweet-and-sour chicken, pork, and pineapple is $6.50. Unfortunately, a pot of mediocre Chinese tea sets you back 70¢. Open all week till 9 p.m.

Battery Point, which you reach by the road winding up from Salamanca Place, is a beautifully preserved complex of colonial residences, some of which have been converted into restaurants. They tend to be plushly intimate and rather expensive. One of the finest is **La Guillotine,** 41 Hampton Rd., specializing in Provençale cuisine. For its equivalent in Anglo steak fare—meaning exceptionally good—there's **Dirty Dick's Steak House** at 22 Francis St., which has no connection with the various theater restaurants of the same name on the mainland. The management offers free liqueur to all visiting Americans.

Sights and Attractions

Hobart has two quite delightful shopping scenes standing in complete contrast to each other. The first is the **Cat and Fiddle Arcade,** which runs from Elizabeth to Murray Streets. Highly contemporary in design, it is centered by a tree-shaded fountain plaza where an animated mural enacts the old nursery rhyme every hour on the hour. The second is **Salamanca Place** at the waterfront. The warehouses along there, all built between 1835 and 1860, are probably the best preserved colonial structures in Australia. One of them houses the famous **Ball and Chain Tavern,** a very classy restaurant decorated with grim memorabilia from the convict era. Every summer Saturday morning the place becomes the **Salamanca Market,** the most joyously colorful street market on the continent, where bands play, singers sing, and dozens of little stalls sell trash, treasure, and edibles.

The **Tasmanian Museum,** 5 Argyle St., was built in 1863. Inside you'll find the tragic and fascinating relics of the fate of Tasmania's Aborigines and Tasmania's whales. Both vanished into oblivion. The art gallery has a good collection of contemporary Australian paintings. Open seven days a week, admission is free. The **Allport Library,** inside the State Library, 91 Murray St., contains a wonderful array of 18th-century books, prints, and maps, plus antique furniture, glassware, ceramics, and silver—once the property of the Allport family, who were among the cultural pioneers of the island.

The **Model Tudor Village,** Tudor Court, Sandy Bay (bus stop 30), is a faithful reproduction of an English 16th-century hamlet, authentic to the last detail, including the garb of the two-inch-high populace. The scale model was constructed over ten years by a polio victim. The village is electronically lit with colors that subtly change from dawn to dusk. Open daily till 5 p.m. Admission is $3.50 for adults, $1.50 for children. The **Shot Tower,** Channel Highway, Taroona, is a historic landmark built in 1870 and simultaneously one of the finest lookout spots in Hobart, offering magnificent views of the entire Derwent Estuary. The tower also contains a museum and a tea room. Open daily till dusk. Admission costs $2 for adults, $1 for children.

The **Van Diemen's Land Folk Museum,** 103 Hampden Rd., Sandy Bay, is housed in one of Hobart's earliest colonial homes. The place was built by Captain Haig in 1836 and is a carefully preserved example of how well and tastefully the gentry lived in this "hell on earth." The exhibits consist of period furniture, costumes, an entire nursery of the times, and a kitchen with all the gleaming utensils required to satisfy the Dickensian appetites of the age. On the grounds, you'll find carriages, tools, and a complete smithy. Open Monday to Friday till 5 p.m., weekends 2 to 5 p.m. Admission is $1 for adults, 20¢ for children.

Anglesea Barracks, Davey Street, was built in 1811 for the original garrison of the island and is today the oldest military establishment in Australia still occupied by the army. It contains the restored officers' quarters and mess, the Georgian-Colonial drill hall (and did they *drill* in those days) and the awesome military jail. The barracks can be visited on weekdays from 9 a.m. to 5 p.m., admission free. The **Tasmanian Maritime Museum,** Secheron Road, Battery Point, has a splendid collection of material on the state's nautical history. Open weekdays from 1 till 4:30 p.m., on Saturdays from 10 a.m. till 4:30 p.m.

The **Postal and Telecommunications Museum,** 21 Castray Esplanade, shows the history and development of Tasmania's mail and telegraph services, including some interesting equipment. Closed Sunday; open other days from 10 a.m. to 4 p.m. Admission free. **Runnymede,** 61 Bay Rd., New Town, is a late Georgian-style mansion built in 1844. The house illustrates the period furnishings of its three 19th-century owners: a lawyer, a bishop, and a sea captain. Closed Monday; open other days from 1:30 to 4:30 p.m. Admission is $2 for adults, 50¢ for children.

After Dark

Most of Hobart's nightlife is concentrated on the lavish premises of the **Wrest Point Hotel-Casino,** an ivory-colored tower complex soaring 21 stories above the Sandy Bay boat harbor. The place houses everything from the gambling casino to Tasmania's finest hotel, plushest show club, and swankest restaurant. For good measure it also contains a swimming pool, shopping arcade, and grill.

The interior is elegant but not overwhelming, more stylishly *gemütlich* than palatial, with cascading chandeliers and gloriously comfortable settees and armchairs, noble woodwork polished to a splendid gloss. Above all, an atmosphere of relaxing quiet—no banging of slot machines to assault your eardrums. These vibes radiate from the staff as well, the coolest casino workers I've ever experienced. They have neither the chilling hauteur of their Monte Carlo brethren nor the slightly sinister condescension of the Las Vegas boys. Here they're just amiably relaxed, very friendly, and remarkably knowledgeable. The only dress regulations in force state that gentlemen must wear jackets after 7 p.m. and no one gets in wearing jeans, sneakers, or sandals.

The cabaret room, which was inaugurated by Jerry Lewis, stages Australia's most dazzling floor shows. The cost of the production I witnessed was around $1.3 million. The hotel rooms feature closed-circuit color TV films from the establishment's own studios. And up in the sky there's the only revolving restaurant on the island.

The unique portion of the casino is the "Two-Up" Room. That's where they play Australia's national game, outlawed everywhere except here. A lot of mainland visitors come simply in order to gaze at those widely visible signs with an air of pleased incredulity, like first-timers in a nudist colony.

The Aussies call two-up swy (from the German word *Zwei*, meaning two) and consider it as much a part of their military tradition as the famous Digger hat. You could allegedly spot Australian trenches and foxholes in two World Wars by the two coins perpetually whirling in the air above them. And when a Sydney primary school class was asked to name the greatest local celebrity, half the kids wrote "Tommo" (which happens to be the tag of Tommo's, the oldest floating swy game in town). To the best of anyone's knowledge, no such person ever existed.

Two-up is a fast game and an honest one. It's fast because all you do is bet whether two spun pennies will land heads or tails. And it's honest because it's safer that way. One operator reputedly tried using a two-headed penny. He was last seen locked in his own car in the process of being rolled off Port Melbourne pier. There hasn't been a double-header around since.

The swy sanctum at the casino consists of a round pit and a surrounding circle for the gamblers. The walls are appropriately hung with huge photos depicting World War I and II Diggers playing, guess what? You can learn the rules in about one minute flat, although it helps to know that the "spinner" is the coin tosser, the "kip" is the wooden board with which he tosses them, the "boxer" is the pit boss, and a "standoff" means all bets are frozen. The game is simple, but it hooks you. The speed of it, the breathless pace at which tension evaporates into triumph or loss, the split-second acrobatics performed by those whirling coppers. The immemorial cry that some folks say should be elevated into a national motto, "Come in, spinner . . . !"

The casino opens at 1 p.m. and operates Sunday through Thursday till 3 a.m., on Friday and Saturday till 4 a.m.

Tours and Excursions

Hobart is the only Australian city for which the Tourist Bureau operates walking tours. The **Battery Point Walk,** a guided hike around the historical area, sets out at 9:30 a.m. every Saturday from Franklin Square, opposite the General Post Office. The guide fee of $3 includes morning tea. The Tourist Bureau also runs a **City Sights** coach tour that includes the environs and a glorious view from Mount Nelson. The tour takes three hours and departs at 10 a.m. Tickets are $11.

Other Tourist Bureau excursions:

A visit to **Richmond,** where you can see the bridge built by convicts in 1823 and the Old Gaol, built in 1825 for convicts considered too dangerous to run loose even in chains. Tickets cost $11, not including admission fees.

A three-hour coach tour to the panoramic vantage point of Mt. Nelson to view the city below you. Then on to Battery Point, a cross between suburb and village with a great many historic sites. Then a tour of Hobart's city sights, including the beautiful Botanical Gardens, Salamanca Place, and Parliament

House (built in 1840). The coach fare is $11 per person. For further information ring the Tourist Bureau at 30-0211.

Useful Information

The **Tasmanian Government Tourist Bureau,** centrally located at 80 Elizabeth St. (tel. 30-0211), is open Monday through Friday from 8:45 a.m. to 5:50 p.m. and Saturday and Sunday mornings and public holidays from 9 to 11 a.m. Bookings can be made for tours and accommodations anywhere in the world. . . . For information on current activities throughout Tasmania, consult *This Week in Tasmania,* free from the Tourist Bureau. The *Mercury* gives a good roundup of nighttime activities. . . . **Tasmanian Redline Coaches** is the interstate bus line located at 96 Harrington St.; phone 34-4577 for information. See Travelways for "other coaches". . . . The **Overseas Sea Terminal** is at Princes Wharf, approximately 500 yards from the GPO on the south side of the city, and at Macquarie Wharf which is about 600 yards from the GPO. . . . **Ansett Airlines** coach terminal is at 178 Liverpool St. (tel. 34-7466) and **TAA** coach terminal is at 4 Liverpool St. (tel. 38-3511). . . . The main taxi rank is opposite the GPO and also by main hotels in shopping area. . . . The **General Post Office** (GPO) is fairly centrally located on the corner of Elizabeth and Macquarie Streets. Open Monday through Friday from 8 a.m. to 6 p.m. Telegrams can be sent from there (or by phoning 015) and Post Restante service is available.

FROM HOBART VIA QUEENSTOWN TO DEVONPORT: The Tasmanian coastline west of Hobart is rugged, sparsely populated, and wildly beautiful, the roads rather difficult. But the stretch from coastal **Strahan** to inland **Queenstown** is absolutely spectacular, winding down the steep slopes of Mount Owen in a series of hairpin bends with brilliantly colored mineral rock glowing on all sides. Queenstown is an old mining community gone quiet. Only six of its former 14 hotels are still functioning. But the green-blue mountain ranges loom over the main street so close you feel you could touch them.

Before leaving the coast at Strahan you could take in one of the scenic river cruises departing from Strahan pier daily during the summer season. The **James Kelly** is a high-speed catamaran, specially designed for the job. The fully carpeted modern craft takes you over Macquarie Harbour and the Gordon River, past the Marble Cliffs and Hells Gates—a distance of 85 miles. The price includes Devonshire tea on all trips. The cruise sets out at 9 a.m. and returns at 12:30 p.m. Adults pay $20; children, $10. For bookings, call 71-7187.

Proceeding clockwise to the east, we come to **Devonport,** the harbor town where the ferry liner from Melbourne docks. Devonport is the launching pad from which the seaborne tourists swarm over the island and does its best to hang on to them for a while. The town lies by the Mersey River as well as on the Bass Strait, and the combination of river and ocean give it double charm.

Devonport is very much a shipping town, as demonstrated by the **Maritime Museum** in Victoria Parade. The building houses an interesting collection of minutely detailed marine models, from antique windjammers to the present streamlined passenger ferries. Open Tuesday to Sunday.

For railroad buffs there is the *Don River Railway,* a working, steam-puffing railroad museum at the edge of town on the Don Highway to Ulverstone, with vintage trains you can ride on, an array of steam locomotives dating back to 1879, collections of old passenger carriages, and early industrial diesel locs to delight the hearts of all those who mourn the passing of the Iron Horse. Open daily from December through February, but closed Saturday.

PRENTICE HALL PRESS   Date_____
ONE GULF + WESTERN PLAZA, NEW YORK, NY 10023

Friends, please send me the books checked below:

$-A-DAY GUIDES
(In-depth guides to low-cost tourist accommodations and facilities.)

☐ Europe on $25 a Day $12.95
☐ Australia on $25 a Day $10.95
☐ Eastern Europe on $25 a Day (avail.
  Oct. '86) $10.95
☐ England on $35 a Day............... $10.95
☐ Greece on $25 a Day............... $10.95
☐ Hawaii on $45 a Day................ $10.95
☐ India on $15 & $25 a Day........... $9.95
☐ Ireland on $35 a Day............... $10.95
☐ Israel on $30 & $35 a Day $10.95

☐ Mexico on $20 a Day $10.95
☐ New Zealand on $35 a Day.......... $10.95
☐ New York on $45 a Day............. $9.95
☐ Scandinavia on $40 a Day........... $10.95
☐ Scotland and Wales on $35 a Day...... $10.95
☐ South America on $25 a Day $9.95
☐ Spain and Morocco (plus the Canary
  Is.) on $40 a Day $10.95
☐ Washington, D.C., on $40 a Day $10.95

DOLLARWISE GUIDES
(Guides to accommodations and facilities from budget to deluxe, with emphasis on the medium-priced.)

☐ Austria & Hungary $11.95
☐ Egypt............................. $11.95
☐ England & Scotland $11.95
☐ France $11.95
☐ Germany $11.95
☐ Italy.............................. $11.95
☐ Japan & Hong Kong $11.95
☐ Portugal (incl. Madeira & the Azores) . $11.95
☐ Switzerland & Liechtenstein $11.95
☐ Bermuda & The Bahamas............ $10.95
☐ Canada $12.95
☐ Caribbean $12.95

☐ Cruises (incl. Alaska, Carib, Mex,
  Hawaii, Panama, Canada, & US) $12.95
☐ California & Las Vegas $11.95
☐ Florida........................... $10.95
☐ New England $11.95
☐ Northwest $11.95
☐ Skiing in Europe (avail. Oct. '86) $12.95
☐ Skiing USA—East $10.95
☐ Skiing USA—West $10.95
☐ Southeast & New Orleans........... $11.95
☐ Southwest........................ $11.95
☐ Texas (avail. Oct. '86).............. $11.95

THE ARTHUR FROMMER GUIDES
(Pocket-size guides to tourist accommodations and facilities in all price ranges.)

☐ Amsterdam/Holland $5.95
☐ Athens........................... $5.95
☐ Atlantic City/Cape May $5.95
☐ Boston........................... $5.95
☐ Cancún/Cozumel/Yucatán $5.95
☐ Dublin/Ireland $5.95
☐ Hawaii $5.95
☐ Las Vegas $5.95
☐ Lisbon/Madrid/Costa del Sol........ $5.95
☐ London $5.95
☐ Los Angeles $5.95

☐ Mexico City/Acapulco $5.95
☐ Montreal/Quebec City $5.95
☐ New Orleans $5.95
☐ New York......................... $5.95
☐ Orlando/Disney World/EPCOT........ $5.95
☐ Paris............................. $5.95
☐ Philadelphia....................... $5.95
☐ Rome $5.95
☐ San Francisco $5.95
☐ Washington, D.C................... $5.95

SPECIAL EDITIONS

☐ Bed & Breakfast—N. America $7.95
☐ Fast 'n' Easy Phrase Book
  (Fr/Ger/Ital/Sp in *one* vol.) $6.95
☐ Guide for the Disabled Traveler....... $10.95
☐ How to Beat the High Cost of Travel ... $4.95
☐ Marilyn Wood's Wonderful Weekends
  (NY, Conn, Mass, RI, Vt, NJ, Del, Pa). $9.95
☐ Motorist's Phrase Book (Fr/Ger/Sp) ... $4.95
☐ Museums in New York $8.95

☐ Shopper's Guide to the Caribbean
  (avail. Oct. '86).................... $11.95
☐ Shopper's Guide to the Best Buys in
  England, Scotland & Wales.......... $10.95
☐ Swap and Go (Home Exchanging) $10.95
☐ Travel Diary and Record Book........ $5.95
☐ Where to Stay USA (Lodging from $3
  to $30 a night) $9.95

In U.S. include $1 post. & hdlg. for 1st book; 25¢ ea. add'l. book. Outside U.S. $2 and 50¢ respectively.

Enclosed is my check or money order for $_____

NAME_____

ADDRESS_____

CITY_____ STATE_____ ZIP_____